D1289556

WOMEN AND POLITICS IN THE ISLAMIC REPUBLIC OF IRAN

WOMEN AND POLITICS IN THE ISLAMIC REPUBLIC OF IRAN

ACTION AND REACTION

Sanam Vakil

continuum

The Continuum International Publishing Group
80 Maiden Lane, Suite 704, New York, NY 10038
The Tower Building, 11 York Road, London SE1 7NX

www.continuumbooks.com

Library of Congress Cataloging-in-Publication Data
Vakil, Sanam.
  Women and politics in the Islamic republic of Iran : action and reaction / Sanam Vakil.
    p. cm.
  Includes bibliographical references and index.
  ISBN-13: 978-1-4411-9734-4 (hardcover: alk. paper)
  ISBN-10: 1-4411-9734-6 (hardcover: alk. paper) 1. Women–Political activity–Iran.
2. Women political activists–Iran. 3. Iran–Politics and government–1979-1997.
4. Iran–Politics and government–1997– I. Title.

HQ1236.5.I7V35 2011
320.955082–dc22   2010034886

ISBN: 978-1-4411-9734-4 (HB)

Typeset by Newgen Imaging Systems Pvt Ltd, Chennai, India
Printed and bound in the United States of America

To Iran's empowering women

Contents

Tables

Acknowledgments

The generosity, patience, and time of many people were essential for the completion of this book. The research for this study would not have been possible without the financial support of the Smith Richardson Foundation and the assistance of Dr. Nadia Schadlow. The Johns Hopkins University School of Advanced International Studies (SAIS) provided me an extended home while I completed my research.

I am grateful to many friends and colleagues who assisted me in this endeavor offering their encouragement, assistance, information, ideas, informal readings, and editorial advice. Fouad Ajami, my mentor and advisor at SAIS, supported me from the beginning of this project with his guidance, suggestions, and constant encouragement. I shall be forever in his debt.

I would also like to thank many valued colleagues especially Fariba Davoudi-Mohajer, Haleh Esfandiari, Farideh Farhi, Mehdi Khalaji, Mohsen Milani, Karim Sadjadpour, and Ray Takeyh who helped me brainstorm throughout the project and offered their expertise. The suggestions and constructive criticism of a number of anonymous reviewers was also instrumental in improving my manuscript. I wish to thank Marie Claire Antoine at Continuum Books who gave me a chance to publish my work.

A number of colleagues and friends read through chapters and offered helpful comments. I feel a special debt of gratitude to Roxanna Faily, Jacquelyn Johnstone, Sheila Shahriari, Angela Stephens, and Christiane West. I am most grateful and beholden to Megan Ring. As a coworker and dear friend she was instrumental in her editorial feedback, commentary, constant motivation and humor. I am ever thankful for her keen eye and valued insights. Kent Davis Packard helped me gather and comb through much of the English literature. Hamid Rassouli and Ava Hajjrassouli assisted in finding some Persian sources. Naghmeh Zarbafian assisted with some Persian translation. Many family members and friends in Iran helped me connect with my interviewees. My family in Tehran and Isfahan welcomed me for prolonged periods.

This book is a tribute to my mother an inspiring activist woman in her own right, and both my grandmothers. These strong, empowering women each profoundly influenced me and awakened my passion for my culture, my gender, and my heritage. My father provided me with every educational opportunity laying the foundation for my interest in politics.

This project could not have been completed without the unyielding support of my husband and soulmate, Simone Di Giovanni. His valued insights, patience, encouragement, and solidarity gave me the motivation to complete this project. Through the process of writing, I took much time away from my family and my newborn daughter, Leila. She in particular proved to be a patient and easy baby affording me the time to finish this narrative. I hope she can be proud of this work and inspired by the activism of Iranian women.

Countless Iranian activists both in Iran and abroad shared their time, memories, personal experiences, and insights. Out of respect for their confidentiality they shall remain unnamed, but this book is an homage to their courage and commitment. Now more than ever, I am proud to be an Iranian woman.

Glossary

Abadgaran Developers
Allah o Akbar God is great
Anjomane Islamie Kargaran Islamic Workers Society
Anjomans Societies
Ayatollah Sign of God
Ayatollah al-Ozma Grand Ayatollah
Bad-hejabi Improper veiling
Banovan Ladies
Basij Volunteer paramilitary section of the army
Basij Mostazafin Mobilization of the Disinherited
Bi-hejabi Without a veil
Chador It literally means a tent. It's a long veil that covers women from head to toe and is normally held under the chin.
Daftare Tahkim va Vahdate Anjomanha-ye Islami Office of Consolidation and Unity of Islamic Associations
Danesh It literally means knowledge. Danesh was the first women's journal edited by a woman.
Dard-o del A heart to heart
Diyeh Blood money
Dovome Khordad May 23 is the date of Muhammad Khatami's reformist victory
Enghelabe edari Administrative revolution
Faqih A high-ranking cleric who is an expert on *feqh*
Farmandar Director
Farzaneh Wise
Fatwa A religious edict offered by a *mojtadeh* or *faqih* on any matter
Fegh (Fiqh) Islamic jurisprudence
Fegh-e pooya Dynamic Islamic jurisprudence
Fegh-e sonnati Traditional jurisprudence
Fitna Chaos

Gham be gham Piecemeal

Ghanun Ghesas (Qanun Qesas) Retribution for killing or injuring another party. The law of *retribution* is the basic penal law in the Islamic Republic based on the right to retribution for the victim or the victim's family against the perpetrator of a crime.

Gharbzadeghi Westoxification; influenced by Western culture

Hadith The collected record of sayings and actions of the Prophet. The *hadith* ranks second in importance to the Qur'an as the basis for Islamic *feqh*.

Hamgaraee Zanan Convergence of Women

Hijab (Hejab) It literally means curtain or screen. It the general term that refers to the women's Islamic covering.

Hezb e Kargozaran Executives of Reconstruction Party

Hokumat-e Islami Islamic government

Howzeh Seminary

Howzehe elmieh It literally mean scientific sphere, but refers to religious university.

Huquq-e Zanan Women's rights

Ijtihad (Ejtehad) The Shi'a practice of exercising religious binding opinion exercised by *mojtaheds*.

Imamzadeh Shrine honoring the descendents of a Shi'i Imam.

Jalaseh Religious gathering

Jame'at al Zahra The largest theological seminary for women

Jame'eh-ye Rowhaniyat-e Mobarez Militant Clerics Association

Jameh Society

Jamiyatei Isargarae Enghelabe Islami Islamic Revolution Devotees Society

Jebheye Moshakerate Iran Islami Islamic Iran Participation Front

Jens e Dovom Second Sex

Jihad Literally means struggle. Religious duty of all Muslims to pursue a spiritual struggle to understand the faith

Jihadi Combative

Jomhuri-yeh Eslami Islamic Republic

Jundallah God's Soldiers

Khanevadeh Family

Layehe Hemayate Khanevadeh Family Protection Bill

Maktab Doctrine

Majlis The Iranian national parliament

Majmae Rowhaniyue Mobarez Militant Clergy Society

Majma Tashkise Maslehate Nezam Expediency Discernment Council

Maqna'eh A form fitting headscarf similar to a nun's habit that covers the hair and neck of a woman

Marja'e Taqlid The highest source of imitation within the Shi'i faith

Markaz Mosharekat Zanan Center for Women's Participation

Mehrieh The bride price agreed between the families of the bride and groom and included in the marriage contract

Mellat Nation

Mostakberin The oppressors

Mosta'zafin The dispossessed

Mujtahid (Mojtahed) A Shi'a cleric who has attained the highest level of religious knowledge and expertise enabling him to practice *ijtihad*. Each *mujtahid* has his own followers and can issue his own *fatwas*.

Naghafeh Alimony payable by a husband to a wife if she has child custody

Namous Honor

Ojrat-ol Mesal Wages for housework

Pasdaran Guardians of the revolution

Payam-e Hajar Hajar's message

Qods Jerusalem

Qur'an (Koran) The Islamic holy book

Rahbar Leader

Rejal Man or person

Roopush Loose tunic worn over clothing

Roosari Scarf used to cover hair

Rouzeh-khani Religious gatherings to commemorate religious events

Salam Hello

Sardar e Sazandegi Leader of the reconstruction

Sepahe Pasdaran Islamic Revolutionary Guards Corps

Shahnameh Book of Kings written by Ferdowsi

Shariah Islamic law that encompasses the totality of Islamic jurisprudence

Shi'ism A branch of Islam whose founders were the partisans and followers of the Prophet's son in law, Ali. Shi'is believe that after the Prophet's death the leadership of Islam should have been transferred to Ali. There are many branches of Shi'ism but the largest includes Twelver Shi'ism, which follows the teachings of the twelve Shi'i imams beginning with Ali and ending with Imam-al Mahdi who is believed to be in occultation. Twelver Shi'ism has been the official religion of Iran since the sixteenth century.

Shorayeh Khobregan The Assembly of Experts

Shorayeh Negahban Guardian Council

Sigheh (Muta) Temporary marriage

Sunnah Tradition

Sura Chapter of the Qur'an

Taqlid A source of religious emulation

Tarhe Amniyat Ejtema'i Social Morality Plan

Tasbeeh Prayer beads

Ulama Relgious scholars

Velayat-e faqih The guardianship of the Islamic jurisprudence. It refers to Ayatollah Khomeini's theory on the guardianship of the *faqih* as the head of state in absence of the twelfth imam.

Zanan Women

Zanan-e Berlin Women of Berlin

Zan-e Ruz Woman of Today

Zena Adultery

To My Sister

Sister, rise up after your freedom,
why are you quiet?
Rise up because henceforth
you have to imbibe the blood of tyrannical men.

Seek your rights, Sister,
from those who keep you weak,
from those whose myriad tricks and schemes
keep you seated in a corner of the house.

How long will you be the object of pleasure
in the harem of men's lust?
How long will you bow your proud head at his feet
like a benighted servant?

How long for the sake of a morsel of bread,
will you keep becoming an aged haji's temporary wife,
seeing second and third rival wives.
Oppression and cruelty, my sister, for how long?

This angry moan of yours
must surly become a clamorous scream.
You must tear apart this heavy bond
so that your life might be free.

Rise up and uproot the roots of oppression.
Give comfort to your bleeding heart.
For the sake of your freedom, strive
to change the law, rise up.

Forough Farrokhzad[1]

---

1. Forough Farrokhzad, *Sin: Selected Poems of Forough Farrokhzad*, trans. Shohleh Wolpe, Little Rock: University of Arkansas Press, 2007.

1

Introduction: A Female Awakening Through a Century of Struggle

On June 12, 2005, hundreds of women in Iran gathered in advance of the presidential elections protesting against the gender segregation policies of the Islamic Republic. The government responded to this open challenge by deploying security forces to arrest and disperse the crowd. This gathering, one among a growing series after almost three decades of limited quiet, revealed the impending confrontation between women and the Islamic government of Iran. A week earlier, a group of women activists forced their way into Tehran's Azadi stadium to watch a soccer match between Iran and Bahrain, a first since the Islamic government banned women from watching games at stadiums. For four hours, they carried signs that read, "My right is also human rights," and "Freedom, justice and gender equality."[1] On the one-year anniversary of this demonstration in June 2006, women again gathered to protest their unequal legal, political, and social status. This time, the state dispatched a female police force to contain and arrest the demonstrators. Most shocking were the images of women police beating women activists that were distributed and circulated on the Internet. On March 4, 2007, 31 Iranian women were arrested for gathering peacefully outside Tehran's Revolutionary Court in support of five fellow activists on trial for demanding changes in laws that discriminate against women. They were also accused of receiving foreign funds to stir up dissent in Iran, which led to the arrest and detention of many female activists.[2] These events set the stage for greater female political participation and activism in and around the tenth presidential elections coincidentally held on June 12, 2009.

During this presidential election campaign and in the post-election protests, women were again prominent participants. Their active involvement is a reflection of women's social and political gains during the past 32 years as well as their growing grievances against the Islamic Republic. Women turned out by the thousands to vote as well as to demonstrate in the postelection upheaval. Moreover, when Neda Agha-Soltan, a philosophy student, was fatally shot while attending a demonstration on the streets of Tehran on June 20, 2009, she became the iconic martyr in the protests. Zahra Rahnavard, former chancellor of Tehran University, activist, academic and also wife of opposition candidate Mir Hossein Musavi became a symbol of hope for women. As the first Iranian woman to campaign alongside her husband in a presidential election, Rahnavard's presence offered a promising example for political change. The other candidates, acknowledging the importance of the female vote, also tailored their campaigns to appeal to women. Mehdi Karroubi, in particular, promised to improve women's social status and appoint a female minister to his cabinet. Conservative candidates Mohsen Rezai and Mahmoud Ahmadinejad were forced to adapt by also bringing their wives along to campaign events.

These recent political episodes highlight how gender rights and female activism, prominent issues for Iranian women, have ebbed and flowed with the momentum of Iranian politics. Activists say that while world attention has focused on the West's standoff with Iran over its nuclear program, abuses of women's rights have intensified, as the regime has used fear of a U.S. attack as a pretext for its crackdown. Indeed, as suggested by Azadeh Kian, the arrest of dozens of women's rights activists, the closure of several women's magazines and women's non-governmental organizations (NGOs) —the number of which has increased from 54 in 1995 to over 600 in 2009—and many other attempts by the government to intimidate women's rights activists attest to the increasing political importance of women's issues.[3] These events also point to the contradictions apparent not only within the Iranian political system but also among women in Iran. Activist and journalist Fariba Davoudi Mohajer stated, "Women have a common discourse that is based on demands for equality. We have reached the conclusion that we have to work together, and this is a very positive development in the history of Iran's women's movement. This is a continuous movement with [solid] roots. The community of Iranian women has also accepted the costs [women] must pay for their actions. They have accepted that a social movement has its price, and they have to pay for it."[4] Shirin Ebadi, the 2005 Nobel Prize winner, has echoed that; "We can drive. We can vote. We've proved in these demonstrations that the world had the wrong idea about Iranian women. We don't sit in the corner and wait for the men to make change. We make change for the men. Iran has had enough male leaders. We are the mothers of Iran."[5] For the Iranian state though, the threat brought on by this domestic pressure has propelled the regime to react aggressively.

As suggested by one women's rights journalist and activist, "The women's issue reveals an inherent weakness apparent in the Iranian regime. Its behavior toward women is a primary example of this frailty. It goes without saying that when you back a cat into a corner, of course it's going to scratch and attack you in self-defense. This is analogous to the behavior of the Iranian government that feels backed into a corner."[6] Indeed, a government observer commented, "The Islamic Republic is experiencing one of its weakest periods in the realm of domestic policy and economics."[7] The political tension and public outcry surrounding Iran's 2009 presidential election has shed light on the fragile relationship between state and society in the Islamic

Republic. This weakness is further evidenced in the state's attempts to control civil society, curb public dissent, contain the post election protests, and is reflected in many of its policies, including those toward women.

Gender issues are at the center of contemporary Iranian politics. Since the revolution, Iranian women have commenced a quiet revolution of their own against the Islamist status quo. They have played a decisive role in elections, assumed political posts, and now outnumber men in all arenas of education. Moreover, their income contributions are considered vital for the economic survival of many families. Ironically, the state has been no innocent bystander in this process but rather an unintentional facilitator. Needing female legitimacy to justify the moral, Islamic, and political nature of the revolution, the state co-opted women by preserving their right to vote, originally granted by Muhammad Reza Pahlavi in 1967. During the Iran-Iraq war, recognizing that female support was again essential for the national defense, they too encouraged female education, and labor participation while also enshrining the exalted position of women as mothers and wives. These initial policies set in motion a cycle of reaction and action on the part of both women and the state—each responding and adapting to the other. Today, the Islamic Republic can no longer ignore women's strength as a political constituency and as promoters of change. Indeed, women's rights are one of the main battlegrounds for domestic change within the factional political system.

The imagery associated with the Islamic Republic of Iran most prominently draws upon the revolution and Islamic symbolism. The black-turbaned, long-bearded, scowling revolutionary leader, Ayatollah Ruhollah Khomeini, is among the foremost icons of Iran and its Islamic Revolution. Illustrations of young Iranian boys running across Iraqi minefields during the eight-year Iran-Iraq war screaming "*Allahu akbar!* ("God is great!") along with photos of the 1979 American hostages, held for 444 days, blindfolded, hands tied behind their backs have also colored the imagination. Figures of women shrouded in long black chadors chanting in defense of Iran's unpredictable revolution point to the dualities of a revolution that was supported by women but resulted in a reversal of many female legal protections. The vitriolic statements of President Mahmoud Ahmadinejad do not dim these grim memories. In fact, Ahmadinejad has only solidified world opinion against the dark and contradictory policies of the Islamic Republic. Yet, these images reveal only a part of Iran and the Iranian story that has played out since the inimical 1979 revolution.

Shahrough Akhavi wrote, "The Iranian revolution of 1979 presents a case in which religion has stimulated profound social change, rather than served only as a basis for social integration."[8] For the Islamic government, which has struggled to keep the passion of its revolution and religious fervor afire after 32 years, this statement astutely points to an unexpected phenomenon of social and political transformation. The impact of a theocratic government dramatically altered Iranian society, but these changes were anything but predictable. Indeed, rather than a monolithic fundamentally religious society, Iran is an amalgamation of its diverse and long history bound together by its myriad of identities—50 percent Persian with ethnic groups including Arabs, Kurds, Azeris, and various tribal associations consisting of the other half, Shi'a Muslim, modernist, nationalist, and reactionist. Over the centuries, these often-competing identities have been woven together, bringing to life the contradictions and dynamism evident within Iranian politics and society.

The Islamic Republic has endured for over three decades amidst the tensions of these competing trends. Many international observers continue to see Iran as unchanged. Despite regular elections and even electoral protests, the revolutionary elite continues to hold its monopoly on power. The government continues to espouse virulent anti-Americanism and support terror organizations in the Middle East. At weekly prayer gatherings and demonstrations, participants and revolutionary loyalists continue to denounce the "Great Satan" (the United States) as well as the "Little Satan" (Israel). Women continue to be subject to patriarchal interpretations of Islamic law all imposed after the onset of the revolution. Human rights violations continue to be an ingredient of life within the Islamic Republic. However, coupled with the revolutionary rhetoric and ideological passions that have come to be associated with the Islamic Republic of Iran, so too has there been a story of vibrancy and change, resilience and resistance, confrontation and conciliation.

Most evidently, the nature of politics, religion and society has evolved. In effect, these changes have been circular. The government has been forced to adjust to the changing nature of society. Since the revolution, Iran has experienced a demographic boom that led to a doubling of the population, leaving 70 percent of the population under the age of 30.[9] This 70 percent has little or no memory of the revolution and its ambitions, adding not only social and economic pressures to the mix of government responsibility, but also political ones, as the youth hope for a new and dynamic future amidst the confines of an autocratic Islamic state. These confines, while restricting movement, action, freedom, and accountability, have also sparked creativity. Many Iranians are continuously pushing the boundaries—legal, social, political, economic, and religious—to find new methods of expression and opportunity within the Islamic state. The state regularly censors films, music, art, dance, and books that are considered anti-Islamic and critical of the state. Yet, aspiring actors, musicians, artists, and writers are persistently finding novel outlets of expression. Of course, the government does indeed catch on to these new methods, and has thus curbed Internet access, closed magazines, banned websites, and prevented writers and musicians from performing. But the collective power of young people to resist regulations they do not condone is immeasurable. A young, politically apathetic generation watch bootleg DVDs of the latest Hollywood films, write blogs about their social lives, and pass phone numbers through car windows during interminable traffic jams. In the wealthy suburbs of northern Tehran, women go out wearing long coats over miniskirts and low-cut tops as they make their way to the parties that take place almost every night with effortless access to drugs, alcohol, and sex.

The pendulum swings widely in Iran. And while the constrictions of social and political life are indeed frustrating, this circle of action and reaction has not constrained the vigor of Iranian society. What's more is that these youth have benefitted from the government's massive investment in education. Approximately 85 percent of the nation is literate, a figure that exceeds 90 percent among those younger than 25.

There are 22 million students, including around 3 million enrolled in universities, of which over half are women.[10] In general, the urban, middle-class youth maintain little connection to the regime's Islamic revolutionary ideology. As the state's Islamist ideology has lost its luster, society has—paradoxically—experienced a form of "secularization" from below and given birth to what is now openly referred to as "Islamic feminism." Islamic feminists contend that women should be afforded equal but not the same rights as men. They boldly call for the reinterpretation of Islamic law, using Shi'a jurisprudence. The paradox of Iranian history is ever potent, as the reaction to a theocratic government has also inspired intellectual and popular movements for the separation of the institution of religion from that of the state, if not of faith from politics. Clearly, in spite of the not-so-hidden hand of the state, new boundaries are being pushed and explored every day.

In its first decade, the Islamic Republic was focused on the struggle of revolutionary consolidation. Amidst the threat of war, sanctions, and international isolation, the government was consumed with the survival of the regime. Policies were implanted to protect the nascent Islamic Republic from threats looming both inside and outside Iranian territory. Domestically, Kurdish and Arab ethnic groups and political adversaries were repressed in the interest of regime consolidation.[11] Internationally, the American hostage crisis and the war with Saddam Hussein had extended into a regional and international conflict as neighbors and nations around the world allied against Iran. The government used these events to successfully purge the regime of opponents and unite in the face of isolation.

In 1988, after eight years of intense fighting that decimated Iran's economic and political stability, Ayatollah Khomeini agreed to "drink from the poisoned chalice" of peace, finally yielding to a cease-fire. This concession was a blessing for Iran's population, which had suffered and sacrificed through the years of war, losing lives, limbs, freedom, and prosperity. For the revolutionary government, however, peace brought the burdens of statecraft and bureaucracy to reality. The regime was forced to shift from revolution and cross-border war to the ordinary business of governing. Iraq's assaults on Iran had enabled the Islamic Republic to unify Iranians in the shared goal of repelling Saddam Hussein's forces and protecting the new government. When the war ended, that unifying mission was replaced by competing ideological visions of Iran's future.

In the decade after the revolution, Ayatollah Khomeini united the country through his charismatic presence and his powerful ideology. Upon his death in 1989, though, factionalism and ideological discord broke the façade of unity that had held the country together. Traditionalists known today as "principalists" or "strict constructionists" have pushed to preserve the revolutionary ideology Khomeini espoused. Seeking to hold fast to the ideals and promises of the revolution, the hard-line revolutionaries along with fledgling offspring, such as President Mahmoud Ahmadinejad, have advanced policies and platforms designed to safeguard the integrity of the Islamic Republic. Two other groups, pragmatists and reformists (or "judicial activists"), have instead pushed for moderate reinterpretations of policy in order to preserve the longevity of the Islamic state through reform. These politicians while equally active and devoted to the ideology of the revolution, support policies of economic and political liberalization. To them, moderate policies would alleviate tensions with the West, thereby opening the door to much-needed foreign investment that would aid Iran's economic woes. This ultimate struggle over the future and direction of the regime continues to dominate both domestic and international politics and is most acutely evidenced in the 2010 post-presidential election protests. This split is reflected in the post-election stalemate where the political elite is divided in their loyalty to the system, the need for political reform, and in their support for President Ahmadinejad. The most immediate consequence of this struggle is seen in the arbitrary and conflicting domestic and foreign policies that emerge from the state and its varying institutions.

On the religious front, the theocratic regime exploited religion as a powerful tool of integration—the unifying glue in society. Through religious sanction, government policies were ordained, lending popular credibility to the revolution and its policies. Time and again, religious fatwas or edicts have been used to endorse political decisions. At the same time, though, the diffuse nature of Shi'a Islam has also facilitated contending interpretations of this fluid religion. Shi'ism has no cohesive religious structure nor a pope-like authority. Moreover, unlike their Sunni counterparts, Shi'a clerics are free to interpret the traditional texts, oftentimes providing modern applications to traditional laws. In fact, after attaining the position of an ayatollah, or "sign of God," with the credentials to interpret the religion and its law and traditions, religious leaders are free to innovate. Shi'a adherents are also free to follow the teachings of one ayatollah over another. As such, the multitude of religious leaders coupled with their competing analysis has undoubtedly been a challenge for the Islamic regime. Indeed, decisions both political and religious can appear arbitrary based on the interpretation of one cleric over another. The controversy surrounding Ayatollah Ali Khamenei's ascent to the post of the Supreme Leader, a man with insufficient religious credentials, has also clouded the unity of the state. It is clear that in mixing together, politics has mired religion. The result has left the regime struggling to retain its ideological and religious identity, often amidst popular resistance.

In dissecting these powerful changes, women have also played a significant and active role in forcing change in Iranian society. These transformations are not limited to the period following the revolution, but date to the past century, as women's activism has been intertwined and even motivated by the political and social changes affecting society. Since 1979, women's issues—be they political, social, economic, or religious—are wrapped up in the identity of the Islamic Republic and represent the contradictions that lie at the heart of the Iranian regime. For the leadership, the question of women—their legal status, their equality and place in society—brings to light the balance between the ideological versus practical determinations of the governing elite. For women, their struggle reflects not only the change and tenor apparent in Iranian society, but also provides a lens focusing on the dynamics of activism, compromise, and confrontation. The emergence of female activism highlights the paradox between social change and integration that is often overlooked when examining the consequences of this religious revolution.

This study draws together the components of change in Iranian politics and society. Through the prism of gender, a crucial variable for understanding politics in Iran, cultural, social, political, and religious forces driving civil society will be analyzed to draw attention to Iran's multifaceted social transformation. Hence, a focus on women, gender issues and activism will shed light on the larger dynamic and dialectic of politics in the Islamic Republic of Iran. The force and evolution of female activism within the Iranian political arena is connected to domestic, international, social, economic, and religious developments. It will be important to characterize and define women's activism in Iran. Is there indeed an Iranian women's movement? What experiences and policies have motivated female solidarity? Particularly, which domestic policies have impacted women? How, if at all, have foreign policies influenced women and women's activism? How have women collaborated to effect political and social change? What gains have women made?

Some scholars and many of my interviewees contend that there is no women's movement in Iran.[12] Ali Akbar Mahdi argues that women have created a movement "without direction, leadership, and structure." At the same time, according to Mahdi, this movement reveals women's "greater awareness of human rights, individual rights, individual autonomy within marriage, family independence within the kinship network, and a form of national consciousness against the global diffusion of Western values." Farhad Khosrowkhavar describes the women's movement in Iran as one of the three new social movements to emerge in the late-1990s—the other two being students and intellectuals.[13] Homa Hoodfar and Fatemeh Sadeghi have advanced,

> The women's movement in Iran does not fit into the classic model of a centralized and coordinated organization with clear leaders. Neither does it subscribe to any grand theories. However, its diverse organizations have demands that are shared across class, ethnicity and generation, and even across ideological and secular/religious boundaries. Its priorities are the tangible issues affecting women's daily lives.[14]

According to Valentine Moghadam,

> [W]omen in Iran are in a pre-movement phase, without the large public mobilizations and independent organizations needed to constitute a social movement. The discourse and consciousness, however, are present. In time, the contradictions between women's legal status and their social reality and aspirations, along with the blocked opportunities for employment and economic independence, could trigger a wider movement. Positive signs of women's activism and indicators of movement formation can be discerned.[15]

A number of my interviewees made the distinction between a *harekat*, or movement, and a *jonbesh*, or a leap. Both Persian words could portend that a movement indeed exists, and both were used repeatedly and interchangeably to point to the pervasive trends of female activism and gender consciousness in Iranian society. However, the subtle differences of these words can expound upon the contending arguments surrounding the existence of an Iranian women's movement. It is argued that the growth in gender consciousness coupled with the socioeconomic shifts evident in Iranian society could facilitate a strong women's movement comparable to those evidenced in the West. The fundamentals are there. However, limitations abound regarding this kind of growth. Indeed, the state poses the biggest obstacle. Government reaction to women's activism exposes their concern for the impending threat from women. At the same time, while society has become more gender conscious, female activism has remained confined to the educated urban middle class where it has been dependent on the mobilizing success of Islamist and secular elites. By analyzing the impact and effect of these forces on women and within the political sphere, I will endeavor to build upon and contribute to contemporary studies of Iranian politics.

It is important to distinguish that in this analysis of Iranian women and their activism; there is no monolithic group of "women" in Iran. Indeed, it is impossible to make generalizations about Iranian women. Although the term "women" will be used frequently as a method of generalization, as much specificity as possible will be provided, including a chapter defining and detailing the strategies, differences and goals of each group. Support for women's activism is drawn from disparate social, demographic, economic, religious, and political classes. The uniqueness of such activism is its diversity. However, it is critical to distinguish between the various divisions among women in order to better understand the history and evolution of gender-based activism.

In this study, three general typologies will be used to delineate the different political and religious leanings of women—traditional, Islamist, and secular. Traditional women were supporters and initial collaborators with the Islamic Republic. They tend to be religious and come from religious families who have staunchly supported the revolution and its ambitions. Moreover, their families have been among the principal economic beneficiaries of the revolution. While prior to 1979 many of these women came from lower- or lower-middle-class families, through their government patronage and familial support, they have risen in economic status. Traditionally, many of these women resided in smaller cities and rural areas throughout the country but since the revolution have partaken in the large-scale urbanization. Plus, while not always in agreement with the Islamic and political decisions of the regime, they have worked and continue to work within the system to advance, protect, or alter laws and policies affecting women. Moreover, they subscribe to the literal interpretation of Islamic laws. Many of these women work in collaboration with the state supporting the state ideology.

Essentially, this group of women seeks to define and reinterpret gender issues grounded in an Islamic framework or as stated by Margot Badran "a feminist discourse and practice articulated within an Islamic paradigm."[16] These women use the Qur'an and its teachings to challenge patriarchal interpretations of women's issues. In reaction to political decisions and events, this group has splintered, bringing Islamist women and Islamist feminists into the fore. It is important to note that a woman can be Islamist without subscribing to feminism. Moreover, women who identify with Islamic feminism as a strategy to challenge gender issues do not always claim an Islamic feminist identity. Feminism carries a negative connotation within Iran's patriarchal society, as it is associated with a foreign ideology, one that was often invoked under the reign of Muhammad Reza Pahlavi. In general, these women were also supporters and participants in the Iranian revolution. However, unlike their traditional counterparts, these women were disappointed with the gender policies of the Islamic government. Many of these women demand that Islamic law be reinterpreted using exegesis as well as adapted to the contemporary needs of a modern society. In general, many of these women do not oppose the theocratic nature of the government but rather seek greater gender equality and political reform. In the second decade of the revolution, these women coalesced around the reform movement supporting the election of President Muhammad Khatami in 1997.

The third group, known as the secularists, has been marginalized from the political system due to their objection to the imposition of Islamic law. Secular women are not necessarily irreligious or non-Muslim, but they support the separation of the political and religious spheres. Many secular women are practicing Muslims, but they fervently reject Iran's theocratic system of government. They support equal rights for women. After a decade of social marginalization during the years of the Iran-Iraq war, they sought out alternative spheres of influence, gaining ground in journalism, the arts, music, film, and grassroots organizations. Secular women are predominantly urban based, although I did encounter women in small cities and rural provinces who shared these similar sentiments. Many secular women are young, literate, and educated coming from lower-middle, middle and upper classes.

Defining the varying groups of women is necessary, as each has played a critical role in advancing women's issues over the subsequent three decades. At the same time, the collective female experience is also vital to this study. Indeed, not all Iranian women are activists, in fact the majority of Iranian women are not involved in any political or social activism. Most women continue to shun and eschew activism and political participation. However, as argued by Asef Bayat, female activism in Iran has generated momentum because of the collective experiences of Iranian women since the revolution, and in reaction to the government's gender policies. Women in general collectively suffered from the Islamic legal restrictions but benefited from educational opportunities. Many women revolted in the aftermath of Khatami's reformist marginalization, using social outlets to express their political frustrations. As such, both Iran society and Iranian women are more gender conscious. As stated by Bayat:

> what underlined Iran's women's activism was not collective protest but collective presence . . . it subsisted on the *power of presence*—the ability to assert collective will in spite of all odds, by circumventing constraints,

utilizing what exists, and discovering new spaces of freedom to make oneself heard, seen, and felt. In this movement, women did not usually take extraordinary measures to compel authorities to make concessions; in a sense, the very ordinary practices that they strove for accounted for the actual gains. Not only did the element of ordinariness make the movement virtually irrepressible, it also allowed women to gain ground incrementally without seeming to constitute a threat.[17]

Indeed, the development of female activism in Iran diverges from patterns prescribed in traditional social movement theory. However, Charles Tilly points to the importance of "history . . . because it identifies significant changes in the operation of social movements . . . and because it calls attention to the shifting political conditions that made social movements possible."[18] For Iran, the historical variable is ever pertinent. Tilly also delineates the conditions of a movement based upon worthiness, unity, numbers, and commitment. Building on this, Sidney Tarrow calls attention to the "cycles of contention . . . when changing political opportunities and constraints create incentives for social actors who lack resources of their own."[19] He also emphasizes the rise and fall of social movements as part of political struggle and as the outcome of changes in political opportunity structures, of which he lists five that are pertinent to the case of Iranian women's activism: increasing access, shifting alignments, divided elites, influential allies, and repression and facilitation. Tarrow writes that unlike political and economic institutions, social movements have an elusive power, but one that is no less real. These ideas combined with Bayat's analysis of "informal, every day form of resistance," will provide the methodological backbone to analyze the convergence of female activism.[20] In this story of contention, the disparate groups, their motivations and collaborations will be explicated alongside the status, activism, and evolution of women and politics in Iran.

Since childhood I regularly visited Iran on summer holidays. I was unaware then that subtle changes experienced at the airports or the relaxation in Islamic standards of dress had such drastic political implications. I continued to return to Iran for graduate and doctoral research. While I focused primarily on foreign policy issues and U.S.-Iranian relations, I became increasingly interested in the changing role of women in Iranian society.

I grew up resenting the confines of my gender likely due to the cultural, socio-economic, and religious boundaries limiting women in Iran and the Middle East. In Iran in particular, I could not travel, explore, or fraternize freely. Moreover, I hated the gender cordoning at Iranian gatherings where men spoke of politics and where women discussed more superficial issues. A study conducted by Manuchehr Mohseni in 2000 suggested I was not alone in my sentiments, as 53 percent of Iranian girls would prefer to be boys.[21] Yet with time, I came to recognize that my gender afforded me access to the female world—a world that was inaccessible for many men and a world that was regularly evolving. This admission was not limited to parties in northern Tehran but extended to rural villages, mosques, female seminaries, mourning ceremonies, card playing gatherings, universities, beauty salons, and government and private offices. I began to seek out Iranian women beyond cousins and friends questioning them on their political and religious beliefs, cultural values and ambitions. Having observed and partaken in "northern Tehrani" life, I was particularly interested in connecting with traditional women and supporters of the Islamic government. With each encounter, I discovered the deeper complexities behind gender issues, that I took for granted, including the contours and characterization of female activism.

My initial interest was to better understand the political, social, and religious orientations of politically conservative, pious, and traditional women. I was interested in understanding how these women, many of whom were educated and religious, reconciled Islamic teachings and law that subjugated women. Particularly, I hoped to study and spend time in female Iranian seminaries. While I succeeded in interviewing many young women who had graduated and studied in the numerous seminaries, my research became subject to political scrutiny. I decided to build on this work by broadening the scope of my study. While it was important to understand the conservative, traditional Iranian woman and her political and religious identity, I realized that these women were only part of the Iranian female narrative and a story addressing the diverse range of social, economic, political, and religious women needed to be told.

Confronting political and social obstacles is routine for most Iranian women and such obstacles are not limited to class, background, or religiosity. Indeed, the mundane tasks of banking, commuting, and dressing are among the long list of daily ordeals for women. Yet, for over three decades now, women have succeeded in transforming daily adversities into opportunities. I am in awe and inspired by the passion and motivation of the many women I have encountered through the years. In the face of continued constraints, they have not yielded. Instead, they have become more empowered, more organized, more creative and more directed. Through these encounters I began to appreciate the value of my gender and sought to officially document my research.

In the subsequent chapters, I build upon the seminal works of Eliz Sarnassian's *Women's Rights Movement in Iran: Mutiny, Appeasement, and Repression from 1900 to Khomeini* and Parvin Paidar's *Women and the Political Process in Twentieth Century Iran*. Both books provide formative contributions to the field of women's and Iranian studies in tracing the history of female politics in Iran. In this vein, I sought to identify the links between gender and politics in the Islamic Republic of Iran. The control of gender policy and subsequently the control of Iranian women were among the foremost political decisions of the Islamic state. The state has used gender issues for domestic and international policy objectives and legitimacy. The long-term consequence has led to gender consciousness and female activism. Qualifying these links and distinguishing the evolution and sources of government policy as well as female motivations and strategies is the goal of this chronological study.

I officially began researching in summer 2006, building on my informal field-work conducted since 1997. My research was conducted over the course of four trips to Iran through May 2008. Through familial and professional contacts, I began interviewing women in the hope of tracing the sources and tracking the growing female momentum evidenced in Iranian society. This energy was inspired not only by women but also in reaction to government policy. As such, my conversations with subjects focused on their personal and professional lives, political and religious beliefs as well as reactions to the state and political issues. Each subject was asked to indentify sources of personal and social change experienced by women and society in general. Meeting settings varied. Often I was invited into subject's homes or met with women in their offices while on many occasions I met women in public settings, such as parks and coffee shops. Female gatherings or *jalasehs* were opportune settings to interact and converse in a group.

These interviews and discussions were conducted in Persian. Despite the innocuous nature of our conversations most women were reluctant to be taped because of the tense political and social environment that had taken hold since the presidential election of Mahmoud Ahmadinejad in 2005. Interviews were conducted with female parliamentarians from the sixth, seventh, and eighth Majlis, with female journalists, university students, housewives, seminary students, professors, scholars, female preachers, one female *mujtahid* (religious scholar competent to interpret Islamic law), and a number of male mujtahids, female lawyers, artists, and school-teachers. The interviewees were based in Tehran, Qom, Isfahan, Karaj, Shahre Kord, Hamedan, Mashad, and abroad.

Over the course of the two-year period, this research became more methodologically challenging. In 2007, four Iranian-American scholars had been arrested and accused of endangering national security. In this tense domestic political climate, many traditional and Islamist women became increasingly reluctant to meet with me, an Iranian-American academic. By my last trip in April 2008, more often than not, politically active or politically connected Islamist women would agree to an interview and then "fall ill" at the last moment proving more difficult to reach on the phone when I would call to reschedule. Those that did agree to meetings spoke in coded innuendos or deflected questions on domestic issues. One female professor handed me her published articles instead of responding to questions. Others spent the scheduled time inquiring about my background, my connections abroad, and ideological affiliations. A number of women intimated that they were "*zeer e nazar*" or under surveillance and insisted on anonymity. For this reason, the names and identities of my subjects have been kept anonymous. More so, in light of the domestic crackdown on politicians, activists, and students in the aftermath of the tenth presidential elections, their anonymity will be protected.

In addition to these interviews, I have studied and drawn from articles and interviews written in the prominent women's magazine, *Zanan* (Women). Published by Shahla Sherkat, *Zanan* is a reflection of the changing trends in women's activism. The journal began publishing in 1992 and was shut down by the state in 2008.

Through the years it has reported on social, political, legal, economic, cultural, and international issues affecting women and society. Moreover, *Zanan* provides significant insight into the dynamism and diversity of women's activism.

XXX

Women have become a formidable political force in the Islamic Republic since 1979, but that was not the starting point of female activism in Iran. Iran has had an active women's movement since the mid-1800s. The history of female activism will be traced in Chapter 2. Bibi Khatoon Astarabadi founded the first school for girls in Tehran and in 1895 published the first declaration of women's rights in Iran, the *Failings of Men.*[22] Women participated alongside their male counterparts in boycotts and protests as early as the 1891–92 Tobacco Rebellion, when public anger erupted over the shah's award of a concession to England to produce, sell, and export Iran's tobacco crop, forcing him to revoke the deal. The momentum of this early movement propelled women to also participate in the 1905 Constitutional Revolution, when they not only struggled to advance the popular political and social ambitions of the day, but also agitated for women's rights—a campaign that has become a century-long struggle.[23] Iranian women started attending university in the academic year 1935–36, gained the right to vote in 1963—earlier than in some European countries—and were a major force in the Islamic Revolution that toppled the shah in 1979. But the history of women in Iran is complicated. While the shah was in power, women had more freedom and greater legal rights, but such change had not altered the patriarchal culture.

Through the monarchical days of the Pahlavi dynasty, women continued to agitate for greater legal protection, enfranchisement, and social opportunities. Their gains were incremental as women's issues were absorbed as state ones. Both Reza Pahlavi and his son, Muhammad Reza Pahlavi, addressed women's concerns as part of their modernization and development campaigns. Despite subtle advancements in education and eventually in legal gains and enfranchisement evidenced in 1967 with the adoption of the Family Protection Law, the public attitude was subsumed under patriarchal norms.[24]

Women continued their activism, often relegating their political and social goals behind broader societal ones. In this vein, women were involved in the mounting antimonarchical opposition. On the eve of the revolution, women once again were intimately involved in the demonstrations calling for the return of Ayatollah Khomeini. At the time, there was little attention given to the question of the post-revolutionary political system, although Khomeini's intentions and ambitions had been foreshadowed in his writings and speeches. Equally ignored was the critical impact of such female activism that also foreshadowed the momentum of change gaining among women. These issues will be examined in Chapter 3.

This female activism has been among the most stimulating development that has taken force over the last 32 years. The story of Iranian women—their triumphs and travails, much of which will be recounted on these pages, is very much intertwined with the story of the revolution and the changing nature of the Islamic government. While a myriad of women were among the supporters of the Iranian Revolution, it is common knowledge that despite their overwhelming support, women have been most negatively affected by the imposition and constraints of life under Islamic law. Chapter 4 will assess these changes describing and dividing women's groups and their modes of activism since the revolution. There exists a general consensus in Iran that whatever the legacy of the revolution's political agenda or economic goals, its deepest impact will be on Iran's social order. Such a prediction is most relevant when observing Iran's women. This sentiment has been echoed by Azar Nafisi, who stated, "If you want to know how much society is changing, look at the women."

That's not, of course, what the clerics intended. Their original goal was similar to gender segregation or gender apartheid. While in theory legal and religious policies sought to restrict women to the maternal sphere, in practice such policies could not be absolutely imposed. The political realities of the day necessitated female political support, education and labor participation. Hence, the pragmatism of politics forced the political leadership under President Hashemi Rafsanjani to balance their patriarchal vision with a practical one. What began as an attempt to marginalize women, soon changed into a plan to integrate them. Chapter 5 will assess these efforts.

In the aftermath of the revolution, as part of the consolidation and Islamization campaign, the state marginalized all women who had collaborated with the Pahlavi past—including 22 members of parliament, 330 in local councils, 5 mayors and thousands of civil servants and diplomats.[25] Rejecting the Western role and image of women supported during the Pahlavi regime, the Islamic government put forth their own ideal revolutionary female model drawing on the influence of Prophet Muhammad's daughter, also the wife of Shi'a Imam Ali, Fatemeh. Women were encouraged to emulate the Prophet's daughter—the ideal wife and mother. Veiling and gender segregation were legally enforced in schools, offices, ski slopes, beaches, and beyond. Adding to these regulations were the social restrictions imposed on society. Roadblocks were set up at night to make sure female passengers were related to the male drivers they accompanied. Families suspected of hosting private parties in their homes with unmarried couples or youths in attendance were raided. Morals police commissioned to enforce these rules patrolled the streets. Bad *hijab*—meaning exposed hair and skin, plus the wearing of makeup—was punished with 70 lashes or 10 days to 2 months in jail. Islamic laws were revived such that women and men convicted of adultery were stoned to death, the legal marriage age for girls was reduced to nine years, and legal protections for divorce, child custody, inheritance, and testimony were reversed.

Inevitably, women were the primary targets of these campaigns. Legally and socially, they were marginalized and forced to accept their limited roles in society as mothers, wives, and sisters. A woman's testimony in court is worth half that of a man's, women receive only half the inheritance of men, and if a man dies without having children, the wife inherits only a quarter of his wealth while the remaining portion is allocated to the state. Although Morocco, Egypt, and Turkey provide better legal protection for women, Iranian women still fare better than those in many countries in the Persian Gulf. Unlike Saudi women, for example, Iranian women have the right to vote, to drive, and to become members of parliament. Women are active in all parts of Iranian life, ranging from agriculture to engineering to nuclear physics.

In recent years, Iranian women have achieved some improvements in their civil status. For example, they won the right to keep custody of their male children until the child turns seven. Previously, custody automatically went to the father in all circumstances upon divorce. Divorce reform continues to be a pressing issue for many women's rights activists. Men still have the exclusive right to end a marriage, although Shi'a law specifies exceptions; such as if it is expressly written into the marriage contract that the woman can herself seek a divorce. On the other hand, if the wife initiates a divorce, she must prove her husband is guilty of misconduct, addiction, imprisonment, not paying her subsistence expenses, or a variety of other grievous situations. Most know that justifying such things in a court is difficult. In most cases, the wife can only demonstrate such failures after many years of pressuring the legal system.

Ironically, though, these broad-ranging policies coupled with demographic and educational shifts have forged greater unity among women and throughout Iranian society. Bound together by common fate and experience, more women and men are conscious of gender, and the issues and obstacles that surround it.[26] At the same time, this consciousness coupled with the bonds of common fate have motivated women to challenge the legal and political norms regarding their rights. Issues such as divorce, child custody, employment, and education, among others, affect all women, no longer just women of a certain class or background. Such issues undoubtedly impact Iranian fathers, brothers, husbands, and sons as well. The common cause and shared experiences have bonded women together, bringing momentum to Iranian female activism.

The passions that emerged from disparate corners of Iranian society to inspire a vibrant women's activism are just as deep as the emotions of the 1979 revolution. The impact has been visible in every aspect of Iranian life. In 1996, an unprecedented 200 women ran for the 290-seat parliament, and 14 were elected. In 1997, four women registered to run for the presidency. A year later, nine women tried to stand for the Assembly of Experts, the political body empowered to elect the Supreme Leader. In both elections, all the women were rejected by the Council of Guardians, which has the power to vet candidates. The official reason for their disqualifications was their lack of religious or political experience, but it was common knowledge that their gender was the real source of constraint. Building on this momentum, in the 2000 presidential election, 100 nominated themselves as candidates, and in 2001, 47 women put themselves forward, though in 2009 only 42 were compelled to run.[27] To balance against these legal limitations, Supreme Leader Ali Khamenei has called for "greater participation of women in social and political affairs" urging families to educate their daughters and to promote female employment. At the same time though, he has also cautioned that, "A blind imitation of Western women is noxious."[28]

On the thirtieth anniversary of the revolution, a third of government employees were female—a major achievement compared to Iran's regional neighbors. Five thousand women ran during the first-ever municipal elections held in 1999, and more than 300 won. In the 2006 municipal elections, 44 seats out of the 264 on provincial capital councils went to women.[29] Increasing numbers of Iranian women had also become lawyers, doctors, professors, newspaper and magazine editors, engineers, business executives, economists, coaches, and television newscasters. By 1999, Iran had 140 female publishers, enough to hold an exhibition of books and publications produced only by women. In the arts, they had become painters, authors, designers, photographers, movie producers, actors, and directors—and winners of international awards in all categories.

In education, Iran was cited in 1998 as one of ten countries worldwide that had made the most progress in closing the gap between boys and girls in the education system.[30] More than 95 percent of Iranian girls were enrolled in elementary school. Over 68 percent of university students were women—compared with 28 percent in 1978. And more than a third of university faculties were female. A third of all physicians are women. In 1998, Zahra Rahnavard, a writer and the wife of former Prime Minister Mir Hossein Musavi, became the first female university chancellor at the women's Al Zahra University.

Just as important was the general sense of power shared among Iran's women. Millions had begun to define the way Islam was applied and to put their own imprint on widely diverse aspects of Iranian life. Using Islamic tools of interpretation and taking advantage of their access to education, women have pushed for modern and moderate interpretations of Islamic law. In essence, they have used the same tools as those used by the government to seek new religious interpretations. Since 1994, female pressure had changed laws on employment, divorce, child custody, alimony, and maternity leave. The overwhelming turnout and unity of the female vote was among the principal factors behind the 1997 victory of President Muhammad Khatami in the biggest election upset since the revolution.

An unexpected benefit of state-imposed religion was that by forcing women to wear the hijab, or Islamic cover, many young women who were previously kept at home were given new opportunities to go outside. Veiled women from conservative and religious families could study and work—to such an extent that women now comprise about two-thirds of university students, a shift that has led to calls for quotas to protect the enrollment of men.[31]

Women began to feel more hopeful during Muhammad Khatami's reformist presidency. His promise of a "dialogue of civilizations" and greater attention to civil society gave hope to the overwhelming female and youth constituency that swept Khatami to office. With women holding multiple posts in the inner political circle and cabinet for the first time since the revolution—including Massoumeh Ebtekar as Khatami's vice president for environmental protection,

Zahra Shojai as his women's affairs adviser, and Zahra Rahnavard as his senior adviser on cultural affairs—and with greater support for NGOs and increased leniency toward the press, women took advantage of the open atmosphere during this period to agitate for greater political and social change. Subtle changes and promises advanced by the Khatami administration motivated women, and their activism grew significantly during this period, as they felt more confident that the reformist political environment would allow change. Legally, though, during Khatami's tenure, no significant advancements for women were made. As will be detailed in Chapter 6, Khatami's hands were tied almost from the outset of his presidency, by the constitutional constraints limiting his power as well as by increasing power of the office of the Supreme Leader.

Chapter 7 highlights the pendulum swing that came with the election of Mahmoud Ahmadinejad in 2005 on a pledge to revive revolutionary values. His administration and its policies, including a widespread social and political clampdown across society, reflect the schizophrenic approach often pursued by the Iranian state. Initially, the new administration refrained from the wholesale rollback of women's rights that was anticipated by women's groups.[32] In fact, in a much-lauded populist move, the president argued that women should be allowed to watch sporting events alongside men. This suggestion was not well received among the conservative clerical community of Qom and elsewhere, forcing Ahmadinejad to backtrack from his remarks. The government is also slowly amending laws that are discriminatory toward women. New laws allow women suffering injury or death in a car accident to the same insurance compensation as men, whereas previously women received only half the compensation given to men.[33] The conservative eighth parliament in February 2009 went further, voting to allow widows to inherit land from their husband, reversing the age-old civil code that prevented inheritance of real estate.[34] Another bill passed by the parliament and awaiting approval of the Expediency Council, could clarify legal discrepancies over female candidacy for president. Changes such as this have given some activists hope that legal equality can be achieved as subtle reforms are setting a precedent for the future.

At the same time, though, Ahmadinejad's government has been trying to quash discussions about women's rights and has violently suppressed demonstrations. He has also tightened enforcement of Islamic dress, supported further segregation of Iranian society, recently inaugurating the first female-only park and exercise ground, and supported parliamentary initiatives that would further restrict women's rights.[35] A prominent effort has been dubbed "the anti-Family bill" and has caused much controversy and uproar. Under Islamic law, men are permitted to take up to four wives. This provision, though, is based on a number of conditions, including a Shariah requirement to obtain the permission of the first wife before any such union is fulfilled. The new bill proposes to remove the requirement of the first wife's permission. Currently the bill has been returned to parliamentary committee, suggesting that popular opposition has forced this initiative to be shunted.[36] Efforts such as this one, point to the glaring contradictions apparent in Iranian society with regard to women's rights. As suggested by one female activist, "The Iranian government has created squadrons of policewomen, bus drivers, and female university students, but at the same time, they want to turn women into housewives and make them accept polygamy. There is a big paradox here."[37]

This paradox is also reflected in the results of the last parliamentary election held in March 2008. Despite the fact that women are overtaking men in education and are now considered paramount to the financial backbone of a family, women performed miserably in the parliamentary election. Surprisingly, or perhaps alarmingly, women now account for a mere 2.8 percent of this new conservative-dominated parliament, compared to the already low 4.1 percent representation in the previous Iranian parliament.[38] This decline in female representation reflects the double-edged challenge for women. Iran is listed 134 out of 140 countries in a ranking of female representation in world parliaments.[39] In order to participate within the political system, women must accept the predominant patriarchal political and religious norms. At the same time, they must contend with the factional and competitive nature of Iranian politics thereby making their entry into the political foray twice as difficult. Ahmadinejad, like his conservative entourage, encourages women to stay at home and focus on the institution of family. Only two women hold secondary cabinet positions, the Center for Women's Participation has been renamed the Center for Women and Family Affairs, and Ahmadinejad has publicly encouraged a pronatalist policy with women staying at home to take care of children. After the 2009 presidential election, President Ahmadinejad nominated three women to head cabinet ministries. Only one, Marzieh Vahid Dastjerdi won approval as health minister, making her Iran's first woman minister since the revolution. While secular activists and reformist politicians have criticized the president for nominating unqualified women to cabinet posts, Dastjerdi herself reflected "today women reached their long-standing dream of having a woman in the cabinet to pursue their demands . . . this is an important step for women and I hold my head high."[40]

At the same time, though, the government is clearly threatened by the increasing tenor of female activism. There is growing support for greater gender equality in Iran. A recent poll conducted by World Public Opinion and Search for Common Ground finds that 78 percent of Iranian respondents believe that it is "somewhat or very important for women to have full equal rights with men and 70 percent think that the government should make an effort to prevent discrimination against women."[41] In light of external pressure with regards to its nuclear program, the Iranian government has come to view domestic women's groups as a threat to national security, accusing women's groups of receiving controversial U.S. government funding aimed at promoting democracy abroad. There have been crackdowns on the One Million Signatures Campaign, a grassroots effort aimed at collecting one million signatures in support of gender equality in Iran, peaceful women's rights demonstrations, and reform of the dress code. Moreover, the premier women's magazine, *Zanan*, was shut down in January 2008 allegedly because it offered a negative picture of the Islamic Republic and compromised the psyche and the mental health of its readers by providing them with "morally questionable information." Headlines continue to report the regular arrest and detention of women's activists, who despite these setbacks continue to push forward with their agendas. As stated by one woman activist, "When Ahmadinejad became president, a lot of people predicted that the women's movement would be marginalized, but over the last two years the movement has shown surprising growth."[42]

In fact, these women, along with male allies, have chosen to abandon a long strategy of cooperation with the system, concluding that this cooperation has left their ambition for female equality stifled and stalled. While they clearly articulate that they are not interested in challenging the political nature of the government, they assert that the past strategy of conciliation is over.[43]

In the aftermath of the thirtieth anniversary of the Iranian Revolution on February 1, 2009, the issue of women's rights continues to top the government agenda. In advance of the tenth presidential election, Iranian women activists formed a coalition to force gender issues onto the political platform of the presidential candidates. They issued two demands: 1) Iran's acceptance of the United Nations Convention for the Elimination of Discrimination against Women (CEDAW) and 2) the elimination of discriminatory laws enshrined in the Iranian constitution. It is also clear that despite government efforts to contain or placate women, women's activism is gaining momentum. This activism came to the fore in reaction to gender policies that have been monopolized by the state. The effect of such state control where compromises or concessions have been piecemeal coupled with legal, social, and cultural obstacles for women have stimulated greater gender consciousness in society. The result has facilitated greater activism and collaboration among women through formal means and in informal contexts. Here lies the inherent story of confrontation, conciliation, and contradiction in Iran, the story of action and reaction.

This story of conciliation is evident on both sides. The government has attempted to placate women through political, legal, and social concessions in an effort to retain female political support. Women have spent years working for and within the Islamic government in an effort to advance women's rights. It is only after years of frustration and obstruction that many women, both Islamist and secular, have been propelled to confront the government directly. Here lies the story of confrontation, as neither side can completely reconcile its ambitions, bringing these tensions to a head. Despite the overwhelming female support for the revolution, it is clear that activist women seek to challenge the legal, political, and social norms of the Islamic Republic. An Islamic government that draws legitimacy from and identifies with its ideologically Islamic pillars is undoubtedly threatened by any such efforts that seek to challenge the foundation of the Islamic state. Women, both Islamist and secular, have discarded their conciliatory approach in favor of more aggressive means of pressure and reform. In defense of the political and ideological balance, the government has struck back against women's activism. It has pitted women against women in an effort to divide the movement, putting forward policies and proposals that attempt to relegate women to the domestic sphere.

Here also lies the story of contradiction, where in spite of the legal and political limitations imposed on women since the revolution, they have profited in terms of educational advancement and social penetration. Not only has the imposition of the hijab enabled religious women to move more comfortably in society, but women have also made use of their educational achievements to challenge patriarchal, traditional, and religious interpretations of Islamic law. The common fate and experience of women subject to the legal and social constraints of Islamic law has brought together Islamist and secular women, despite their contending ideological leanings, adding momentum and unity to female activism. Furthermore, state policies that encouraged the population to go forth and multiply—leading to a demographic crisis with demand for education, jobs and housing outpacing the government's ability to provide them—have not only posed economic and social challenges for the government but ironically also political ones, as this youthful population, which is the majority, is at the forefront of reform efforts. The very nature of the Islamic Leviathan evident in the competition and ideological disunity of political and religious establishment poses the ultimate paradox for the regime. With little political unity or coherence within the government elite on the future of the Islamic Republic, arbitrary and incongruous policies continue to dominate the political sphere, leaving room for continued domestic unrest and momentum against the regime. It is here where the fragile fault lines of the Islamic Republic are most vulnerable. A government effort to muffle and control the growth and expression of civil society during the Khatami administration, which has been restrained since the election of Ahmadinejad, continues to be at the forefront of the political agenda. Despite such efforts, civil society continues to flourish. This growth was evidenced in the day-to-day resistance and political pressure advocated not only from women's groups, but also from students, merchants, activists, and workers. It is the fortitude of this activism that threatens the fundamental balance in Iran, bringing to the fore the ultimate contradiction and challenge for the future of the Islamic Republic.

Notes

1. Nazila Fathi, "Hundreds of Women Protest Sex Discrimination in Iran," *The New York Times*, June 13, 2005. "Zanan Jayegaheshan ra dar Azadi Gereftan" [Women Took Their Place in Azadi Stadium], *Zanan*, 39, 2.

2. Scheherezade Faramazi, "Iran's Rising Conservatives Roll Back Women's Rights," *Los Angeles Times*, April 29, 2007.

3. Azadeh Kian, "Social Change, the Women's Rights Movement and the Role of Islam," *Viewpoints* Special Edition, The Iranian Revolution at Thirty, Middle East Institute, Washington, D.C., 2009, 55. These statistics include the trials of Parvin Ardalan, Mansoureh Shoja'i, Khadidjeh Moghaddam, Jelveh Javaheri, Nahid Keshavarz, Maryam Hosseinkhah, and Jhila Bani-Yaghoub, to name but a few, include the closure of the *Zanan* in January 2008, including closure of the Training Center for Women Non-Governmental Organizations led by Mahboubeh Abbasqolizadeh and the Raahi Center led by Shadi Sadr, in 2007.

4. Golnaz Esfandiari, "Iranian Police Forcibly Disperse Women's Rights Protest in Tehran," *Payvand News*, June 14, 2006.

5. Suad Jafarzadeh, "Iranian Women Take Front and Center," *The Washington Times*, July 23, 2009.

6. Interview with Iranian journalist by Author, Washington, D.C., September 12, 2008.

7. Kaveh Afrasiabi, "Iran's Long Road to Sharm al-Sheikh," *Asia Times Online*, May 1, 2007.

8. Shahrough Akhavi, "The Ideology and Praxis of the Iranian Revolution," *Comparative Studies in Society and History*, Vol. 25, No. 2. 1983, 195--21.

9. National Census 1385 (2006–2007), Population and Housing Yearbook, Statistical Center of Iran.

10. UNESCO, Institute for Statistics, Iran, Education.

11. Although Iran's state religion is Shiite Islam and the majority of its population is ethnically Persian, millions of minorities from various ethnic, religious, and linguistic backgrounds also reside in Iran. Among these groups are ethnic Kurds, Baluch, and Azeris. Many of them face discrimination and live in underdeveloped regions. Though they have held protests in the past, they mostly agitate for greater rights, not greater autonomy. Most are integrated into Iranian society, participate in politics, and identify with the Iranian nation. For more on Iran's ethnic minorities see Eliz Sanasarian's *Religious Minorities in Iran*, 2000.

12. Interview with Iranian blogger, London, April 12, 2007. Interview with former politician, New Haven, February 8, 2007. Interview with journalist and activist, Washington, D.C., November 12, 2007.

13. Farhad Khosrokhavar, "New Social Movements in Iran," *ISIM Newsletter*, no. 7, 2001: 17; Ali Akbar Mahdi, "Caught Between Local and Global: Iranian Women's Struggle for a Civil Society," paper presented at the CIRA annual meeting, Bethesda, MD, April 2000 (http://www.owu.edu/~aamahdi/globalization-final.doc).

14. Homa Hoodfar and Fatemeh Sadeghi, "Against all Odds: The Women's Movement in the Islamic Republic of Iran," *Development*, 52, 2009, 221.

15. Valentine M. Moghadam, "Women in the Islamic Republic of Iran: Legal Status, Social Positions, and Collective Action" *Woodrow Wilson International Center for Scholars Conference*. November 16–17, 2004.

16. Margot Badran, *Feminism in Islam: Secular and Religious Convergences* Oneworld Press, Oxford, 2008.

17. Asef Bayat, "A Women's Non Movement: What It Means to Be a Women's Activist in an Islamic State," *Comparative Studies South Asia, Africa & the Middle East*, Vol. 27. No. 1, 2007.

18. Charles Tilly, *Social Movements, 1768-2004*, 3.

19. Sidney Tarrow, *Power in Movement: Social Movements and Contentious Politics*, 2002.

20. Asef Bayat, "Un-civil Society: The Politics of Informal People," *Third World Quarterly*, Vol. 18, No. 1, March 1997, 53–72.

21. *Kar va Kargar*, August 22, 2000.

22. Afsaneh Najmabadi, editor, *Bibi Khanum Astarabadi's Ma'ayib al-Rijal: Vices of Men*. "Madreseh Dosheezgan" (The School for Girls: Interview with Dr Mah-Laghā Mallah Maternal Granddaughter of Bibi Khatoon Astarabadi), *Deutsche Welle Persian* August 11, 2006.

23. Hamideh Sedghi, *Women and Politics in Iran: Veiling, Unveiling and Reveiling*, 2007.

24. Sedghi describes patriarchal cultural trends from154–60.

25. Haleh Afshar, *Islam and Feminisms: An Iranian Case Study* (Women's Studies at York), 1998.

26. Charles Kurzman, "A Feminist Generation in Iran?" *Iranian Studies*, Volume 41, Number 3, June 2008.

27. Nayereh Tohidi, "Women's Rights in the Middle East and North Africa: Iran Draft Chapter," *Gozaar.org*, September 2, 2009. http://www.gozaar.org/template1.php?id=1343&language=english. Accessed March 25, 2010.

28. "Iranian Leader Warns Women Against Copying Western Feminist Trends," *Agence Free Presse*, October 22, 1997.

29. Noushin Tarighi, "Zanan va Shoraha" [Women and the Councils], *Zanan* 139, 2–5.

30. "The Shape of Things to Come: Country Case Study, Iran," Population Action International report, October 1998.

31. Shirin Ebadi, "Hoghugh-e Zanan dar Ghavanine Jomhuriye Islamiye Iran" [Women's Rights in the Laws of the Islamic Republic of Iran], Tehran: Ketabkhaneh-ye Ganj-e Danesh, 2002, 48.

32. Roxanna Saberi, "Women's Rights on Iranian Agenda," BBC News, March 9, 2006.

33. Diyeh Zan Va Mard Dar Tasadofat, Yeksan Shod" [Equal Blood Money in Accident Injury], *Mardomak*, May 29, 2008, http://www.mardomak.org/news/dieh_zano_mard.

Accessed December 28, 2009. Shahindokht Molaverdi. "Tasavee e Diyeh Zan Va Mard," [Equality of Blood Money Between Men & Women], *Zanan*, 109, 2–4.

34. "Iran Enforces New Women's Inheritance Law," *Press TV*, March 12, 2009.

35. Parvin Ardalan, "Iran: The Women's Movement in a Game of Snakes and Ladders," *Payvand News*, December 1, 2008.

36. Hugh Sykes, "Iran Rejects Easing Polygamy Law," *BBC News*, September 2, 2008.

37. Quoted in Thomas Erdbrink, "Iranian Parliament Delays Vote on Bill That Upset Judiciary, Women's Activists," *Washington Post*, September 3, 2008, A09.

38. http://www.washingtonpost.com/wp-srv/special/world/women-in-parliament/. Accessed March 18, 2010.

39. Ibid.

40. Quoted in "Dream Win for Female Minister," *Gulf Daily News*, September 4, 2009.

41. "Public Opinion in Iran and America on Key Public Issues," World Public Opinion, April 7, 2008.

42. "Public Opinion in Iran and America on Key Public Issues," World Public Opinion, January 27, 2007.

43. Interviews with Women Activists in Tehran, April, 27, May 12–13, 2008.

2

The Revolutionary Century Through the Eyes and Lives of Women

No force can bind us: pull of moment, arrows flying home,
Nor any wild nostalgia that seized our hearts whilom.
Though my soft braids turned chains of steel and anchored in your heart,
Could any chain keep me at home if I should wish to roam?

Mahasati Ganjavi[1]

The success of the 1979 Iranian Revolution is considered to be the culmination of a century-long revolutionary struggle. For some, this struggle is defined by Iran's attempt to reclaim and define its own path of history. For others, this struggle has been an effort to balance the contending narratives that have dominated Iranian history. Most significant was that despite the dramatic political changes that emerged at the outset of Iran's revolutionary century, so too came equally profound social and cultural transformations, including the rise of Iranian female activism.

Using the broader political arena as their initial stage, women have agitated against conventional norms, joining men in demanding political and social change. Through such mobilization, women began to discover ways and means to assert their interests. In effect, female activism drew strength and motivation from political and social developments. This link has been carried forward through this revolutionary century. The history connecting women and popular political activism has both advanced and hindered their goals. Repeatedly, the state, both under the leadership of Reza Pahlavi and then under his son Muhammad Reza Pahlavi as part of their modernization and development campaigns, has used women to enhance its political agenda, absorbing women's issues as part of the state's vacillation between policies of championing or constraining women's causes. This ebb and flow and dependency on the state has colored Iranian history and the history of female activism. Ultimately, it has set a precedent in which these similar trends are perpetuated under the tenure of the Islamic Republic.

Iranian national identity has been a defining feature dividing state society relations in Iranian nineteenth- and twentieth-century history. Particularly prescient during and after the Iranian Revolution, the trends that came together in 1979 and continue to dominate Iranian politics today are evidenced in the turmoil of Iranian history where religion, tradition, culture, nationalism, and modernity have repeatedly clashed in the battle for a decisive national identity. Unraveling these trends is critical to understanding the currents driving Iranian society today and dissecting the social and political transformations that have driven the debate on gender issues and led to greater female activism.

If one travels through Iran, a visitor might observe that Iranians are pilgrims of their past. Checkered throughout the country are homages, shrines, and archeological sites that pay tribute to the nation's multifaceted identity—a Persian, a Shi'a, and a modern. There is Iran's imperial history that dominates the Iranian imagination with dreams of resurrected grandeur and glory. A trip to Persepolis, the ceremonial capitol of the Persian Empire located in southern Iran, can bring to life the stateliness of the Achaemenid Empire.[2] Considered by many to be the first great superpower with domains stretching east and west, the majestic legacy of Iran's early empires has left a profound historical mark of Iran as a great civilization. As the forbearers of an effective administration espousing tolerance and religious freedom, the Achaemenids impacted both the regional successor states and the religions that would follow.[3]

The dynamism of religion in Iran has also left a deep impression on Iranian society. The blossoming of Shi'a Islam on the Iranian plateaus played a unique role in uniting Iran under the fifteenth century Safavid Dynasty. While Islam came to Iran centuries earlier under the Arab conquest in the seventh century, Iran has prided itself on challenging the Arab Umayyad aristocracy through support of the Abbasid rule—a period dominated by Iranian ascendancy and political and cultural influence. Most revolutionary was the mass transformation of Iranian society to Shi'ism during the Safavid reign. The effects of this metamorphosis were not only relegated to the religious sphere but to the political, too. Iran's new religious identity created a newfound unity that would ultimately separate Iran from its regional neighbors through its delineated territorial and religious boundaries. While Iran's conversion into a Shi'a sanctioned state took centuries, its impact left a profound mark on the social and political levers of society. This is most clearly noted in the religious traditions so deeply rooted in Iranian society and culture. Pilgrims flock to the many religious shrines and mosques paying tribute to Iran's Shi'a distinctiveness. In northeastern Iran, in the city of Mashad[4] lies the mausoleum and enormous complex dedicated to the eighth Shi'a imam, Imam Ali ibn Musa-al-Reza, known to Iranians as their beloved Imam Reza. In Qom, the religious heart of the country, one can honor the revered sister of Imam Reza, Fatemeh Masumeh.[5] *Imamzadehs,* or shrines, marking the burial sites of the descendents of Shi'a imams color the religious landscape, and regularly receive visitors for worship.

This profound history is not without cultural influences, too. Iran's poetic tradition holds a special place within society. Most Iranians can recite quatrains of their favorite poet. Saadi, Rumi, Hafez, Khayam, Rudaki, and Ferdowsi are revered as national icons who used the power of their pen to revive the language and customs of ancient Persia. This is evidenced most prominently in Ferdowsi's *Shahnameh,* or Book of Kings, in which the mythological history of Iran from the first fitful moments of creation to the Arab conquest of the Persian Empire is meticulously documented. Ferdowsi was a member of Iran's aristocratic class, which maintained a strong attachment to the heritage of pre-Islamic Iran. Children are named after the book's heroes, and political enemies are likened to its villains. For many Iranians, the *Shahnameh* links past and present, forming a cohesive mytho-historical narrative through which they understand their place in the world. The poem is, in a sense, Iran's national scripture and is the key to unlocking the Iranian imagination. In deference to these poetic gods, Iranians frequent the tombs of Ferdowsi near Toos, Saadi in Shiraz, and Khayam in Nishapur.

These historical, cultural, and religious pillars come together to forge the foundation of Iranian national identity. Balancing these inclinations has often been a challenge for the varying rulers of Iran. Each leader with his own agenda, has supported an incomplete vision of Iran. For the Pahlavi shahs who strove to modernize Iran, they neglected and even suppressed the religious character of Iranians. Under the Islamic Republic, the clerical leadership has attempted to promote its religious roots over Iran's pre-Islamic identity and history. These varieties of national character have also impacted the female Iranian identity where the defining features of gender were linked to that of the state. Examples of such imbalances are also evidenced throughout Iran's turbulent and often contradictory history, where indigenous efforts at reviving Iranian glory, cultivating nationalism, or modernizing society have highlighted these trends.

The road to the 1979 revolution is riddled with historical repetition and mired with these conflicting visions of Iran. Indeed, these inconsistencies are prevalent today in contemporary Iran. The revolutionary crusade began in the nineteenth century, when popular nationalistic movements took strikes against the political structure. The oppressive combination of foreign interference and absolutism evidenced during this period unleashed a revolutionary fervor that, in turn, facilitated dramatic shifts in society. Influenced by contact with the West, education, communication, travel, trade, and Western thought, Iranians were no longer passive in the face of national and international developments. Their road to modernity commenced with this historic struggle designed to reform a traditional society, to access greater political representation, and to limit the authority of the absolutist government.[6] Amidst the political and social changes that emerged in the nineteenth century, one of the most noteworthy has been the political participation of women.

The political realm in nineteenth century Iran was controlled through the power of the Qajar monarchy.[7] Unlike many of its neighbors, Iran was not officially a colonial domain, although the country was not excluded from European competition over resources and markets. Russia slowly encroached on Iranian territory in the early nineteenth century, forcing the weak government of Fath Ali Shah to capitulate to the humiliating Treaty of Golestan in 1813 and the Treaty of Turkomanchy in 1828 ceding territory in the Caucuses and Central Asia. By the late nineteenth century, the Russian military had a decisive presence in the northern Iranian cities of Tabriz and Qazvin. Promoting their interests, Russian interference was critical in disrupting the constitutional gains evidenced from 1905–11. Only in the aftermath of the 1917 Russian Revolution would Russia withdraw, albeit temporarily, from Iranian territory and from interference in Iranian affairs.

British interests by contrast, were focused on access to Iranian terrain around the Persian Gulf. Entry to these ports was essential for Great Britain's trade route to India. Humiliating treaties and concession agreements opened the door to a large British presence on Iranian soil particularly in the aftermath of the Anglo-Persian War of 1856, where Iran lost control over its Afghan domains. With such a defeat, Iran was forced to accept redefined southern and eastern boundaries and with it continued British intrusion. Several trade concessions by the Iranian government, including the infamous 1901 D'Arcy concession, which allowed for the exploration for oil, put economic affairs largely under British control. Because of these interests, Britain would continue to play a prominent role in Iranian domestic affairs into the mid-twentieth century.

By the late nineteenth century, many Iranians believed that their rulers who were reputed to be corrupt and profligate were beholden to foreign interests. Coupled with the economic and political impact of the Western presence that ultimately undermined the economic welfare of merchants and laborers, popular resentment was exacerbated. Increased elite and intellectual contact with Western ideas of modernity and nationalism also fueled a domestic backlash. Nationalism played and would continue to play a primary role in the Iranian revolutionary struggle. For women, too, nationalistic sentiments and movements opened doors, permitting them to join, to demonstrate, and to agitate alongside men. The downside though of these nationalistic bonds, as suggested by Deniz Kandiyoti is "that [nationalism] reaffirms the boundaries of culturally acceptable feminine conduct and exerts pressure on women to articulate their gender interests within the terms set by nationalist discourse."[8] This dynamic too would perpetuate through the years of colonial, nationalistic, and revolutionary opposition.

The first episode of organized involvement against exploitative rule is found in the food riots of the late nineteenth century, including opposition to the Reuter concession of 1872 and the Tobacco Protest of 1891, when the monarchy bartered away a monopoly over Iran's tobacco production and sale.[9] Participating in the revolt were *ulama* (religious scholars), secular reformists, and merchants. There were many women among them. This grassroots coalition would come together repeatedly in demanding political change throughout Iranian history. Crucial to this coalition was the religious class, which provided sanction against political activities of the government, including concession granting. During this period, the ulama and secular groups reconciled their ideological visions becoming allies in mutual cause. This alliance would also repeat over the course of Iran's revolutionary century. Indeed, so too would the fracturing among these groups be repetitive. In particular, it was women who would see their ambitions for suffrage and education quashed by the clerical class. Needless to say, women were perceived to be central to these movements, as the growing participation of women foreshadowed increasing societal changes linked to modernization.

Although not the first example of female empowerment, the Tobacco Protest saw women marching against the concession, even leading other women in the closing of the Tabriz bazaar.[10] Women in the shah's harem stood in solidarity with ordinary Iranians in boycotting tobacco. Nasir-al Dinh's most influential wife, Anis-al Dowleh, was among the most prominent facilitators of the resistance. In response to what became a nationwide boycott, the shah was forced to cancel the concession and lose his much-coveted revenue stream. One woman, Zainab Pasha was an early activist and organizer of the female opposition from Tabriz. She challenged men, "If you men do not have the courage to punish the oppressors . . . wear our veil and go home. Do not claim to be men; we will fight instead of you."[11]

The Tobacco Protest marked a turning point in Iranian history.[12] Not only did the event cement relations among the disparate social classes, but it also revealed the emergence of a newfound nationalism among the population. Contact with the West through travel, translations, and greater education had helped form a new middle or intellectual class inspired by enlightened European ideas. These intellectuals implanted the ideas of a modern and developed society free of despotism and foreign imperialism within Iranian society.

These ideals would be absorbed in the goals of the 1905–11 Constitutional Revolution—the penultimate movement in reaction to foreign interference and despotism. Dreams of constitutional checks and balances would reign in monarchical injustice, bringing the ideals of constitutionalism to Iran. Through protests, a coalition reminiscent of the one seen during the Tobacco Protest, merging together the religious, merchant, and disparate social classes, forced the shah to accept restraints on his power.

Again, during this popular uprising, women were avid participants. Initially they organized street protests, participated in some fighting, joined underground activities against foreign forces, and spearheaded the boycott against foreign goods. They raised funds to be used in the establishment of the first National Bank. During the revolutionary zenith, some women had organized separate and often secret societies known as *anjomans,* through which they began to articulate their hopes for female enfranchisement.[13] Most noteworthy are the women who took up arms in support of the public's petition for a constitution. Morgan Schuster, the American financier and treasurer-general sent to Iran during this period, recounts in his memoirs how vocal women were in making demands. "Straight to the Majlis they went . . . and demanded of the President that he admit them all . . . in the reception hall they confronted him and lest he or his colleagues should doubt their meaning these cloistered Persian mothers, wives and daughters exhibited threateningly their revolvers, tore aside their veils and confessed their decision to kill their own husbands and sons and leave behind their own dead bodies if the deputies wavered in their duty to uphold the liberty and dignity of the Persian people and nation."[14]

Recent studies have suggested that female participation was initially motivated by clerical instruction—a pattern that would be repeated in other popular movements, including in the fateful 1979 Islamic Revolution.[15] However, such statements do not account for the diversity of female participation, including that of upper-class women, which is also relevant in drawing comparisons with 1979. Indeed, clerical sanction was important for traditional women who were often confined to their homes under the guise of their protective husbands. It is with clerical approval that they were permitted to rally alongside men. Important to note though is the collective female support during this period. Despite their initial motivations, women would soon deviate, using these initial forays out of the confines of the home to redirect their ambitions toward the political sphere. Indeed, lower-class and upper-class women were divided in their political and religious support. Such differences would hinder the collaborative efforts of women as would be evidenced in the aftermath of the Iranian revolution. However, the political participation of women would inspire female *anjomans* (organizations), the birth of the female press, and female education. Interestingly, in the aftermath of the 1979 revolution, a similar pattern of female awakening would reappear.

In the course of this national struggle, some women drew on the strength of female mobilization to incorporate demands for a constitution, education, and suffrage rights.[16] Seizing on the political momentum, women hoped to gain greater political and social rights. In this vein, some women took up arms for the cause while others provided moral support and "kept the spirit of liberty alive."[17] It is now recognized by scholars that women played a unique role in transforming the essentially political revolution of 1905 into the beginnings of a social revolution. Women were participants and collaborators at the political and social realm seizing on political motivations to challenge social conventions on gender issues including suffrage, education, and equality.

A *Majlis,* or parliament, was created as a result of the revolution and a constitution similar to the Belgian one institutionalized this parliamentary system of government. It curbed the power of the king by granting extensive legislative power to the Majlis. While the constitution emulated Western ideas, it was deferent to Iran's religious influence, too. All constitutional provisions were to be in conformity with Shariah law (Islamic law based on the Qur'an and *sunnah* or tradition of the Prophet Muhammad) and clerical approval. This condition in effect imposed an additional check on parliamentary power, thereby enshrining a clerical role in politics.

Also meaning *path* in Arabic, Shariah guides all aspects of Muslim life including daily routines, familial and religious obligations, and financial dealings. It is derived primarily from the Qur'an and the *Sunna*—the sayings, practices, and teachings of the Prophet Muhammad. Precedents and analogy applied by Muslim scholars are used to address new issues. The consensus or *ijma* of the Muslim community also plays a role in defining this theological manual. Specifically, Shi'a legal exegesis was unique compared to Sunni Islam. The practice of *ijtihad* or interpretation, where a *mojtahed* or religious scholar could use his own reasoning in addition to that of the Qur'an and *hadith* to arrive at legal decisions in the form of a *fatwa* is the most important and most relevant for gender issues. According to traditional Shariah law, despite declarations of the equality of the sexes before God, women are considered inferior to men, and have fewer rights and responsibilities. A woman counts as half a man in giving evidence in a court of law, or in matters of inheritance. Her position is less profitable than a man's with regard to marriage and divorce. Women have little or no autonomy and are subject to the protection and direction of their fathers, husbands, or other male relatives throughout their lives.

To the dismay of Iran's activist women, female participation and contribution to the Constitutional movement was not rewarded. In the electoral law of September 1906, women were barred from the political process. Again in 1911, a parliamentarian, Vakil ul-Ruaayaa, proposed a bill in support of the female right to vote and establishment of societies. However, the clerical establishment offered no backing for the goal of female education or recognition of their societies, stating that their ambitions were counter to the laws of Islam. Sheikh Assodollah deplored that "God has not given them [women] the capacity needed for taking part in politics and electing the representative of the nation. They are the weaker sex, and have not the same power of judgment as men have."[18]

Combating the patriarchal culture as well as the conventional interpretations of Islam would become an early and ongoing challenge for women. Female education was particularly feared by clerics who used historical examples as their guide. Considering the political influence of women in history such as Ghoratolain, who became a leader in Iran's Babi religious movement in the mid-1800s, a movement rejected and denounced by the Shi'a establishment, and even Aisha, the Prophet Muhammad's favored wife, who led an army into battle in 656, among others, clerics feared the deleterious effects of female influence.[19] Women were informed that their "education and training should be restricted to raising children, home economics and preserving the honor of the family."[20]

Despite these setbacks, the events surrounding the Constitutional Revolution only propelled women forward, laying the groundwork for a nascent women's movement to take hold through the political events of the twentieth century. Developments such as the spread of the Bahai religion, which advocated women's freedom, increased contact with Europeans, the Russian Revolution, the emergence of the women's movement in Turkey and Egypt, and the victory of British and American women in gaining the right to vote in the late 1910s all impacted Iranian women. Drawing influence from the works of pioneering women such as Bibi Khatoon Astarabadi (1895) and Taj al Saltaneh (1914),[21] who linked Iran's latent development with its treatment of women, initially women focused their efforts towards education. Shaikh Fazlullah Nuri, a respected cleric who had mobilized female participation in the Constitutional Revolution, issued a *fatwa* against women's education, arguing that it would lead to undesirable changes in gender roles. Ayatollah Shushtari organized protests against women's education and distributed a leaflet entitled "Shame on a country in which girls' schools are founded."[22] Nevertheless, women's schools continued to thrive in Tehran and smaller towns. Some activist women published letters in the newspapers of the period in which they condemned the actions of the religious-conservative opposition and called for greater recognition of women's rights to education.

At the time, a handful of radical male journalists, Majlis delegates, and poets supported the women's movement. Together they would speak out on other issues, such as child marriage, polygamy, and male divorce rights, and even call for women's suffrage in the Majlis. While most men subscribed to the vision of women as primarily mothers and wives, some stressed that a more educated woman would become a better mother and housewife and produce children who could lead Iran to modernize quickly and productively. Shuster observed that "The Persian women since 1907 had become almost at a bound the most progressive, not to say radical, in the world; that this statement upsets the ideas of centuries makes no difference. It is a fact . . . In Tehran alone, twelve women's associations were involved in different social and political activities. [Iranian women] overnight have become teachers, newspaper writers, founders of women's clubs and speakers on political subjects."[23]

While frowned upon by the clerical and patriarchal establishment, formal education became the primary vehicle for female empowerment. Among the first female pioneers in favor of educating women was Toubi Azmoudeh, who was the first Iranian woman to establish a girl's school, called *Namous* (Honor) in Tehran in 1907.[24] Azmoudeh first held classes in her home, believing that there was no contradiction between women's education and Islamic teachings. As such, she even incorporated religious texts and Qur'anic study with mathematics and home economics. Despite clerical attempts to close Azmoudeh's school, she was able to increase her outreach by adding secondary and evening education. Others followed Azmoudeh's example, beginning their initiatives in the home and then expanding to include larger portions of the community. Often women provided both the staff and budget for the schools themselves.[25] Indeed, by 1910 there existed over 50 private girls' schools and literacy and night classes for women.

The emergence of women's activism can also be tied to the formation and growth of women's associations and publications over a period of 20 years, from roughly 1910 to 1932. During this period, women established a number of *anjomans* and published a variety of weekly or monthly magazines dealing specifically with issues related to the condition of women's lives. By the mid-1930s, these issues included women's rights, education, and veiling. *Zaban-e-Zan*, published by Sedigheh Dowlatabadi in 1918, was the "first publication that used the word woman and could be written by a woman about women and for women's interests."[26] Dowlatabadi challenged social norms by printing political articles that attacked government policies. Eventually and inevitably, the government censored the journal. Dowlatabadi was, according to the chief of Isfahan police, "born 100 years too soon."[27] Despite these setbacks, she continued to challenge social norms not only through her work but through her actions too. In fact, Dowlatabadi was the first woman to publicly abandon the veil even before the legal ban imposed in 1936. For many, Dowlatabadi is considered "the founding mother of Iranian feminism. She was a nationalist, progressive and a determined woman who dared to tell the truth and to struggle against foreign domination of Iran."[28] In her will, Dowlatabadi instructed women to attend her funeral only if they were unveiled.

It was women like Astarabadi, Dowlatabadi, and Azmoudeh, among others, who had the courage to push for change within the patriarchal, religious culture of Iran. Seeking to bring Iranian women out of the shroud of seclusion, they challenged the patriarchal social and religious order, setting into motion the wheels of female activism. While immediately unsuccessful in combating repression or attaining meaningful women's rights, they succeeded in bringing attention to women's issues and demands.

The transfer of power that took place after World War I established the Pahlavi monarchy under the guise of Reza Shah. This change in government, though, only perpetuated autocracy under new leadership. In fact, Reza Shah disregarded the fleeting constitution and parliamentary authority to exert greater control over the clerical establishment and society in general. He had little tolerance for any independent and nonconformist organizations including women's groups. Reza Shah's concerns were oriented towards the rapid modernization of Iran.[29] Impressed by the reforms and secular plans of Turkey's Kemal Ataturk, Reza Shah sought to emulate these Western-inspired initiatives in forcing a massive modernization program. He sought to create a capitalist Iran free from foreign and religious influence. To achieve this end, Reza Shah sought to contain clerical power, which according to him was the root cause of Iran's political and social stagnancy. His modernization campaign was effective in striking against the clerical class although, unlike Ataturk, he never fully divested the clergy of power. He created his own model of modernization and Westernization, which was not based on a constructed secular state with a strong civil society. Instead, he coupled repression with an overreliance on the military to defend state power.

Women's issues were included in Reza Shah's modernization plans. Seeking to curtail clerical power, Reza Shah made use of his secular ambitions to promote female ones. As Tavakoli-Targhi points out, "the early twentieth century Iranian modernists tied the progress and moral strength of the nation (*mellat*) to educating and unveiling of women, and encouraging their participation in the public sphere."[30] Indeed, for Reza Shah, modernization was linked to gender issues as women's emancipation was grounded in the need for national progress. Legal provisions advanced in 1931 introduced a number of changes to marriage and divorce laws. A bill was passed in the Majlis giving women the right to ask for divorce under certain conditions and increased the marriage age to 15 for girls and 18 for boys. More challenging to the clergy's authority was the movement of marital issues from religious to civil courts. Efforts to expand women's participation in the economic and public affairs of the country were also encouraged. The government invested money and resources in the expansion of schools for girls, including in 1934 the establishment of the University of Tehran, where women were admitted alongside their male counterparts in 1935. A number of female teacher training colleges were also opened, ushering in women to fill the void in education. Important to note, though, is that despite gaining protection through the new Civil and Penal Codes, women were still subject to the legal constraints of Shariah law, which is considered patriarchal by most interpretations.

Tehran was the site of the 1932 Congress of Oriental Women. Women from around the Middle East gathered in Tehran to assess and discuss the state of Muslim women. Iranian women were championed for their passionate speeches arguing for economic independence as a first step toward emancipation.[31] Iran Erani criticized the existing system for "treating women like animals" and contended that women's emancipation was contingent on their economic independence.[32] A year later, Iranian women submitted some of the congress's recommendations for electoral rights to the Iranian parliament. Other resolutions included equal rights for women in the family, the abolition of polygamy, compulsory elementary education for women, and equal compensation for equal work. The Majlis rejected the demand for emancipation but implemented a series of reforms encouraging protection of women in the social arena.

Although Reza Shah favored improvements to women's status, his efforts were tied to his broader ambitions of modernization rather than a benevolent concern for women's rights. Clerical opposition combined with the government's fear that any social protest would threaten the political sphere obstructed women's activism in the form of organizations, education, and the press. Many women's organizations were forced to close, with the last independent women's organization banned in 1932. Instead, Reza Shah, in an effort to control "the feminist movement," sponsored his own government-controlled women's organization, *Kaanoon e Baanovaan*—The Ladies Center—headed by his daughter Ashraf Pahlavi. The organization commenced a series of welfare activities designed to both depoliticize the women's movement and link women's involvement and participation in society to modernity—the latter being a major concern of the new king.

Most noteworthy in Reza Shah's reforms was the 1936 edict forcefully ordering women to abandon their hejab or headcovering.[33] Many secular and urban women championed this move. A small number of elite and upper-class women supported and benefited from the unveiling law, and welcomed the change, taking advantage of some of the educational and employment opportunities offered by the modern state. However, because the state had little presence in the countryside, and since most rural women dressed in their traditional clothing, the law had little immediate impact on their lives. On the other hand, for lower-middle-class and low-income urban women, who were socialized and educated to embrace veiling as the only legitimate, acceptable way of dressing, the unveiling law was far from liberating.[34] Many felt obliged to stay home, and gave up their public activities, including shopping for the family, engaging in economic pursuits outside the home, visiting neighbors, and going to the public baths. The de-veiling law and its harsh enforcement not only failed to liberate women of these classes, but rather sequestered them by forcing them to rely on their husbands, sons, and male relatives for public tasks they normally carried out themselves. From this period onward, "the veil slowly came to symbolize in the resistance narrative, not the inferiority of the culture and the need to cast aside its customs in favor of those of the West, but, on the contrary, the dignity and validity of all native customs, and in particular those customs coming under fiercer colonial attack—the customs relating to women—and the need to tenaciously affirm them as a means of resistance to Western domination."[35]

Indeed, veiling and female education amplified tension between the state and clergy. Reza Shah viewed the clerical monopoly of education as a limitation to his development ambitions. Delinking clerical control would empower women and girls to be part of a more productive population. In the absence of the state's active intervention, low-income and traditional middle-class social groups remained under the cultural influence of conservative religious leaders who considered modern schooling to be a source of corruption for girls. They advised parents against educating their daughters revealing a dividing line between state and clerical influence on gender relations.

At the same time though, the state's reforms did not interfere or challenge the patriarchal familial patterns particularly within the legal sphere. By limiting the scope of legal reform, in effect by only adding protections for female education, Reza Shah endorsed a modern and traditional role for Iranian women. While secularization, education and employment were essential to national progress, Iranian women were to retain their primary roles as wives and mothers. A cultural and social dichotomy persisted. Educated women were important for nurturing Iran's future generations. Female employment and social inclusion was necessary for projecting a modern nation state. He fell short of introducing whole scale gender reform likely because of his own patriarchal vision. Years later, his son would endorse this view stating:

> Reza Shah never advocated a complete break with the past, for always he assumed that our girls could find their best fulfillment in marriage and in the nurture of superior children. But he was convinced that a girl could be a better wife and mother, as well as a better citizen, if she received an education and perhaps works outside the home long enough to gain a sense of civic functions and responsibilities.[36]

The divergence between the national vision for women and the familial position of women would become part of the national gender debate. During the reign of Muhammad Reza Shah and in the aftermath of the Iranian revolution, state policy again would endeavor to balance these two vision.

After World War II and the abdication of Reza Shah (1924–41) in favor of his son Muhammad Reza Shah, the veil remained illegal although the law enforcement was relaxed. Gradually, women wearing scarves and chadors appeared side by side with those without any head covering. While de-veiling had negative consequences for many women, educational and employment opportunities for urban women improved through their increased social integration.[37] In this more open environment, religious women who observed veiling returned to the public sphere partaking in educational opportunities. Even then, women argued that there was no contradiction between observing hejab and acquiring an education—an argument that would be reiterated after the 1979 revolution. However, as the government ban on veiling extended to places of work, these women were excluded from employment opportunities in the public and modern sectors of the economy.[38] In the face of the state-sponsored modernization efforts, the veil remained a symbol of backwardness and ignorance even though many urban women continued to adhere to veiling. This perpetuated the alienation of this social group.

While directly impacting women, veiling issues were aimed at restraining clerical power. It became abundantly clear that Reza Shah's reforms, including those affecting women, were part of a grand modernization campaign and not intended to challenge societal norms or eradicate patriarchal dominance. Reza Shah's policies on "women's emancipation was thus a means, not an end."[39] His forced abdication at the hands of the Allied powers in 1941 opened a new frontier for women to yet again demand greater social and political change.

World War II opened another page in the history of the women's movement in Iran. The political instability coupled with the insecure reign of the new Muhammad Reza Shah provided a new opportunity for women to reassert their demands. The political environment of the time though was tense. The young shah was considered inexperienced and in the postwar environment, a growing communist shadow loomed over the Iranian terrain. Taking advantage of the vacuum of power, religious radicals also emerged onto the political scene demanding respect for the Islamic traditions and laws, including that of the veil.

Here, women took advantage of the permissive political atmosphere. Several prominent women's organizations emerged.[40] The most salient feature of women's organizations in the period, in addition to their independence from the government, was their close associations with various political parties, including those affiliated with the communist Tudeh Party. Safiyeh Firouz in 1942 formed the National Women's Society, and the newly formed Council of Iranian Women in 1944 strongly criticized polygamy. The Tudeh Party women's league was the best-organized women's organization of the period. In 1944, Huma Houshmandar published *Our Awakening,* and in 1949 the women's league was changed to Organization of Democratic Women and branches were opened in all the major cities.[41] They campaigned in favor of education, economic equality, and mobilization, linking women's emancipation to issues of class and gender.

Women again became active in the national struggle against foreign forces and were even involved in the political events of 1945 in Azerbaijan when Soviet forces refused to withdraw from Iranian territory in accordance with the Allied Tehran agreement signed in 1943.[42] In the politicized atmosphere of the day, another new development was the participation of younger females in the student movement in universities. Many women joined student organizations and took part in repeated demonstrations associated with political events.

Between 1942 and 1951, the Majlis was presented with three bills supporting female enfranchisement. The Democratic Union of Women called on the government to offer voting rights to women. In support of their effort, they collected over 100,000 signatures in favor of this reform. None of the three initiatives succeeded though, mostly due to clerical obstruction. Muhammad Mossadegh, the nationalist prime minister, also failed to include women in the 1951 electoral reform bill presented to the Majlis designed to increase popular representation. Again, these proposals were defeated through extensive lobbying of the clergy who continued their opposition to female suffrage in accordance with Shariah law. Yet, women were offered a piecemeal victory winning the right to vote in municipal councils in 1952. Women's suffrage would not be revived at the legislative level until 1959—long after Mossadegh's forced downfall.

The 1953 CIA-engineered coup against Prime Minister Mossadegh had ramifications for Iranian society and its women.[43] The young shah, having been returned to his throne, began to assert and protect his power more aggressively. Among his first steps was the elimination of all oppositional and independent political parties and organizations. Since most of the women's organizations in the 1940s were attached to various political parties, by default they became subject to this political purge. Organizations that remained intact were those controlled by the central government, including those supporting women. It was these organizations that would influence the nature and direction of women's activities in the following three decades.

During this period, the government centralized women's organization, unified their leadership, and depoliticized their demands. In 1959, 18 women's organizations were brought under the umbrella of the Federation of Women's Organizations—a federation later transformed into a new and more centrally organized body: the High Council of Iranian Women. Under the direction of Ashraf Pahlavi, the council was then transformed into a new organization called Women's Organization of Iran (WOI), which lasted until the end of the Pahlavi regime in 1979.[44] The WOI developed branches in major cities and cultivated smaller health and charity offices. It established committees responsible for health, literacy, education, law, social welfare, handicrafts, international affairs, provincial affairs, membership, and fund-raising. It, too, played a critical role in the political process, merging its activities with that of the government sponsored Rastakhiz (Resurgent) Party. Mahnaz Afkhami, who was appointed Secretary General in 1970, was essential in linking the state sponsored gender policy to the organization's mandate. "The creation of the [WOI] organization brought Reza Shah's gender policies full circle: the complete transformation of women's initiatives into a loyal organization."[45]

Throughout the shah's reign, women's activities were channeled through these government-controlled organizations. These societies were incorporated into the government bureaucracy and were basically involved in aid, health, and educational activities. Afkhami and others were responsible for promoting "positive" policies in line with the state apparatus. The only political demand advanced by these organizations was that of women's enfranchisement—a right finally granted to women by the Pahlavi government in 1963 in the face of clerical opposition.[46]

In the face of these organizational developments, limited legal or social changes took place during the twenty-seven-year period between 1936, the year of de-veiling and 1963, when Iranian women's enfranchisement was approved in a national referendum. To bolster his own popularity in the midst of international criticism, the shah introduced a program known as the White Revolution—a series of measures designed to attain Iran's rapid development ambitions. The 17-point program included land reform, and the formation of a health and literacy corps, among other statutes. The White Revolution programs allowed female graduates to serve in education and health corps.

Important to note that despite the monarchical determination to force rapid modernization, female enfranchisement occurred almost 30 years after the recognition of Turkish women's right to vote and participation in parliamentary politics. In Iran, though, this measure was still met with considerable opposition from the Iranian clergy, including Ayatollah Khomeini himself, who viewed this as the complete corruption of Muslim mores. In fact, the opposition of the clergy, the bazaar merchants, and some landlords to the reform package led to a brief and unsuccessful uprising, which resulted in the exile of Ayatollah Khomeini to Turkey and then Iraq.[47] The shah's motivation for female enfranchisement resulted from his ambitious program of Iranian development that was inextricably linked to modernization and secularization of society. Unlike his father though, Muhammad Reza Shah, a weaker and more detached leader, had limited control over the women's movement and its development and demands. However, he envisaged that a move such as enfranchisement would place him on equal footing with his father's de-veiling laws granting him greater access and authority to define gender reform within Iran.[48]

However, in 1967, a Family Protection Law was also passed applying tougher conditions for polygamy, raising the marriage age for girls to 18, placing divorce under the authority of the courts, and creating more safeguards against male vagary in male divorce. While the civil code of Reza Shah had mostly codified Shi'a Islamic law in matters of marriage, divorce, and child custody, the Family Protection Law moved legal practice in a more gender-egalitarian direction. It placed strict limits on polygamy where husbands could no longer divorce with only a thrice-repeated statement of "I divorce you"; both husbands and wives had to go to court for a divorce; and grounds for divorce were similar for both. Child custody, which under Shi'a law went to the husband and his family, though the mother kept boys to age two and girls to age seven, now went to family courts for adjudication, and could go to either parent. As Shi'a jurisprudence, allowed special conditions to be put in the marriage contract that might protect wives, the main provisions of the Family Protection Law were put into every marriage contract as a way to try to render them legitimate by Islamic law. In the same period, increasing numbers of women were educated and began to work in a variety of jobs outside the domestic sphere. Although these changes, which had been promoted by activist women, affected mostly the new, Western-oriented middle class, they also began to have trickle down effects on the urban lower-middle and lower classes too, who benefited from increased access to education, employment opportunities, and legal reform. On the other hand, the effect of these state-sponsored gender policies spawned further conflict within the social and religious spheres.

From 1966 to 1977, in the midst of a growing autocratic political environment, women's organizations and associations were forced to assume an apolitical, charitable, and educational character. Despite official recognition, the state remained the major source for change in the status of women—policy supported by the belief that without the endorsement of the modernizing state and its political organs, which were controlled by men, women's rights were unattainable in an Islamic society. As argued by Afkhami, "the law as the expression of the will of the state was indispensible to secure women's rights in Iran."[49] Thus, access to education and work outside of the home was made easier for women despite the lack of any serious efforts to create job opportunities for them.

The state continued to increase the number of women in executive positions, enhance their opportunities in the public area, and appoint women as judges—a practice also condemned by Shi'a theologians. Forough Parsa was appointed as minister of education from 1968–74. In 1975, the family law was further modified to give women custody rights, ease earlier penalties against abortion, and offer free abortion on demand. In the same year, the office of women's affairs was raised to ministerial status and Mahnaz Afkhami was appointed to the position.

While significant, these appointments served as symbols with marginal influence in their scope. In the last 20 years of the Pahlavi reign, the number of women in managerial positions in the government never passed 2.8 percent.[50] Moreover, these developments took place in an atmosphere of contradictions between women's freedom and patrimonial dominance. Women were appointed to executive positions in male-dominated environments with strong male cultures and structures. Imperial bureaucracy was a male institution intolerant of independent decision-making by women. Opposition to male decisions was not tolerated, especially on political issues.

In practice, these reforms primarily benefitted only women who had access to information as well as the social and economic support necessary to take advantage of the legal system. Yet, it would be a mistake to belittle the considerable ideological, symbolic, social, and psychological significance of these reforms, which indicated to women and to society at large that women deserved more rights than tradition had accorded them. This had a substantial impact on women's self-perception and psychology. The swift cancellation of these reforms by Ayatollah Khomeini in 1979 became a major burden for the regime such that over the years, incremental steps have been taken by the Islamic Republic to reinstate and expand on most of these reforms.[51]

Female integration into the labor market also affected female image perception and the socially accepted preconceived female societal role. Initially, the Ministry of Education was the primary employer of women as teachers, but gradually, and especially after 1963, the government pursued a more whole-scale policy of integrating women into the public sector. The implementation of this policy was made possible as increasing number of women graduated from high school and university. An outgrowth of more active women in the public sector facilitated the formation of women's professional associations, particularly the associations of lawyers and teachers. Theoretically, the labor law guaranteed equal treatment for men and women, and also entitled women to paid maternity leave. During the 1970s, large companies and ministries were required to provide day care centers in order to facilitate women's employment. Nonetheless, according to official statistics women continued to occupy only eight percent of the office workforce.[52]

The shah's development ambitions coupled with his authoritarian rule increased the ire of the clerical class, which remained a regular target as the monarchy sought to solidify and strengthen its power. It is amidst this tense political climate that gender issues became a battleground between the state and clergy. Leading this charge against the shah was Ayatollah Ruhollah Khomeini, an activist cleric who challenged Shi'a quietist norms in demanding clerical participation in political activities. Khomeini captured the reigns of Shi'a leadership in the aftermath of the reigning *marja'e taqlid* (literally meaning source of imitation and a title assigned to a Grand Ayatollah) Ayatollah Borujerdi's death in 1961.[53] As early as 1963, Khomeini stood sentry in challenging the shah's modernization program—a confrontation that eventually led to his arrest and exile. As part of the shah's ambitions, Muhammad Reza Shah sought to restrict clerical power as well as advance a more liberal development and political agenda. For Khomeini, these reforms were proof of the illegitimacy and corruption rife within the government. Among his main criticisms of the shah's policies was the banner of women's rights, which Khomeini considered inimical to the Muslim faith. Indeed, Khomeini supported the imposition of Shariah law. Moreover, he considered the Pahlavi monarchs to have flouted Islamic law and tradition bargaining away Iranian independence in exchange for greater security from the imperialistic United States. As such their attempts at modernization and reform were rejected due to the nature of the government itself. For Khomeini, political and social reform, including that related to women, could only be accepted should the government be legitimate and Islamic. He responded to the 1967 Family Protection Law by declaring that the "law that has been recently passed by the illegal Majlis under the name of the Family Protection Law in order to destroy Muslim family life, is against Islam."[54] The clergy built on this example denouncing women's suffrage, among other issues, organizing protests against such radical policies.

In the 1970s, drawing from the anti-Western discourse, diverse Islamic political movements became popular among opponents of the shah. In arguing for an alternative to the corrupt monarchy, intellectuals and religious scholars effectively modernized Shi'a ideology, particularly those concepts relating to gender. Many scholars were the predominantly young followers of the lay Islamic reformer, Ali Shariati. Islamic clerics considered more moderate on women's issues than Khomeini, like Ayatollahs Motahari and Taleghani; and the young, leftist, urban guerillas; the Mojahedin-e Khalq also retained popular support. Shariati and

Motahari were known for their treatises on women where they interpreted Islamic teachings in a more gender-egalitarian way. Shariati in particular expanded on writer and critic Jalal al Ahmad's concept of *gharbzadeghi* or Westoxification—a condition and obsession that had come to dominate Iranian society—to redefine a woman's role away from the sexual and cultural imperialistic definitions that he saw overtaking traditional culture and values.[55] He argued that women had been reduced to "breeding machines" and "washing machines" and in these roles they could not participate in a revolutionary struggle to return Iranian society to its authentic nature.[56] Motahari argued that women's participation has led to three historical periods. In the first period, women were confined to roles as "adored precious objects relegated to the hearth and home. In the second period though, women gain greater opportunity and responsibility as a partner to men in education and employment but at the same time they have sacrificed their value through their greater accessibility. Motahari never completed this discourse on women, but scholars have deduced that his third period is reflective of the revolution's goals for women where women would participate alongside men in political and social life without abandoning their responsibilities as wives and mothers.[57] In essence, Motahari argued that gender issues should be moved from the realms of the family to that of nature adapting social issues to modern norms. He concluded that monogamy was the natural form of marriage and polygamy was reserved for only special circumstances.

Despite these more moderate opinions, they were still considerably less egalitarian than the women's groups working with the state or the secular opposition.[58] Secular opposition parties often had their own women's groups and displayed women in their program. Though their stated aims promised equality, they actively discouraged any targeted campaign for women's rights, fearful of a divisive platform, reassuring that once they attained power, all such issues would be solved.[59] Hence, many who most visibly worked for gender equality were middle-class activists at least partially allied with an increasingly disliked autocratic government. Those allied with the opposition during the revolution accepted the leadership of Khomeini, who stood against Westernizing reform, and invoked female interest by challenging the exploitation of women as sex objects, instead encouraging the independence and authentic nature of both women and Iran.

The growing divide between state and society as well as among divergent political groups intensified amidst the political and economic tensions of the 1970s. The increasing autocratic nature of the shah, who was supported by the United States, coupled with the country's corruption and economic inefficiency fueled popular discontent among the middle, lower and religious classes. Political opposition was further enabled through the effects of the White Revolution where the trends of urbanization and literacy brought dislocated Iranians together in urban centers.[60] As suggested by Arjomand "the facile presumption of a worldwide secularization of culture is one of the more important commonly held misconceptions convincingly dispelled by the upheaval of the Iranian revolution."[61] The clerical class used these trends coupled with their religious bonds to facilitate greater contact. The circulation of religious publications increased during this period, as did the emergence of religious associations. The mosque also provided a fertile ground for an organizational network for the opposition.[62]

Despite his exile, Khomeini continued to garner popular support as he called on the people to oppose the creeping Westernization that had begun to smother the traditional culture and religious nature of Iranian society. An opposition similar to the diverse coalition brought together during the turn-of-the-century Constitutional Revolution banded together. In defiance of Western political standards, Khomeini orchestrated a merger of religion and state in the creation of the Islamic Republic of Iran. Indeed, almost a century later, the 1979 Islamic Revolution had brought Iran full circle. And despite the Islamic dimension of the revolution, popular support was still directed towards social, political, and civil transformations.

Notes

1. Twelfth-century Iranian poet, Gladys Evans *Online Article on Azeri Literature: Mahsati Ganjavi,* Gladys Evans translator, 2001.

2. For more on the Achaemenid Empire see A.T. Olmstead, *History of the Persian Empire,* 1959.

3. For the most comprehensive description and analysis of Iran's competing identities see Roy Mottahedeh's *The Mantle of the Prophet: Religion and Politics in Iran,* 2000.

4. Mashhad grew as a city because Imam Reza, the eighth in a line of twelve Shi'a Imams, Imam Reza, died there in 818 CE.

5. The Hazrat-e-Masumeh shrine is considered Iran's second holiest site.

6. For more on the Constitutional Revolution see Janet Afary, *The Iranian Constitutional Revolution: 1906–1911,* 1996.

7. The Qajar monarchy ruled Iran from 1794 to 1925. They ruled over a period that saw British and Russian advances into Iran, creating frustration among the Iranian people. Reaction to such foreign encroachment led to the Constitutional Revolution. For more on this period including the modernization efforts pursued by Nasir-ed-Dinh Shah, see Abbas Amanat, *Pivot of the Universe: Nasir al-Din Shah Qajar and the Iranian Monarchy, 1831–1896,* 1997.

8. Deniz Kandiyoti, "Contemporary Feminist Scholarship," in *Gendering the Middle East: Emerging Perspectives,* Deniz Kandiyoti ed., 1996, 9.

9. Nikki R. Keddie, *Modern Iran: Roots and Results of Revolution,* 2003, 61.

10. Hamideh Sedghi, *Women and Politics in Iran: Veiling, Unveiling and Reveiling,* 2007, 42.

11. Parvin Paidar, *Women and the Political Process in Twentieth-Century Iran,* 1995, 51.

12. Keddie, *Modern Iran,* 2003, 61–64.

13. Two of the most important secret societies were *Anjomane Azaadiye Zanan* [the Women's Freedom Society] and *Anjomane Zanan e Negahposh* [The Society of Masked Women].

14. W. Morgan Schuster, *The Strangling of Persia: A Story of European Diplomacy and Oriental Intrigue,* Washington, D.C.: Mage Publishers, 2007, 192.

15. Sedghi, Women and Politics in Iran, 2007, 44; Mangol Bayat, "Women and Revolution in Iran, 1905-1911," In *Women and the Muslim World*, Lois Beck and Nikki Keddie, eds., Cambridge: Harvard University Press, 1978, 299.

16. Hassan Morsalvand, "Zan dar Jombeshe Bidari" [Women in the Awakening Movement], *Zanan* 58, 22–24.

17. Schuster, *The Strangling of Persia*, 2007, 191.

18. *The Times of London,* August 28, 1911.

19. Sedghi, *Women and Politics in Iran,* 2007, 52. For more on Babism see Abbas Amanat's *Resurrection and Renewal: The Making of the Babi Movement in Iran, 1844–1850,* 1989; Farzaneh Milani, *Veils and Words: The Emerging Voices of Iranian Women Writers,* 1992.

20. Ali Akbar Mahdi, "The Iranian Women's Movement: A Century Long Struggle," *The Muslim World,* Vol. 94, October 2004.

21. For more on the life of Taj al Saltaneh see her *Crowning Anguish: Memoirs of a Persian Princess From the Harem to Modernity: 1884–1914,* 1993. Some scholars debate the authenticity of these memoirs. Regardless of the authorship, it is clear that Taj al Saltaneh lived a progressive life as reflected in her memoirs. She is critical of polygamy, veiling, the seclusion of women, and prescribes education and political participation.

22. Paidar, *Women and the Political Process,* 1995, 70.

23. Schuster, 2007, 191.

24. Women decided to organize their own schools for female education drawing from the example of missionary activity. Prior to this initiative, mostly upper-class women learned at home from tutors. Some girls, mostly from clerical families received Qur'anic training. In March 1838, American Presbyterian missionaries had opened the first girls' school in Urumiyeh, Azerbaijan. Religious minorities, mainly Armenians, attended the school. Similar schools had opened in Tehran, Tabriz, Mashhad, Rasht, Hamedan, and other cities. However, Muslim girls were pressured from attending the missionary schools by the religious authorities. In the 1870s, the first Muslim girls graduated from the missionary school in Tehran and by 1909, 120 Muslim girls attended.

25. Bayat, 1978, 299.

26. Sedghi, *Women and Politics in Iran,* 2007, 54.

27. Cited in Sedghi, *Women and Politics in Iran,* 2007, 56.

28. Pari Sheikholeslami, *Zanan-e Rooznameh va Negar va Andishmand-e Iran* [The Iranian Female Journalists and Intellectuals], 1351/1972.

29. For more on Reza Shah, his modernization programs and impact on Iranian society see Cyrus Ghani, *Iran and the Rise of Reza Shah: From Qajar Collapse to Pahlavi Power,* 2001.

30. Mohamad Tavakoli-Targhi, "Women of the West Imagined: The Farangi Other and the Emergence of the Woman Question in Iran," in *Identity Politics and Women,* Valentine M. Moghadam, ed.,1994, 105.

31. Stephanie Cronin, *The Making of Modern Iran: State and Society Under Riza Shah 1921–1941,* 2003. 184.

32. Charlotte Weber, "Between Nationalism and Feminism: The Eastern Women's Congresses of 1930 and 1932," *Journal of Middle East Women's Studies,* Winter 2008, Vol. 4, No.1, 83–106.

33. There is no uniform veil in Iran, although as part of the veiling requirement, women should cover their hair and dress modestly. Women have the choice of different hejabs or headcoverings. The most traditional form is the chador or black tent held under the chin or in

one's teeth covers a woman from head to toe. In general, more religious women use this form of hejab. A roosari or headscarf and a manteau or loose fitting coat is another option often worn by less religious women. Veiling will be discussed in detail in Chapter 4.

34. Bamdad Badrol-Molouk. *From Darkness into Light: Women's Emancipation in Iran.* Translated from Farsi and edited by F. R. C. Bagley, 1977.

35. Leila Ahmed, *Women and Gender in Islam: Historical Roots of a Modern Debate,* 1992, 164.

36. Muhammad Reza Pahlavi, *Mission for my Country* London: Hutchinson, 1960, 231.

37. Eliz Sanasarian, *The Women's Rights Movement in Iran: Mutiny, Appeasement, and Repression from 1900 to Khomeini,* 1982, 64.

38. Homa Hoodfar. "The Veil in Their Minds and on Our Heads: The Persistence of Colonial Images of Muslim Women," in *The Politics of Culture in the Shadow of Capital,* David Lloyd and Lisa Lowe, eds., 1997, 266–67.

39. Sedghi, *Women and Politics in Iran,* 2007, 90.

40. Tashkilaat-e Zanan-e Iran [The Organization of Iranian Women], Hezb-e Zanan, [Women's Party], and Jamaiat-e Zanaan [Women's League] were the most influential.

41. Massoumeh Price, "A Brief History of Women's Movement in Iran 1850–2000," *The Iranian.com,* March 7, 2000.

42. Sedghi, *Women and Politics in Iran,* 2007, 93.

43. For more on the fateful 1953 Operation Ajax coup against nationalist Prime Minister Mossadegh, see Mark Gasiorowski & Malcolm Byrne's *Mohammad Mosaddeq and the 1953 Coup in Iran,* 2004; Sepehr Zabih's *The Mossadegh Era: Roots of the Iranian Revolution,* 1986, James Bill and W. Roger Louis (eds.). *Mussadegh, Iranian Nationalism and Oil,* 1988.

44. Eliz Sanasarian, *The Women's Rights Movement in Iran: Mutiny, Appeasement, and Repression from 1900 to Khomeini,* 1982, 83–93.

45. Sedghi, *Women and Politics in Iran,* 2007, 169.

46. Eliz Sanasarian, *The Women's Rights Movement in Iran: Mutiny, Appeasement, and Repression from 1900 to Khomeini,* 1982, 83–93.

47. For more on Khomeini's opposition and tactics used to garner public support against these initiatives see Keddie, *Modern Iran: Roots and Results of Revolution,* 2003, 149–69; Paidar, *Women and the Political Process,* 1995, 143.

48. Paidar, *Women and the Political Process,* 1995, 142.

49. Mahnaz Afkhami, "Women in Post-Revolutionary Iran: A Feminist Perspective," in *In the Eye of the Storm: Women in Post Revolutionary Iran,* Mahnaz Afkhami and Erika Friedl, eds., 1994, 192.

50. Ali Akbar Mahdi, "The Iranian Women's Movement: A Century Long Struggle," *The Muslim World,* Vol. 94, Issue 4, 427–48.

51. Mehrangiz Kar and Homa Hoodfar, "Personal Status Law as Defined by the Islamic Republic of Iran: An Appraisal," *Women Living Under Muslim Laws Special Dossier 1,* 1996, 7–35.

52. Valentine M. Moghadam, *Modernizing Women: Gender and Social Change in the Middle East,* 1993, 210–13.

53. *Marja' e taqlid* is the label provided to a *Grand Ayatollah* with the authority to make legal decisions within the confines of Shariah law for followers and less-credentialed clerics. After the Qur'an, Prophets and Imams, *marjas* are the highest authority on religious laws in Shi'a Islam. Grand Ayatollah Seyyed Hossein Borujerdi was the leading Shi'a marja from 1947 until his death in 1961. Ruhollah Khomeini was a student of Borujerdi

who forbade him to take part in political activities, a ban which only ended with Borujerdi's death.

54. Ruhollah Khomeini, *Resaleh Towziholmasael* [The Book of Religious Instructions] J. Borujerdi, trans. Boulder:Westview Press, 1984, 466.

55. For more on Jalal al-Ahmad see al-Ahmad's *Gharbzadeghi: Westruckness*, 1982, and Mehrzad Boroujerdi's chapter on Al-Ahmad in *Iranian Intellectuals and the West: The Tormented Triumph of Nativism*, 1996. For more on Motahari see *Nezam Hoghugh Zan dar Eslam* [The System of Women's Rights in Islam], 1978, and his posthumously published book *Masaele Hejab* [The Problem with the Hejab], 1979.

56. Paidar. *Women and the Political Process*, Cambridge: Cambridge University Press, 1995, 179–84; Ali Shariati [Tahrike Tarsile], *Fatima is Fatima*, Quran, June 1982. http://www.al-islam.org/rightsofwomeninislam. Accessed May 2, 2009.

57. Hammed Shahidian, *Women in Iran: Gender Politics in the Islamic Republic*, Volume 1, 2002, 110.

58. Paidar, *Women and the Political Process*, 1995, 168.

59. Haideh Moghissi, *Populism and Feminism in Iran*, 1996, 93.

60. Said Amir Arjomand, *The Turban for the Crown: The Islamic Revolution in Iran*, 1988, 198.

61. Arjomand, 1988, 91.

62. Charles Kurzman, *The Unthinkable Revolution in Iran*, 2004, 34.

3

Khomeini: The Paradox and Politics of Religion

I am a woman who dwells in grace,
Covered and veiled but audacious.
O, you who behest me to abide by his rules
Do not veil me! Enthrone me! Thus
Live Eve and the Empress
To zephyrs travel, those who are pretentious
Fairness and goodness are my resting place.
Not every able one is a seaman or has a face,
Not everyone disguised is as pure or chaste.

Padeshah Khatun, thirteenth-century poetess[1]

Sociologist Max Weber poignantly observed that, "religious . . . behavior or thinking must not be set apart from the range of everyday purposive conduct."[2] Such a statement is relevant when describing the politics of religion that came to light in the Islamic Republic of Iran. Considering the radical policies pursued by the revolutionary regime, this statement might seem counterintuitive. Indeed, these preconceptions are easy to make as the Iranian government neglects human rights, sponsors terror groups, opposes the Israeli state, and pursues a controversial nuclear program. Erroneous assumptions abound regarding the monolithic nature of the government as well. The Iranian reality, though, is more complex and mired in factional, ideological, and religious politics while also constrained by the complex system of government. Finding means to balance the pragmatic considerations of politics with the ideological claims of the revolution continues to pose a challenge to the government. Equally daunting for the revolutionary elite has been the obstacle of sustaining the ideological passions of the revolution and its ambitions amidst growing popular and international discontent. Thirty-two years on, in the face of these and other political challenges and pragmatic realities, the Islamic Republic continues to stumble forward. Such an anniversary is championed as a revolutionary feat lauding the success of Ayatollah Khomeini's Islamic vision for Iran. Indeed, this achievement not only marks a success for the Islamic Republic, but also acknowledges the durability and adaptability, rather than consistency, of this regime. It has survived through a mix of fluidity and rigidity—using a balance of pragmatism and ideology—that points to the regime's contradictory nature. These contradictions are best expressed in the relationship between the Islamic government and women.

Women of all walks of life—religious, secular, urban, rural, middle and lower class, young and old—supported and participated in the Iranian revolution. During the post-revolution consolidation period, women also voted in the government referendum in favor of an Islamic government. Their dynamic presence and collaboration empowered the current government providing a greater aura of legitimacy for the Islamic government that would come to the fore. In return, the state acknowledged that female support was critical to the success of the revolution and the durability of the Islamic Republic. In fact, this realization facilitated a unique and enduring relationship between women and the government. The state found itself caught between Islamic ambitions and the political need to accommodate women. The ebb and flow between ideology and pragmatism was not limited to the relationship with women, but extended to all matters of state. Women, in turn, struggled to pursue their activism in the wake of this Islamic resurgence that would curb their rights, positions, and advancements. What developed over the subsequent 31 years has been a contest between society and the state over women's changing roles, images, and opportunities.

The Iranian Revolution of 1979 was an event that defied all expectation.[3] A heterogeneous coalition of social forces including fundamentalists, merchants, Westernized intellectuals, students, women, Marxists, and liberals came together with the goal of deposing the Pahlavi monarchy. Chanting slogans such as "independence, liberty, and Islamic Republic," this diverse coalition was unified against the monarchical days of despotic rule. This unity was only limited to ridding the country of the Pahlavi ills. As became evident shortly after the shah's exile, there was little agreement among those disparate elements on the framework of the post-revolutionary government.

After decades of monarchical rule with which the government implemented a rapid modernization and development plan, the resulting theocratic government that emerged from the ashes of the revolution was a shocking feat. It was none other than the firebrand cleric Ayatollah Ruhollah Khomeini, who succeeded in imposing his particular type of Islamic ideology and Shariah law on Iran. Following the deposition of the Pahlavi Muhammad Reza Shah, Khomeini transformed the Iranian state into an Islamic one. Street names, billboards, school curricula all exhibited this conversion as society was remade to reflect the Islamic nature of the revolution. Activist clerics and religious revolutionaries who held fast to an ideological interpretation of Shi'a Islam would now guide the country.

Ideology has played an integral part in political life within the Islamic Republic of Iran. In Khomeini's revolutionary message was the merger of Shi'a Islam with populism, providing the ideological framework and identity of the post-revolutionary Iranian state. Khomeini recognized that Shi'a Islam—a religion infused with symbolism, a dramatic history, and strong ethics—could effectively unite Iran's diverse opposition. Seeking to stir the passions of Iranian nationalism, he forged together his personal vision for an Islamic government with the dominant trends found in socialist discourse. His movement, while directed toward the Iranian people, simultaneously provided a call to revolution for all Muslims to rise against the despotism—both domestic and international—that had come to overwhelm their societies.

Ayatollah Khomeini, unlike his clerical contemporaries, was a man ahead of his time. In challenging Shi'a norms of political passivity, Khomeini argued that there existed a clerical responsibility to defend the faithful against injustice. Upon the death of the venerated Marja'e Taqlid Ayatollah Borujerdi in 1961, Khomeini catapulted himself onto the political scene in the first of many confrontations against monarchical injustice. To attract popular support, the astute Khomeini infused his dialectic with Marxist and leftist themes seeking to address the inequities of the international and domestic political system and avaricious nature of imperialism. Conveniently, Khomeini benefited from the work of the French-educated sociologist Ali Shariati, who inspired and reinvigorated a religious spirit among the Iranian masses. Shariati, despite his revolutionary Islamic vision, opposed a clerical monopoly of religion, but his influence set the wheels of a radical momentum in motion.

Critical to Shariati's allure was his adaptation of Islam to appeal to urban youth, focusing on students in general and socialists in particular. As stated by revolutionary leader Ayatollah Mahmoud Taleghani,[4] "Shariati created a new *maktab* (doctrine). It was he who drew the youth of Iran into the revolutionary movement."[5] Prior to his sudden death in 1977, Shariati linked Islam to "Third worldism," infusing his vision with both political and cultural anti-imperialism, chastising Iranians for their *gharbzadeghi* or "Weststruckness."[6] Seeking to return Iranians to the authentic culture that had dissipated during the Pahlavi modernization push, Shariati called upon Iranians to rise against such imperial domination corrupting society. No longer was a passive, black Shi'ism shrouded in the memory of Imam Hussein's martyrdom at Karbala the guiding inspiration of this Muslim society, but rather it was a red Shi'ism based on activism and unyielding in fidelity to the revolutionary cause. This distinction, presented in a group of lectures by Shariati, was relevant in delineating between what he called Alid Shi'ism and Safavid Shi'ism. The former draws on the tenets of progress, revolution, and social justice evidenced in the original Islam as advocated by the Prophet Muhammad and the first Imam Ali. Safavid, or black Shi'ism, is reflective of the institutionalization of the religion that began during the reign of the Safavids, where religious interpretation and ritual were monopolized by the monarchy and the clergy.[7] Here, under the guise of the state, Shi'ism was transformed into a passive faith dominated by mourning and martyrdom rather than drawing upon the active revolutionary spirit championed during the religious leadership of Imam Ali. In rejecting this traditional approach of waiting for the return of the twelfth Imam,[8] he called upon his brethren to actively work to hasten the Imam's return by fighting for social justice, even to the point of embracing martyrdom, saying "every day is Ashura, every place is Karbala."[9]

Despite clerical antagonism towards Shariati, Khomeini seized upon his legacy in the hope of welcoming the socialist base attracted to Shariati's philosophy.[10] Merging together these principles, Khomeini's populist call to revolution was made in the name of the *mostazafin*, or dispossessed, members of Iranian society—those that bore the burden of social, political, and economic injustice. At the same time, he attacked the oppressive nature of American cultural and capital imperialism dominant throughout the Middle East and particularly prescient in Iran as the root source exacerbating the injustice evident in society. Using Islamic symbols of struggle to unite Iranians against the monarchy, Western imperialism and capitalism, Khomeini solidified the ideological foundations of his movement. The challenge to the ruling order would be fulfilled through the implementation of Khomeini's Islamic vision—in the creation of a just Islamic government that would bring freedom, independence and Islam to Iran and Iranians alike.[11] Indeed, Khomeini's ideology was all encompassing "rather than clinging to any single creed, he combined these ideas into an ideology that was at once eclectic, even contradictory and on another level deeply alluring precisely because it was so heterogeneous."[12] In effect, he provided something for everyone, thereby increasing his base of support. This base would also fracture, creating permanent fissures among the revolutionary elite. Factional groups would in the aftermath of his death contest the true meaning of his ideology seeking to be the rightful heirs of his rule and proprietors of his legacy.

The Iranian regime fashioned together in the halcyon days of revolutionary fervor was based on Khomeini's vision of a Shi'a Islamic government—a radical interpretation of Shi'a political thought. First articulated in his 1970 treatise *Hokumat-e-Islami* (Islamic Government), Khomeini called for a government based on Shariah law where the arbiters of the state would be those who held expertise in such legal precepts.[13] For Khomeini, only an Islamic jurist or a *faqih* in the absence of the divinely inspired twelfth imam was the right candidate to interpret Islamic law. The *velayat-e faqih* (guardianship of the Islamic jurisprudence) justified political rule by the clergy, where the faqih would serve as the ultimate authority in the political system wielding absolute religious and political power. The novelty of this system, though, lay in the empowerment of the clergy, endowing them with the authority to rule beyond the scope of Islamic law.[14] The Shi'a use of *ijtihad*, or interpretation of religious doctrine, was essential to Khomeini's reading of Islamic law.[15] He proposed new interpretations to this religion, gaining support from low-level clerics, often over the heads of the leading theologians of the day. With widespread approval through a popular referendum that voted in favor of an Islamic government in 1979, he made his new creed the ideology of the Islamic Republic and the philosophical backbone of the Islamic regime in power.

Equally important to note that despite the overarching emphasis on religion, the theocracy could not discount or neglect the importance of nationalism in mobilizing and rallying the populace. As suggested by Ali Ansari, "Iranian nationalism has never been far beneath the political surface, although at the onset of the Islamic

Revolution it tended to be buried within layers of Islamicized rhetoric. While many have debated the relationship between religion and nationalism, and particularly the importance of Shi'ism to the development of a specifically Iranian identity, there has perhaps been less appreciation of the process by which religion has effectively been nationalized over the last 30 years, such that now more than ever we can talk of an Iranian Shi'ism."[16] This feature of nationalism then would also play a pivotal role in the new government cultivating both pride and activism at the same time.

The structure of the Islamic state is notoriously complex. Initially supported by a broad range of revolutionary groups, the system is stabilized by multiple centers of power—a diffuse polity where ultimate authority lay with the religious and revolutionary institutions, not the central government. Understanding the purpose and character of the various political bodies requires an appreciation of the theological underpinnings of the state and the competing interests of the institutions and their leaders. The Constitution recognizes that Islam is the comprehensive political, social, economic, and religious guide for the Islamic state. Moreover, the Constitution combines Islamic theocracy with democratic accountability where a system of checks and balances is imposed on the contending institutions of the state, as do elections, which provide popular endorsement of the system. These theological and democratic principles often clash, as seen in the post-2009 presidential election protests, leading to conflict between Iran's elected and unelected rulers.

At the top of the pyramid structure of government is the Supreme Leader of the revolution—a cleric selected by the *Majlis Khobregan* (Assembly of Experts), which is comprised of 86 high-ranking clerics popularly elected for an eight-year term after the vetting process imposed through the *Shoraye Negahban* (Guardian Council). The Assembly of Experts is empowered to oversee the Supreme Leader's work and to remove him should he act against Islamic or constitutional precepts. The Supreme Leader, known as the *rahbar* and assuming the position of the faqih, has absolute power over the total system. Specifically, he oversees the armed and security forces and the media and intervenes in legislative, executive and judicial matters of state when appropriate. The Supreme Leader's influence extends to his power of appointment among the oversight bodies, including the head of the judiciary and the Guardian Council, among others. The latter is composed of six senior clerics appointed by the Supreme Leader and six nonclerical layman nominated by the judiciary responsible for approving the Islamic credentials of election candidates and assessing the Islamic compatibility of the laws passed by the *Majlis* (parliament). The *Majma Tashkise Maslehate Nezam* (Expediency Discernment Council) is charged with arbitrating between the parliament and the Guardian Council.[17] These institutions serve as the checks and balances over the elected legislative and executive ones. The President and members of parliament and the local and municipal councils are elected from candidates approved by the Guardian Council. The president and the parliament are elected through universal suffrage every four years, with the president's tenure limited to two terms. Any legislation passed by the parliament must be approved by the Guardian Council, but any Guardian Council decision can be overturned by the Expediency Council.

The Islamic nature of the theocracy is the glue holding this Leviathan state together. Clerical approval in the form of *fatwas* (edicts), provide religious justification for political necessities. However, Shi'a ideology not only unites the Islamic realm but so too does it divide. Subscription to the overarching ideology of government has not restricted the subtle quality of the religion. In fact, the fluidity of interpretation has been both useful and harmful to the regime. The merger of Shi'a jurisprudence with the tools of ijtihad, has led to the fluctuating explanations of political and religious issues. To respond to the changing needs of Muslim societies, Muslim jurists and scholars have relied on the well-established process of innovation. This process is based not only on the Qur'an and religious tradition, or sunna, but also on reason, deduction, and prioritization. Indeed, the use of ijtihad has been controversial throughout Islamic history. In the early days, ijtihad was a commonly used legal practice. Over time and in response to the growing wave of conservatism and competition, "a closing of the doors of ijtihad," took place in the tenth century. In the words of Joseph Schact, "hence a consensus gradually established itself to the effect that from that time onward no one could be deemed to have the necessary qualifications for independent reasoning in religious law, and that all future activity would have to be confined to the explanation, application, and, at the most, interpretation of the doctrine as it had been laid down once and for all."[18] Such limitation took place primarily within the Sunni schools of thought. Although today there are many scholars who advocate for the reopening of these doors in order to adapt to modern times, there remains a debate within the various schools over these issues.

Shi'a theologians, however, have continued to assert their right to interpret. While ijtihad has brought modern analysis to traditional Islamic law, it has also been used to advance political or religious policies. The dispersed nature of Shi'ism with no overarching religious authority or institutionalized structure has fueled contending religious interpretations. Independent ayatollahs have the ability to assert their personal religious opinion, oftentimes in conflict with those of their contemporaries. Devotees can follow the interpretations of any one ayatollah, fueling the multiple interpretations and practices within the faith.

To balance these contending visions, the new constitution pledged to remain true to the noble values of Islam. Here, Khomeini's system of the velayat-e faqih would provide the model of just government. At the same time, the Constitution endorsed the republican values of government enshrining the importance of an electoral mandate. In the initial years after the revolution, to enable this vision, Khomeini forced through a consolidation of his revolution. Daniel Brumberg argues though that Khomeini's revolutionary vision was "anything but straightforward, coherent or consistent." Rather, "Khomeini's religiopolitical views swung from one perspective to another; . . . [and] during the last years of his life—and with nearly competing notions of authority to advance various agendas of their own."[19] As suggested by Amin Saikal,

All this reflected Khomeini's two-pronged approach to Iran's transformation from a pro-Western monarchy to a Shia Islamic republic, based on empowering what he called *mosta'zafin* [the 'have-nots' or dispossessed] against *mostakberin* [the 'haves' or oppressors]. One element of Khomeini's approach embodied a *jihadi* [combative] course of state-building, which Khomeini applied, especially in the early years of the Islamic Republic, to enforce a thorough re-Islamisation of politics and society and purge all opposition to his Islamic vision. Another element was *ijtihadi* [based on creative interpretation and application of Islam through independent human reasoning] to construct a strong modern Islamic Iran with a degree of domestic political pluralism and foreign policy flexibility to make Iran palatable in a changing international order.[20]

Mixing together Islamic imagery and populist discourse, the government implemented a thorough Islamicization of Iranian society where changes to the school syllabi, street names, dress codes, and the new legal system all reflected the return to Islamic norms. At the same time, political events such as the 1979 hostage crisis and the outbreak of the Iran-Iraq war in 1980 allowed the government to purge the political and social system of disloyal and threatening opponents.[21]

Reconciling the pragmatic needs of the state with dogmatic religious precepts became the ultimate paradox of this new government. Again Brumberg states, "Khomeini articulated a utilitarian instrumentalism that viewed religion as a useful tool for attaining collective political and social ends."[22] In a clear deviation from the creed of the revolution, the regime was forced over time to give greater weight to national interests and practical considerations over purely rigid convictions. Though these moves were reconciled. Through the creation of the Islamic government—one sanctioned by God and religious interpretation—the Shi'a faith and its malleability was the backbone and justification for all policy. In the end, the religious justification could supersede any argument. However, at the same time, through calculated and innovative interpretation, Khomeini proved that his religious authority in his role as the faqih enabled him to implement practical decisions that often went counter to Islamic traditions.[23] Faced with the challenge of governance, Khomeini himself often intervened to sanction the authority of politicians at the expense of prominent clerics, in recognition of the practical needs of the state. He pressured the Guardian Council to reverse rulings against legislative efforts deemed inconsistent with Islamic law. Because of its conservative approach, the Council vetoed many laws that the government deemed essential for the effective running of the government, to the point of obstructing government functions. In another more significant decision, just prior to his death, Khomeini sanctioned the supra-authority of the state even "to destroy a mosque" or suspend the exercise of the "five pillars of the faith," if state interest so required—positions seemingly at odds with his revolutionary philosophy that the state and religion are best merged.

By limiting the scope of the clerics and clerical institutions, Khomeini in fact sanctioned the supremacy of the state over the philosophy of the revolution, which was whittled down in the face of harsh political realities. Such a decision "in favor of state paramountcy in society's affairs" gave "dramatic new power to the state," sanctioned its dominance over society, and even "permitted the state to violate citizens' rights for common good."[24] In 1988, Speaker of the Parliament, Hashemi Rafsanjani interpreted Khomeini's guidelines in a revealing way: the "law should follow Islamic doctrine. However, if necessary, priority will be given to government decision over doctrine."[25] The interests of the state became the defining precepts over Islam. Khomeini's rulings effectively demonstrated that his rhetoric, along with Islamic jurisprudence could be modified, depending on the political circumstances. As suggested by Ervand Abrahamian, Khomeini's ideological creation "should be seen as a flexible political movement expressing socio-economic grievances, not simply as a religious crusade obsessed with scriptural texts, spiritual purity and theological dogma."[26] It was "a political struggle," and Khomeini's motives had "little to do with theological traditions."[27] He "instituted political innovation in the garb of traditional religion," scholar Mangol Bayat maintains. He has, in fact, "effectively revolutionized Shi'a Islam."[28]

The endurance of Khomeini's vision and ideology is apparent in the institutions and constitution fashioned together in the revolutionary heyday. Thirty-one years on, these institutions have more or less retained their integrity. The revolutionary elite loyal to the Imam and his religious ideology sustained its hold over the reigns of state power. However, despite the resilience of the bureaucratic Islamic state, the Imam and his clerical counterparts have been forced to confront political realities. The revolutionary unity among the diverse coalition of supporters cracked during the period of consolidation. Khomeini's devotees would fracture over economic, political, and religious policies leading to "competing interpretations about the characteristics and role of an Islamic state."[29] Ironically, it was Shi'a ideology used by the Khomeini to support his Islamic government that also permitted and facilitated vigorous debate. As such, factional discord would become a political norm within the Islamic state. To balance against these trends, the exigencies of politics would often overpower the ferocity of ideology. Early on, the Imam himself would have to break from Shi'a tradition in favor of political pragmatism. Indeed, the preservation of the state would regularly trump ideological fervor. A balance of pragmatic considerations with Islamic ideology would reveal the Janus-like face of politics in the Islamic Republic of Iran. This fluidity and pragmatism would prove essential to the many challenges facing the government. Among the first was that of women's activism.

The victory of the Islamic revolution profoundly altered Iranian society. Early on in the revolutionary consolidation, Islamization plans and a cultural revolution were the first steps toward strengthening the position of the new government while simultaneously rejecting the secular notions of the Pahlavi state and society. Women were the primary targets of these efforts, as they saw their legal and social gains overturned. Rejecting the Western image of women, the new government advanced an Islamic model of women as nurturers, mothers, and daughters of society. Part and parcel of the Islamization policies of the state was the gender segregation of Iranian society visible in schools, universities, and throughout the workplace. And most evident to the Western eye was the imposition of the *hijab* or veil mandated for all women.[30]

In the early days of the revolution, government policies toward women were extreme as the revolutionary Islamic ideology was imposed over society. Indeed, women were affected in every realm; women's issues were tied to the ideological foundations of the theocratic government. Religious legitimacy was among the main institutional pillars and foundation of the new theocracy. Due to the Islamic nature of the new government, religious conformity was at the forefront of many political, social, and economic decisions. Specifically, with the imposition of Shariah law and the mandatory return to the veil, women were inimically connected and impacted by the nature of the government. However, over time, with the revolution's consolidation underway, the radicalism associated with women's issues was tempered in favor of the pragmatic considerations of the day. Through the multiple power centers, competing ideologies and policies emerged. It became clear that the government policy toward women was anything but uniform. One the one hand, Islamization had instituted traditional legal, social, cultural, and political norms on women. At the same time, though, the necessities of the state in maintaining female support opened opportunities for women. In this vein, women exploited these contradictions to force open greater space for themselves in the unfolding drama of Iranian politics.

X X X

Women were prominent participants in the 1979 revolution. Attracted to the prospects of a change in government, a myriad of female groups from diverse political, economic, and religious backgrounds participated and were absorbed by the revolutionary momentum. The Pahlavi monarchy had supported many legal and social efforts that favored the advancement of women, including the education and literacy campaigns, the long sought after right to vote obtained in 1967 as one of the many changes brought about under the shah's White Revolution, and the implementation of the Family Protection Law expanding women's legal rights to divorce and custody. However, despite the slight gains in literacy attained during this period, public attitudes toward women changed very little during the monarchical days. Education had yet to alter the perception of women's traditional roles. Here, the patriarchal culture and socialization played a huge hand in society. [31] These traditional views were held by middle- and lower-class Iranians but were also evident among the elite. Indeed, the Shah had revealed his cultural bias toward women in an infamous interview with Italian journalist Orianna Fallaci. "In a man's life, women count only if they are beautiful and graceful and know how to stay feminine . . . and this women's lib business, for instance. What do these feminists want? Equality, you say? Indeed! I don't want to seem rude, but . . . You may be equal in the eyes of the law, but not, I beg your pardon for saying so, in ability."[32] Evident at the top echelons of society, statements such as these reflected the predominant patriarchal views. Indeed, despite the shah's support of female education and suffrage, there was little change in social attitudes towards women and their place in society—clearly facilitating female frustration.

The revolution offered a unique opportunity to women. Women of diverse ethnic, political, social, and economic backgrounds supported the Iranian Revolution, pouring onto the streets in support of a new government that seemed to promise everything to all. "Women sometimes constituted more than one-third of . . . demonstrators."[33] Secular and Marxist women demanded further opportunities and equality not seen under the Pahlavi policies of state-sponsored feminism but offered by the prospect of political agitation and change. More religious women donned their conventional black chador, making the garb a symbol of opposition against the former regime rallying for the return to a just and Islamic government. While others influenced by the growing tide of antimonarchical opposition equated political change with the prospect of democratic tidings. Seeing flaws in the political and social limitations of the Pahlavi government, through their support of the Islamic revolution, they were looking for an alternative to the shah.

Women were mainly active in the antimonarchical demonstrations and strikes. While not involved in the leadership of the movement, women chose the means of participation. Some were active in peaceful protests, while others took part in more violent mass demonstrations.[34] Some women, including members of the WOI, took part in boycotts and strikes, while others participated in guerilla attacks against government installations.[35] Women were often seen leading the protests as a means of preventing government violence. In August 1978, six women were indicted for disrupting the activities of the Tehran bazaar and many women lost their lives in street clashes and the "Black Friday" events.[36] In addition to these activities, most women provided both moral, physical, and logistical support to their revolutionary brethren. Similar to female activities during the Constitution Revolution, women were the social backbone.

For Khomeini, the presence of women among the revolutionary opposition did not go unnoticed. The visibility of women directly confronting the status quo was a powerful image. Despite his traditional views Khomeini "insisted on the legitimacy and even necessity of women's political mobilization" in the new political landscape.[37] He took advantage of statements such as those promulgated by the shah to draw disenchanted women into the growing revolutionary movement. He countered the shah's views with his own, telling Fallaci, "the Shah declared that women should only be objects of sexual attraction. It is this concept that leads women to prostitution and reduces them to the status of sexual objects. Religion is opposed to this view of women, and not to their liberty and emancipation. The fact that women from all levels of society took part in the recent demonstrations . . . shows the falsity of these allegations. Women fought side by side with men in the struggle for their independence and their liberty."[38]

From abroad, Khomeini had recognized the importance of women among his constituency of support. He appealed to them by promising them respect in a new government that would celebrate the virtues of women. Reaching out through his religious network, he sought to mobilize women. He acknowledged the social and historical challenges faced by women commending their strengths in facing adversity. He repeatedly stated that "Islam made women equal with men; in fact, it shows a concern for women that it does not show for men."[39] Moreover, he championed, "That which was most significant than anything else in Iran was the change which took place in Iranian women."[40]

Not only did women's participation have a profound effect on the politics of the era, it had an even deeper impact on women themselves. The sanctioning of their participation by undisputed religious authority changed the traditional view of women in the minds of both women and their families. The idea that women had a place in the public sphere sent a powerful social message. The result was the "altered . . . consciousness of many women and particularly popular-class women, about their political potential."[41]

Because religious forces gave gender issues a key role in differentiating between life under the Islamic government from that of the monarchy, after the success of the revolution, gender issues were immediately included on the government's agenda. While the subject of women remained central to the new government, there was no clear view of how to resolve the discrepancies of opinion and contradictions as well as maintain unity among the disparate factions. Indeed, Khomeini sought to Islamize Iranian society and through the application of these policies to provide new gender standards for women in the Islamic Republic. These dramatic changes were designed to distinguish the new regime from the old. Consequently, Islamization opened a new battleground for the fledgling state. Pre-revolutionary unity quickly eroded. The diverse coalitions that had come together in support of an indigenous Iranian identity during the revolution divided over Islamization and gender issues. "The issue of women's rights became the point on which the internal and external political boundaries of gender intersected."[42]

Initially, as suggested by Parvin Paidar, "women were praised as revolutionaries . . . [but] afterwards they were asked to go back to their homes." It became clear to women that Khomeini's pre-revolutionary commitments to women were not to be taken at face value. Indeed, "no group experienced the post-revolutionary change so rapidly and thoroughly during the transitional period as did women."[43] Women awoke to the realities of life in the Islamic government of Iran where overnight the Family Protection Law that granted women protection in divorce and custody had been withdrawn. Then came the decision that barred women from holding positions as judges. Female students were excluded from 69 fields of study, including law, singing, engineering, and agriculture. Women were banned from participating in some sports activities and from watching men on the playing fields. The new Shariah laws gave men absolute right to divorce, revoking the prior need for justification. Child custody laws were also amended in favor of men, such that in the aftermath of divorce, women were entitled to keep their boys until the age of 2 and the girls until the age of 7. Women's judgment as evidence in court was worth only half of a man's and blood money for a murdered woman was equal to half of a man's. And if a murdered woman's relatives demanded retribution in kind, her relatives would be obliged to pay the killer's family the full blood money in compensation.[44] Khomeini announced that women were required to wear the veil in the workplace, a move that would eventually be uniformly instituted throughout society.

These changes were codified in the legal documents of the government. The Constitution of the Islamic Republic reflected the government ambiguity with regards to women's issues due to the post-revolutionary conflicts over gender issues. Primarily the Islamic link between the nation and women was codified under the control of the clerical leadership. As a result, prior opposition to women's political, social, and economic participation was reversed. However, gender issues and equality while delineated and enshrined in the Constitution were left to the interpretation of experts, thereby avoiding concrete clarification. In writing the constitution, the revolutionary leaders promoted motherhood and domesticity, stressing in the preamble the importance of the family as "the fundamental unity of society" and emphasizing a woman's "important duty" as a "wife and mother." Indeed, women and the family were prominent in the Constitution that established the foundation for the ideal Islamic society. "The widespread solidarity between men and women of all segments of society, belonging to both religious and political wings of the movement, played a clearly influential role in the struggle. Women were active and massively present in a most obvious manner in all stages of this great struggle."[45] As seen in Article 3, women were treated equally with rights granted for education, employment, and equality. Although Article 20 of the Constitution provided for "equal protection before the law," it also states that "all human, political, economic, social, and cultural rights will be based upon Islamic precepts," thus enshrining women's unequal position with regard to polygamy, divorce, and child custody.[46] Article 21 further enshrined women's rights as mothers and future mothers and as protectors of the sacred Islamic family. At the same time though, the state was given the responsibility to ensure that the rights of women were "in conformity with Islamic standards." Numerous examples of contradictory articles ascribing rights would enshrine the contradictory and conflicting government response to women's issues moving forward.

These edicts came as a surprise to many women who had overwhelmingly supported the revolution and its goals of freedom, equality, and Islamic government. Despite these setbacks, so too did the government recognize the power and potency of its female constituency. The revolution and its consolidation would not have triumphed without the support of women. In fact, Valentine Moghadam stresses this, stating, "it may be said that Iran had two revolutions."[47] The first overthrew the shah and the second firmly established the Islamic Republic. Achieving the unity and activism of all Islamist forces, which included many women, meant substantial changes in respect to Khomeini's discourse on women. When he first began challenging the shah in 1962, he openly declared female enfranchisement as un-Islamic. However, after the revolution, he said women had undergone "an amazing transformation" in which they "served Islam [even] exceed[ing] the service of men." He even suggested that female participation in politics was "one of the blessings of this movement."[48] Going further, Khomeini lauded women encouraging them to "Stand together all of you, you must stick together. You play an important part in this movement, one can even go so far as to say that it was the ladies who took this movement forward because they poured into the streets even though they were not expected to do so. This dispelled any fears the men may have had, it emboldened them seeing the women doing something, it gave them courage. It was you [women] who gave Islam this victory; you participated in this triumph. Keep on participating."[49] On another occasion he stated, "We are indebted to you the courage of your lionhearted women."[50]

Yet, the new regime did not initially conceive that women themselves would be active in the post-revolutionary state. Because of such confusion, the gender policies of the early Republic were neither coherent nor consistent. While in theory the Constitution had provided a general framework for gender issues, in practice "the formulation and implementation of gender policies were closely tied with the Islamic Republic's political and economic development and reflected the heterogeneity of state policy, the diversity of Islamic thought, the political debate, and the power struggle."[51] Many policies that emerged came from "legislative debates or fatwas of influential clerics, Friday prayer leaders and personal interventions of Shi'a leaders and state officials."[52] And "the dominant conceptions of gender were . . . in the context of immediate social and political relations and processes in the post revolutionary society."[53]

During and after the revolution, the need to mobilize and retain all his popular support led Khomeini to urge women to remain politically active. He asked women to come out to vote, first for a referendum on the structure of the post revolutionary government in March 1979, then on the constitution of the Islamic Republic approved in December 1979, and again in January 1980 for the election of the president and in March 1980 for the election of the parliament. He stated, "Women in the Islamic Republic must vote. Just as men have the right to vote, women too have that right."[54] He stressed even further that for women, voting was a "religious, Islamic and divine duty."[55] Ultimately, women were essential as they "like men have a part to play in building the Islamic society of tomorrow. They enjoy the right to vote and be voted for. Iranian women participate in Iran's current struggle just as the men do."[56]

In addition to retaining women's suffrage despite his earlier opposition, Khomeini also addressed other aspects of women's life in the Islamic Republic. He told women that Shariah could in fact give them the right to initiate divorce, pointing out the procedural means whereby a woman could influence her right to divorce in the marriage contract delineating her unilateral rights. He said religion supported women's activity in the public sphere: "Islam urges women to strive and reach perfection which has no limits, nor does it stop at any point and therefore has granted them the right to serve society as a scholar, inventor, philosopher, teacher, physician or even an active politician." Women were included among candidates for the Majlis, with Khomeini saying, "Today is not like the former period when women of uncertain repute ... were brought into the Parliament. Women enter the parliament today, but the circumstances are totally different."[57]

The contradictory steps taken in regards to women might be contextualized as part and parcel of the revolutionary consolidation. Was it opportunism or was it pragmatic growth? In either case, the result, as Paidar suggests, "was a total reversal of the history of clerical opposition to women's participation in the economy, politics and society."[58]

Women's political participation was encouraged at the highest level; their mobilization sanctioned as divine. The gender ideology of the new republic, in other words, was not summed up by a return to Shariah. Aside from the external symbol of the hijab visible throughout the society, there was no consensus on the praxis or politics relating to women's issues. What was demonstrated though by these changes to women's status was "the centrality of gender relations in the political ideology of Islam and in the creation of the new government."[59]

Simultaneously, other realities fostered conservatives to be more generous toward Islamic gender visions. Before the revolution, Khomeini had promised justice for women. As Islamic leaders continued to encourage women to participate in street demonstrations and show support for the regime and its policies, women became more politicized. Given the abysmal performance of the economy and the burdens imposed on the population by long years of the Iran-Iraq war, the government was wary of public criticism and further alienation of their constituencies. In this atmosphere, the shrewd religious and political leaders grew more amenable to offer compromises on gender issues.

Traditional patriarchal views were cast aside for political necessity. Specifically, in the decade of revolutionary consolidation, Khomeini would make many political concessions to women in order to retain the patronage of this important constituency. Despite strong conventional views regarding gender roles, Khomeini and his cadre of associates would support female political mobilization in the public sphere, encourage female education, and promote women's public participation in support of the Iran-Iraq war. These early actions seemed paradoxical when contextualized amidst simultaneous dismissal of female judges and large numbers of women from the public sector. However, women seized the opening to increase their presence in the public sphere while concurrently raising objections to the imposition of *fiqh* or Islamic jurisprudence in every aspect of social life. As Ziba Mir-Hosseini poignantly notes, "a door from within was opened that could no longer be closed."[60]

Changes such as these did not occur overnight nor did they happen smoothly; the decade from 1979 to 1989 was one of revolution and war. Issues of importance to women, such as widows' pensions and child custody, women's working conditions, day care and equal access to education, became part of the public discourse. The eight-year Iran-Iraq war was a turning point for society. Indeed, the Iranian population and the economy were devastated as thousands upon thousands of brothers, sons, fathers, and husbands were lost on the battlefields. To ensure the success of the new government, it was crucial that women supported the wartime efforts. Khomeini spoke on numerous occasions to encourage female support of the national war efforts.[61] At the outset, women were expected to "refrain from over-consumption and boycotting luxury good."[62] As the war progressed denying Iran an early resolution to the conflict, women were recruited as active participants in the economic, social, political, and military realm. Women were involved in assisting in battle areas in providing food, transport, and medical support, and in distributing arms as members of *Basij Mostazafin* (Mobilization of the Disinherited). At home they aided the wounded as part of the *Emdad Pezeshki* (Medical Aid), participated in meetings, demonstrations and conferences to support the war effort, resettled refugees on the war front, and were active in the government sponsored *Nehzate Savadamuzi* (Literacy Campaign).

In 1984, at Khomeini's behest, the *basij*, the regime's volunteer paramilitary arm, started recruiting women. As the war spread from the heartland into urban centers, Khomeini urged women to volunteer for military training in order to "double the strength of men" already fighting. Khomeini argued that "With [female] presence at the war front, women not only bring extra human power, but they also create special sensitivity in men to fight even harder. So, if you participate in the defense of Islam in military and non-military ways, you will create great strength in our soldiers."[63] To further support his call for female military training, the Society of Al-Zahra, a religious women's organization in Qom, called for a demonstration in honor of Khomeini's edict.[64] Four thousand women were trained for information gathering tasks and security missions as part of the volunteer mobilization force.[65] While women received munitions training, their main tasks throughout were limited to administrative, educational, and nursing assistance.[66] Ayatollah Yusef Sanei'i supported female participation stating, "Although Islam does not allow women to participate in jihad, it allows women to take part in defensive jihad. The present war is an imposed one. Our youth make sacrifices and women too should defend the country. But women's defense takes the form of nursing, cooking and washing for the wounded and encouragement of husbands and sons to go to the front. A young woman whose husband became a war martyr, played an equally important role in the national defense."[67] Khomeini furthered in a speech to female members of the war effort, "Today we see that the respected ladies of Iran through-out the country are useful members (of our society) and form a committed and devout community serving their country. They are the mainstay of this country. I hope that, mindful of Islamic precepts and armed with the weapon of faith and devotion to Islam, they will carry this victory forward and will be the mainstay of this revolution too."[68] The Basij also continued to play a critical role in maintaining the revolutionary spirit inspired by Khomeini. In 2009, it is estimated that of the 10 to 14 million Basij, 5 million of them are women.[69]

Moves such as this led the government to implement policies more favorable to women. An early example of the influence of women and the government's awareness of the importance of their support relates to custody of the children of martyrs. Women's advocates gave publicity to heartrending cases of war widows whose children had been taken from them by paternal relatives. Shariah law sanctioned custody struggles where a widow's children are transferred to the deceased husband's family. The law further stipulated that if a woman remarried, she would lose all parental rights. During the war years, female Majlis deputies such as Goharolsharieh Dastgheib and Maryam Behrouzi brought attention to this discriminatory law against women.[70] As early as 1981, female deputies attempted to change the law in favor of women. The bill was referred to the Guardian Council, which rejected the measure on the grounds of its incompatibility with Shariah law. Three years later, in an attempt to address the Guardian Council's concerns, the bill was revived. The bill known as *Layeheh Hagh Hezanat Farzandan Saghir va Mahjur Beh Madaran* (Mothers' Right to Foster Minor and Forlorn Children) empowered the special civil courts to punish fathers who did not respect the decision of the court to award custody to mothers. Despite Guardian Council support, female Majlis deputies opposed this measure as it did not directly address the right of maternal custody.[71]

But, in 1985, at Khomeini's request, the Majlis revised the law. The new law allowed the surviving parent, regardless of gender, to have fosterage or physical custody of children both immediately after the spouse's death and upon remarriage and to receive the government financial support provided for war orphans. Though the deceased father's male relatives retained legal guardianship, the substance of the custody was all but hollow.[72] The pragmatism on display in this move indicated the extent to which the leadership of the Islamic Republic was prepared to bend religious practice to retain the support of women.

An even larger change occurred in respect to women's economic activity. When men did not come home, or came home wounded, it was the mothers, wives, sisters, and children who provided the means of subsistence. The impact on women's employment was substantial and the influence of this change in female status was equally important for the state. Paidar argues that "No other aspect of women's social involvement presented so much difficulty for the Islamic Republic's policy makers as women's employment . . . [where] different and often conflicting ideological, political and economic pressures" led to massive pressure.[73] The state struggled to justify its reversal of its previous opposition to women's employment, particularly during the Pahlavi reign when critics claimed that women's employment was pursued in blind imitation of the West.[74] Further complicating the change in policy was the state's veneration and preservation of the family with women holding the primary role as mothers and wives. Conservative parliamentarians argued "certain professions were considered as damaging to the moral integrity of the family."[75] Additionally, others argued that female employment would increase male unemployment.[76]

At the same time though, women had been economically active in Iran for quite a while. Lower-income women, who were loyal revolutionary supporters, were among the largest segment of females employed. Marginalizing this group would in effect reduce constituent support for the Islamic Republic. Official statistics indicated that only 12.9 percent of all women over the age of 10 in 1979 and 8.1 in 1986 were wage earners. However, it was estimated that a larger percentage of women contributed to the family income in non-formal sectors.[77] Additionally, more women had to work outside the home, either because their husbands were at the war front, or because the escalating inflation of the war years required families to have two incomes. The image of female employment also proved beneficial for the regime, which was under constant attack from critics and the international community who opposed the state's gender policy.

During the post-revolutionary consolidation phase, women were particularly affected by the state policy toward female employment. In March 1979, women were prohibited from becoming judges. Part and parcel of this process was a cleansing of the workforce in Khomeini's *enghelabe edari* (Administrative revolution). Through Islamization policies such as the imposition of the hijab, gender segregation, the replacement of Pahlavi bureaucrats, many women were removed from their posts. Child-care facilities were closed and the workday was extended from 5 to 6 days.[78]

With time, these ad hoc initial plans evolved to a more systematic and practical approach to women's employment. In the midst of the war, women who never had been employed outside the home were encouraged by the state to enter the workforce so that they could support their families. At the same time, Khomeini recognized that female employment was essential to retaining female political support. "Women's employment proves their political presence. The Muslim women's presence in the workplaces, which happen to be less penetrated by Islam, is a sign of their political support for the Revolution."[79] Additionally, he stated, "Of course there is no objection to women taking up employment, sound employment, but we do not want a repeat of the way it was during the Pahlavi era. Then they did not have employment in mind for women, rather their aim was to degrade both men and women, pulling them down from that position they occupy. They did not want a natural growth for either sex."[80] Hashemi Rafsanjani, then speaker of the Majlis, even declared that Iran was "in need of a women's labor force."[81] Such activities also perpetuated popular support for the war, as the female effort was imperative for the defense of the nation.

The early position of the Islamic Republic that had discouraged women from working outside the home was then reversed quickly to adjust for the changing national and economic interests of the nation. Labor practices favorable to working mothers, such as part-time jobs with significant full-time benefits, and requirements that workplaces provide day care, were adopted to make work and motherhood compatible.[82] Moreover, the Islamist ideology of gender segregation enhanced the demand for female teachers, doctors, and social workers. This was a major determinant in the policy shift toward female employment.[83] Hojatoleslam Mahdavi Kani, the head of the special civil courts clarified the legal position of female employment stating:

A women does not have the right to work without the knowledge and permission of her husband especially so if her work interferes with her matrimonial responsibilities. But on the other hand, the husband cannot withdraw permission unreasonably. If the women [was] in employment before marriage and had made it clear to her prospective husband that she intends to continue to work after the marriage, then the husband does not have a valid excuse to prevent her from working.[84]

By 1987, the Labor Law was amended giving greater rights to women with regards to maternity leave, child care, and health and safety.[85] Restrictions on subjects that women could study were removed, increasing women's access to higher education that had not grown since before the revolution, when about 30 percent of university students were women. A campaign was also introduced to bring health care and literacy to isolated areas. This effort focused directly on women and consciously sought to mobilize them to support governmental efforts.

The first years of the Islamic government set a precedent for the subsequent decades to come where contradictory policies would persist toward women. Sidney Tarrow describes the encounter with authority as important for activists. "Much of the history of movement-state interaction can be read as a duet of strategy and counterstrategy between movement activists and power holders."[86] The government empowered women by lauding them as the guardians of the revolution, of the state, and of the society, through their venerated roles of mother and sisterhood, but at the same time constricted them, imposing Islamic laws that sought to restrict women to the home and hearth. This Janus-faced relationship would also be evidenced in legal, social, economic, and cultural policies. With the conclusion of the Iran-Iraq war and the death of Ayatollah Khomeini in 1989, the revolution would move into a new phase. The economic and social effects of these initial war-torn years had profoundly scarred Iranian society. The years that followed would be directed toward reconstruction and rehabilitation. Here, too, women were impacted by these political changes, taking advantage of these contradictions to advance their position within the political, social, and economic spheres. The impact of this first decade where gender policies were conceived in a reactive manner under the guise of Ayatollah Khomeini would set a precedent for gender politics in the years to come. The pragmatism of the state coupled with the multiplicity of ideological and gender visions would further complicate the reaction and action between state and society.

Notes

1. Sheema Kalbasi, *Seven Valleys of Love: A Bilingual Anthology of Women Poets from Middle Ages Persia to Present Day Iran*, 2008, 6.

2. Max Weber, *The Sociology of Religion*, 1993, 1.

3. There is a vast literature on the wide-ranging and highly complex issues that led to the revolution of 1978–1979. See Shahrough Akhavi, *Religion and Politics in Contemporary Iran: Clergy-State Relations in the Pahlavi Period*, 1980; Ervand Abrahamian, *Iran Between Two Revolutions*, 1982; Said Amir Arjomand, *The Shadow of God and the Hidden Imam*, 1984; Nikki R. Keddie, *Religion and Politics in Modern Iran*, New Haven: Yale University Press, 2003; Mohsen M. Milani, *The Making of Iran's Islamic Revolution: From Monarchy to Islamic Republic*, 1994.

4. Ayatollah Taleghani was a prominent ayatollah and activist in the 1979 Iranian revolution. While not the most prestigious cleric, Taleghani had much popular support evidenced in the 1979 Assembly of Experts election where he received the highest number of votes. He was active in the Islamic opposition and jailed on numerous occasions for his links with leftists. During the revolution, he served as the nexus between secular and religious groups. He died in 1979 and is remembered for his numerous contributions on Islam and the economy.

5. Cited in *Ettelaat*, June 17, 1980.

6. See Ali Rahnema, *An Islamic Utopian: A Political Biography of Dr. Ali Shariati*, 2000, 65.

7. For more see Rahnema 300–6. An independent translation of Shariati's *Tashayyo'e' Alavi va Tashayoo'e' Safavi* appears in Shahrough Akhavi's *Religion and Politics in Contemporary Iran* , 1980, 231–3.

8. The twelfth Imam, Muhammad al Mahdi, also known as the Hidden Imam or the Mahdi (the guided one) is the last of the twelve direct descendents of the Prophet Muhammad, venerated by Shi'ites. He went into occultation in the ninth century and is said to be returning as the spiritual savior after a period of chaos and confusion.

9. See Vali Nasr, *The Shia Revival: How Conflicts Within Islam Will Shape the Future*, 2006, 128–9.

10. Shariati criticized the clerical monopoly of religion accusing clerics of misinterpreting Islam.

11. See Ervand Abrahamian, "Ali Shariati: Ideologue of the Iranian Revolution", in *Islam, Politics, and Social Movements*, Edmund Burke, III, and Ira M. Lapidus, eds., 1988, 289–97.

12. Daniel Brumberg, "Khomeini's Legacy: Islamic Rule and Islamic Social Justice," in *Spokesmen for the Despised: Fundamentalist Leaders of the Middle East*, Scott Abbleby, ed., 1997, 19.

13. Ruhollah Khomeini, *Hokumat-e Islami* [Islamic Government], Najaf, 1971.

14. See Said Amir Arjomand, "The Rule of God in Iran," *Social Compass* 36 (4), 1989, 539–48; Hamid Dabashi, *Theology of Discontent: The Ideological Foundations of the Islamic Revolution in Iran*, , 409–85; Daniel Brumberg, *Reinventing Khomeini: The Struggle for Reform in Iran*, 2001, 98–120; Baqer Moin, *Khomeini: The Life of the Ayatollah*, 1999, 199–223; Hamid Algar, *Islam & Revolution: The Writings and Declarations of Imam Khomeini*, 1981.

15. A characteristic of Shi'a Islam is the continual exposition and reinterpretation of doctrine known as *ijtihad*. The most profound example is Khomeini's doctrine of *velayat-e faqih*.

16. Ali Ansari, "Iranian Nationalism Rediscovered," *Viewpoints*, "Special Edition, The Iranian Revolution at Thirty," Washington, D.C.: Middle East Institute, 2009, 83.

17. The Expediency Council is an advisory body to the Leader with an ultimate adjudicating power in disputes over legislation between the parliament and the Guardian Council. The body was created upon the revision to the Constitution of Islamic Republic of Iran on February 6, 1988. The Supreme Leader appointed its members, who are prominent religious, social, and political figures. While the Guardian Council is tasked with assessing the Islamic mandate of the state, conversely the Expediency Council must advance the state's interests. For more information on Iran's multiple power centers, see Wilfried Buchta, *Who Rules Iran? The Structure of Power in the Islamic Republic*, 2002.

18. Joseph Schacht, "Law and Justice," in *The Cambridge History of Islam*, P.M. Holt, Ann Lambton, and Bernard Lewis, eds., Volume 2, Cambridge: Cambridge University Press, 1977, 563.

19. Daniel Brumberg, *Reinventing Khomeini: The Struggle for Reform in Iran*, 2001, ix.

20. Amin Saikal, *Islam and the West: Conflict or Cooperation?*, 2003, 76–88.

21. For the first years of the Islamic Republic see David Menashri, *Iran: A Decade of War and Revolution*, 1990; Vanessa Martin, *Creating an Islamic State: Khomeini and the Making of a New Iran*, 2000; Shaul Bakhash, *The Reign of the Ayatollahs: Iran and the Islamic Revolution*, rev. ed., 1989.

22. Brumberg, *Reinventing Khomeini*, 2001, ix.

23. Menashri, *Iran: A Decade of War*, 1990, 386.

24. Farhad Kazemi, "Civil Society and Iranian Politics," in Augustus Norton (ed.), *Civil Society in the Middle East* , 1996, II, 123–4.

25. British Broadcasting Corporation (BBC), Summary of World Broadcasts, The Middle East, February 3, 1988.

26. Ervand Abrahamian, *Khomeinism: Essays on the Islamic Republic*, 1993, 57. Ahmad Ashraf, "Theocracy and Charisma: New Men of Power in Iran," *International Journal of Politics, Culture, and Society*, 4 1990, 139.

27. Ibid., 57.

28. Mangol Bayat, "Mahmud Taleghani and the Iranian Revolution," in *Shi'ism, Resistance, and Revolution*, Martin Kramer, ed., 1987, 67–8.

29. Parvin Paidar, "Gender of Democracy: The Encounter Between Feminism and Reformism in Contemporary Iran," United Nations Research Institute for Social Development, Democracy, Governance and Human Rights, Program Paper Number 6, October 2001, 2.

30. Ibid., 3.

31. By 1976, despite some gains, almost 60 percent of Iran was still illiterate, and the majority of that number was comprised of women.

32. Quoted in Anne Betteridge, "To Veil or Not to Veil: A Matter of Protest or Policy," in *Women and Revolution in Iran*, ed. Guity Nashat, 1983, 115.

33. *Iran in Revolution: The Opposition Reports*, Middle East Reports # 75, 76 Middle East Research and Information Project (MERIP) Reports, March/April 1979, 15.

34. *Keyhan Havai*, August 3, 1978.

35. Eliz Sanasarian. *The Women's Rights Movement in Iran: Mutiny, Appeasement, and Repression from 1900 to Khomeini.* 1982, 117.

36. *Ketab Jomeh*, March 1980.

37. Nikki Keddie, *Modern Iran: Roots and Results of Revolution*, 2003, 408.

38. Oriana Fallaci, "An Interview with Khomeini," *The New York Times Magazine*, October 7, 1979, 8.

39. The Position of Women from the Viewpoint of Imam Khomeini," *The Institute for Compilation and Publication of Imam Khomeini's Works*, translated by Juliana Shaw and Behrooz Arezoo, 2001. 116.

40. Shaw & Arezoo, 2001, 91.

41. Nikki Keddie, *Modern Iran: Roots and Results of Revolution*, 2003, 408.

42. Parvin Paidar,. *Women and the Political Process in Twentieth-Century Iran*, 1995, 233.

43. Ibid., 353.

44. Ibid., 233.

45. Constitution of the Islamic Republic, 1980, 17.

46. Asghar Schirazi, *The Constitution of Iran: Politics and the State in the Islamic Republic*, 1998, 139–42.

47. Valentine Moghadam, "Islamic Feminism and its Discontents: Toward a Resolution of the Debate," *Signs*, Volume 27, 2002, 1135–71.

48. Vanessa Martin, "Creating an Islamic State: Khomeini and the Making of a New Iran," 2000, 156.

49. Shaw & Arezoo, 2001, 93.

50. Shaw & Arezoo, 2001, 96.

51. Paidar, *Women and the Political Process*, 1995, 271.

52. Haleh Afshar, "Behind the Veil: The Public and Private Faces of Khomeini's Policies on Women," in ed. B. Agarwal's *Structures of the Patriarchy*, India: Kali for Women, 1988.

53. Paidar, *Women and the Political Process*, 1995, 271.

54. Ibid.

55. Nesta Ramazani, "Women in Iran: The Revolutionary Ebb and Flow," *Middle East Journal* 47, 1993, 409.

56. Shaw & Arezoo, 2001, 38.

57. Shaw & Arezoo, 2001, 156.

58. Paidar, *Women and the Political Process*, 1995, 167.

59. Ibid., 232.

60. Ziba Mir-Hosseini, "Islam, Women and Civil Rights: The Religious Debate in the Iran of the 1990s," in *Women, Religion and Culture in Iran*, Sarah Ansari and Vanessa Martin, eds., 169–88, 2002, 186–87.

61. *Keyhan*, May 24, 1981.

62. *Keyhan*, April 7, 1980.

63. *Ettelaat*, March 3, 1986.

64. *Ettelaat*, February 12, 1986 and March 15, 1986.

65. Maryam Poya, *Women, Work and Islamism*, 1999, 86.

66. *Zan-e Ruz*, April 14, 1984.

67. *Zan-e Ruz*, March 18, 1984.

68. Shaw & Arezoo, 42.

69. Fatemeh Sadeghi, "Foot Soldiers of the Islamic Republic's 'Culture of Modesty,'" *Middle East Report 250*, Spring 2009.

70. *Keyhan*, January 28, 1982.

71. *Ettelaat*, January 23, 1985.

72. *Zan-e Ruz*, December 2, 1989.

73. Paidar, *Women and the Political Process*, 1995, 322.

74. *Zan-e Ruz*, June 9, 1984.

75. *Keyhan*, February 24, 1983.

76. *Zan-e Ruz*, August 22, 1987.

77. Statistical Center of Iran, 1988, 65.

78. *Zan-e Ruz*, August 25, 1984.

79. *Zan-e Ruz*, June 9, 1984, & September 5, 1987.

80. Shaw & Arezoo, 2001, 40.

81. Ramazani, "Women in Iran: The Revolutionary Ebb and Flow," 1993, 411.

82. *Zan-e Ruz*, July 17, 1988.

83. Paidar, *Women and the Political Process*, 1995, 325.

84. *Keyhan*, February 24, 1983.

85. *Ettelaat*, October 24, 1987.

86. Tarrow, 2002, 3.

4

Defining and Redefining Activist Women

You are a strong man of high authority with a vast land, and a great kingdom.
I am a proud woman, a follower of logic and wisdom.
If yours are all good, you could deserve to be flourished.
If mine is imperfect, I would certainly be rebuked and punished.

Tahereh Ghoratolain[1]

Women, like the variety of political and social groups participating in the revolution, adhered to conflicting political ideologies, some secular, others religious, some leftists, others right. Although united in the objective of the revolution, many women were divided along political, social, and religious lines. Women did not participate in the revolution as a monolithic bloc, nor did they advance their cause through a political platform on women's issues.[2] Instead, similar to the female activism evidenced during the turn of the century, women subordinated the gender cause to that of the larger goal of the revolution. Women's issues were left to be addressed by the post-revolutionary regime. Despite the lack of a decisive gender platform, women had high hopes that their political, economic, and social goals would be achieved through the promise of the revolution and the establishment of a new, just government. In the aftermath of the revolution, though, women both secular and religious emerged divided in the post-revolutionary atmosphere. Parting ways over their conflicting ideologies and the policies and programs of the new Islamic government, it was abundantly clear that even for women the revolutionary unity was short lived.

Islamization of Iranian society created vast schisms among women. Indeed, religious and secular tendencies in Iran have often been at odds with each other, and are a reflection of the broader ideological currents competing within Iranian society. In the post revolutionary atmosphere, women, whether traditional, Islamist, or secular, would emerge with distinct strategies, methods, and political ambitions to advance their gender visions. Initially, traditional women collaborated with the state while secular ones were effectively marginalized. Understanding the distinctions between women and the goals of each female group is essential to the narrative of female activism. Fundamental to this account is the emergence of a new discourse on Islam and feminism. This chapter contextualizes these changes through the first two decades of the Islamic Republic.

The story of female activism also reflects the political dynamics and domestic developments of action and reaction in the Islamic Republic of Iran. In the first decade of the Islamic Republic, the state assumed responsibility of gender issues, controlling the gender debate and women's groups to bolster its legitimacy with women. During this period, women were also party to political influence. Traditional women sought to collaborate with the state while secular women were isolated from the national gender debate. In spite of the vast schisms between these two groups, traditional women who embraced Islamization and traditional gender policies, refused to be marginalized within the political system. Through deference to Ayatollah Khomeini and the revolutionary ideology, these women collaborated with the state to guarantee a legitimate female social and political role. In the second decade, some traditional women splintered and evolved into Islamist women who supported gender reform within an Islamic framework and were more accepting of the feminist and secular discourse. The birth of this group came both in response and in reaction to the political and economic failures of the first decade. Islamist women called for a reinterpretation of gender policies, often collaborating with secular women. This rapprochement was facilitated by the economic reconstruction and more open political and cultural atmosphere of the 1990s where education, employment, and legal gains had empowered women. The reform movement of President Muhammad Khatami, which was supported by both Islamist and secular women, enabled activists to directly confront the state. The tide of reform though was constrained by the ideological and factional political divide. With reformists marginalized in the third decade of the Islamic Republic, so, too, were many female collaborators. Here, women would again part ways on strategies of confrontation versus conciliation. Many Islamist women continued to support the latter tactic believing that long-term results would come from greater cooperation with the state. Others in cooperation with secularists believed that confrontation was the only means to effect decisive gender change. The actions of women in the first two decades of the Islamic government set in motion the responses of the following decade. This trajectory while incongruous has laid the foundation for Iranian female activism. Part action, part reaction, women—traditional, Islamist, and secular— "had imposed themselves as public players."[3] The 'power of presence' coupled with the power of pressure has yielded recognition from the "political authority . . . of women's role in society and thus, their rights."[4]

Gender Politics Through the Prism of Veiling

The Islamization of Iranian society impacted women most profoundly by highlighting the centrality of gender relations in revolutionary politics. The most visible sign of this policy was the imposition of the veil, or *hijab*, on women although men also respected Islamic modesty requirements by wearing long pants and long-sleeved shirts. In Western parlance, the veil is associated with subjugation, tradition, and backwardness. Non-Muslim Western observers commonly assume that women wear the veil because they are forced to, not out of their personal choice. In Muslim countries, though, the veil has come to represent a myriad of meanings. In fact, the veil was politicized in Iran long before the revolution. Members of the reformist Babi (later Baha'i) movement early on advocated improvement in the status of women. In 1848, Tahereh Ghoratolain, a poet and an outspoken member of the Babi movement, appeared in public unveiled.[5] She was arrested for her affiliation with this outlawed religious group and for removing her veil; in 1852 she was executed.[6] In 1936, Reza Shah banned the veil linking his policy of unveiling with that of modernization similar to the reforms evidenced in Kemal Ataturk's Turkey.[7] A consequence of this forced unveiling inevitably politicized the choices and concept of veiling. The compulsory nature of veiling was exacerbated by Reza Shah's use of force to unveil women. Ataturk in contrast merely encouraged women to remove their veils. Although unveiling was a progressive measure and provided many women with choice in their public attire, the manner in which it was implemented was undemocratic. Unveiling was a major religious offense and an emotional challenge to many women who were not ready or willing to appear in public unveiled. For these women, "the veil was a source of respect, virtue, protection, and pride."[8] They viewed unveiling as a moral violation. Forcefully unveiled women felt as if they were naked,[9] and many women decided not to leave their homes.[10]

To further guarantee the success of his unveiling mandate, Reza Shah ordered veiled women barred from theaters, offices, and restaurants. A further unplanned outcome of the unveiling policies was the seclusion of many religious women in their homes. An additional consequence was the preclusion of female children of religious families from education, due to the government restrictions.[11] When again the veil was made permissible under the reign of Muhammad Reza Pahlavi, the veil became a prominent symbol of resistance against the political and Western values of the monarchy. During this period, many women voluntarily returned to traditional veiling practices.[12] Religious leaders also encouraged women's veiling in an effort to reclaim some ground with the state.[13] For some women caught between the state and the religious establishment, the choice of wearing a headscarf or *roosari* along with a loose-fitting overcoat or *roopush* became a means of negotiation or compromise between the veiled and the unveiled state.

From 1941 to 1978, women exercised choice in their public attire. But the image and the social meaning that each group of women conveyed with their presence and dress was totally different: although veiled women were seen in public, unveiled women had a social and political "presence" supported by the state's modernization and development ideology. Each group through the external symbols of dress conveyed contesting narratives. Through female attire general stereotypes could be made about the education, class, and religious background of women. Women who wore the traditional black sheath over the clothing known as the chador, and who were known as *chadori* women, were considered to be from religious, middle- and lower-class families with limited education. Some middle-class women wore a *roosari* and a *roopush* or *manteau* (taken from the French word). Those who opted to wear no veil (known as *bi-hejabi*, or without veil) wore Western clothing and makeup. They were assumed to be from middle- and upper-class families. Some of these women had obtained university degrees and were employed.

The 1979 revolution politicized the issue of veiling even further. The symbolism of the veil was heightened not only for women, but also for men at the helm of the revolution. The veil, considered so controversial by Western standards, came to represent the authentic nature of the revolution and its Islamic identity. In opposition to the creeping Westernization so prevalent during the Pahlavi monarchy, women donned their black veils in support of the resistance ideology of the revolution. Issues such as freedom of movement, freedom from subjugation, and freedom from exploitation were all wrapped up in the controversy of veiling. Moreover, the veil represented the immense possibility of freedom for the many pious women sequestered in their homes during the decades of Pahlavi rule. A multitude of women, clutching their chadors as weapons of defiance, were overwhelming in number and support of the revolution. Many were to become the vanguard women of the Islamic Republic.

For secular women, though, the veil represented the very opposite of freedom— that of restriction. Considered a patriarchal misreading of religion, the veil brought attention to the predominant patrimonial influences in Iranian and Muslim society. Indeed the Qur'an does not mandate veiling, but states:

> And say to the believing women
> That they should lower
> Their gaze and guard
> Their modesty; that they
> Should not display their
> Beauty and ornaments except
> What (must ordinarily) appear
> Thereof; that they should
> Draw their veils over
> Their bosoms . . .[14]

The other relevant *sura* in the Qur'an regarding veiling says:

> O Prophet! Tell Thy wives and daughters
> And the believing women,
> That they should cast
> Their outer garments over
> Their persons (when abroad):
> That is most convenient,

That they should be known
(As such) and not molested.[15]

These citations emphasize modesty and covering the bosom and neck. There is no reference to covering female hair or to specifically veil female hair. What is more, the word hijab (literally meaning screen) in the Qur'an refers to the etiquette of interaction with the Prophet's wives (Sura 33:53). The use of the screen, according to Ali, "was a special feature of honor for the Prophet's household." Nevertheless, over time, covering female hair was promoted as part of Islamic tradition. The Prophet Muhammad adopted veiling first to shield his plethora of wives from the public eye—a move that then spread through Muslim society, advancing values of female piety and respect.

Veiling though was practiced three millennia before the arrival of Islam.[16] The "first known reference to veiling" is believed to be in an "Assyrian legal text of the thirteenth century B.C."[17] The isolating effect was the same with the goal being to distinguish between classes of women. Upper class and royal women were veiled against the gaze of the commoners. Contrary to common belief, veiling was not common in Arab communities before Islam. At the advent of Islam in the seventh century, the custom of veiling was present in the Greco-Roman, Judaic, Persian, Byzantine, and Balkan cultures. One can deduce that early Muslims adopted veiling as result of their exposure to the culture of societies they conquered.[18]

Secular women, including those who supported the Iranian revolution, were dismayed by the early foreshadowing of the state-gender policies. Khomeini's first edict required veiling in the workplace. Women displayed their opposition by participating in a public protest on International Women's Day, March 8, 1979. Thousands marched against the newly imposed governmental decrees affecting women, particularly those on veiling.[19] They voiced their opposition to the veil with slogans such as "freedom of choice in clothes."[20] Such uproar did not alter government policy as a mandatory veiling edict came down in 1981 and dimmed secular hopes for greater women's rights and opportunities promised by the new government. By 1983, the Majlis passed the Islamic Punishment Law where the lax observance of the veil would render a punishment of 74 lashes.[21] Through this mandate of obligatory veiling, it became clear that the Islamic Republic like its monarchical forbearers had politicized and taken the helm of women's issues.

Ironically, the issue of veiling points to the contradictions apparent within the Islamic government. The creed of veiling was used to promote Islamic values of justice, modesty, and piety. In this vision, women had a particular role in advancing these values in society. Khomeini suggested that women, as wives and mothers, were the most important contributors to a successful Islamic society. Khomeini and his clerical contemporaries connected Iranian women to the Islamic role models of Fatima, the wife of Shi'a Imam Ali and daughter of the Prophet. Zeinab, the sister of the martyred Imam Hussein, was also a role model for Iranian women holding the mantle as the revolutionary champion against injustice and oppression. Both served as exemplars for Iranian women as wives, as mothers, as sisters, and as revolutionary supporters.[22]

It was Ali Shariati, the influential sociologist and socialist who gave a lecture entitled "Fatima is Fatima," reviving her image as the ideal female one. He describes Fatima as a manifestation and symbol of pure Islam, stating that even in the ever-changing world in which people's views towards life constantly change, as a role model Fatima can still be emulated by women around the world.[23] Shariati extended his argument on cultural authenticity to suggest that "cultural imperialism" was the source of women's subjugation. By shirking Western fashion and culture, Muslim women would protect their integrity and seek equal stature in society working side-by-side with men. Such close proximity with men would require women to desexualize their bodies by wearing headscarves and loose-fitting clothing.

Shariati's conception of a culturally authentic Muslim woman appealed to younger women, particularly those of traditional middle-class background who wanted to pursue education and have an active presence in society.[24] The mid-1970s witnessed the ever-growing presence of female students in universities wearing the new Islamic attire. These women were claiming their social and political space with a new identity and a novel perspective on Islamic society. In this vein, the chador and headscarf found a new political meaning, conveying rejection of the shah and Westernization. Many secular and modern women took up the veil in solidarity with religious women and in support of the politics of veiling. These women did not necessarily adhere to the religious values represented by the veil, but they subscribed to the political metaphor registering their opposition to the shah.[25]

Compulsory veiling became an essential part of the state gender policy in the Islamic Republic. Khomeini himself stated, "You must remember that the veil, which Islam has prescribed for you is to protect your status. Whatever God has decreed for man or for woman is to keep alive the true values they possess, values that may be destroyed by the devil's insinuations or at the corrupt hands of imperialism and its agents."[26] The regime made use of all mediums of mass communication to justify the hijab, propagating the link between the veil, morality, and Islamic virtue. Slogans such as "Veiling is divine duty," "The worth of a woman is in her veil," and "The stronghold of the Muslim woman is her veil" covered billboards and public places.[27] Women who did not comply with the compulsory veiling laws or who wore an improper hijab were subjected to harassment and violence. Slogans such as "Death to the improperly veiled woman" or "The improperly veiled woman is a stain on the Islamic Republic of Iran who must be eliminated immediately" give a sense of the political atmosphere.[28]

What began in 1979 and continues even in 2010 is a state-imposed campaign to force women to appropriately wear the veil. At times the government has been lax in its control of society. At other times, though, checkpoints and morals police have been dispatched throughout cities to monitor and punish those slighting the rules. At the apogee of the revolution and during the decade of consolidation from 1979–1989, the morals police was vigorous in their detention of women. Through the years, such social control has waxed and waned contingent upon domestic policies and the waves of revolutionary fervor. Indeed, with the 2005 election of Mahmoud

Ahmadinejad so too came a crackdown on Islamic dress as solidifying the bond between gender issues and the state.

In urban centers, a generation of young women who have known nothing but a life of veiling have taken to use the veil as a means of flouting government control.[29] Similar to women before the revolution who put on their veils as a symbol of resistance, so too do young girls today use the veil and their choice of dress as a challenge to the regime. Instead of wearing the chador, which is among the most conservative method of veiling seen commonly in Iran,[30] these women wear loose headscarves and formfitting overcoats. Other common symbols such as wearing makeup, revealing their hairstyles, and undergoing plastic surgery are also part of this social subversion. As evidenced during the Pahlavi era, veiling mores also portend stereotypes of class and religious affiliation. In general, lower-middle- and lower and middle class religious women wear the chador while middle- to upper-class women gravitate to the roosari and roopush. Women active within the political establishment mostly wear the chador. A most significant change though is that educational attainment and political affiliation can no longer be generalized through female dress.

As argued by Louise Halper, "Where patriarchal families previously resisted women's education and employment because they took place within a corrupt public space, the Islamic Republic's commitment to hijab and Islamic morality now constructed public space as morally safe for women."[31] Indeed, for many religious families, it was because of the veil that they felt comfortable enough to send their daughters to be educated or integrated in the communal sphere. Further, Nayereh Tohidi poignantly states, that women used "the veil to facilitate their public presence."[32] Here lies this ultimate paradox, in which the veil that is designed to shield and protect women and even isolate them in society had the contrary effect in Iran. Under the protection of the veil, women were in fact liberated and through this liberation also educated and incorporated in society.[33]

The contours of veiling continue to be controversial in the political realm and amidst public life. In 2000, Elaheh Koulaee, one of the newly elected female reformist parliamentarians refused to wear the chador in parliament. For the first time, a female deputy participated in the legislature wearing the roosari and roopush. Indeed, Koulaee is remembered by many for her stance on the hijab. Koulaee's appearance drew criticism from male members of the parliament, but male members acceded as two other female parliamentarians also chose to abandon their chadors. This political statement eventually led to Koulaee's disbarment from reelection in 2004, when the Guardian Council disqualified her based on her choice of dress.[34] The subsequent seventh parliament inaugurated in 2004 was composed of only chador-clad women. Fatemeh Aliyah, a representative elected from Tehran, rejected Koulaee's supposition stating, "This election was not about chador or non-chador issues. I believe the female voters investigated the candidates and, at the end of the day, they voted for those whom they believed were more active and akin to women issues."[35] Most relevant here is that in conjunction with the politicization of dress, politically active women are reflecting popular social norms that had gained momentum during the reformist period of President Khatami.

The hijab, a male government official asserted, is "the symbol of the Islamic Republic and its values. Compromise on most anything is possible, aside from the veil."[36] Statements such as this are confirmed by government action. In 2000, a young cleric, Hassan Yousef Eshkevari stated while attending the Berlin conference[37] that women should have choice regarding the hijab.[38] While many women championed Eshkevari's bold remarks, Eshkevari's statement was ill received back in Tehran. Upon his return, he was arrested and convicted of heresy by a special clerical court.[39]

Equally important is that even among the female supporters of the revolution there never existed a wholesale embrace of compulsory veiling. Moreover, veiling choices no longer reveal a woman's political association. Many elite Islamist women spoke out early on in an effort to challenge Khomeini's compulsory veiling edict. Indeed, the issue of veiling would cause divisions also among the elite. Veiling would continue to cause a divide as in 2003 when Zahra Eshraghi, Ayatollah Khomeini's granddaughter whose husband Muhammad Reza Khatami was head of the reformist faction in parliament, stated, "I'm sorry to say that the chador was forced on women—in government buildings, in the school my daughter attends. This garment that was traditional Iranian dress was turned into a symbol of revolution. People have lost their respect for it. I only wear it because of my family status."[40] In 2008, Fatemeh Sadeghi, daughter of Ayatollah Sadeq Khalkhalli,[41] echoed these sentiments, in a widely circulated essay, "Why We Say No to Forced *Hijab*," the veil has "nothing to do with morality and religion. It is all about power."[42] After the publication of this article, Sadeghi was removed from her teaching post at University of Karaj. Trends such as these are also evident in the grassroots Green Movement where women wearing chadors and roosaris have stood together to challenge the 2009 election results.

While many young, urban women I interviewed dream of having a choice regarding the veil, many conservative women see the veil as the integral symbol of the revolution and its success. Moreover, for many traditional Iranians the veil is not only a cultural or political symbol but a religious one as well. One female politician insisted that "the veil enabled women to be gender neutral giving them more freedom of movement."[43] Discounting and dismissing the veiling practices of the conservative and traditional portion of the Iranian population is a regular phenomenon, particularly among international and Western analysts who view the veil through their own ideological prism. Despite continued Western disdain toward veiling, the religious, political, and cultural significance of the veil should not be diminished. Should the veil become optional for Iranian women, it would be likely that half of the female population would continue to veil—an assumption that points to the prevalence of tradition, custom, and religion within Iranian society. [44] There remains as much adherence to veiling as there is rejection of it. As such, while veiling continues to draw discussion and debate, women have not legally challenged the state on compulsory veiling. One political activist suggested that "veiling is part of the struggle but does not encapsulate the totality of women's issues. Because of the ideological importance of the veil for the regime, a focus on compulsory veiling would result in a rejection of critical legal issues that impact the livelihood of women more profoundly than veiling."[45] The legal terrain has indeed been among the most decisive battlegrounds between women and state evidenced in the progressive efforts to overturn regressive gender laws. While the issue of choice has gained increased momentum, veiling continues to be part of the subterranean battleground between women and the state.[46] Women have used creative means of dress to subvert and contest the state imposition of the veil and the regime itself. In turn, the regime views this challenge as a contest over its very existence. The imposition of hijab is crucial for the regime, its identity as an Islamic nation, and its Islamic ideology. This ideology has served to empower some women, yet it has also marginalized women who do not accede to the state-sponsored female image.

In effect, the dialectic of the veil serves as a useful analogy to understand the paradigm of gender politics in Iran. Over the past 31 years, fashion surrounding the hijab has changed significantly. Today, women contravene through external and physical symbols among them being the veil. At the same time, the government regularly sponsors fashion shows displaying colorful and alternative veiling possibilities for women. Ultimately, the veil remains the most subtly contested arena between women and the Islamic Republic. As early as March 8, 1979, on internationally recognized Women's Day, the massive demonstration suggested that gender issues would unite and divide women. While ineffectual at forcing the government's hand on veiling, the female presence and challenge foreshadowed a larger conflict to come. This conflict would not only loom between the state and women but also among women themselves.

X X X

In reaction to the Islamization of Iranian society, a myriad of women's groups emerged both to support and to subvert government efforts. One must first distinguish between the mass support of women in general versus the selected efforts of female activists. The state sought to cultivate both groups since it needed a female constituency for its legitimacy and female leaders to promote the Islamic ideology. In general, women's groups can be divided into two broad categories—secular women and traditional women. Over time, a third group known as Islamist women also emerged. There have been many terminologies and typologies used to define female groupings and affiliations. While categorization of women can obscure the commonalities between them, such labeling is necessary to define the goals and strategies of each female group. In this study, the terms secular, traditional, and Islamist are employed to categorize women's groups. However, other scholars have utilized characterizations such as conservative, conformist, and proponent to describe traditional women while using the terms *nonconformist* and *reformist* to categorize secular women. Women who are divided among these categories are predominantly urban based although rural and small-town women have become increasingly active in gender issues through their day to day activities, electoral, grassroots activities, education, and labor participation. While they are not the principal focus of this book, these women are important to the female narrative and exemplify the larger gender and social changes affecting Iranian society.

In the aftermath of the revolution, the contradictory nature of government policy toward women was on full display. Seeking to limit gender activism, the Islamic government made use of the Iran-Iraq war and threats of infiltration as opportunities to repress organized political groups, including those of women. Secular women in particular were targeted, arrested, and jailed as they were seen as part of the opposition. The intense political attention on women's organizations forced many women either into exile or to distance themselves from their activist ambitions.

One cannot underestimate the role of the state and the religious institutions in dividing women. While the state benefited from the patronage of women, it also sought to undermine any independent activity that threatened governmental control and consolidation of the revolution. As such, the state countered women's activism through paradoxical tactics. It suppressed all activities that were considered a challenge to government policy. Demonstrations, petitions, lobbying efforts were all considered incendiary. At the same time, similar to their Pahlavi predecessors, the Islamic government presented itself as the champion of women's rights and the major source of social change in the status of women. The Islamic Republic formulated policies on women's education, employment, and political participation to ensure their political support. Further, women's patronage of the Islamic Republic was critical to the wholesale implementation of Islamization policies. Concurrently, the regime cultivated the emergence of an indigenous women's group to counter efforts made by secular women. The disassociation of religious women from secular ones along with their strong association with the Islamic government gave momentum to a state-sponsored women's activism.

These reactions toward women took place in the context of a diversity of Islamist options, political power struggles, factionalism, political repression, economic stagnation, war, and international isolation. These developments affected the ability of the state to establish coherent policies or ensure their effective implementation. Although the general framework of state policies on women was defined in opposition to the Pahlavi regime, actual policies of Islamization were formulated in a heterogeneous and ad hoc manner by a variety of agents with different and conflicting interests. Indeed, this inconsistent approach both benefited and hindered women. On the one hand, such arbitrariness left women frustrated by a system that had promised equality, and on the other, women recognized that they could exploit these inconsistencies to demand greater access, rights, and clarification. The way this affected women can be seen in the pattern of their education and employment in this period. Although strongly encouraged in official rhetoric, in reality, women's education and employment suffered from incongruous policies, the imposition of gender quotas and support for male institutional dominance, combined with lack of coordination between multiple centers of decision-making and lack of financial resources. Nevertheless, while the opportunities available to women were reduced, Islamization policies and mismanagement did not stop women's participation in social and political life.

Equally important to note is that the Islamic government facilitated and encouraged the ideological divide between women in its consolidation and Islamization plans, seeking to shore up political support while simultaneously marginalizing dissenters. Despite these governmental attempts at dividing women amongst themselves, over time, female groups slowly merged forces responding and reacting to the social, political, and economic changes of life in the Islamic Republic. The combined effects of women's participation in the revolution, their presence on the social scene of the post-revolutionary society, forced Islamization policies of the government and the failure of women's groups to forge concrete alliances to safeguard women's rights, all facilitated the gradual reconstruction of female activism. Common experiences shared by Iranian women in the aftermath of the revolution brought them together in a collective cause. In order to understand the momentum of this movement, it is critical to contextualize the boundaries uniting and dividing women.

Traditionalists

Traditional women are pious female supporters of the Islamic Republic and the theocratic government. These women are devoted to the traditional interpretations of religion although their views and activities are by no means monolithic. This group does however support the institutions and policies of the state. Choosing to work within the political system, these women, who are often the daughters, wives, and sisters of the political revolutionary elite, have used their influence to challenge the government on the failed social, economic, and political promises of the revolution. However, their work must be contextualized with their support for the revolution and its Islamic progeny. Careful not to directly criticize the government, they continue to work through institutional confines in order to advance women's rights within a traditional Islamic paradigm.

Many of these women have received official and unofficial religious education either in government-supported seminaries or from their clerical families. A number of traditional women have advanced through the clerical ranks while others have become politically engaged due to their familial connections. Despite the adherence to traditional interpretations of Islam particularly with regards to women, this group *does* support the active participation of women in public and political affairs. By maintaining allegiance to the state, traditional women guaranteed their relevance and in turn worked to enforce the Islamization policies. The state mobilized women from this group in an effort to retain support of the female constituency. Through education, employment, support for the Iran-Iraq war and political participation, traditional women were the initial collaborators of the state.

Since the revolution, the government mobilized traditional women through a variety of means. Most effectively, through education, the state has encouraged female religious study and supported *Howzeh* (seminary) education throughout the country. It was during the apogee of religious and revolutionary momentum that Khomeini, in collaboration with leading religious figures in the clerical community of Qom, sanctioned female religious seminaries. Female clerical education in Iran began long before the 1979 Islamic Revolution. Mujtahideh Fatemeh Amin founded the first official religious seminary for women Maktab-e-Towhid in Qom in 1972 under the supervision of Ayatollah Kazem Shariatmadari and Ayatollah Ghodosi. Only a number of women were educated at this time as their access to the religious seminaries was controlled.[47] Those who did have access either through familial connections or through perseverance struggled to continue their studies in the male dominated environment where women were not permitted to have contact with male students.

The government advanced the cause of female education in order to create a loyal cadre of women within the Islamic Republic of Iran. For the regime, religious education of women was to be powerful tool of indoctrination and inclusion for the regime. The government, in cooperation with the religious community in Qom, invited women to participate in an environment where they had not previously been welcome. It is important to note that the Islamic government embarked on the program of female religious education not with the direct intent to promote women's interests within the seminaries. The regime sponsored female clerical education to maintain support from an important community that was discouraged by the setbacks brought on by the revolution.[48] At the same time, Khomeini sought to enhance the Islamic nature of Iranian society. By educating women in their religion, then women, in the roles as mothers, could in turn serve as models and educators to their children. In this vein, the government granted women concessions to stimulate female education and labor participation in the primary years of the revolution thus ensuring their participation during the trying times of war and isolation.

Iranian women have benefited from the opportunities of religious education. Through years of rigorous study, women are entitled to achieve the status of a *mujtahed*[49] where once they attain this rank they can interpret Islamic law. Only one woman has had the fortune of fulfilling their requirements to accede to the rank of a mujtahed since the significant decision of the regime in 1984.[50] Many female seminarians have opened personal seminaries to educate women and initiated campaigns to reverse patriarchal misinterpretations of Islamic law.[51]

For over a century a number of intellectual Islamist women have chosen to challenge the patriarchal and negative interpretations that the male dominated religious institutions have presented of their faith. They have insisted on their entitlement to interpret the teachings of the Qur'an and have reaffirmed their right to participate fully in the public domain. Among the most accomplished and recognized Iranian women is Mujtahideh Nosratolmoluk Amin Esfhani. Born in 1886 to a religious family, she was educated despite the obstacles in the way of women's education. Amin continued her studies to the highest level, obtaining the status of *ijtihad* at the age of 40. From then until the end of her life, Amin devoted her life to writing different books, studying, teaching religious courses, and responding to religious questions. In 1965, she established the School of Hazrat-e Fatima and a high school for girls in Isfahan. Other schools were formed in later years. Through political and social adversity, she paved the way for advanced female clerical education in Iran.[52]

Since her death, Iran has been devoid of leading female religious authorities. This shortage has led some religious women, who believe that such undertakings require the training of women to create religious seminaries for women. One of the implications of this undertaking has been the self-determination of women in the realm of religion. Young women, including university or high school students, increasingly seek religious training and enroll in seminaries. The state has made a religious diploma equal to a university one. Considering the challenge of university enrollment, many women have opted for a seminarial education.[53] In 1996, out of 62,731 students in religious seminaries, 9,995 or 16 percent were women, 34 percent of whom were in the 20 to 24 age group, and 20 percent in the 15 to 19 age group.[54] Almost 90 percent of these women resided in urban areas. It is estimated that over 25,000 are currently pursuing religious studies in Iran today.[55]

After 1984, female mujtahids, such has Fatemeh Amin founded religious seminaries around the country. After opening her first seminary, she founded three more, including Maktab-e Ali, for which she enjoyed the moral and financial support of Ayatollah Haeri-Shirazi, the Friday Prayer leader in Shiraz. She also founded Maktab-e Zahra in Yazd with the support of the late Ayatollah Saddouqi. After the revolution, when Ayatollah Khomeini ordered all seminaries to unite and appoint a council of management, Amin moved to Tehran and founded an independent religious seminary called Fatemeh-ye Zahra in 1986. While initially male teachers entered the building through an underground passage and taught the women from behind a curtain, today only female educators lead schools and males are not allowed inside.[56] In addition to the Al-Zahra center, five theological schools for women were in operation during Khomeini's leadership. Under the tenure of Ayatollah Khamenei, who has increased the seminarial dependence on the state, female seminaries expanded to 270 schools across Iran. Between 2003 and 2007, the number of women in the seminaries increased by 50 percent from 20,000 to 30,000. In 2007 alone, 13 new women's seminaries were established.[57]

The challenge of religious study within the seminary is daunting. The contradictions that exist between female and male religious education continued to pose obstacles for women to attain high religious rankings. One female cleric, who began her studies in 1974 and slept in the dormitory for her first years of study was still in pursuit of her ultimate degree when I interviewed her in 2008.[58] Female theological students technically have only five years to complete their studies while their male counterparts have no limitations. Social and cultural barriers continued to obstruct women from advancing in their religious studies. Inevitably, these duties often interfere with their religious commitments. With advanced levels of religious education, for some, it has been difficult to marry. Others who come from religious families feel constrained within the patriarchal nature of Islam.[59] Most of these women have varying interpretations on important issues that affect them such as polygamy, temporary marriage, the veil, custody, and divorce.

One traditional woman I interviewed was a student and companion of Fatemeh Amin. She was nearing 90 but her age had not dimmed her memories and religious convictions. I visited her in her home where she was attended to by a number of devout traditionalists. I had limited time with this cleric as her day was filled with female visitors coming to pay their respects and seek counsel from this respected scholarly woman. Upon learning of my American education, she spoke disdainfully about the history of American and British occupation and influence in Iran. She championed the revolution and Khomeini for returning "Iran to Iranians." Having studied from the age of 16 with Amin, she spoke in admiration of this pioneering woman who she judged to be an equal to many male clerics. Despite her veneration of Amin's achievements, she maintained a strict interpretation of Islam and its traditions. For her, a woman's primary responsibility was the family. Only with the permission and support of one's husband could and should a woman pursue religious studies.[60]

Another energetic traditional woman I encountered in Isfahan spoke of the dualities of her life and ambitions. She married a conservative man who constrained her curiosity and energy. She was neither permitted to drive nor pursue further study and such limitations brought on depression. After eight years, she sought psychological counseling where her therapist helped convince her husband that her depression was situational. With his permission, she was able to pursue religious studies at the seminary (*howzeh*) where she engaged in Qur'anic exegesis. Her education enabled her to work as a female preacher providing guidance to other female devotees.

Her energy was reflected in her passionate "defense of the Qur'an as a complete guide for life." Through her study, she maintained that the laws of custody, inheritance, polygamy, and representation are justified by nature. For her, in order to be awarded custody of children, women must be economically viable. She furthered that polygamy is justifiable in certain conditions putting the onus on women to prevent their husbands from wanting a second wife. For her, women are the "*farmandar* or director of the family." When women cannot manage their families another woman is needed to help. Her traditional approach and views were counterbalanced by her vivacious style of dress. In the company of women, she removed her chador revealing a stylish and colorful roosari and matching outfit. While she has overcome her depression and isolation, she remained beholden to her husband who even after her years of education and work prevented her from driving. To justify these limitations, she spoke of a man's need to protect women even at the expense of female freedom.[61]

A young religious student in the company of a young mojtahed and professor spoke of the importance of maintaining positive connections with the Iranian youth. For him, Islam was also the solution to society's moral corruption. The female student spoke of the immense respect for women in Islam. Despite her piety, she wore a roosari and roopush stating that the chador was not a reflection of her beliefs. For her, women were held to such high standards that children were permitted a break in their prayers only in response to a mother's call. "Women have been spared the responsibility of equality out of respect." At the same time, she stated that while "there should be more female mojtaheds, women were too emotional and often incapable of managing the stress of politics and religion." Needless to say, she had ambitions to translate her religious education to serve as a female preacher. She thought it her duty to explain and contextualize the traditional Islamic guidance from the time of the Prophet. In this vein, women would have the tools and knowledge to protect themselves. She poignantly used the example of beating ones wife as misappropriated by men. To buffer against familial conflict, she counseled that first a couple should spend one night away from each other even seeking the mediation of a cleric. Should physical violence be necessary then men should be cautioned to leave no mark when hitting their wives.

Through educational gains including that of religious education, women have challenged the social, religious, and political barriers. As stated by journalist Nahid Moussavi, "Many women from conservative families are taking courses in higher education and taking part in social, economic, and political life. They want to increase their status. But if Islam is rigidly interpreted, they can't leave their homes without permission from their husbands or fathers. And if they talk to men outside their families, they must place a pebble under their tongue so their voices are indistinct. The presence of ten Islamist women in parliament who address men without pebbles under their tongues shows that, despite setbacks, these women have made real progress since the revolution".[62] Here the contradictions associated with supporting female clerical study emerge. For many young female clerical scholars, the opportunities associated with religious education have strengthened gender consciousness.[63]

Over the years, the government has worked hard to retain the support of this female constituency using their presence as validation for their gender programs. Formal political participation was yet another arena for traditional women to serve and support the state ideology. In the first decade, women who made inroads into politics came from strict religious backgrounds. The parliament proved to be the only venue open to women, and that led to the election in 1980 of three women whose candidacy was supported by pro-Islamic parties.[64] These women, Azam Taleghani, Monireh Gorji,[65] and Goharolsharieh Dastgheib, were active in the revolution, devout Muslims, and connected to the clerical elite through familial or personal relations. This trend of male patronage would continue to be important for female politicians in the decades to come. In the first decade, six female representatives would repeatedly dominate the parliamentary scene. In addition to the above three were Maryam Behrouzi, Marzieyh Dabbagh, and Ategheh Rajai. During this period female parliamentarians had minimal influence in the male dominated environment and their presence was often considered perfunctory. Moreover, women's issues were considered secondary to the larger domestic preoccupations of the war and economic problems. Despite these limitations, female parliamentarians of the first decade were the initial pioneers of female oriented legislation.

In recent years, the Supreme Leader's office has cultivated employment and patronage efforts supporting groups such as the Zeinab Society. Founded in 1986, the Zeinab Society has promoted national political, cultural, social, and ideological activities for women. Active in parliament as a political organization, the Zeinab Society is notorious for advocating conservative restrictions on female clothing and banning male/ female fraternization.[66] The Zeinab Society is headed by former parliamentarian Maryam Behrouzi, whose stance has evolved toward one of an Islamist. Nevertheless, women members must be committed to the principles of Islam, the revolution and the velayat-e faqih.[67] Through education, propagation, and research, the organization provides women with theological, religious language including English and Arabic, Qur'anic translation and art courses.[68] The Zeinab Society has branches in 2 provincial centers, 60 towns, and 22 areas of Tehran. The organization also oversees eight women's seminaries in Qom and some Qur'anic centers. While not a conventional political party, the society has become a lobbying arm to advance gender issues within an Islamic prism.

The Women's Basij, which was created to defend the ideals of the Islamic Revolution, and women's police force are other examples of government patronage of women. The Basij, the regime's paramilitary organization and the effective eyes and ears of the state has groups in schools, universities, public, and private offices and factories. The group organizes military training courses for women, improves female military knowledge and skills, and involves women in national defense. Although there is no exact figure on the number of women involved in the Basij, it is estimated that 5 million of the total 13.6 million members of the Basij are women.[69] The Women Basij is the largest women's organization in the country. The women provided logistical and relief support during the Iran-Iraq war and as many as 4,470 women died during the eight-year conflict.[70]

A third and equally important group is the female police corps. For several years, the Iranian security forces have been recruiting women candidates and holding special courses to provide them with military training.[71] In 1999, the first female police cadets were admitted for training to the police academy; 400 women graduated in 2003.[72] The Iranian authorities have presented this activity as an innovation within the male-dominated system that controls the Iranian security forces, and have carried out an intensive propaganda campaign as evidence of the inclusive nature of the Iranian security forces. However, during a peaceful female protest on June 12, 2006, the government employed women police officers to suppress these demonstrations. Iranian women were beaten with clubs and sticks by the women of the security forces—representing the ultimate contradiction and antifeminist achievement of the regime.

Through recruiting initiatives such as these, women have often proved to be the roadblocks to reform. Important to understand is why these women join groups that seem opposed to women's interests and that subscribe to the gender bias of the state. Many support the regime's revolutionary ideology. Others receive financial compensation and job security in a country where the economy is the regime's major Achilles heel. The financial benefits of food and housing subsidies have assisted female financial contributions to the family. Collaborating with the clerical regime for many is a matter of personal survival as women and their families are dependent on the patronage system of the government. The government has exploited this element of dependency in return for continued political support—in essence a quid pro quo.

For the state, the consequences of such patronage though have been costly. Most painful has been the financial burden. Traditional women and families, particularly those whose children died in the war, were beneficiaries of stipends and subsidies. The state also employed these women and provided educational privileges to their children. The long-term outcome was evidenced in the social changes observed in this group. Many women who had participated in the war effort and supported government policies refused to return to the traditional female sphere of the home. Young women benefited from access to education and pursued theological degrees also seeking to be relevant within the gender discourse of the state while demanding employment and independence. The irony for traditional women is that while supporting the regressive state sponsored gender policies, these women have not accepted a marginalized role for themselves and their female counterparts.

Secularists

Secular women were the first to secede from the semblance of revolutionary unity voicing objection to the process of Islamization of the government and its institutions. Clearly, secular women were disappointed by the resurrection of Islamic law and the removal of legal protections that had been gained during the Pahlavi realm. The imposition of the hijab further incensed secularists who were forced to live under patriarchal interpretations of Islamic law. The ultimate dividing line, though, went beyond the external issues of hijab. For secular women, it is the overarching merger of religion and politics that facilitated their break.[73] As stated by a female activist, "it was as if we had to start pressing for change all over again but this time the bar was lower than zero."[74] Mehrangiz Kar, one of the most articulate secular advocates, questioned the passion of traditional women in forcing equality in Iran, stating that no equality exists in Islam—rendering their goals untenable.[75] Kar, a human rights advocate and lawyer, was initially marginalized like many secular women. Her narrative is representative of many secular women who found means to participate in gender activism. With time and perseverance she returned to the court system defending women in cases of divorce, adultery, and human rights abuses. Like many of her contemporaries she embraced the opportunities for collaboration with other female activists and began to critique women's rights in the reformist press of the 1990s.

For Kar and other secularists, their arguments centered around the need for universal acceptance of human rights as evidenced in the CEDAW adopted in December 1979 which states that "all member countries must in all respects, particularly in terms of political, social, economic and cultural activities ensure that the appropriate legislations are in place to facilitate the extensive and successful development of opportunities for women to participate fully and equally and obtain the maximum benefit from their human rights and liberties, on an equal par with those of men."[76]

Within weeks of the revolution's success, many secular women realized the consequence of not having their own independent organizations, and scrambled to organize themselves. Small organizations were formed to better equip women to deal with the political crisis and put forward their long-term demands. Women also tried to arrange themselves around their professional associations. Some of the associations, supported by experienced and educated members, became vocal critics of the provisional government. Others attempted to reach women and build awareness through grassroots lobbying, including training and literacy classes. Meanwhile, in

1979 and 1980, women struggled, albeit unfruitfully, to form the Women's Solidarity Committee, a coalition of women's organizations designed to coordinate an organized gender response. The primary reason for the failure was that most of the participants were also active in other political organizations with divergent views, preventing them from appearing publicly on the same political platform even if the issues were gender-related.[77] As a result, it became clear early on that open confrontation with the regime was unlikely.

The state made use of the period of revolutionary consolidation to crush organized political groups including those working on gender issues. Many gender activist members were arrested and jailed. Others, confronted by the reality of repression, went into exile. As part of the diaspora, many women activists continued to write and engage on women's issues. Those female activists who remained in Iran reemerged by the mid and late 1980s, forming small, informal consciousness-raising or training groups, while others continued to write or express their ideas through artistic means.[78] Despite such efforts, it has been challenging for secular women to organize public forums and express their views on gender issues. While limited in their political activity, secular women found alternative means of self-expression and social participation. Over the years, instead of directly addressing gender issues through the political prism, secular women became active in social and cultural modes of expression. Through the arts, literature, and social services, particularly grass roots and non-governmental organizations they raised public awareness on issues of female equality thereby advancing alternate gender visions.[79] Through these mediums secular women gained a voice in the gender dialogue of the 1990s. Lily, a secular Western-educated woman, was among those who channeled her ambitions into the arts. Today, a successful fashion designer, Lily creatively designed traditional tribal roopushes and roosaris. Her business flourished as middle- and upper-class women sought creative veiling alternatives. She recounted that when she began her work she was frustrated by her inability to actively contribute to women's issues. With time, she realized that she was helping women express themselves through nontraditional means.[80]

In the more liberal cultural post-war atmosphere, secular women were asked to contribute to public, journalistic, political, legal, and social debates.[81] Secular women voted overwhelmingly for President Khatami in 1997 actively reemerging on the political and social sphere.[82] In the post-war decade, a reevaluation of the war, economic isolation, and political policies of the Islamic Republic gave birth to reformist and secular trends. These debates opened new ground for secularist women where they could contribute to the gender discourse.[83] Kar scrutinized these changes stating, "All that I observed led me to believe one thing: the need to utilize fully any political opening to discuss and bring to light the issue of women's rights."[84]

Islamists

The role and evolution of Islamist women is critical to understanding the impact of social and political changes among conservative portions of society. Traditional women, while initially supportive of the revolution and its promises, soon divided often against each other over many of the gender-biased policies of the Islamic government. This secession gave birth to an Islamist grouping. In general, Islamist women are also devout believers who subscribe to the tenets of Islam. They consider equality of rights in the family and social spheres compatible with their Islam, but incompatible with the Islam represented by conservative forces. They believe that many of the gender positions attributed to Islam are not in fact Islamic but arise from the patriarchal control of men over women. Over the years, their effort has focused on proving this and detaching Islam from its patriarchal heritage. Their goal has been to bring Islam in line with the requirements of modernity.[85] At the same time, their political views have shifted away from unilateral support of the revolution and its principles toward calls for political reform. Most Islamist women championed the election of Khatami and favored his platform, which encouraged greater women's rights, calling themselves reformists.

Islamist women have played a pivotal role in challenging gender inequality in the Islamic government. Seeking to formulate the government's gender policies, these women were active in defining women's rights and responsibilities in Iranian society. Like traditionalists, these women subscribe to the idea that pre-revolutionary Iranian society reduced women to mere sexual objects. At the same time, they are also critical of Marxist and Eastern models that have focused solely on the economic integration of women without effecting gender equality. Rejecting both the Eastern and Western models, Islamist women sought to formulate an authentic Islamic model for women.[86] Zahra Rahnavard, a prominent Islamist politician who is married to Mir Hossein Musavi, reflected, "Our revolution introduced a totally new thing into the world—not Marxist, not nationalistic, but religious. We could do nothing without Islam. I was not always religious, but now I see it's the only way we can make the changes."[87]

Islamist women were equally critical of women's treatment by historical and modern Islamic societies. In their views, through distortion and manipulation, and by exaggerating some aspects of Qur'anic verses and downplaying others, Muslim societies have oppressed women for centuries and denied them their genuine Islamic rights and dignity.[88] Instead of romanticizing Islam's treatment of women, Islamist advocates targeted many unfair aspects of traditional and conventional religious beliefs and practices, in an effort to demolish the popular conception of a long-ago, just Islamic society, which was being promoted as a model for Islamic Iran. The newspapers and magazines contained many criticisms, but also fresh glimpses of the role and status of women in the "ideal Islamic society" that had yet to be created.[89] Islamist women established branches of women's organizations and charitable organization in provincial towns and engaged themselves in consciousness-raising and the promotion of their own Islamic visions on gender.

Early on, Islamist women who often rose to prominence due to their political or familial connections, as Azam Taleghani and Zahra Rahnavard did, voiced their opposition toward the government's gender vision.[90] Despite their personal support of the hijab as well as many of the other Islamization measures, they criticized the state policy on compulsory veiling.[91] They issued an open letter, warning the government of the consequences of enforcing an Islamic society to hijab and of placing undue importance on it.[92] They advanced their alternative policy suggesting that such an Islamic dress code should affect both genders in an Islamic society. In fact, both men and women should dress modestly creating a balance between the sexes. Islamist women also criticized the cancellation of the Family Protection Law and the return to laws, which according to their interpretation, were even more unjust and un-Islamic because they were based on age-old social norms.[93]

Open criticisms such as these, even though always combined with reiterations of support for the revolution and for Ayatollah Khomeini, put Islamist women activists in disfavor with the hard-line conservatives who believed women to be relegated to the home, and certainly not in the position of defining the gender boundaries of Iran's Islamic society. To their disappointment, Islamist women anticipated greater collaboration with the new government. They expected not only greater financial support that would allow them to continue with their mandate, but also that they would be invited to participate in policy making where they could advise on gender issues. None of these expectations materialized as the government sought to advance its own Islamic vision.[94] Thus, with the tacit support of hard-line conservatives, these Islamist women who had supported and participated in the revolution became targets of attack and marginalization. To further such policies, Islamist women on the newspaper editorial boards such as that of *Zan-e Ruz,* (Woman of Today) were replaced with the state's traditional female supporters.[95] While the hard-liners who pushed for rapid Islamization continued to organize women's demonstrations in support of their policies, they found the idea of an independent Islamic women's organization unpalatable. As such, during the politically extremist years of 1981–1987 the voice of Islamist activism was dramatically silenced.[96]

In the political climate of the first decade of the Islamic Republic, the initial wave of organized Islamist political activities diminished. Shahla Habibi, the first presidential advisor on Women, Azam Taleghani, elected to the first parliament, and Maryam Behrouzi, who held the Chair of Islamic Studies at Shahid Behesti University and was elected to four consecutive parliaments, were the only Islamist women who continued to hold prominent political positions for these beginning years.[97] The challenge of remaining relevant in the political sphere was tenfold for these women as it was for others. Islamist women sought to confront the traditional fear within the patriarchy of *fitna* or social chaos, which was brought upon the Muslim community by a woman. The Prophet's favored wife, Aisha, went to war against the Caliph Ali, the revered Shi'a Imam, cousin, and son-in-law of the Prophet causing massive upheaval within the Islamic realm.[98] Traditional men have argued that women have this proclivity to cause upheaval and should be exempted from the political process in order to protect the national interest. Maryam Behrouzi recalled, "In the early days there was talk about whether or not women could stand for Majlis. Eventually women stood and some were elected. But many men and some of the *ulama* viewed this as being against Islamic law and Islamic practices. They argued that if women got into the Majles then it would not be possible to control them or to implement the rule of Islam.[99] Indeed, changing the political culture proved to be among the biggest obstacles for women. In 1983, one Majlis representative stated, "in my view women have used women's way[s] to get their rights, that [is] to say they have screamed and protested."[100] To counter male fears in the parliament, Khomeini supported female political participation through a verbal statement saying that "women have the right to participate in the political arena and in the law making process, anything else would be unfair and unjust."[101]

Among this group of politically active Islamist women, Azam Taleghani's development from a revolutionary to Islamist activist and prominent political figure in the women's movement provides a reflection of the growth and evolution of women's activism since 1979. Taleghani was an active supporter of the revolution serving time in prison during the Pahlavi monarchy. She is the daughter of prominent Ayatollah Mahmud Taleghani, who influenced his daughter through his intellectual work linking Islam with modernity. She is the co-founder of the Women's Society of the Islamic Revolution (WSIR)—along with Zahra Rahnavard, Fereshteh Hashemi, and Shahin Tabatabai—The Islamic Women of Iran, and has published *Payam-e Hajar* (Hagar's Message), a journal that promoted women's issues within an Islamic paradigm.[102] Taleghani has been subject to much harassment through the years for her gender activism but she has succeeded in safeguarding the autonomy of the first independent women's NGO. Moreover, Taleghani's resilience is marked by her strategic navigation of the dangerous political and social waters within the Islamic Republic. For Taleghani, women's pre-revolutionary political activities and continued support during the war gave them a sense of "collective consciousness."[103] She explained how women's experiences of voluntary work during the Iran-Iraq war politicized women: "During the war we joined the Sisters Mobilization Organization. We worked in the mosques, prepared food, blankets, and medicines for the men at the war front. In the war zone areas, women were involved in the distribution of arms amongst the population and the soldiers. In these areas, women set up mobile hospitals and looked after the injured. As the war continued, women had to return to their homes, but they still continued their voluntary work and had to organize their time in a way to allow them to do their housework and their voluntary work in order to keep family members happy."[104] Taleghani used her influence and visibility to reinterpret Islamic laws in favor of women's political and economic participation. She continued to challenge the patriarchy through her political activism much of which will be discussed in subsequent chapters.

Faced with the reality of government reluctance to promote justice for women, in the first years, Islamist women activists were forced to seek out unconventional channels to promote their gender vision. Seeking creative outlets, many Islamist women took pen to paper, writing for female oriented magazines without direct confrontation of the state. Their goal was to nonetheless address the contradictions of building a just Islamic society through exposing the unjust nature of Islamic gender policies, both within the family and society. In this vein, they continued to raise awareness. The use of the press, as evidenced during women's post-Constitutional revolutionary activism, proved to be a successful strategy and one that would be continued, as activism of this kind gained momentum in the 1990s. As such, a new magazine, *Khanevadeh* (Family) was launched primarily to address family issues. To prevent government interference, the magazine was never advertised to be a woman's magazine, but was focused on providing a forum for women for complaints and legal problems concerning marriage, divorce, custody of their children, and domestic violence. Most articles were printed with limited commentary, making it difficult for opponents to brand the magazine as "political."[105]

Over time, pressure and pragmatism forced the state to be accommodating toward progressive Islamic gender visions. Many women's complaints and hardships were caused and exacerbated through the government policies of Islamization evidenced in the aftermath of new gender-discriminatory laws. The popular debate centered around the notions of "Islamic justice" for women. The outcome of political support and revolutionary participation had politicized women, giving them a new confidence. As women were impacted by the economics of war and the politics of Islamization, they voiced their opposition through protest letters to the leaders, national newspapers, and women's magazines. Given the abysmal performance of the economy and the burdens imposed on the population by long years of the Iran-Iraq war, the government was wary of public criticism and further alienation of its constituencies. In this atmosphere, the state was more amenable to compromise on gender issues.

The international community was also important in affecting some state conciliation. Iranian oppositional forces and secular feminists in exile exposed the dualities of women's rights in post-revolutionary Iran. Through the international media, negative stories of a gender-biased society with compulsory veiling, along with those about the stoning of women, offered tempting headlines. Concurrently, the Iranian regime realized the political and economic value of international acceptance. Particularly in the aftermath of the war and Khomeini's death, the state not only sought to regain lost international legitimacy but also to prove that their "revolutionary solutions benefited women."[106] Pressure from international critics on human rights issues made it hard for the regime to reintegrate itself internationally. Moreover, economic investment was often tied to human rights issues. Thus, slowly the state became engaged in improving its tarnished image abroad, and gender issues were incorporated into the new agenda. For female activists—and particularly Islamist women—these changes created fertile ground in which to sow the seeds of legal reform.

Islamist women began to cooperate with the government in the late 1980s when the strain of the war, economy, and Islamization coalesced.[107] Despite disagreements over the state sponsored women's agenda, Islamists compromised seeking an opportunity to develop and define an Islamic women's discourse. "We thought that once we were included in the political system we would have greater influence so short-term compromise was necessary for long-term change," stated one Islamist former parliamentarian.[108] They drafted a concrete critique of Western feminism, deriding the policies of the Pahlavi government and of women's treatment by historical and modern Islamic societies. They challenged the government's decision to exclude women from the judiciary arguing that female emotionality was not an acceptable ground for their exclusion. Instead, they countered that women should be able to take their legal problems to female judges.[109] These arguments though received little attention from conservative and traditional hardliners in the government. Zahra Rahnavard stated, "Women like myself have continuously campaigned for better conditions. We have made our demands in the Majlis in the press and in the public domain. But no one has taken any notice and our voices are not heard."[110]

Moderate Islamists also took positions under the patronage of the state. Organizations such as WSIR and the popular pro-Pahlavi magazine *Zan-e Ruz* were taken over by a board of Islamist women. The government responded to constant criticism from women activists by establishing of the Women's Social and Cultural Council in October 1987 closely affiliated with the Higher Council of Cultural Revolution.[111] The Council was responsible for "preparing the ground for the growth of women's talents and personality and preserving their rights . . . planning for the fortification of the family . . . and removing obstacles in the way of women's participation in economic, social and political activities."[112] In the venue of these organizations, Islamist women were influential in reformulating national gender policies including those related to female employment.[113] In December 1991, the Bureau of Women's Affairs (BWA) was established reporting directly to the president. This office coordinated the development of government policies and programs and is charged with improving the status of women. Over the years, the BWA established offices in many of the critical ministries such as justice and labor, in order to examine women's issues. While the government appointed members of these governmental organizations, they have emerged nonetheless as forums for women's grievances as well as successful lobbying groups. In the past, the Council has used its visibility to draw attention to women's concerns and gender discrimination.[114]

At the same time, the government continued to encourage women to remain active in the public sphere. State institutions and organizations attempted to harness the mobilized power of women. As stated by Parvin Paidar, "Women's political participation was approved because it legitimized the state's Islamization policies and created an image of popular support and stability both internally and domestically."[115] Women's support of Islamization against secular women was an imperative. Further, the government sought female support in the electoral process and for the war. Islamist women became active in philanthropic, religious, and gender activities. Women ran many of the welfare agencies, the health and education centers, and foundations. Not withstanding the WSIR and the Zeinab Society headed by Maryam Behrouzi, the Women's Sports Organization was established in 1981, and the Women's Committee of the Islamic Republic of Iran was founded in 1986 by Zahra Mostafavi. A decade later, women's committees were active in the provinces.[116] Women who managed such organizations often came from clerical families and were connected to the Islamic leadership through their husbands, brothers and fathers.

Female Collaboration

The Islamic government, not unlike its Pahlavi predecessors, continued to monopo-lize gender issues. Obviously, the state anticipated that this would be the best method to retain power over women's issues and their place in society. Conversely though, this plan backfired. A consequence of the state centralization of women's issues was the prevalence of gender consciousness in Iranian society. Indeed, gender conscious-ness has been one of the great outcomes aiding women's activism. As observed by Nikki Keddie, "the history of women's rights in modern Iran . . . exhibits the features of dialectical development. Activism, encouraged by internal contradictions, brings change and often creates a new synthesis which is not, however, permanent but is continually altered by its own activists and contradictions."[117] The imposition of the hijab and the segregation of women inevitably amplified awareness of gender issues. Moreover, women of all classes or religious and political affiliations were bound together by their common fate. As explained by Mahboubeh Abbasgholizadeh, editor of *Farzaneh* magazine, "issues such as divorce, custody of children and other family laws and regulations affected all women, especially poorer women in urban areas."[118] Similar experiences coupled with female frustration facilitated greater cooperation among women. As stated by a middle-aged, activist, young urban woman, "In a sense, the bond of sisterhood, femalehood, was cemented through compassion. I felt more connectivity with other women, more compassion for my gender, hearing stories of divorce, and other social challenges impacting women."[119] Indeed, many women have become pragmatic and individualistic rather than collaborative. One middle-aged Islamist mother at a women's gathering told me, "of course I feel for other women as I know the impact of female hardships could extend to me, but I don't have time or patience or the heart to listen anymore. This is a survivalist society. You must fend for yourself to protect yourself."[120]

Other Islamist women, many of whom had received religious educations, con-tinued to present a new gender vision based on female-centric interpretations of Islamic texts. While this phenomenon will be discussed further in Chapter 5, for them, "Islam is nothing but patriarchy in Islamic costume."[121] The efforts at reinter-pretation proved effective as Islamization affected more women. Thus, many Islamist views and female interpretations of Islamic texts leading to reanalysis of divorce, custody, and other legal, political and social issues found their way into government circles, slowly facilitating legal change.

Moves such as these lent greater credence to the cause of Islamist activism. To survive during particularly repressive periods, Islamist women remained as non-controversial as possible, and in doing so, they were forced to collude as the state tacitly supported the gender policy of the government.[122] The revolutionary years of the first decade greatly impacted Islamists. Many Islamist women realized that without autonomy to criticize and lobby for gender issues, women would remain subject to traditional Islamic precepts.[123] In this vein, another activist group would materialize merging together Islamist and feminist arguments.

Many Islamists embraced 'feminism', despite the controversial Western connotations surrounding the word, for struggling to overcome patriarchy and achieving equality of women's rights. Merging their Islamic interpretations with their gender values, the ideals behind Islamic feminism have come to represent the ideals of many activist Islamist women in the Muslim community and Middle East.[124] While many traditional and secular women perceive Islamic feminism to be contradictory, however as argued by Margot Badran, "Islamic feminism has a positive role to play as it transcends and destroys old binaries that have been constructed. These included polarities between religious and secular and between 'East' and 'West.'"[125]

For many of the women I interviewed, feminism was still a taboo. Indeed the urban, traditional women both young and old argued that feminism was another Western ideology designed to subvert Iranian and Muslim culture and traditions, if not the state as well. Islamist women were divided. There were young urban, educated women who were not afraid of the label. One women's studies student expressed her pride in having reconciled a respect for her religion and her gender stating, "of course I am a feminist, I am an Islamic feminist!"[126] Older, established political women expressed their trepidations with the term though. Perhaps the years of pragmatism and political requisite of compromise with the state and the patriarchy in order to maintain a political position had taken its toll. One female politician conceded that the feminist label even with the context of Islam would be a concession to the West of the failures of their endeavors. Noushin Ahmadi Khorasani contended that "active Islamist women refuse the feminist label.[127] The sister of a prominent female Islamist politician smiled furtively when I asked her about feminism. Marzieh had a seminary education and came from a religious family in Qom but chose not to pursue her studies in Tehran after getting married. She insisted that the seminaries in Tehran did not offer the same level of education. Her marriage, however, had ended in divorce. More tragic was her story of having lost custody of her two boys to the father who had now remarried. She insisted that her children were better without the instability of two families, two mothers, but I saw the pain in her eyes as she looked away to hide her tears. She maintained that feminism was not relevant as Iran had embraced revolutionary Islam, which defended women. The current phase was extremist with men in control but moderation would return. Her divorce signaled foreshadowing of the positive changes possible for women. Coupled with the work of pioneering women like her sister, Marzieh believed that incongruities for women would be reconciled by faith. I saw Marzieh regularly during my visits to Tehran. She was the most open and welcoming of the women I interviewed. Each time we met, we exchanged little gifts. Her parting souvenir was *tasbeeh*, or prayer beads, and a prayer mat that she had purchased on her pilgrimage to Karbala. She urged me to remain faithful.[128]

Islamic feminists make use of religious interpretation or ijtihad to provide updated analysis of Shariah law as it applies to women. The birth of Islamic feminism in Iran is tied to the birth of reformism and trends of secularism that emerged in the 1990s, a topic that will be explored in detail in Chapter 5. Islamic feminists have employed religious tools as well as secular ideas to reinforce their gender vision and through the birth of the Islamist feminist press were able to begin dialogue and collaboration with other women's activists—secular and Islamist alike.[129]

In particular, on the role of women within the family, these women believe that gender should not validate inequality between men and women. In fact, equal rights if not supplementary rights for women due to their maternal role should be ascribed. Islamists have supported increasing marriage age for women and stand opposed to prearranged marriages. Many Islamists have taken strong positions against polygamy and temporary marriage,[130] a particular Shi'a practice. They support divorce laws based on female autonomy, choice, and economic security, and defended custody laws that promote the interests of mother and child. To increase the independence of housewives, they have campaigned for recognition of housework as paid work. They have also supported family planning.[131] Many Islamist women have condemned the family abuse against women enshrined in the law of retribution, or *ghanun ghesas*, that has legalized punishments such as stoning and considers female life to be worth half that of a man's.[132] On women's social role, Islamists have worked to ensure women's political participation and inclusion in civil society. Many reject hard-line views that allocate less value to women's testimony and prohibit women from becoming judges. As an alternative they agitate for equality in such matters.[133]

In this vein, by the early 1990s, secular and Islamist women came together despite their diverse views on gender, feminism, secularism, and democracy. Tilly suggests that "social movements have proceeded as interactive campaigns"[134] The interactions between and among women played a significant part in activism. An "examination of how women constructed sometimes through conflict with one another, a sense of togetherness . . . [among those] who critique female disadvantage, and who work to improve women's situations" is important to the improvement in women's status.[135] International connections also facilitated the bridge between ideological groups. Deniz Kandiyoti addressed this by pointing out that feminists in the Middle East have been both intensely local, grappling with their own histories and specialties, and international, in that they have been in dialogue, both collaborative and adversarial, with broader currents of feminist thought and activism."[136] Despite Iranian isolation during the war with Iraq, with government support, traditional and Islamist "waged a missionary campaign," to spread or "export" the values of the Iranian Revolution abroad.[137] A second wave of international dialogue began during the 1990s when Islamist and secular women displayed new pragmatism in international and United Nations conferences. Links with international women's organizations and NGOs fostered greater solidarity among Iranian women as they exchanged gender views. Invitations to participate in international academic conferences also connected diaspora Iranians with Islamist and secular ones.[138] These international bonds were critical to the shift in gender activism.[139] "The development of international communications was another critical factor in pushing female activism. International seminars and meetings were a stepping stone for women's networks. Women met in Mexico attended conferences in Copenhagen and from there traveled to Beijing in

1995 and participated in the Beijing +10 . . . These meetings created unique opportunities for Iranian women to engage, learn and take part in intercultural and among civilization discussions," said one female government interviewee.[140]

Indeed, as suggested by Haleh Afshar, "The return to the international arena enabled secular and Islamist women gradually to carve out a mutually acceptable political space for themselves. Secular activists decided to abandon political posturing and to organize and collaborate with whomever was willing to defend women's interests. The goal for both Islamist and secular women was to make it unacceptable for any public figure to oppose women's rights."[141]

While secularists still consider that real reform can only be implemented when there is separation of church and state, merging forces with Islamist women served the greater cause of improved civil society, human and women's rights. The mutual bond forged a collective, collaborative and more pronounced presence in pressing for women's rights. Before long, dissatisfied secular and Islamist women emerged with campaigns in the press, the parliament, employment and education that pushed for reforms. Indeed, such an alliance was not a luxury but a political necessity.[142] Moreover, it should be noted that this ideological reconciliation has not been easy as Islamist women have an Islamic worldview while secular women are Western oriented. However, as expressed by Paidar, "Old ideological enemies may turn into new political allies when it comes to resisting the onslaughts of male supremacy. Although these alliances may be fraught and fragile, they speak of Iranian women's will to act upon their gender interests."[143] The solidarity emerging between Islamist and secular women, which goes beyond their divergences, can open the prospect of new forms of cooperation. Editor of the independent *Zanan* (Women) magazine, Shahla Sherkat noted, "we must all tolerate and respect each other's convictions. Even if we don't share the same philosophy, the same beliefs and thinking, we can and should work together."[144] Zahra Ommi, editor of another well-known women's magazine, *Farzaneh*, also points out: "We know that secular women do not share our convictions but this does not give us any problems, since we're all working to promote the status of women. We Islamists have abandoned the idea that we are sole heirs to the revolution. We realize that our sectarianism during the early years led to the isolation of many competent women and this was detrimental to women in general. We want to make up for our mistakes."[145]

In the post-revolutionary decade, it became clear that the government's tactics were both a blessing and a curse for women, but only with time would these distinctions come to light. In the short run, government policies successfully divided women amongst themselves, thereby limiting their collaborative abilities. In the long run though, women—both secular and Islamist—were able to bridge the divide between them. Time and common experience helped these groups come to a rapprochement. Acknowledging the government's contradictory and piecemeal approach to women's issues, they sought to exploit these discrepancies to their advantage. Effectively and unexpectedly, the government's female agenda, one that was designed to isolate women, instead bound women together through common cause and experience.

It would be naïve to portray this rapprochement between women's groups as without obstacle. In 2000, in the aftermath of the Berlin conference, a number of the attendees, including Mehrangiz Kar were jailed for their criticisms of Islamic law. To the dismay of these secularists, their Islamist female counterparts did not come to their public defense for fear of direct confrontation with the state. Shahla Sherkat, who was fined and released, was accused by Kar of protecting her magazine *Zanan* over her relationships. In fact, Kar stated, "We always sensed there was a gap. It simply became very clear after Berlin that the reformists would never take any risks for us, pay any price for us, or defend us. They used us. Especially after our imprisonment, we felt this with our body and our soul."[146] Indeed political expedience and practicality have guided Islamist activism, but Islamist women have also emerged reflectively from the post-Berlin experience. According to Lily Farhadpour, Islamist activist and author of *Zanan-e Berlin* (Women of Berlin), during this time both religious and secular women began to question whether or not Iranian women could afford to allow a division along religious-secular lines to crystallize in the post-Berlin political climate.[147] While Faradpour and her contemporaries believe that unity is necessary, women's groups—Islamist and secular—have achieved a practical accommodation that is reflective of politics in the Islamic Republic.

While diverse women's groups continued to promote different means in their respective efforts to advance women's issues, their collaboration is oriented to similar ends. These mutual endeavors have resulted in both short- and long-term results for women's activism. As will be explored in the coming chapters, women used access to education, the birth of the press, labor participation, and legal means to affect change both through the power of presence and through the power of pressure. Drawing from cultural openness and the politics of reformism, they drew strength from legal victories, the student movement, the flourishing of NGOs, increased internationalization and globalization, the Internet, and what is known as the "Ebadi effect." It is with this newfound cooperation that women pose an effectual challenge to the state. As suggested by Hamideh Sedghi, "women are threatening the most important pillars of the Islamic state—its control of women."[148]

Notes

1. Ghoratolain was among the first Iranian female activists. She was a Babi convert and was sentenced to death in 1853 for her political activities. M. Saadat Noury, Online article on Iranian Poetesses: Past and Present, 2006. http://www.irandokht.com/editorial/print.php?area=pro&sectionID=8&editorialID=2237 Accessed March 31, 2010.

2. Parvin Paidar, *Women and the Political Process in Twentieth-Century Iran,* 1995, 21.

3. Bayat, A. 2010, 108.

4. Bayat, A. 2010, 112.

5. Farzaneh Milani, *Veils and Words: The Emerging Voices of Iranian Women Writers,* 1992, 3.

6. Paidar, *Women and the Political Process,* 1995, 37.

7. Haideh Moghissi, *Populism and Feminism in Iran: Women's Struggle in a Male-Defined Revolutionary Movement.* Repr. New York: St. Martin's Press, 1996, 86.

8. Milani, *Veils and Words*, 1992, 35.

9. Minou Reeves, *Female Warriors of Allah: Women and the Islamic Revolution*, 1989, 85.

10. Moghissi, *Populism and Feminism in Iran*, 1996, 39.

11. Afsaneh Najmabadi, *Women with Mustaches and Men without Beards*, 2005, 226.

12. Eliz Sanasarian, *The Women's Rights Movement in Iran: Mutiny, Appeasement, and Repression from 1900 to Khomeini*, 1982, 75.

13. Paidar, *Women and the Political Process*, 1995, 133.

14. M.A.S. Abdel Haleem, trans. *The Qur'an*, 2008, 24:30–31.

15. M.A.S. Abdel Haleem, 2008, 33:53.

16. Guity Nashat and Judith Tucker, *Women in the Middle East and North Africa: Restoring Women to History*, 1988, 33.

17. Nikki Keddie, "Introduction: Deciphering Middle Eastern Women's History," in *Women in Middle Eastern History: Shifting Boundaries in Sex and Gender*, Nikki Keddie and Beth Baron, eds., 1991, 31.

18. Guity Nashat, and Lois Beck, eds. *Women in Iran from the Rise of Islam to 1800*. 2003, 38.

19. Haleh Afshar, *Islam and Feminisms: An Iranian Case Study*, 1998, 15.

20. Paidar, *Women and the Political Process*, 1995, 324.

21. *Keyhan*, September 9, 1983.

22. Nesta Ramazani, "Women in Iran: The Revolutionary Ebb and Flow," *Middle East Journal*, 1993.

23. Ali Rahnema, *An Islamic Utopian: A Political Biography of Ali Shariati*, 2000, 120–3.

24. Mohammad Javad Gholamrezakashi, "Zan dar Kalame Siyasi: Tahleely as Olgooye Zan dar Negahe Dr. Ali Shariati," [Women in Political Words: Analysis of the Model of Women in the View of Dr. Ali Shariati], *Zanan*, 54–9.

25. Anne Betteridge, "To Veil or Not To Veil: A Matter of Protest or Policy," in *Women and Revolution in Iran*, Guity Nashat, ed., 1983, 121.

26. Shaw & Arezoo, 2001, 55. [This is not by Paidar but a compiled text by Shaw and Arezoo who are the translators. no listing in bibliography unless "The Position of Women from the Viewpoint of Imam Khomeini," *The Institute for Compilation and Publication of Imam Khomeini's Works*, translated by Juliana Shaw and Behrooz Arezoo, 2001].

27. Faegheh Shirazi, *The Veil Unveiled: The Hijab in Modern Culture*, 2001, 106.

28. Ibid., 2.

29. For more on this see Azadeh Moaveni's, *Lipstick Jihad: A Memoir of Growing up Iranian in America and American in Iran*, 2005.

30. While most religiously devout women wear the chador, in 2008 I witnessed a handful of Iranian women in the city of Isfahan wearing the *niqab* or full veil, which fully covers the face. It is said that these women study at a religious school in Isfahan. The niqab has not been embraced by the Iranian female population and is generally worn in southern Iran among the Arab tribes women.

31. Louise Halper, "Law and Women's Agency in Post-Revolutionary Iran," *Harvard Journal of Law and Gender*, 2005, 124.

32. Nayereh Tohidi, "The Issue at Hand," in *Women in Muslim Societies: Diversity within Unity*, Herbert Bodman and Nayereh Tohidi eds, 1998, 277.

33. Moghissi, 1996, 277.

34. Shahla Sherkat, "Eslahtalaban va Sokhangooee az Jense Digar: Gofto Goo ba Dr. Elaheh Koolaee," [Reformists and a Discussion on the Other Sex: A Conversation with Dr. Elaheh Koolaee] *Zanan*, 3.

35. Shadi Sadr, "Women's Gains at Risk in Iran's New Parliament," Womeniniran.org, June 9, 2004, www.onlinewomeninpolitics.org/archives/04_0608_iran_wip.htm. Accessed January 27, 2010.

36. Personal interview with government official from Interior ministry, Tehran, July 17, 2006.

37. The Berlin Conference, entitled "Iran after the elections," was organized by the Heinrich Böll Institute and held in Berlin on April 7 and 8, 2000. The conference was notable less for its proceedings than for the disruption of them by anti-regime Iranian exiles, and for the long prison sentences given to several participants upon their return to Iran.

38. Other attendants of the Berlin conference, including lawyer and women's activist Mehrangiz Kar, were also arrested.

39. Halper, "Law and Women's Agency," 2005, 128.

40. Elaine Sciolino, "Daughter of the Revolution Fights the Veil," *The New York Times*, April 2, 2003.

41. Khalkhali, a close disciple of Khomeini, was appointed head of the Revolutionary Courts in 1979. His appointment earned him a reputation as the "hanging judge," as he sentenced many former government officials to death including former longtime Prime Minister Amir Abbas Hoveyda and head of the SAVAK Nematollah Nassiri.

42. Fatemeh Sadeghi, "Chera Hijab?" [Why We Say No to the Compulsory Hijab,] Trans. Frieda Afary, *Meydaneh Zan*, [Women's Field], April 14, 2008.

43. Personal interview with former female politician, Tehran, May 3, 2008.

44. Personal conclusion drawn from interviews in 2006, 2007 and 2008 and personal observations over the past 25 years of traveling throughout Iran.

45. Personal interview with female activist, Tehran, May 12, 2008.

46. Ibid.

47. *Zan-e Ruz*, May 26, 1984.

48. Personal interview with activist and journalist, Washington, D.C., November 12, 2006.

49. A person who applies ijtihad or interpretation is called a mujtahid. He or she is someone who has studied Islamic law and describes the process of making a legal decision by independent interpretation of the legal sources, the Qur'an and Sunnah.

50. Personal interview with female seminarian and teacher. Tehran, February, 12, 2007.

51. Mina Yadigar Azadi, "Ijtihad va Marja'iyate Zanan" [Level of Religious Learning and Jurisprudence Among the Women's Clergy,] *Zanan*, 7–9.

52. Ahmad Behishti, *Zanane Namdar dar Qur'an Hadith va Tarikh*, [Important Women in the Qur'an, Hadith and History,] *vol. 1*, 1989, pp. 122–6, and *Zan-e Ruz*, August 15, 1992.

53. Personal interview with female seminarian, Qom, April 29, 2008.

54. The 1996 National Census of Population and Housing, National Statistics Center, 77–81.

55. Personal interview with female seminarian, Tehran, February 23, 2007.

56. Azadeh Kian, "From Islamicization to Individualization," in *Women, Religion and Culture in Iran*, Sarah F. D. Ansari and Vanessa Martin, eds., 2002.

57. Homa Hoodfar and Shadi Sadr, "Can Women Act as Agents of a Democratization of Theocracy in Iran?" *United Nations Research Institute for Social Development*, October 2009, 29.

58. Personal interview with female seminarian and teacher, Tehran, April 12, 2008.

59. Personal interviews with female seminary students, Qom, Isfahan, and Tehran, April–May, 2008.

60. Personal interview with companion and student of Mrs. Amin, Isfahan, May 23, 2008.

61. Personal interview with female cleric, Isfahan, May 23, 2008.

62. Azadeh Kian, "Islamist and Secular Women Unite," *Le Monde Diplomatique.* Nov. 1996.

63. Azam Torab, "The Politicization of Women's Religious Circles in Post-revolutionary Iran," in *Women, Religion and Culture in Iran,* Sarah F. D. Ansari and Vanessa Martin, eds., 2002.

64. *Keyhan,* December 4, 1984.

65. Gorji was the only female representative elected to the Assembly of Experts in 1979.

66. Valentine M. Moghadam, *Modernizing Women: Gender and Social Change in the Middle East,* 2003, 176.

67. Hoodfar and Sadr, 2009, 20.

68. Afshar, *Islam and Feminisms,* 1998, 56.

69. Hossein Arayan, "Iran's Basij Force—The Mainstay of Domestic Security," *Radio Free Europe Radio Liberty,* December 7, 2008.

70. Ibid.

71. "Women Police on Parade in Iran," *BBC News,* October 10, 2000.

72. "Iran: Police to deploy women officers for first time since Islamic Revolution," *Islamic Republic News Agency,* January 4, 2003.

73. Mehrangiz Kar, "Women's Strategies in Iran from the 1979 Revolution to 1999," in *Globalization, Gender and Religion: The Politics of Women's Rights in Catholic and Muslim Contexts,* Jane H. Bayes and Nayereh Tohidi, eds., 2001.

74. Personal interview with secular activist and lawyer, Tehran, May 2007.

75. Kar, "Women's Strategies in Iran," 2001, 178.

76. United Nations Convention for the Elimination of Discrimination of Women, 1979, www.un.org/womenwatch/daw/cedaw/text/econvention.htm. Accessed February 8, 2010. CEDAW became an international treaty in 1981. Moreover, the Convention takes up an important place in bringing the female half of humanity into the focus of human rights concerns.

77. Sedghi, 2007, 252.

78. Hoodfar, Homa, "The Women's Movement in Iran: Women at the Crossroad of Secularization and Islamization." *Women Living Under Muslim Laws.* The Women's Movement Series No. 1, Winter 1999.

79. Moghadam, 2003, 176.

80. Personal interview with female designer, Tehran, April 12, 2008.

81. Kar, "Women's Strategies in Iran," 2001, 97.

82. Ibid., p. 97.

83. Afshar, *Islam and Feminisms,*1998, 39.

84. Mehrangiz Kar, *Crossing the Red Line: The Struggle for Human Rights in Iran,* 2007, 97.

85. Paidar, *Women and the Political Process,* 1995, 307.

86. Afshar, *Islam and Feminisms,* 1998, 40–2.

87. David H. Albert, *Tell the American People: Perspectives on the Iranian Revolution,* 1980, 155.

88. Personal Interviews with Islamist journalist and parliamentarian, Tehran, June 1, 2007, and June 10, 2007.

89. Kar, "Women's Strategies in Iran," 2001, 181.

90. Ashraf Zahedi, "Contested Meaning of the Veil and Political Ideologies of Iranian Regimes, *Journal of Middle East Women's Studies,* Vol. 3, No. 3. Fall 2007, 90.

91. Sussan Siavoshi. "Islamist Women Activists: Allies or Enemies," in *Iran: Between Tradition and Modernity,* ed. Ramin Jahanbegloo, 2004, 181.

92. Paidar, *Women and the Political Process*, 1995, 241.

93. Ibid., 261.

94. Ibid., 239.

95. Hoodfar, "The Women's Movement in Iran," 1999, 5.

96. Afshar, *Islam and Feminisms*, 1998, 42.

97. Ibid., 1998, 43–4.

98. Ibid.

99. *Zan-e Ruz*, May 4, 1994.

100. *Zan-e Ruz*, April 17, 1983.

101. Shaw and Arezoo, 2001, 54.

102. Haleh Afshar, "Women and the Politics of Fundamentalism in Iran," in *Women and Politics in the Third World*, ed. Haleh Afshar, 1996, 129–30.

103. Elaheh Rostamy Povey, "Azam Alaee Taleghani," *Biographical Encyclopedia of the Modern Middle East and North Africa*. Michael R. Fischbach, ed., Vol. 1, 2008, 443–4.

104. Maryam Poya. *Women, Work and Islamism: Ideology and Resistance in Iran*, 1999, 136–7.

105. Hoodfar, "The Women's Movement in Iran," 1999, 7–10.

106. Afshar, *Islam and Feminisms*, 1998, 39.

107. Paidar, *Women and the Political Process*, 1995, 311.

108. Personal interview with former parliamentarian, Tehran, May 25, 2007.

109. Afshar, "Women and the Politics of Fundamentalism", 1996, 134.

110. *Zan-e Ruz*, February 10, 1990.

111. *Zan-e Ruz*, October 17, 1987.

112. *Zan-e Ruz*, October 17, 1987.

113. Afshar, "Women and the Politics of Fundamentalism," 1996, 130.

114. http://www.salamiran.org/Women/NROW/1995/Advancement.html   Accessed February 4, 2010.

115. Parvin Paidar, "Feminism and Islam in Iran," in *Gendering the Middle East*, ed. Deniz Kandiyoti, 1996, 58.

116. Afshar, "Women and the Politics of Fundamentalism," 1996, 134.

117. Nikki Keddie, "Women in Iran since 1979," *Social Research*, Vol. 67, No. 2, 2000, 411.

118. Elaheh Rostami Povey, "Feminist Contestations of Institutional Domains in Iran," *Feminist Review*, 48.

119. Personal interview with female student and activist, Isfahan, May 23, 2008.

120. Personal interview with Islamist housewife, Tehran, May 15, 2007.

121. Afshar, *Islam and Feminisms*, 1998, 41.

122. Personal interview with Islamist politician, Tehran, April 14, 2007 and May 14, 2008.

123. Personal interview with Islamist politician, Tehran, April 16, 2007.

124. Margot Badran, "Islamic Feminism: What's in a Name?" *Al Ahram Weekly*, January 17, 2002.

125. Ibid.

126. Personal interview with female student at Tehran University, Tehran, May 20, 2007.

127. Noushin Ahmadi Khorasani, *Zanan Zir-e Sayeh-e Pedar Khandeh-ha*, [Women under the Protection of Stepfathers], 1380, 2001.

128. Personal interviews with sister of prominent female Islamist, Tehran, February 12, and 17, 2007 and April 12, 2008.

129. Fereshteh Ahmadi. "Islamic Feminism in Iran: Feminism in a New Islamic Context," *Journal of Feminist Studies in Religion*, 22, (2), 2006, 33–53.

130. Temporary marriage (*sigheh*) is a fixed-term marriage contract. The duration of this type of marriage is fixed at its inception and is then automatically dissolved upon completion of its term. This arrangement requires no witnesses, and no registration is needed. This form of temporary marriage, according to its proponents, is a measure for curbing free sex and controlling prostitution. A man can have as many sigheh wives as he can afford, but the woman can be involved in no more than one such temporary relationship at any given time and cannot enter another contract before a waiting period (*edda*) of three months or two menstrual cycles elapse. This obligatory waiting period also applies to divorced women in permanent marriage and is intended to determine paternity in case the woman becomes pregnant. Sigheh has been very unpopular, particularly among the educated middle-class families and among women who tend to associate it with legalized prostitution. It is known to be practiced mainly by widowed or divorced women and is believed to be more common in theological seminaries and among the clergy. For more on temporary marriage see Shahla Haeri's *Law of Desire: Temporary Marriage in Shi'a Islam*, 1989. Ayatollah Rafsanjani caused quite a stir in 1990 when he publicly addressed the sexual frustrations of Iranian youth, going so far as to urge "young men and widows to enter into brief temporary marriage for gratification." Quoted in *Iran Times*, December 1990.

131. Parvin Paidar, "Gender of Democracy: The Encounter Between Feminism and Reformism in Contemporary Iran," United Nations Research Institute for Social Development, Democracy, Governance and Human Rights, Program Paper Number 6, October, 2001, 34.

132. The *Ghesas* law addresses retribution in the case of murder or physical harm. The essence of the law, which contains 199 articles states that should murder or harm be committed by one person on another, then retaliation of an exact nature can be used by the injured party or family. While murder could be punished by retribution, blood money or *diyeh* could be allocated instead. Drawn from the Qur'an, the law justifies that the life of a woman is worth half of a man's in murder, retribution, and in judgment. In this vein, a woman is entitled to half the blood money as a man and two women are needed to corroborate the evidence of one man. Additionally, this law gives a strict interpretation to the concept of "an eye for an eye" reviving age-old punishments such as stoning.

133. Roza Eftekhari, "Chahar Mabhase Asasi dar Feminism" (Four Essential Discussions in Feminism), *Zanan* 32, 30–34.

134. Charles Tilly, *Social Movements, 1768–2004*, 2004, 12.

135. Leila Rupp and Verta Taylor, "Forging Feminist Identity in an International Movement: A Collective Identity Approach to Twentieth Century Feminism," *Signs*, 24, 1999, 363.

136. Deniz Kandiyoti ed. *Women, Islam and the State*, 1991, 123.

137. Nayereh Tohidi. "International Connections of the Iranian Women's Movement," in Nikki Keddie and Rudi Matthee, eds., *Iran and the Surrounding World 1501–2001: Interactions in Culture and Cultural Politics*, 2002, 209.

138. Nayereh Tohidi, "Ta`amol Mahali-Jahani Feminism dar Jonbeshe Zanane Iran" [The Local-Global Intersection of Feminism in the Women's Movement in Iran], in *Arash: A Persian Monthly of Culture and Social Affairs*, October 2007, 163–168. www.arashmag.com.

139. Nayereh Tohidi, "Peyvande Jahaniye Jonbeshe Zanane Iran" [The Iranian Feminist Movement's Global Connections," *Journal of Goft-O-Gu* [Dialogue on Culture and Society], December 2003, 25–49.

140. Personal interview with former female government employee, Washington D.C., November 12, 2007.

141. Afshar, *Islam and Feminisms*, 1998, 39.

142. Personal interview with activist and journalist, Washington, D.C., June 8, 2008.

143. Paidar, "Gender of Democracy," 2001, 64.

144. Cited in Azadeh Kian. "Islamist and Secular Women Unite," *Le Monde Diplomatique*, November 1996.

145. Ibid.

146. Mahsa Sherkarloo, "Interview with Mehrangiz Kar: Settling the Score," *Bad Jens Iranian Feminist Newsletter*, November 21, 2000. http://www.badjens.com/fourthedition/kar.htm.

147. Mahsa Shekarloo, "Government Newspaper? What Government Newspaper? An Interview with Journalist Lily Farhadpour", *Bad Jens Iranian Feminist Newsletter*, November 21, 2000, http://www.badjens.com/fourthedition/farhadpour.htm.

148. Sedghi, 2007, 249.

5

Rafsanjani: The Road to Reform

O you martyr
hold my hands
with your hands
cut from earthly means.
Hold my hands,
I am your poet,
with an inflicted body,
I've come to be with you
and on the promised day
we shall rise again.

Tahereh Saffarzadeh[1]

The death of Ayatollah Khomeini in June 1989 and the loss of his pioneering leadership left a colossal void in the Islamic Republic. Not only was Khomeini the founding father of Iran's revolution, but so too was he critical in preserving the revolutionary momentum as an essential force required to moderate factionalism and maintain a balance within the country's dispersed political system. Mehdi Moslem argues that unlike factionalism in post-revolutionary Russia or China, which remained minor and secondary to the matters of state, in Iran, factionalism has increased rather than abated throughout the post-revolutionary years.[2] Critical to understanding these divisions is that each faction claimed to advance the authentic ideological vision espoused by Ayatollah Khomeini. Khomeini's vacillating policies and pragmatism further enabled such diffusion, as he did not establish pronounced policy principals beyond the encompassing umbrella of Islamic government. His role and influence was essential to keeping the balance and peace between the competing factions.

In all stages and through different means the Imam tried to keep the wings in balance and use the executive, ideological, populist or political power and efficacy of each wing for the benefit of the state. He tried to preserve this balance in order to keep one wing from becoming too powerful and every time he felt that one was aiming to monopolize power he would put his weight behind others to keep the power intact.[3]

As such, the main factional divisions within Iran's political system have vacillated from those espousing radical, or leftist, and traditional, or fundamentalist, ideologies. In the middle, a moderate group of technocrats have taken a more pragmatic position within the revolutionary elite. Amidst this triumvirate, there existed a number of fundamentalist groups, individuals and institutions that advance extreme political visions. At the same time, secular ideologues have also gained prominence. In accounting for this spectrum, it is important to note that affiliations and ideological interpretations promoted by particular individuals have been in constant flux. Moreover, as stated by Moslem, "This lack of cohesion and clear direction has adversely affected Iran in all areas of policy making . . . policy making is a by-product of extended maneuvering and politicking and the final version of any particular policy depends largely upon which faction controls the responsible organization or ministry. In short, for most of its post-revolutionary era, Iran has experienced systemic and ideological disarray because there are multiple centers of power and numerous sources of authority."[4] The ideological streams existent within the Islamic Republic—while split between right, moderate, and left—are more nuanced and generally formed in reaction to domestic or international events. Additionally, each group has claimed to be the legitimate inheritor of Khomeini's legacy fueling competition over the larger ideological vision of the state. Understanding these factional dynamics within the context of post-Khomeini domestic politics is critical to appreciate the unfolding contours of women's activism. Women, secular, Islamist, and traditional subscribed to these various political and factional divides using their political alliances to advance their gender agenda. Factional divides have also hindered female activism as politicians and elites have refused to compromise because of their competing ideological and political views. At the same time, the birth of reformism and secularism are consequences of factional and ideological divisions and disappointments coming to light in the post-Khomeini decade. Coupled with institutional and social changes, the convergence of these trends is particularly relevant for women's activism and gender reform. Tilly suggests that understanding the totality of a social transformation is essential. He states, "Analysts often treat 'the movement' as a single unitary actor, thus obscuring both a) the incessant jockeying and realignment that always go on within social movements and b) the interaction among activists, constituents, targets, authorities, allies, rivals, enemies and audiences that make up the changing texture of social movements."[5] While in the first decade of the revolution women were reactive agents of change, in this period, women became active proponents of change.

X X X

Ali Akbar Hashemi Rafsanjani's ascension to the presidency in 1989, the month after Khomeini's death, ushered in a new era in Iranian politics. Elected by an overwhelming margin, Rafsanjani quickly garnered increased powers for a previously weak executive office,[6] and showed considerable political skill in promoting his pragmatic policies in the face of resistance from Islamic hard-liners. As he departed from the ideological rhetoric and isolation of the first decade of the Iranian revolution, Rafsanjani sought to enshrine a pattern of pragmatism in his policy-making decisions, which were not limited to the political and economic sphere. Rafsanjani has been repeatedly described as a "pragmatic conservative" and a political chameleon. He has been astute at reading the popular pulse and has often been the driving force of moderation within the Islamic Republic. He has held numerous elected and appointed government posts, and continued to wield political power not only from elected office but also due to his imposing reputation and appointed positions.

As part of his liberalization and development program, Rafsanjani realized early on that enhancing women's participation in society would further his agenda. Like Khomeini, Rafsanjani saw that the inclusion rather than the marginalization of women would boost political legitimacy and increase economic productivity. However, factional obstruction would color Rafsanjani's ambitions as clerical conservatives, in the aftermath of Khomeini's death would not tolerate policies that threatened the ideological foundations of the revolution and could possibly constrain the conservative stronghold on power. The result of such factionalism for women led to the subordination of gender issues, leaving women frustrated and discouraged by the gradual pace of change. Although Rafsanjani encountered factional opposition from traditionalists or conservatives that tainted his legacy in effecting political and economic reform, this period was critical in facilitating significant domestic, social, and political transformations.

Rafsanjani sought out practical attempts at moderating domestic and international policy in order to return Iran to the good graces of the international community. He recognized the dire need for economic investment to rejuvenate Iran's ailing industries and weak economy after eight years of revolutionary isolation and war. To attract such investment, it was clear to Rafsanjani and his technocratic cadre that Iran should temper the ideological fervor that had led to its isolation. His efforts were not limited to the political or economic sphere; Rafsanjani also promoted measures to improve the status of women and society in general. His attempts did not result in a wholesale transformation of Iranian society, particularly due to the increased factional atmosphere that took hold in the aftermath of Khomeini's death. However, his policies of liberalization ushered in a new era of political, economic, and social reflection that ultimately gave birth to competing ideological visions for the future of the Islamic Republic. In the wake of this more dynamic atmosphere, women's activism was rejuvenated. Here, women were able to advance in the legal, educational, employment, media, and political realms.

Unlike the first decade of the Islamic Republic, the years 1989 to 1997 are often referred to as the "second republic," distinguished by new policies and programs that departed from the Khomeini years. This period should be categorized as the catalyst decade. Fundamental to Rafsanjani's presidency were his efforts to redeem and revive the Iranian economy through the introduction of pragmatic and moderate economic and political programs designed to restore Iran's tarnished reputation and rejuvenate Iranian society.

The revolutionary theocratic regime under Khomeini had proved threatening to the regional political establishment with its calls to "export the revolution." Moreover, its foreign policy of "neither East nor West"[7] along with the dramatic events of the revolution and the hostage taking of Americans had severed Iranian-American relations. As the United States and Iran's Arab neighbors lined up against Iran, Saddam Hussein took advantage of the country's perceived weakness to challenge its contested borders. With only a few allies not much international support, Iran struggled to rebuff Iraqi advances. After 1982, Iran succeeded in thwarting Iraq. But Khomeini and the clerical establishment did not seize the opportunity to pursue a cease-fire. Instead, they sought to push into Iraqi terrain, prolonging the war for an additional six years. One might question Iranian strategy here; however, for Khomeini this war was not only an ideological one, with Iran defending its revolution and integrity against the world. He was using the war to complete his process of revolutionary consolidation. With the distraction and nationalistic momentum of war, the population could not actively oppose the policies of creeping Islamization and marginalization of opponents. After eight years in which the country suffered not only immense loss of life but also enormous damage, Khomeini accepted a cease-fire. It has been suggested that Rafsanjani, who was then the acting commander of the armed forces, convinced Ayatollah Khomeini to accept the cease-fire offered in UN Resolution 598, ending the Iran-Iraq war.[8]

Since Khomeini's death, factional differences only intensified to the extent that ideological discord has become one of the most prominent features of politics within the Iranian state. Although Khomeini succeeded in uniting the system and its factional groups in times of crisis, his repeated interventions also energized competition and further created ideological groupings within the system. The Iranian polity is composed of contentious ideological groups, with each bloc sharing and advancing its own particular vision for the future of the regime.[9] Indeed, factionalism has fueled a vicious political circle that has impeded the fluidity and unity of the system.

Such governmental disunity in post-Khomeini Iran has been evidenced most clearly in the controversy surrounding the appointment of Supreme Leader Ali Khamenei. Khamenei was not Khomeini's intended successor.[10] In fact, it was the previously anointed Ayatollah Montazeri who fell from grace when he accused the regime of violating freedom and personal rights through its employment of terror tactics.[11] This blatant criticism forced Khomeini to search for a candidate who shared his loyalty and vision of Islamic government. Khomeini found these characteristics in his dedicated revolutionary disciple, Khamenei.

Khamenei had been active in revolutionary politics since the 1970s and held prestigious positions within the Islamic government, including that of President from 1981 to 1989. Khamenei, however, did not possess the religious credentials, as called for in the Iranian constitution, of an *Ayatollah al-Ozma* or Grand Ayatollah, allowing him a smooth accession to the position of Supreme Leader. To facilitate Khamenei's promotion, the Iranian constitution was amended, separating the positions of the *marja'iyat* from the *velayat,* allowing any *mujtahid* or jurist to assume the position.[12] As such, emphasis was placed on political rather than religious experience, catering to Khamenei's resume.[13]

While Khomeini had approved and designated Khamenei to succeed him in the aftermath of Montazeri's defection, the effect of these constitutional amendments upset the ideological and religious foundations of the Islamic government. Despite government efforts to bolster Khamenei's religious credentials, Khamenei lacked the blessing of the clerical community, which viewed his appointment with skepticism. In fact, Khamenei only attained the title of Ayatollah in 1994 through his persistent lobbying of the senior clerics in Qom. Since then, Montazeri, too, has become an outspoken critic of the new Supreme Leader. In 1997, Montazeri delivered a provocative speech openly criticizing the power and authority of the Supreme Leader, targeting him for his overreliance on the country's security forces and disrespect for the clerical establishment. The event sparked demonstrations and clashes culminating in Montazeri's house arrest.[14] With his credibility questioned, Khamenei has also become embroiled in the factional nature of Islamic politics as a means to protect his power and position.[15]

Unlike Khomeini before him, Khamenei did not possess the charismatic qualities needed to unite the country. His power has only been strengthened through the nature of his 17-year reign, during which he has tactically cultivated relations with a diverse group of political figures ranging from Hashemi Rafsanjani to Mahmoud Ahmadinejad and the Islamic Revolutionary Guard Corps (IRGC)—all in an effort to protect his interests and the position of the theocratic government.[16] His political mandate is to "Safeguard the regime [as] a religious duty above all duties."[17]

At the same time, a fierce struggle for power began within the rank and file of the elite. Divergent opinions ranged from varying interpretations of Islamic law to beliefs over the tug and pull between revolutionary identity and the national interest. What once was a contest between two parties that grew out of the ashes of the Islamic Republican Party developed into a challenge between a myriad of groups vying for political power and the ascendency of their ideological vision. Over time and in reaction to political events, ideological affiliations have shifted and given birth to new groupings, further diluting the political system. Since the elections of Rafsanjani and Khatami, and more prominently since Ahmadinejad's ascent to the presidency, the ideological dimension of these groups has evolved to account for domestic and international events affecting Iran. Most of the rivalries and differences are between groups or individuals who remain loyal to the Islamic revolutionary system.

Rafsanjani's political mandate as president was directed to rebuilding the country after the devastating economic and political consequences of the Iran-Iraq war.

Often known as Leader of the reconstruction (*Sardar e Sazandegi*), Rafsanjani directed the economic reintegration of Iran into the global economy along with the refurbishment of the housing, infrastructure, and oil industries. During his tenure as president, Rafsanjani attempted to introduce privatization and liberalizing economic policies to Iran's statist economic system. Under his supervision, Iran's trade with the European Union almost quadrupled.

However, Rafsanjani's term as president was not met without significant internal factional opposition. Traditional factions within the government opposed his economic and social policy, which challenged the fundamental tenets of the ideological basis of the revolution. These internal groups also disputed Rafsanjani's ideas of foreign policy moderation. With Rafsanjani's efforts to encourage foreign investment, stimulate private investment, and renegotiate loans came World Bank and IMF programs that were considered by conservatives to be extensions of "hegemonic Western policy."

Rafsanjani favored reducing Iran's international isolation and renewing its ties with Europe as part of a strategy to use foreign investment and free enterprise to revive the country's war-torn economy. Domestically, he implemented family-planning practices, in effect reversing previous policies encouraging population growth. Since the revolution, despite the consequences of war, Iran had experienced a massive and burdensome population burst, which amidst the post-war economic pressures had further strained the government.[18] Such a program was designed to not only educate the population on birth control but to also assist the government in containing its demographic crisis.

Although human rights abuses and the suppression of dissent continued, there was a degree of cultural openness under Rafsanjani, where a certain level of criticism was tolerated. In order to fulfill his liberalization initiatives, Rafsanjani believed that enhancing cultural openness was necessary to placate Iran's already restless youth. He sought to relax the stringent Islamic decrees in an effort to provide more social freedom to the frustrated youth. Such efforts earned the ire of the hard-line establishment that feared Western cultural encroachment and corruption of society as well as the slow erosion of their power.

The main themes of this new economic policy included privatization and the encouragement of private and foreign investment. In order to implement these policies, President Rafsanjani had to rely on technocrats over ideologues. Generally speaking, religious virtues came second to technical skills as a basis for employment and advancement in public offices during the second republic. Having promised the people an improved standard of living after the injustices of war, public expectation grew in response to Rafsanjani's repeated economic and social pledges. But his programs were thwarted by regime hardliners who were threatened by new moderate policies that could dilute their power. As Ray Takeyh put it, "not for the first time Iran was paralyzed by the core contradiction between factions professing ideology and those pressing the cause of national interest."[19] The end of Rafsanjani's term saw little success in effecting change. The impact of factional politics and pressure of U.S. embargos and sanctions also complicated Rafsanjani's presidential legacy.

The presence of factionalism has undoubtedly both impeded politics within the Iranian state and has also facilitated intellectual debate. As contending groups were vying for political power and ideological ascendancy, so too did politicians, revolutionaries, journalists, and intellectuals undertake serious assessments of the ideological and political foundations of the Iranian state. Amidst this vacillating political environment, marginalized intellectuals, religious leaders, and members of the elite took advantage of the more open atmosphere to reexamine the political, social, and economic status quo. Once revolutionary loyalists, this group found itself excluded from the central arena of politics. In political exile, they began to analyze and question the foundations and legitimacy of the Islamic state in the wake of growing factional, economic, and social stagnation. Seeking new solutions to resuscitate what they believed was a decaying political system they began to break apart the ideological foundation of the Iranian revolution. What emerged through various modes and means of analysis was a realization that the merger of Islam and government was incompatible in the current political system. Giving greater credence to such arguments, scholars sought to modernize religious interpretation so that government too could rely on modern religious analysis.

Those who have contributed to the development of such trends have included high-ranking clerics, such as Ayatollah Yusef Sanei'i and a number of less senior proponents, such as Hojatoleslams Mohsen Saidzadeh, Muhammad Mojtahed-Shabestari, Mohsen Kadivar and Hassan Yousef Eshkevari, as well as intellectuals such as Abdolkarim Soroush. Dynamic jurisprudence is particularly relevant and important because it opens jurisprudence to influence and change. These scholars sought to merge religious tenets with democratic ones using such methods of interpretation.

To update the traditional interpretations of Islamic law, these scholars revived the use of dynamic jurisprudence or *feqh-e pooya*, as opposed to relying on the traditional jurisprudence or *feqh-e sonnati* that the clerical establishment relies on.[20] This method opened up Islamic jurisprudence to new solutions in response to modern problems. With the emergence of new religious interpretation, scholars offered innovative religious, political, and social perspectives. The immediate consequence challenged the political and religious norms while also opening the public landscape to the innovative reinterpretation of politics and religion. An ultimate outcome, though, was the emergence of a growing trend of secularism that took hold at this time. As scholars were criticizing the Islamic foundations of the government while also calling for modern reinterpretations of classical traditions, it became clear that the Islamic foundation of the Iranian Republic was no longer universally embraced.[21]

Abdolkarim Soroush's contribution profoundly challenged the ideological foundations of the Islamic Republic. Having once been a revolutionary supporter arguing in favor of Islamization, Soroush like many of his contemporaries was disenchanted by the failure to translate revolutionary promises into reality. Moreover, through his writings and lectures, it became clear that he no longer subscribed to the merger of religion and politics as the institutional pillar of the Iranian republic. Soroush, a well-known intellectual and professor, led the storm of criticism against the political role of the clergy. His monthly magazine *Kian* became the most visible forum for religious intellectualism. He published controversial articles on religious pluralism, hermeneutics, tolerance, and clericalism. A pillar of Soroush's argument is the distinction between religion and religious knowledge. While Soroush argues that the Qur'an and hadith are part of divine and eternal religion, the interpretation of these texts is a matter of human religious knowledge and is thus open to debate. Drawing from both Western and Islamic sources, Soroush made the case for Islamic pluralism by challenging Khomeini's claim that the clerical establishment has a God-given right to govern. Through this groundbreaking analysis, Soroush in effect called into question the ideological foundation of the Islamic Republic as well as the clerical monopoly of interpreting religion.[22] Instead, he advocated the introduction of rationalism in facilitating a balance between religion and democracy. Arguing that the Iranian state had manipulated religion to advance political control, he asserted that religion and politics belong to alternate realms, where the former should be confined to matters of ethics and beliefs, not to issues of government. Soroush sees democracy and human rights are essential components of contemporary religious knowledge and argued that these principles must be integrated into Iranian society.[23] Statements such as these led to Soroush's marginalization and ultimate voluntary exile as conservatives targeted him for his heretical secular statements. Despite political and even physical attacks on Soroush and his followers, his provided the intellectual foundation of the reform movement.[24] Moreover, Soroush's Islamic revisionism has received much traction among women's activists enabling women to frame their gender discourse within an Islamic paradigm.

Other marginalized elites such as Said Hajjarian and Akbar Ganji, who were also disillusioned by the "political line of the Imam" in the aftermath of the war, came together in support of the concept of reformism.[25] In general, reformists united in their support for a pluralist, democratic political system, emphasizing the promotion of civil society. Thinkers who synthesize Islamic moral concepts with modern Enlightenment political philosophy—arguing that there is no inherent tension between democracy and an Islamic society—also inspire them. Said Hajjarian contributed profoundly to the doctrine of reformism. After leaving the Ministry of Intelligence, Hajjarian established the Institute for Strategic Studies, where he promoted a new discourse on democracy and the rule of law. Hajjarian demonstrated that even Khomeini's pragmatism pointed to the primacy of politics over religion. Hajjarian is credited for being the linchpin in defining the reform movement and its strategy. As such, members of the Ansar-e Hizbullah group, which attacked those it saw as violating Islam, attempted to assassinate him.[26]

Intellectuals such as Mohsen Kadivar, Hojjatoleslam Muhammad Mojtahed-Shabestari, and Akbar Ganji also contributed to the reformist discourse on religion and politics. Kadivar, a philosopher, professor, and cleric, like Soroush, questioned the ideological premise of the theocratic regime, going so far as to challenge the concept of the velayat-e faqih. Kadivar argued that because the concept of the velayat system was conceived by clerics rather than by God it cannot be considered sacred or infallible. And if clerics have no God-given right to rule, that means that Muslims may freely select their government in a democratic Islamic Republic.[27] Shabestari, a theologian and philosopher, challenged the holistic vision of Islam, calling into question the link between religion and politics.[28] In Shabestari's view, what is essential and eternal are the general values of Islam not particular forms of their realization in any particular historic time. He writes that "Religion does not wish to replace science and technology, and lay claim to the place of reason . . . God has only offered answers for some of the needs of human beings. As for other needs, He has left it to reason and human effort to supply the answer."[29] Akbar Ganji was active as a journalist and former Islamic Revolutionary Guard member and jailed for his investigative reporting on the 1999 murders of political dissidents in Iran. Most directly, he called for the replacement of the theocratic system with a democratic one.[30]

For the many women who had a received religious education, these methods of ijtihad were valuable tools to challenge the patriarchal Islamic norms. Using their knowledge of Islamic law, female religious scholars could advance their own interpretations to age-old laws thereby forging a new modern Islamic discourse. Fereshteh Ahmadi stated, "in Iran, male reformists first argued for reinterpretation of the Qur'an and other sacred texts regarding gender issues, but now women are claiming their right to interpret Islamic sources and to leave behind or go beyond classical formulations to develop new paradigms and reformulate Islamic concepts and law from a "feminist" perspective. The result is a lively debate over competing visions of male-female relations and the status and roles of women in Islam and Muslim societies, yielding new understanding of spiritual, professional, and social equality."[31] One such example has been the argument in favor of female clerics. Whereas many conservatives disprove of women entering such a traditional domain, women have drawn from the *sunnah* during the time of the Prophet to show that women, including a number of the Prophet's wives, were actively preaching and spreading the message of Islam. In effect, through this process, Islamist women took the religious tools of the regime and used them to their advantage further diluting government monopoly over religious and political interpretation.[32] Parvin Paidar suggests,

> It was the merging of the social currents of Islamization and secularization that had been moving in parallel since the Revolution. These processes eventually met up and created a "middle ground" polity, referred to as the civil society. On one hand, the Islamization process, which started with the issue of women's position in the immediate aftermath of the Revolution and engulfed the society, made a lasting impact on Iranian society. On the other hand, a parallel current of secularization ran counter to Islamization. The influence of the secularization process opened many windows in Islamism and brought

many supporters of the Islamic Republic closer to secularists. Eventually the merging of these two processes created new opportunities for political development.[33]

It is here, amidst this critical political atmosphere, that women—both Islamic and secular—saw an opportunity to assert themselves. Islamist women seized upon this open political and economic environment to lobby for change from within. Secular women alternatively subscribed revisionism in order to regain lost momentum in championing female rights and equality. Rafsanjani also was selectively encouraging of women's activism. Early on, he asserted, "Women can become philosophers, actors, scholars, Friday prayer imams, researchers and writers. Not only do these things not contradict chastity [of women], they are a means of propagating chastity."[34] New economic policies aimed at attracting foreign investment, increasing exports, and reducing Iran's rapid population growth all also let to improvements in the status of women. Dr. Sohrab Razzaghi summarized,

> One of the main factors is the economic and financial situation of the society. After the excitements of revolution halted, moving away from populist approaches and ideological perspectives toward public issues, emerging necessities after war and return to development discourses led to the glory of the dynamism of women's movement. In new social and cultural context, Iranian women have been able to organize themselves and initiate creative methods in confronting power structures in the society and established many civil organizations and institutions to achieve their rights and express their demands and needs. Losing ideology in the society and moving away from ideological perspectives and emergence of cultural middle class, had a crucial role in acceleration of women's movement in Iran.[35]

In this atmosphere, Islamist feminists were able to campaign for women's rights more directly. Drawing from the more open post-war political environment, they used collaborative efforts to pressure policy makers to revise restrictions on women's legal rights and to consider positive approaches for greater rights within an Islamic framework. They campaigned on issues such as legal rights, the family, education, employment, political participation, and hijab. In describing their efforts, it is clear that these issues are profoundly linked and that no topic can be discussed in a vacuum. To understand such cooperation, the effects and advances of female activism should be analyzed collectively where the flourishing of the press, growth of political participation, new legal interpretations, and increased education and labor productivity converged to impact government moderation. Moreover, the connections between the female press, female legal establishment, women parliamentarians, and the NGO network highlight the collaborative efforts of secular and Islamist activists. These relationships and female cooperation played a substantial role in demanding reform of the gender laws. The institutional, legal, and societal changes that took place during this period mobilized female activists and set a precedent for future female activism. Noushin Ahmadi Khorasani explained, "we are linked together indirectly through theoretical work, practical work, women's NGOs and the media. We work systematically, therefore, we operate like a chain."[36]

Education

With the arrival of an Islamic government in Iran, formal barriers to female education were enforced posing a number of obstacles for women. At the same time though, education was considered an important pillar of the state's gender policy. The contradictory approach to female education aptly represents the incongruities of the Islamic Republic's gender policy. Among the first edicts affecting the education system was the universal gender segregation of schools in March 1979.[37] By 1982, gender segregation had been fully implemented in all levels of education. One such consequence of the segregation policies came from the shortage of teachers often resulting in the dismissal of the female students. In small towns or rural areas where girls' schools were limited, many girls were forced to drop out. Because there were not as many female students at the time, many young women were also obligated to change their concentrations in high school or university to accommodate for the lack of instruction or facilities. Initially, married girls were also barred from attending high schools. At the same time, the marriage age was reduced to 13. Schoolgirls were required to wear the hijab from the age of 6 and girls were under continued pressure to maintain proper hijab.[38]

Concurrently, the education curriculum was rewritten to accommodate the Islamization policies evident throughout the country. As such, teachers and administrators were forced to adhere to the banner of Islamization to retain their employment. Gender stereotyping was evident in all school textbooks where the role of women, motherhood, and the hijab were enforced. The countries' universities were also forced to adhere to similar demands of Islamic cultural revolution and were reopened gradually between 1982 and 1983 under Islamic supervision. At the time, the criteria for admission included a demonstrated commitment to the values of the Islamic Republic.[39]

Despite these early restrictions on female education, women have made massive advancements. A walk through any Iranian university from the classroom to the grounds reveals the powerful presence of women. In fact, the overwhelming success of female education has been one of the significant paradoxes to emerge from the contradictory government policies concerning women. It has been argued that the Islamization of education coupled with mandatory veiling opened the schoolhouse doors to the daughters of conservative and pious families who found the post-revolutionary educational environment acceptable for their daughters.[40] This incidence, coupled with the launch of an adult literacy campaign, has resulted in higher overall female literacy and higher female rate of enrollment among girls.[41]

Table 5.1 Percentage of female students at different educational levels, 1978–2006

Year	Primary	High-school	University
1978	39.72%	36.36%	31.77%
1988	44.34%	42.38%	31.10%
2006	48.19%	49.16%	63.7%

Additionally, female completion and enrollment rates at the university level have surpassed those of men. These developments have been hailed by the state as a reflection of the government commitment to women's rights.

Early after the revolution, in an effort to revive Iranian society throughout the war, Khomeini instituted a campaign against illiteracy that was particularly applicable to women. The literacy campaign brought millions of illiterate women to the mosque to learn reading and writing. These women did not join the Shah's literacy programs promulgated under his White Revolution out of deference to their religious leaders, who warned that education was a tool of Western propaganda and exploitation.[42] However, responding to Khomeini's call making literacy a religious duty for women, the rejoinder was overwhelming. Moreover, with clerically sanctioned education, male relatives could no longer oppose literacy for their female family members. Mass literacy campaigns and free education were major steps toward increasing literacy and education for all Iranians, particularly women.[43] Such policies encouraging education and literacy clearly contradicted those that limited female education opportunities, pointing to one of the many inconsistencies of the new government.

Khomeini and his successors also made staunch commitments to female education. Khomeini stated, "You [women] should endeavor for knowledge and piety. Knowledge is not the monopoly of a particular group but belongs to all and it is the duty of all men and women to acquire knowledge. I hope the authorities will assist you in this and provide the educational and cultural facilities that you need to enable you to succeed."[44] Rafsanjani avowed that in Islam, "there are no barriers to the education of women in any field," and as president in 1989, he emphasized the need to create "greater education opportunities" for Iran's youth as well as "equal pay for equal work by women."[45] The supreme leader, Ali Khamenei, has said, "an Islamic environment cannot tolerate even one illiterate person."[46]

In the early years of the revolution, women's higher education was also the target of government restrictions. Initially, the state had closed off subjects of study considered inappropriate for women including those in the technical, engineering, and experimental sciences. Quotas were also placed on female admission to medical, environmental, and human sciences. Married women were also prevented from studying abroad without the presence of their husbands.[47] However, after the war, in response to pressure from women, including from Khomeini's daughter, Zahra Mostafavi, higher education became less restrictive. Zahra Rahnavard, as a member of the Women's Social and Cultural Council part of the High Council of Cultural Revolution (HCCR), was among those responsible for demanding change to the state educational policy. After lobbying President Khamenei, in May 1989, the government began to remove earlier policies that closed geology and agriculture programs to women. Then the medical and engineering quotas were removed.[48] By 1994, all barriers to specific fields of study were lifted for women. Again here the change of state education requirements reflected the ad hoc manner of the state's gender policy. Paidar argues that "the personal goodwill of political leaders and the receptivity of the demands of the Islamic women's movement" were essential ingredients for further change to female legislation.[49]

While the census of 1976 showed that only 10 percent of rural women aged 20 to 24 were literate, this rate increased to 37 percent in 1986, 78 percent in 1996, and 91 percent in 2006. The same success can be applied to university education where in 1975 some 462,000 women aged 20 to 29 had secondary or higher education; by 2005, this number increased more than tenfold to 4.8 million.[50] In 2010, an estimated 70 percent of university students were women. In 2000, after almost a decade of lobbying, the sixth parliament was able to reform the education law allowing unmarried female students to study abroad.[51] Also in 2000, the first women's studies institute, the Iranian Society for Women's Studies was established.[52] Through the efforts of women's rights advocates in Iran, in 2001, Allameh Tabatabai Unversity, Tarbiat Modares University, and Al Zahra University started women's studies programs at the Master of Arts level, and shortly thereafter Tehran University organized a similar program. Within the discipline, three sub-specialties are offered: women and family, history of women, and women's rights in Islam.[53]

Iranian authorities have tried at different times to control the impact of the demand by the new generation of school-age women for higher education. For nine years, from 1989 until 1997, they imposed quotas on the number of university slots for women in order to provide space for male war veterans. Additionally, they have been slow to build new dormitories on big campuses where out-of-town women are required to live. To control the activities of women on campus, for example, the universities enforce strict rules at dormitories. Young women are required to wear the hijab not only outside the dorm but inside as well. There are curfews, bans on visitors and music, and constant supervision of reading material brought into the dormitories. But even with the regulations, many women say they have acquired an independent way of thinking that cannot be unlearned.[54] A young sociology major, relayed how the pressure and challenge of admittance to university has fueled rather than abated female university enrollment. Living in a dorm away from home and surrounded by friends and the hazards of city life had further awakened her hopes for the future. She hoped to work as a writer and had no plans to return to her small-town roots.[55] Marriage too was no longer an immediate concern for her. Like many of her contemporaries, a career had come to trump the conventionalities of the former generation. Recent research has confirmed such a trend where young women are prioritizing employment over marriage.[56] This unintended consequence of the state educational policy has alarmed conservatives who seek to limit the female public presence and also policy experts who recognized that the state does not have the means to create additional employment.[57]

Alarmed that women are overtaking men, some conservative officials proposed a new quota system to limit the number of women entering medical schools and other areas of higher education. A report released by the Parliament's research center stated that over over a 20-year period they had observed a 23 percent increase in the number of girls taking university entrance exams, with the number of girls who passed the tests nearly doubling—to 65 percent—over the same period.[58] On university campuses throughout Iran, it is clear that women are outnumbering their male counterparts. To counter the unexpected flourishing of female education the government of President Ahmadinejad in 2006 introduced a quota that reserves 40 percent of university slots for men. Efforts have also been made to reduce women's access to engineering fields. Justification for such measures centers on the principle of a "gender equilibrium" in the labor market, within the family and society.[59] The state is also considering reducing the number of years required for female schooling so that women could graduate earlier. Limits such as this would render women ineligible for a number of university programs because they would not have adequate math and science training.[60]

It is interesting to note that opposition to university enrollment for women started several years before women outnumbered men, exposing the Janus-faced attitude of the government toward women. Former President Rafsanjani revealed this paradox in an interview in 2000 describing the political pressures on him to limit women's access to universities when he was in office in the 1990s: "They asked why women should study if they are not going to work. And even some radical representatives spoke from the tribune of the Majlis questioning why we should give the seats in universities to women who when they finish their education must go home and take care of children. I said if we have one educated mother without a job she will be effective in the society because of the children that she will educate."[61] Indeed, the circular realities surrounding female education point to the political, social, cultural, and economic obstacles for women.

Labor

Khomeini's campaign against illiteracy was coupled with another one promoting social reconstruction and self-sufficiency in society. To further this aim, many women responded to the government's call and mandate to fight the war. Millions of women worked as volunteers to help build the country's economy and win the war against Iraq, which brought them into the public arena just as the world wars brought many American women into the U.S. labor force. Once the Iran-Iraq war ended, women who had put such hard work into the revolution and the defense of their homeland could not easily be sent back home.

The economic benefits of including women in the labor force were easily evidenced in the post-war period. The economic crisis of the post-war era led to the decline in real incomes of urban households, the majority of which relied on a single source of income. Women, whose financial contribution proved essential, were thus compelled to participate in the labor force. As a result, the representation of women in the economic arena began to expand. In addition to the increasing importance of the Islamic professionals, the implementation of reconstruction policies also resulted in the return of secular women professionals who had been dismissed from their posts during the revolutionary period.

President Rafsanjani suggested that women should play a larger role in Iranian arts, sports, politics, and religion, and said, "we are in need of a women's labor force."[62] Indeed, Islam sanctions women's economic activities, as women were active during the time of the Prophet Muhammad. The Prophet's first wife, Khadijah, who was a self-sufficient businesswoman, is regularly cited as a role model for women who seek to gain increased access to the labor market. However, at the same time, deeply entrenched cultural norms made it difficult for women to enter and integrate in to the workforce in large numbers.

The policies implemented during this period were in opposition to those exalting the reproductive capacity of women that was introduced at the outset of the revolution. Women, in their biological roles as mothers, were responsible for the nurturing of Iran's Islamic society. Drawing an analogy from Fatemeh, the Prophet Muhammad's daughter, who was the quintessential devoted Shi'a wife and mother, women were encouraged to go forth and multiply. This pro-natalist policy, designed to strengthen the Islamic and moral foundations of Iranian society, proved untenable for the Iranian government. The demographic outcome of this policy led to such a dramatic rise in Iran's birth rate that Iran's population doubled since 1979. Iran's 1986 national census, the first taken since the revolution, revealed a population growth of about 15 million. By 1990, the population had reached 59.5 million growing at an average annual rate of 3.9 percent.[63]

Responding to the economic, social, and political effects of this demographic crisis, the government reversed its pro-natalist agenda in favor of what is referred to as a *pro-family* one.[64] In accordance with a fatwa from Ayatollah Yusef Sanei'i who stated, "None of the wise and learned people has ever said that it is good and desirable to have lots of children,"[65] the ban on family planning was lifted and clinics began distributing contraceptives and family planning advice, launching one of the most successful state-sponsored family planning campaigns in the developing

Table 5.2 Population growth, 1978–2008

Year	Population	Growth Rate
1978	36.5 million	3.23%
1988	51.8 million	2.88%
2008	71.9 million	1.31%

world. State assistance was reduced for families with more than three children, as was maternity leave. Vasectomies were subtly encouraged and in 1992, the abortion law was amended to allow for abortions in the case of fetal defects or risk to the mother's life under the guidance of a doctor in the first trimester.[66] Here the economic imperatives of the state together with the tools of Islam were used to influence female politics.[67] To obtain a marriage license in Iran, couples must partake in a marriage seminar that includes family planning.

Additional family-based initiatives were also introduced during this period to promote social and familial harmony amidst the changing domestic social, economic, and political climate. Female sponsored programs to educate men and women on maintaining a harmonious relationship in the familial domain. Emphasis was placed on the concept of partnership between husband and wife rather than that of male guardianship enshrined in the civil code. Islamist activists objected to the lack of policy to "protect the rights of unprotected women and remove obstacles in the way of women's participation in economic, social, and political activities."[68] The policies sponsored initiatives for state recompensation for housewives and unmarried women, against polygamy, custody rights for mothers, female protection and consent against arbitrary divorce, increase in inheritance rights, and women's rights to pursue education, employment, or travel without the consent of husbands or male guardians.[69]

Here again, Zahra Rahnavard was active from her post in the HCCR encouraging a female and family friendly labor policy. She cautioned the state that without a precise employment policy, female support for the regime would decline. "We have no strategy for including women in this country's destiny and in this respect we have fallen short of our political aspiration. . . . In the Five Year Plan women are only mentioned once . . . despite all our protests we have remained invisible. It is essential that women's role[s] in the development process is clearly defined."[70] The Council issued a resolution demanding equal pay for equal work and recognition of female familial responsibilities. Additionally, the declaration sought job security and unemployment and welfare benefits for women.[71]

Islamist women like Rahnavard, who asserted that Islamic texts and traditions could be reinterpreted and enacted into law, pursued employment rights. The *Ojrat-ol mesal* campaign (wages for housework law) passed in December 1991 served as an ideal example of such interpretation and activism of Islamist women.[72] Islamist women argued that women were entitled to be compensated for their housework on the grounds that Islam opposed exploitation. Drawing on Islamic tradition, they argued that fidelity is the only duty of a wife to her husband. Housework and even breast-feeding were not required without payment. As women do in fact work in their husbands' homes and take care of children, they are entitled to such compensation.[73] The novel argument was based on Islamic texts. Conservatives in parliament initially resisted the bill calling it an unconventional interpretation of Islamic law. However, opponents were unable to prove the un-Islamic nature of the legislation. Female lobbying garnered much popular support and the law was eventually passed in December 1992. Also included was a revision of the divorce law to account for this provision. The new law stated that if the marriage contract failed to include the wealth-sharing provision, then the husband must pay his wife wages for household work performed during the marriage.[74]

With pressure for further consideration, Iranian religious authorities began to acknowledge women's economic activity outside the household but continued to consider housework and child care as women's primary responsibility. "The Islamic Republic's Supreme Leader, Ayatollah Ali Khamenei, argued: "Islam authorizes women to work outside the household. Their work might even be necessary but it should not interfere with their main responsibility that is child rearing, childbearing and housework. No country can do without women's workforce but this should not contradict women's moral and human values. It should not weaken women, nor compel them to bend or to stoop low."[75] Often such resistance to women's financial independence can be explained by the patriarchal culture and the legal restrictions that have conditioned the limited mobility of women.

However, in order for a woman to work, if she receives compensation for housework, she also must have her husband's permission. Moreover, only the financial and economic dimension of women's activity is recognized, whereas the social is neglected. This is clearly enforced by a traditionalist opinion reflecting that, "Islam prefers that women take care of housework. . . . But if the husband's earnings are not enough to meet his family's needs then his wife is authorized to work in order to complete her husband's earnings provided that her work corresponds to her condition as a woman and that she maintains her chastity. If the costs of marital life prevent a young man from getting married, then woman's work outside the family becomes even compulsory in order to enhance marriage which is the tradition of our Prophet."[76] Nevertheless, formal female labor participation continues to be minimal. According to the results of the 2006 Iranian census, only 3.5 million Iranian women are salaried workers, compared with 23.5 million men constituting only 15 percent of the workforce and well below the world average of 45 percent.[77]

Maryam Poya suggests that official statistics underestimate women's labor participation particularly in rural areas. She writes, "my interviews show that official statistics do not include categories of women workers who effectively contribute to their families and to the national and international economy. These are unpaid agricultural workers and carpet weavers, petty commodity producers, and a large

Table 5.3 Percentage of formal female labor participation, 1978–2006

Year	Formal Female Labor Participation
1978	13.6%
1988	9%
2006	18.5%

number of women workers who are employed by many medium or small private enterprises, who[se] employers do not declare them as their workforce in order to avoid paying tax and insurance."[78] Informal labor participation including beauty services, language and computer lessons, tailoring, catering, and design could account for the greater female visibility in the workforce. Moreover, while labor participation remains particularly limited, women have expanded their occupational profiles, entering male dominated professions such as industry, engineering, agriculture, political, and entertainment sectors. The virtuous circle of such changes are demonstrated by the linkages between female employment and the impact of female labor participation on matrimonial and family relations as women have access to a better education, economic independence, and social participation.[79]

Legal Rights and Interpretations

For many Islamist women, the use of religion became a primary tool in the struggle to advance women's rights. Faced with limited government reluctance to support its own program of promoting justice for women, Islamist women sought alternative channels to gain political support. Using the same religious tools supported by the state, they adopted surreptitious strategies to advance their gender agenda.

A first part of this approach led many women to address women's issues through commentary in women's journals. While initially their commentary was nonconfrontational, through this writing Islamist women sought to highlight the contradictions of the state's gender policies. They pointed out that much of what is being presented to women as authentically Islamic was nothing but "patriarchy in Islamic costume."[80] These efforts proved effective in raising public awareness. As Islamization policies impacted all women, uniformly critical voices emerged from all segments of society, including among traditional and Islamist women. The convergence of awareness with gender consciousness began to take hold. Thus many Islamist views and woman-centered interpretations of Islamic texts found their way into conservative circles, contributing to legal change.

"Increased Islamic knowledge and expertise has enabled women to use religion and Islamist history against the religious establishment," said a religious scholar.[81] Not only have women made use of the Islamic government's religious schools, but they have also joined women's organizations, such as the Zeinab Society, which have sponsored meetings of Islamic scholars. The purpose of these meetings, similar to one held in 1992, is to "help bring about a profound educational change in Iranian society and to study the application of Qur'an teachings to the lives of women."[82] Other women attend *jalasehs*, or gatherings of religious study led by a female cleric who has pursued religious education. Convened in mosques or in women's homes, these gatherings offer women the opportunity to address and question religious edicts and rulings impacting women. I attended a number of jalasehs both in local mosques and in private homes. The religious gathering, while principally designed to address social and political concerns, has also provided women with a social venue. Initially, the first hour is allocated to Qur'anic reading followed by questions to the female cleric. Following this, women socialize and share common experiences or *dard-o del* (a Persian expression literally meaning pain and stomach, that means having a heart-to-heart.) Despite the light conversation, Mrs. Ziain, a female cleric I visited regularly, counseled women to "not be shackled by the comforts of jewelry and cars but rather be lifted up by the knowledge and wants of religion." Yet she, too, admitted the gatherings served important social purposes beyond that of religious transmission and enquiry.[83] The exchange among women has enabled greater gender consciousness. "Women's religious gatherings and associations—in addition to feminist magazines and women's publishing collectives—have become platforms for secular and religious feminists to debate and negotiate legal status and social positions of women and to deal with harsh social, political and economic realities."[84]

In this vein, Islamist women, through their knowledge of religious scholarship, have presented a new gender vision based on a woman-centric interpretation of Islamic text. Instead of adhering to the traditional interpretation of Islamic law, or *fegh*, they began to draw from a new interpretation of the legal tradition using dynamic Islamic jurisprudence. From their perspective, much of what is being presented to women as Islamic and authentic has been advanced and interpreted by men. Islamist women, seeking new interpretations of traditional laws, have sought to draw on the "intent rather than the literal meaning of the Qur'an . . . and *sunnah* or tradition" in the hope of adapting Islam to the modern world.[85]

The seminary for some is perhaps the most surprising environment for such dialogue. However, religious women, having studied the doctrine, are reflecting on the misinterpretations that have been imposed upon them. Issues such as polygamy, divorce, veiling, child custody, marriage, and women's rights in general, and political issues are openly discussed. Because several articles of the civil code such as men's unilateral right to divorce and polygamy find their origins in Qur'anic verses, these educated women are challenging the dominant readings by the clergy that they consider distorted.

Indeed, women with religious training are best equipped to address such religious issues. For example, *Payam-i Hajar*, edited by Azam Taleghani, was the first to publish an article in 1992 refuting the legalization of polygamy and proposing a new interpretation of the Qur'anic verse that supports it. Using her religious background to her advantage, Taleghani has challenged the concept of polygamy by using Qur'anic precepts. Arguing that a man may take up to four wives as long as he treats those wives equally, Taleghani pointed to the fact that even the Prophet Muhammad was not able to practice this tenet of equality. As the revered Prophet could not fulfill such a requirement, she argued that it would be unlikely for an average man to achieve this either.[86]

With limited political and religious allies, this task has been challenging. However, through continued education, many of these Islamist women have influenced the perceptions and interpretations of religion among women. Islamists have played an important role in broadening the "discursive universe" while expanding "legal literacy and gender consciousness." Islamic reinterpretation as such is "a legitimate—and historically necessary—strategy to improve the status of women and to modernize religious thought."[87] These women are among the future reformers of Islam. Khomeini himself argued "We should keep pace with the times if we wish not to reach a dead end," lending further credence to the strategy of reinterpretation.

The first demonstration of this successful campaign of reinterpretation was seen in the introduction of a new family law. While many Islamist women activists hoped that the new law would rewrite the inequities toward women, the legislation gave women a stronger negotiating position. Under the new legislation, through the use of an official marriage contract women stipulate the conditions of marriage. Traditionally Muslim marriage has been a contractual relationship. As such both parties have always had the opportunity to insert conditions into the marriage agreement. In the contract, the bride is entitled to include provisions for divorce and child custody to protect her rights.[88]

A further example of such reinterpretation has been on the issue of female judges. In 1979, Khomeini had barred women from the legal profession yet female lawyers refused to be marginalized. Islamist women blamed centuries of misreading the patriarchal interpretation of Islam. Marzieh Dastjerdi, a Majlis representative stated, "those who head the judiciary and those who sit as judges in court must be people who have a clear Islamic vision in matters concerning women ... unfortunately what we see is that our courts are run by men who have a patriarchal approach and their rulings tend to be to the advantage of men."[89] In 1992, women were permitted to practice law. After years of lobbying, together with pressure on the parliament and the judiciary, a system was introduced whereby women could act as counsel to male judges in family court. Women were also permitted to become legal advisors in government legal affairs offices. While this compromise was welcomed, it did not satisfy critics who continued to lobby for the removal of those obstacles that prevented women from becoming judges. In 1995, after much debate, discussion, and pressure, it was announced that women could be employed as legal consultants and the judiciary employed the first 100.[90] While this move nationally and internationally celebrated as yet a further achievement for women, female activists continue to press for women to become full-fledged judges with the power to issue final verdicts. Nobel prize winner Shirin Ebadi and Mehrangiz Kar have written about the challenges and humiliation they faced as women pursuing their legal careers.[91] Ebadi who was appointed to the court in 1975 was dismissed after the revolution. They both became lawyers in the post revolutionary state taking on controversial female cases. Their exposure to the system enabled them to challenge the system through legal means also offering new legal interpretations to contest Islamic law. Activists viewed these changes as part of a piecemeal victory, reflective of the gradually evolving state policy toward women, while they continued their struggle to rectify the law and remove all legal and social obstacles for women to serve as judges.

Press

The role of the women's press should not be discounted in the struggle to advance women's issues. In fact, it has been argued that the women's press has been most prominent and an effective means of advancing gender awareness through the publication of articles reflecting on the condition and treatment of women in Iran. Even before the Iranian revolution, women used the press to address issues of gender consciousness and reexamine laws and policies. It was in the aftermath of the Constitutional Revolution that the first women's journal began publishing. In those early days of the women's press, women experienced difficulties getting licenses and maintaining a circulation beyond four or five editions. "These publications played a major role in bringing previously private matters into the public domain and informing women about the literature, history, culture, and politics of Iran as well as Europe and the rest of the world."[92]

Since the revolution, women's access to education, political institutions, and public domain has brought to light the glaring contradictions and legal and moral limitations to women's activism and political participation. Important to these advancements has been the increase in female literacy and education. The press has also been an important outlet for women's employment, but such employment has come with its challenges.[93] Neda, a young journalist I interviewed, chose her profession because of the activism and opportunities promoted by Iranian female journalists and activists. She spoke admiringly of the pioneering nature of her female colleagues who were not limited by their gender and sought creative means to circumvent the press restrictions.[94] Although Neda was from a traditional family, wore the chador and had received a seminary education, the female press provided a political and social outlet. Journalist Banafsheh Samghis reflected in an interview on women's journalists in *Zanan* magazine, "This culture does not easily accept women journalists." Lily Faradpour commented, "I have paid a lot . . . Men that I used to work with believed that they were more knowledgeable than women. I had to prove that we, too, have intellect."[95] The growing demands for a free and active women's press should be contextualized amid Iran's wider social transformation, where women have made gains in education, labor, and political participation.[96]

The women's press has been subject to the same scrutiny and challenges of the media in Iran. During the first decade, the press was subject to strict government control and censorship. The state through the Ministry of Culture and the Islamic Republic of Iran Broadcasting agency monopolized reporting. Under the Rafsanjani period of reconstruction and liberalization, the media while still under strict government control, experienced a gradual flourishing. Then, President Khatami who had promised increased press freedoms and civil society appointed an ally Ataollah Mohajerani as Minister of Islamic Guidance and Culture who was responsible for regulating the press. Under his tenure, the licenses were granted for new publications and many media restrictions were removed.[97] New titles pointed to the the new cultural mood and the "blossoming of the press," with titles such as *Jamee* (Society),

Neshat (Joy), *Mellat* (Nation), *Azad* (Free), *Hayat-e no* (New Life), *Aftab* (Sun), *Hamshahri* (Citizen), among others. From 1998 to 1999, the government approved 168 new licenses.[98] The conservative response to this "Tehran Spring" resulted in a backlash against the press including the vibrant female press that had developed in tandem. In July 1998, the parliament ratified a law "prohibiting the publication of women in pictures and contexts deemed humiliating and insulting, promoting the use of luxury, and creating conflicts between men and women by using non Shariah standards to defend women's rights."[99] As part of a government effort to restrict civil society, closures and suspensions of newspapers and journals soon followed. The press, however, remained an important arm of women's activism.

Table 5.4 Percentage of female journalists, 1971–2006

Year	Percentage of Female Journalists[100]
1971	2.5%
1997	10%
2006	22%

In the aftermath of the revolution, Islamist women who were involved in the Islamization of institutions played a decisive role in launching an Islamist presence in the press. Azam Taleghani's *Payam-e Hajar* (Hagar's Voice) represents the voice of early Islamic activists who have embraced reform for women within an Islamic context. Taleghani has been an active promoter of women's rights, yet her journal reflects the confines of her political and religious ideology where factional politics have always overshadowed discussion of gender and women's rights.[101] Taleghani has acknowledged, "I believe that in our country, women's problems are secondary to political ones. What our people need is a correct analysis. Women are part of society, and when its problems are solve, women's issues will be solved."[102] Parvin Ardalan observed, "when censorship in the country relaxes, *Payam-e Hajar*'s coverage of women's rights diminishes."[103] Like many other women's journals, *Payam-e Hajar* was banned in 2000. The women's magazine *Zan-e Ruz* was also remade under an Islamic guise. Although not independent, the magazine continued to advocate for gender reform using articles to publicize information. Indeed, partly as a result of a publication campaign organized in 1984 by *Zan-e Ruz*, women lobbied for changes to the family law that resulted in amendments relating to the marriage contract, including grounds for divorce.[104]

Within the context of political and economic liberalization promoted during the presidency of Hashemi Rafsanjani, women found a more open environment extending to the press as well. In this new environment, liberal Culture Minister Muhammad Khatami who served from 1989 to 1992 approved permits for many new publications. During his tenure, the number of newspapers and journals more than doubled from 102 in 1988 to 369 in 1992.[105] *Kian* the leading reformist periodical began publishing during this time. Shahla Sherkat, the editor of *Zan-e Ruz* from 1984 to 1991, launched a new magazine, *Zanan*, in February 1992. *Zanan* was the first journal that promoted an unequivocal gender egalitarian stance. Sherkat unlike Taleghani supported the links between Islam, feminism, and gender. Although Sherkat grew up in a modest religious family where she wore the hijab, she considered herself to be a feminist. Through her mother's encouragement, she attended the University of Tehran after which she pursued a career in journalism. In the revolutionary years, Sherkat played a role in the women's press joining *Zan-e Ruz* in 1982. By 1991, she became disillusioned with the limited portrayal of women as homemakers and mothers and resigned.[106] Carrying articles by women and men, *Zanan* has reported on social and cultural taboos including women's sports initiatives, temporary marriage, drugs, prostitution, physical punishment, and polygamy, while also analyzing legal and judicial issues affecting women. Having studied the majority of *Zanan's* publications, the magazine provides comprehensive and creative insight into gender issues in Iran advancing a revisionist approach to women's issues. International gender issues and focused articles on women's issues abroad presented links to domestic gender ones. One section entitled "A Month With the Women of the Parliament" provided an update on parliamentary efforts affecting women. The last section includes a list of recently published books by women. Interviews with politicians, authors, artists, and activists provided access to the subtle spread of gender consciousness. Legal and political issues were explained to a wider readership, exposing the patriarchal nature of existing laws on education, marriage, divorce, custody, and employment.[107] The magazine also promoted alternative and modern readings of the Qur'an and Shariah publishing controversial articles about the impact of women on Iranian family and civil law by Mohsen Saidzadeh, a young liberal cleric. Secular activist, Mehrangiz Kar was also asked to contribute. Kar reflects in her book over the shock of Sherkat's new focus "something was happening which is no lesser in significance than the Islamic Revolution itself. Cultural and intellectual forces [were] openly engaged in a challenge with those forces from the regime."[108] The journal ran for 16 years, producing 152 issues, forced to close in February 2008 under the administration of Ahmadinejad. Indeed, over the course of these years, *Zanan* became the most popular women's publication in Iran and played a critical role in changing laws and regulations by publishing articles on women's rights issues within family law and the wider society. As *Zanan* editor Sherkat argued, "Our aim is not to destabilize families and family relationships. Our aim is to bring about equality between women and men."[109]

Another important women's magazine, *Farzaneh* (Wise), began publishing in 1993. The license holder, Massoumeh Ebtekar, and its editor-in-chief, Mahboobeh Abbas Gholizadeh, were members of the Women Studies Center in Tehran. The editors of *Farzaneh* hold a similar beliefs as Sherkat. "We support the equality of rights between men and women and believe that according to the Qur'an, men and women are equal. We should make a distinction between Islam and patriarchal traditions.

Our laws are largely founded on some unreliable *hadith* narrated by religious authorities. Several articles of the civil code, including those concerning the right to divorce, guardianship of children after divorce, and those prohibiting women's access to judiciary are among them. Religious reformists examine the authenticity of these laws and purify the civil code from spurious articles."[110] *Farzaneh* printed articles illustrating the Prophet's respect for women as reflected in the Qur'an, and highlighted the political and religious roles that certain women played during his lifetime. Based on such evidence, the magazine made an argument for the incompatibility of the Qur'an and existing religious interpretations. *Farzaneh* has served as a bridge between policy makers and activists addressing debates on Islamic feminism but also practical issues impacting women.[111] The magazine appeared sporadically as Ebtekar was appointed a deputy to President Khatami's Organization for Environmental Protection. Yet the journal, published both in English and Persian, released a number of editions with the latest published in summer 2009.

Rafsanjani's youngest daughter, Faezeh Hashemi was also an important contributor to the flourishing of the female press. She launched the first ever woman's daily newspaper in 1998.[112] *Zan* (Woman) survived only through April 1999 due to the restrictive press environment and the controversial articles published by the newspaper. Because Hashemi was also an elected member of the parliament serving in the Fifth parliament from 1996 to 2000, she was able to use the newspaper as a mouthpiece for women's issues although the newspaper also addressed wider social issues to expand its readership. Hashemi stated, "If men are our problem we should get them to read these issues."[113] In addition to providing information, the newspaper provided a forum where women could voice their concerns and express their reflections on social and political developments. Its editorials included criticisms of child-custody laws, stoning as a form of punishment allowed in the constitution, and other repressive legal or social practices applied to women in discriminatory ways. The newspaper advocated allowing women to stand as candidates for the Assembly of Experts and encouraged women to advance their names in the coming election.[114] At the time, ten women decided to participate but the Guardian Council rejected all. Hashemi, like Sherkat and her other contemporaries, agreed that the rigid readings of Islamic teachings have constrained female advancement. She called for reinterpretation of Islamic law, stating, "It's not Islam which forbids women from attaining office, but the interpretation of its teachings by the clerics."[115] Months later, the daily was ordered to halt operations due to its publication of an interview with Farah Diba, the widow of the former Shah, and for publishing a satirical cartoon criticizing the *ghesas,* (retribution law). According to the eye-for-an-eye policy, blood money for a murdered woman is only half that for a man. The cartoon showed a gunman pointing at a couple and the man shouting, "Kill her, she is cheaper." Ten years later, in May 2008, however, the judiciary passed a bill that entitles women victims of car accidents to receive the same amount of blood money as men.[116]

Jens e Dovom (Second Sex) launched in 1998 by Noushin Ahmadi Khorasani was an example of an influential secular woman's journal. Ahmadi Khorasani was also the director of Nashr-e Towseh publishing house. She used her journal to focus on international women's issues as well as to collaborate with Iranians in exile publishing interviews with Iranian academics and activists. It provided extensive coverage of the Fourth World Conference on Women in Beijing in 1995, International Women's Day, and the 2000 Berlin Conference. In 2001, the journal was closed.[117]

Sports Initiatives

At the same time, Hashemi advocated advancements in female sports and sporting activities both before and during her election to the Majles. In her own words, the reasons that triggered her interest in women's sports are that "sporting activities have tremendous impact on women and prepare them for social activities. It offers them the courage they need to get involved in the country's affairs." Through her initiatives, she remained increasingly popular among women, especially the youth, for courageously defending women's outdoor cycling—a sport considered controversial by the clerical establishment because the movements of the female body while riding a bicycle are considered provocative to men. In fact, her forthright views run contrary to the traditionalists, whose opposition has politicized the issue: "Women's outdoor cycling is neither illegal nor illicit . . . It has become a political issue because it was proposed during the legislative elections, and those who opposed it bestowed a political dimension on it. After all, their opposition was beneficial to outdoor cycling, for now there is a significant demand for it."[118]

Hashemi served as a member of Iran's High Council of Sports and she also founded and presided over the Islamic Countries Women's Sports Solidarity Council, which took place in 1993. Hashemi's opening speech at the games stressed the compatibility of their athletic activities with the values of Islam and noted the importance of sports for the health, strength and joy of Muslim women. On the world stage, Hashemi has been most recognized in connection with her contributions to promoting Muslim women in sports. The Islamic Countries Women's Sports Solidarity Games are officially recognized by the International Olympic Committee and have been held every four years since 1993.[119] She has also served as the vice president of the Iranian Olympic Committee. Domestically, she defended women's rights to ride a bicycle in public challenging the Supreme Leader and has supported the formation of women's sport teams including soccer.

Political Participation

Ayatollah Khomeini disagreed with women's formal political participation as evidenced in his 1963 denunciation of female enfranchisement. Yet once in power he did not question women's inclusion in the political system. The massive participation of women in the revolution demonstrated the potential political force of women to the revolutionary leaders. The Islamic government successfully incorporated ordinary women as a principle constituency recognizing that female participation legitimized the state's policies. In practical terms, women were encouraged to vote and participate in politics. As such, the Council of Guardians would have to accept the nomination of at least some women candidates for political office. While female political participation has substantially declined since the revolution, women have been elected to all eight parliaments.

Women's formal presence in politics regressed immediately after the revolution, as many secular women were purged from the state. Indeed, the first post-revolutionary government, the Provisional Government, did not have a single woman member. But in later years, women advanced in the state apparatuses through active political participation in presidential, parliamentary and local politics. Women's active participation has played a principle role in reapportioning the gender balance and in advancing gender-oriented legislation.

During President Rafsanjani's tenure, an office for women's issues was set up under the new president and Shahla Habibi was appointed as advisor to the president for women's affairs. In 1995, the government announced the appointment of a woman as deputy minister of health. All ministries and provincial governments were instructed to set up offices for women's affairs.[120]

According to Article 115 of the constitution, women are not permitted to become president by virtue of the interpretation of the law. Despite this, in 1997, nine women sought to challenge this restriction by placing their names on the ballot. Such a move was designed to force the state to acknowledge its own contradictory policies. Indeed, women succeeded in bringing this issue to a head as reformist and conservative theologians issued fatwas both in favor and against women. Azam Taleghani was one of these female candidates who sought to expose the contradictions in the constitution. She announced that her intention was first "to clarify the interpretation of the term *rejal* (statesman or man depending on the interpretation. Islamist women believe rejal refers to a qualified candidate regardless of gender while traditionalists insist that rejal means a man. Hence, for them, women are not qualified to run), which is ambiguously defined in the Constitution"; and second, she said, "It was my religious duty to stand for the presidential election, otherwise the rights of half of the population of this country would have been wasted and I would have been responsible and accountable to God for such an injustice."[121] Taleghani's candidacy was rejected propelling the reform parliament to seek legal clarification through the implementation of a new law—a move that was also blocked. In 1998, women also sought to challenge the ban on women advancing into the elected Assembly of Experts.[122] The Guardian Council continued to limit women's election to these two bodies, but at the same time prominent ayatollahs such as Ayatollah Sanei'i and Bojnourdi have supported female elections to all positions including that of the Supreme Leader.[123]

Despite other institutional limitations for women, the Majlis has been among the primary venue for female activism. From early in the Islamic Republic's history, women have been active and elected into the parliament. During the reform period, female representation peaked and it was during this period where gender

Table 5.5 Percentage of women elected to the Iranian parliament, 1963–2008

Year	Number of female parliamentarians	As a Percentage of all parliamentarians
1963: female enfranchisement granted		
1963–1967	7	3.5%
1963–1971	10	3.5%
1971–1976	17	6.5%
1976–1979	18	7%
1979: formation of Islamic Republic of Iran		
1979–1983	4	1.5%
1983–1987	4	1.5%
1987–1992	4	1.5%
1992–1996	9	3.3%
1996–2000	14	3.7%
2000–2004	13	4.4%
2004–2008	13	4.1%
2008–2012	9	2.8%

Table 5.6 Female candidacy for Parliamentary elections 1979–2008[126]

Year	Number of female candidates	Total candidates	Women as a % of total candidates
1979–1983	66	3694	1.79
1983–1987	28	1592	1.76
1987–1992	37	1999	1.85
1992–1996	81	3223	2.51
1996–2000	320	5366	5.96
2000–2004	513	6853	7.49
2004–2008	829	4679	5.64
2008–2012	585	7168	12.2

reform also crested. However, women continue to hold only limited seats of the 290-member parliament and have only marginally increased their representation since enfranchisement in 1963. Moreover, in the 2008 parliamentary elections, women's representation had officially declined.

Through the years though, with the levers of education, employment, and the press working in tandem, women took advantage of their suffrage rights both in voting and in electoral participation. During the decade of reconstruction in particular, women's candidacy and political involvement moved into a new frontier. In the fifth Majlis elections, in 1996, 320 women announced their candidacy for the

Majlis; 179 of these women were approved by the Council of Guardians to run in the election, and 14 women were elected into the 290-member body. Moreover, Faezeh Hashemi received the second-highest number of votes among all candidates in her district.[124] Farideh Farhi asserts "the first sign of a visible shift in women's political assertiveness came in the fifth parliamentary election."[125] This shift is a likely reflection of the larger gender consciousness resulting from converging social, economic, and political trends.

Women members of parliament have played a primary role in the direction and promotion of gender legislation. These women have found themselves in the precarious position of being expected to focus on women's issues while at the same time having to be loyal to the state and their patrons. Under pressure to represent women's interests and issues, some parliamentarians have developed gender awareness even embracing feminism. Some female parliamentarians have used this awareness to promote reform while others continue to support traditional gender views.[127] As such, female oriented legislation has been limited in scope as women have been either unable to convince the male majority to support their efforts or have been thwarted by the Guardian Council. Despite their diverse socioeconomic backgrounds and political and religious views, Afshar argues that Iranian women politicians have generally been able to work together and have made important strides in "gradually clawing back rights denied to them by "assiduously formulating their demand in terms of Islamic teachings."[128]

However, it can be said that no female legislation has been passed without the initiatives of women members of parliament. Most legislative efforts were directed to overturning the Islamization measures enforced after the revolution. They have focused on education, such as the reversal of the earlier ban limiting female areas of study and overturning gender quotas, access to professions such as the reversal of the earlier ban on women becoming judges and on their recruitment as police officers, standard marriage reforms that enable women to negotiate the terms of the marriage contract, reevaluation of alimony set at the time of marriage in line with inflation at the time of divorce, and provisions reinstating women's conditional right to divorce. Particular aspects of these legislative victories will be discussed further in Chapter 6.

Non-Governmental Organizations

These political achievements should be placed alongside women's participation in welfare organizations and awareness-raising ventures. Although many Iranian NGOs are affiliated and dependent on the government, NGO activities have ranged from domestic to international, from charity to education, environment, literacy, and vocational training. While Iran has a long historical commitment to community-based charitable organizations evidenced through the social work of pioneering women like Sattareh Farman Farmaian among others,[129] the growing crop of NGOs reflected global trends as well as domestic demand for greater social and political activism. Female participation through these sociopolitical organizations has been important for spreading gender consciousness, providing employment and for promoting linkages among women. Moreover NGO participation and collaboration has provided many young women with team-building skills, goal oriented activism, and grass roots experience.[130] "The emergence of new types of female social and political activists with modern discourses and agendas was yet another outcome of the post-war era and was tightly linked to broader transformations."[131]

An estimate of the number of official, government-affiliated women's NGOs active in the mid-1990s was 40 while in 2003 NGOs numbered over 5,000.[132] In line with the liberalization policies promoted by Rafsanjani, the government sponsored increased female participation in the global NGO network. One female scholar has suggested that such networks were critical for the maturation of women's activism during this period.[133] Through such networks, women were given greater access to the international community in general and women's organizations in particular. Greater cooperation and collaboration led to increased interconnectivity among women's activism. The government collaborated by dispatching female representatives to important international conferences on women and encouraged other official government delegations to include women among their members.[134] Mahboubeh Abbasgholizadeh criticized the state for cosmetically supporting NGOs to alleviate international pressure. "I suddenly understood that NGOs has become instruments of the government's propaganda. . . . NGOs were firmly glued to the government and the government enjoyed it too. . . .The result has been NGO passivity."[135]

However, according to Zahra Shojai, who ran the Office for Women's Participation under President Khatami, the pro-NGO policies of the government also facilitated the mushrooming of NGOs. The growth of these organizations led to increased education and awareness among women. Moreover, the interconnectivity of these networks has eased cooperation even among groups with divergent ideological leanings.[136] The Office for Women's Participation supported many NGO activities, including the sponsoring of conferences and research, while the State Welfare Organization recruited NGOs and private-sector organizations as contractors to deliver social services to disadvantaged populations. With an increase of government support for NGO activity, youth-initiated NGOs, human rights advocacy, environmental NGOs and women's NGOs mushroomed. Official NGO statistics suggest that one thousand NGOs were established during this period however it is likely that more organizations were operating without government approval due to the restrictions and long registration period.[137] Elaheh Rostami Povey suggests that while women's NGOs have not engaged in structural reform efforts, "they are challenging gender specific access and influence over institutional power, matters that are crucial to the process of democratization."[138]

Through these concentrated efforts, the battles fought and accomplishments won by women in the realms of education, labor, law, media, and politics extended well into Iranian society. As such, female activism became a circular endeavor as momentum trickled down to the streets and into the homes, where women slowly began to assert themselves consciously and unconsciously against conventional social and religious norms. The impact of the reconstructive decade further enabled women to demand gender reform and economic integration. Despite avowed government efforts to contain the spread of such activism, the social transformation among women and within society became irreversible. Again, the Islamic government unwittingly facilitated female activism through its own disjoined political and economic policies as well as through its own factional and ideological disputes. "While the Islamic Republic ha[d] not opened the gates, women [were] jumping over the fences."[139] Once these gates were open, the cycle of action and reaction could not be stopped.

Notes

1. Saffarzadeh is a twentieth-century Iranian poet. Quoted in Farzaneh Milani. "Revitalization: Some Reflections on the Work of Saffar-Zadeh," in Guity Nashat, ed. *Women and Revolution in Iran*, 1983.

2. Mehdi Moslem, *Factional Politics in Post Khomeini Iran*, 2002, 3.

3. *Ettelaat*, September 26, 1998.

4. Moslem, *Factional Politics in Post Khomeini Iran,* 2002, 5–6.

5. Tilly, 2004, 13.

6. In 1989, prior to Khomeini's death, the constitution of the Islamic Republic of Iran was amended abolishing the office of the Prime Minister and empowering that of the president with more authority.

7. Ayatollah Khomeini pursued a foreign policy characterized by the statement "neither East nor West" advocating Iranian independence from foreign imperialism relying neither on the United States nor the Soviet Union.

8. For more details on the war, including the particular military campaigns, regional reaction, and the cease-fire accepted in 1988, see Shahram Chubin and Charles Tripp's *Iran and Iraq at War,* 1988; Farhang Rajaee's *The Iran-Iraq War: The Politics of Aggression,* 1993; Lawrence Potter and Gary Sick ed., *Iran, Iraq and the Legacy of War,* 2004; Efraim Karsh, "From Ideological Zeal to Geopolitical Realism: The Islamic Republic and the Gulf," in *The Iran-Iraq War: Impact and Implications,* ed. Efraim Karsh, 1989; and Saskia Gieling, *Religion and War in Revolutionary Iran*, 1999, 40–107.

9. Literature exists on the ideological orientation of factional groups in Iran. For more information, see Mehdi Moslem, *Factional Politics in Post Khomeini Iran,* 2002; Wilfried Buchta, *Who Rules Iran? The Structure of Power in the Islamic Republic,* 2002; David Menashri, *Post Revolutionary Politics in Iran: Religion, Society and Power,* 2001; Shaul Bakhash, *Reign of the Ayatollahs: Iran and the Islamic Revolution,* 1986; Ervand Abrahamian, *Iran Between Two Revolutions,* 1982; Said Amir Arjomand, *The Turban for the Crown: The Islamic Revolution in Iran,* 1988; Ray Takeyh, *Hidden Iran: Power and Paradox in the Islamic Republic,* 2006; Nikki Keddie, *Modern Iran: Roots of Revolution,* 2003; Ali Ansari, *Iran, Islam and Democracy: The Politics of Managing Change,* 2001.

10. For more details on the life and ideology of Ali Khamenei, see Mehdi Khalaji's "The Last Marja: Sistani and the End of Traditional Religious Authority in Shi'ism," The Washington Institute for Near East Policy, 2006; and Karim Sadjadpour's "Reading Khamenei: The World View of Iran's Most Powerful Leader," The Carnegie Endowment for International Peace, 2008.

11. It is rumored that Montazeri's association with Mehdi Hashemi also called into question his revolutionary credentials. Hashemi was executed in 1987 for sedition and murder

most likely for his duplicitous involvement with the United States related to the Iran-Contra affair. Since Montazeri's house arrest, he has continued to criticize the policies of the government, including those proposed by President Ahmadinejad.

12. The initial stipulation that the Supreme Leader be "recognized and accepted" by the "majority of the people" was also dropped.

13. David Menashri, *Post Revolutionary Politics in Iran: Religion, Society and Power* 2001, 17.

14. Buchta, 2002, 125–7.

15. See Shahrough Akhavi, "Elite Factionalism in the Islamic Republic of Iran," *Middle East Journal*, Volume 41, Number 2, 1987.

16. For details on the Revolutionary Guards and their political role in Iran see Ali Alfoneh, "The Revolutionary Guards' Role in Iranian Politics," *Middle East Quarterly*, Fall 2008, 3–14.

17. See Mehdi Khalaji, "Apocalyptic Politics: On the Rationality of Iranian Policy," The Washington Institute for Near East Policy, Policy Focus 79, 2007, 28.

18. Since the revolution, Iran's population has increased from 25 million in 1978 to over 70 million in 2010.

19. Ray Takeyh, *Hidden Iran: Paradox and Power in the Islamic Republic*, 2006, 43.

20. Fereshteh Ahmadi, "Islamic Feminism in Iran: Feminism in a New Islamic Context," *Journal of Feminist Studies in Religion*, 22, (2), 2006, 33–53.

21. Parvin Paidar, "Gender of Democracy: The Encounter between Feminism and Reformism in Contemporary Iran," United Nations Research Institute for Social Development, Democracy, Governance and Human Rights, Program Paper Number 6, 2001, 18–24.

22. Abdolkarim Soroush and M. Sadri, *Reason, Freedom and Democracy: The Essential Writings of Abdolkarim Soroush*, 2000, ix.

23. Abdolkarim Soroush, 2000, 7. For analysis of Soroush's views, see Valla Vakili, *Debating Religion and Politics in Iran: The Political Thought of Abdolkarim Soroush: Occasional Paper Series*, No. 2, 1996.

24. Said Amir Arjomand, "The Reform Movement and the Debate on Modernity and Tradition in Contemporary Iran," *IJMES*, 34, 2002, 719–31. Afshin Matin-Asghari, "Abdol Karim Soroush and the Secularization of Islamic Thought in Iran," *Iranian Studies*, 30 (2), 1997, 95–115.

25. See Mahan Abedin, "The Origins of Iran's Reformist Elite," *Middle East Intelligence Bulletin*, Vol. 5, No. 4, April 2003. The Organization of Mojahedin of the Islamic Revolution that had been founded in 1979 but was later dissolved was reactivated. Its leader, Behzad Nabavi, served as minister of industry from 1982 to 1989.

26. See Farhad Khosrokhavar, "New Intellectuals in Iran," *Social Compass*, Vol. 51 No. 2, 2004, 195–7. For more on vigilante groups in Iran, see Michael Rubin, *Into the Shadows: Radical Vigilante's in Khatami's Iran*, 2001.

27. Mohsen Kadivar, *Vela'ie Based State*, 1999.

28. Muhammad Mojtahed Shabestari, *Naqdi bar Ghira'ate Rasmie Din* (A Critique of the Official Reading of Religion), 2000.

29. Muhammad Mojtahed Shabestari, *Iman va Azadi* (Faith and Freedom), 1997. Mohammad Mojtahed Shabestari. "Zanan, Ketab va Sonnat," (Women, Books and Tradition), *Zanan*, 57, 19–22.

30. Akbar Ganji, *Ghosts' Darkhouse: Pathology of Transition to the Developmental Democratic State*, 1999. Khosrokhavar, "New Intellectuals in Iran," *Social Compass*, 191-2004. See also Farzin Vahdat's, "Post-revolutionary Discourses of Mohammad Mojtahed Shabestari and Mohsen

Kadivar: Reconciling the Discourses of Mediated Subjectivity: Part 1 Mojtahed Shabestari," *Critique Journal for Critical Studies of the Middle East,* 16, Spring 2000, 31-54; "Post-revolutionary Discourses of Mohammad Mojtahed Shabestari and Mohsen Kadivar: Reconciling the Discourses of Mediated Subjectivity: Part 2 Mohsen Kadivar," *Critique* 17, Fall 2000.

31. Ahmadi, "Islamic Feminism in Iran, 2006, 33–53.

32. Personal interview with female seminarian, Tehran, February 11, 2007.

33. Paidar, "Gender of Democracy," 2001, 3.

34. Nesta Ramazani, "Women in Iran: The Revolutionary Ebb and Flow," *Middle East Journal,* Vol. 47, No. 3, 1993.

35. Quoted in Dr. Kathryn Spellman, "Civil Society and Women Movement," Tehran: Volunteer: Iran CSO's Training and Research Center, Spring 2005.

36. Quoted in Elaheh Rostami Povey, "Feminist Contestations of Institutional Domains in Iran," *Feminist Review,* Volume 69, Winter 2001, 55.

37. *Ayandegan,* June 3, 1979.

38. *Zan-e Ruz* published a report of suicide by girls due to the psychological pressure and humiliation over maintaining Islamic behavior. *Zan-e Ruz,* June 3, 1989.

39. Golnar Mehran, "Socialization of School Children in the Islamic Republic," *Iranian Studies,* Vol. 22, No.1, 1989.

40. Golnar Mehran, "The Paradox of Tradition and Modernity in Female Education in the Islamic Republic of Iran," *Comparative Education Review,* Vol. 47, No. 3. 2003.

41. "The Review of Women's Advancement 1975-2005," The Office of Women and Family, Tehran, 2006.

42. Roksana Bahramitash, "Revolution, Islamization, and Women's Employment in Iran," *Browns Journal of World Affairs,* Winter/Spring 2003, Volume IX, No. 2.

43. Golnar Mehran, "Lifelong Learning: New Opportunities for Women in a Muslim Country (Iran), *Comparative Education,* Vol. 32, No. 2, 1999.

44. *Ettelaat,* March 14, 1985.

45. Quoted in Ramazani, 1993.

46. Ibid.

47. Parvin Paidar, *Women and the Political Process in Twentieth-Century Iran,* 1995, 321.

48. *Zan-e Ruz,* May 27, 1989 and June 24, 1989.

49. Paidar. *Women and the Political Process,* 1995, 321.

50. Iran Statistics Center, 2006 National Yearbook.

51. Zahra Ebrahimi, "Ezame Dokhtarane Daneshjoo be Khareje Keshvar Tasveeb Shod" [Ratification of Legislation Permitting Female Students to Study Abroad,], *Zanan* 74, 8–9. Golnar Mehran, "The Paradox of Tradition and Modernity in Female Education in the Islamic Republic of Iran," Comparative Education Review, Vol. 47, no. 3, 2003. See also National Census, Statistical Center of Iran and documents available at the Ministry of Education and Zahra Mira Elmi, "Educational Attainment in Iran," *Viewpoints* Special Edition, "The Iranian Revolution at Thirty," Middle East Institute, Washington, D.C., 2009.

52. *Aftab-e Yazd,* December 17, 2000.

53. Shams al Sadat Zahidi, "Moqiyate Zanan dar Jame'e Daneshgahi," [Status of Women at University] *Zanan,* 24, 3–6.

54. Personal interviews, students from Tehran University, February 23, 2007.

55. Personal interview with female student, Tehran, March 1, 2007.

56. Charles Kurzman, "A Feminist Generation in Iran?" *Iranian Studies,* Vol. 41, No. 3, 2008.

57. Hoodfar and Sadr, 2009, 13.

58. Iraj Gorjin, "Does Iran fear Educated Women?" *Radio Free Europe Radio Liberty,* February 10, 2008.

59. Homa Hoodfar and Shadi Sadr, "Can Women Act as Agents of a Democratization of Theocracy in Iran?" *United Nations Research Institute for Social Development,* 2009, 13.

60. Ibid.

61. *Hamshahri,* January 10, 2000, 15.

62. Ramazani, "Women in Iran," 1993, 417.

63. Haleh Afshar, "Women and the Politics of Fundamentalism in Iran," Haleh Afshar ed. *Women and Politics in the Third World,* 1996, 135. See also World Bank, World Development Indicators.

64. Farideh Farhi, "The Contending Discourses on Women in Iran," Third World Network, Third World Resurgence No. 94, June 1998, 5.

65. *Zan-e Ruz,* February 3, 1990.

66. Afshar, "Women and the Politics of Fundamentalism," 1996, 137.

67. Farhi. 1998, 6.

68. Quoted in Parvin Paidar, "Feminism and Islam in Iran," in Deniz Kanidyoti ed., *Gendering the Middle East.* 1996, 62.

69. Valentine Moghadam, "Women, Work, and Ideology in the Islamic Republic," *International Journal of Middle East Studies,* Vol. 20, No. 2, May 1988, 221–43.

70. *Zan-e Ruz,* February 10, 1990.

71. Afshar, "Women and the Politics of Fundamentalism", 1996, 132.

72. *Ojrat-ol-Mesal* is similar to the wages for housework movement that developed in the US in the 1970s but never succeeded in winning compensation for housewives.

73. Homa Hoodfar, "The Women's Movement in Iran: Women at the Crossroad of Secularization and Islamization." Women Living Under Muslim Laws. The Women's Movement Series No. 1, Winter 1999.

74. Afshar, "Women and the Politics of Fundamentalism," 1996, 130–134.

75. From Ayatollah Khamenei's sermon on December 16, 1992, in *Cheshmeh-ye Nur,* Tehran, 1995, 269.

76. Seyyed Javad Mostafavi, *Beheshte Khanevadeh,* Qom, Qods, 10th ed., 1995, Vol. i, 117.

77. Statistical Center of Iran, National Census 2006.

78. Maryam Poya, *Women, Work and Islamism: Ideology and Resistance in Iran,* 1999, 19.

79. Azadeh Kian, *Les Femmes Iraniennes entre Islam, Etat et Famille,* 2002.

80. Hoodfar, 1999, 7.

81. Personal interview with female seminarian, Tehran, February 2007.

82. Ramazani, "Women in Iran," 1993, 424.

83. Personal interview with female preacher, Tehran, May 3, 2007.

84. Kathryn Spellman, "Civil Society and Women Movement," Tehran: Volunteer: Iran CSO's Training and Research Center, Spring 2005.

85. Halper, 2005, 133.

86. Afshar, "Women and the Politics of Fundamentalism," 1996, 138.

87. Valentine Moghadam, "Islamic Feminism and Its Discontents: Toward a Resolution of the Debate", *Signs,* Vol. 27, No. 4, Summer, 2002, 1162.

88. Haleh Afshar, *Islam and Feminisms: An Iranian Case Study,* 1998, 132.

89. *Zan-e Ruz,* September 29, 1996.

90. Afshar, *Islam and Feminisms,* 1998, 126.

91. See Shirin Ebadi, *Iran Awakening: A Memoir of Revolution and Hope*, New York: Random House, 2006; and Mehrangiz Kar, *Crossing the Red Line: The Struggle for Human Rights in Iran*, 2007.

92. Gholam Khiabany and Annabelle Sreberny, "The Women's Press in Contemporary Iran: Engendering the Public Sphere," in Naomi Sakr's *Women and the Media in the Middle East: Power Through Self Expression*, 2004.

93. Nazanin Shahrokni, "Zanan-e Khabarnegar: Zendegi az Noeh Digar" [Women Journalists: A Different Life], *Zanan* 54, 2–7.

94. Personal interview with female journalist, Tehran, May 13, 2007.

95. Roya Karimi-Majd, "Zanane Khabarnegar: Kargaran Arzan Matbooat" [Women Journalists: The Inexpensive Workers of the Press], *Zanan* 101, 2–9.

96. Zahra Mira Elmi, "Educational Attainment in Iran," *Viewpoints* Special Edition, The Iranian Revolution at Thirty, Middle East Institute, Washington, D.C., 2009, 63.

97. Gholam Khiabany. "Politics of the Internet in Iran," in *Media, Culture and Society in Iran: Living with Globalization and the Iranian State*, edited by Mehdi Semati, 2008, 26.

98. *Islamic Republic News Agency*, August 28, 1999.

99. Zahra Ebrahimi, "Ma Vazeefeye Ghanoonee Khod Midaneem" [Confrontation Is Our Legal Duty], *Zanan* 42, 3–5.

100. Lily Faradpour, "Women, Gender Roles and Journalism in Iran," A paper presented at the Development Studies Association, Women and Development Study Group 6th May, 2006, York University, UK.

101. Ziba Mir-Hosseini, "Debating Women: Gender and the Public Sphere in Post-Revolutionary Iran," in *Civil Society in the Muslim World,* ed. Amyn Sajoo, 2002, 102.

102. Quoted in Mir-Hosseini, 2002, 102.

103. Parvin Ardalan, "Zanan Nashriyate Zanan ra Mo'arefi Mikonad: In Bar Payam-e Hajar" [Zanan Introduces Women's Journals: This Time Payam-e Hajar], *Zanan* 53, June 1999, 16–17.

104. Paidar, *Women and the Political Process*, 1995, 282–93.

105. Forough Jahanbaksh, *Islam Democracy and Religious Modernism in Iran*, 2001, 141–3.

106. Shahla Sherkat, "Chashmahe Agahi Agar Bejushad . . ." [If Opened Eyes Only Boiled . . .] *Zanan*, February 1992.

107. In 1997, *Zanan* organized and reported on one such discussion, entitled "What Are the Most Important Problems of Women in Iran?" Featuring feminists such as Farideh Farahi and Mehrangiz Kar, this discussion touched on issues such as the reform movement in Iran, the limited nature of women's rights, and the need for the press to enjoy more freedom.

108. Mehrangiz Kar, *Crossing the Red Line: The Struggle for Human Rights in Iran* 2007, 109.

109. Elaheh Rostami Povey,"Feminist Contestations of Institutional Domains in Iran," *Feminist Review*, Volume 69, Issue 1, 2001, 59.

110. Cited in Azadeh Kian, "Women and Politics in Post-Islamist Iran: A Gender Conscious Drive to Change," *British Journal of Middle Eastern Studies*, Vol. 24, No. 1, 1997, 75–96.

111. Parvin Ardalan, "Zanan Nashriyate Zanan ra Mo'arefi Mikonad: In Bar Farzaneh" [Zanan Introduces women's journals: this time Farzaneh,] *Zanan* 69, June 2000, 16–17.

112. Shahla Sherkat, "Faezeh Hashemi Che Migooyad?" [What Does Faezeh Hashemi say?] *Zanan* 28, 8–17.

113. Elaheh Rostami-Povey, "Feminist Contestations of Institutional Domains in Iran," *Feminist Review*, Vol. 69, No. 1, 2001, 58.

114. Ziba Mir-Hosseini, "The Rise and Fall of Faezeh Hashemi: Women in Iranian elections," *Middle East Research and Information Project*, Middle East Report, No. 218, 2001, 9.

115. Haleh Esfandiari, "The Politics of the 'Women's Question' in the Islamic Republic, 1979-1999" in Esposito, John L. and Ramazani, R.K. (eds.), *Iran at the Crossroads*, 2001, 110.

116. "Iranian Women to Get Equal Blood Money in Car Crashes," *Reuters*, May 27, 2008. Shahindokht Molaverdi, "Tasavee e Diyeh Zan Va Man" [Equality of Blood Money Between Men & Women], *Zanan*, 109, 2–4.

117. Ziba Mir-Hosseini, "Islam, Women and Civil Rights: The Religious Debate in the Iran of the 1990s," in *Women, Religion and Culture in Iran* ed., Sarah F. D. Ansari, Vanessa Martin, 2002, 116.

118. Women in Iran are obliged to wear the hijab to hide their hair and body contours. Female athletes must also follow this rule when participating in sporting events, even during international events such as the Olympic Games they must wear scarves and gowns. In 2007, Iran reportedly made a plan to have special bicycles designed for women with a cabin to cover half of the rider's body and hence not exposing their body movements while riding. See Farzaneh Milani, "Islamic Bicycle Can't Slow Iranian Women," *USA Today*, June 29, 2007; and Azadeh Kian, "Women and Politics in Post–Islamist Iran: A Gender Conscious Drive to Change," *British Journal of Middle East Studies*, February 1997.

119. Ziba Mir-Hosseini, "The Rise and Fall of Faezeh Hashemi: Women in Iranian Elections," *Middle East Research and Information Project*, No. 218, Spring 2001, 11.

120. Afshar, *Islam and Feminisms*, 1998, 43.

121. Elaheh Rostami Povey, "Feminist Contestations of Institutional Domains in Iran," *Feminist Review*, Vol. 69, No. 1, 2001, 49.

122. Azam Taleghani. "Mikhaham Taklife Rejal ra Roshan Konam" [I Want to Make Clear the Role of Statesmen], *Zanan* 34, 6–7.

123. "Iranian Women Seek Equality," *BBC News*, February 23, 2000 and Ayatollah Mohammad Mousavi Bojnourdi, "In Madehye Ghanuni Irad Darad" [There is an Error with this Legal Clause], *Zanan*, 87, 11.

124. Ziba Mir-Hosseini, "The Rise and Fall of Faezeh Hashemi: Women in Iranian Elections," *Middle East Research and Information Project*, No. 218, Spring 2001, 10.

125. Farideh Farhi, "The Contending Discourses on Women in Iran," *Third World Network*, Third World Resurgence No. 94, June 1998, 7.

126. Data from www.iranwomen.org/zanan/charts/politics/majis and Islamic Republic of Iran Ministry of Interior, "Ettela'iyeh Shomarehye 8 Setade Entekhabate Keshvar Adar Khosouse Amare Ghat'iye Sabte Nam Shodeh Gane Entekhabate Majlese Hashtom" [Bulletin Number VIII of the Headquarters for Elections on the Final Statistics of Registered Candidates for the Eighth Parliamentary Elections], available in Persian at www.moi.ir/Portal/Home/ShowPage.aspx?Object=Standard&CategoryID= da3dfedf-2133-461e-8f0b-90dd22bf18a3&LayoutID=52012b04-039d-4115-8d1b- 3562c062764c&ID=085f2469-1e2a-4e35-b122-a1cea2b49175. Accessed February 17, 2009.

127. Afshar, *Islam and Feminisms*, 1998, 64.

128. Haleh Afshar, "Competing Interests: Democracy, Islamification and Women Politicians in Iran," K. Ross (ed) *Women, Politics and Change*, 2002, 110.

129. For more on Sattareh Farman Farmian's work, see Sattareh Farman Farmaian and Dona Munger, *Daughter of Persia: A Woman's Journey from her Father's Harem through the Islamic Republic*, 1993.

130. Mehrangiz Kar, "Women and Civil Society in Iran," in *On Shifting Ground Muslim Women in the Global Era,* Fereshteh Nouraie-Simone (ed.), 2005, 221.

131. Azedeh Kian, "Women and Politics in Post-Islamist Iran: A Gender Conscious Drive to Change," *British Journal of Middle Eastern Studies,* Vol. 24, No. 1, 1997, 84.

132. Bagher Namazi. "Non-Governmental Organizations in the Islamic Republic of Iran: A situation analysis" United Nations Development Program, Tehran, 2000.

133. Personal interview with NGO activist, Tehran, March 3, 2007.

134. Nayereh Tohidi, "'Fundamentalist' Backlash and Muslim Women in the Beijing Conference" in the Canadian Women Studies, Vol. 16, No. 3, 1996.

135. Ardalan, 2000, 17.

136. Personal interview with activist and journalist, Washington, DC, March 12, 2008.

137. Bagher Namazi, "Non-Governmental Organizations in the Islamic Republic of Iran: A situation analysis" United Nations Development Program, Tehran, 2000.

138. Elaheh Rostami Povey, "Trade Unions and Women's NGOs: Diverse Civil Society Organizations in Iran," *Development in Practice,* 14, 1–2, 2004, 254.

139. Moghissi, "Women in the Resistance Movement in Iran." *Women in the Middle East: Perceptions, Realities and Struggles for Liberation,* Haleh Afshar (ed.), New York: St. Martin's Press, 1993, 183.

6

Khatami: The Momentum and Challenge of Reform

No one is thinking about the flower,
no one is thinking about the fish,
no one wants to believe that the garden is dying,
that the garden's heart has swollen under the sun,
that the garden is slowly
being drained of green memories.

Forough Farrokhzad[1]

The presidential election of 1997 marked a profound turning point for political and social activism that built on the changes and momentum of the previous decade. This "was the first election after the revolution in which the public will expressed at the ballot box overturned the writ of the conservative leadership."[2] Indeed, the results of May 23, 1997, can be seen as the expression and apogee of two decades of social and political frustration. Millions of Iranians, many of whom had never voted before, stood in polling lines to cast their ballots. The energy throughout the country was electric and contagious as hope and optimism for political change emanated from the hallowed voting halls.

Women played a fundamental role in the election. For the first time in the history of the Islamic Republic, gender issues were prominent among the candidates' platforms in a presidential election. The women's vote was critical in securing a victory for Muhammad Khatami against his opponent and front-runner, Majlis Speaker Ali Akbar Nateq Nuri. Khatami seized on the needs of many voters, including that of women, the youth and the underprivileged. His message and persona were essential factors in generating new optimism as his campaign was directed at promoting civil society, rule of law, and dialogue with the West—moderate views that galvanized voters.[3]

The outcome left no doubt of a reformist victory: Khatami won with over 20 million votes—70 percent of those who showed up at the polls.[4] Although voter turnout in Iranian presidential elections had always been high, the 1997 elections expanded the size of the electorate further by capturing the votes of those who had eschewed previous elections.[5] In so doing, the election did not legitimate the Islamic Republic so much as it produced a pro-democracy, civil society movement.

The decisive and surprising election outcome suggested initially that the reform era would alter the power balance. The results ushered in an innovative, ambitious group of politicians into office on the hope and promise of change. The reform movement also brought a new discourse to the political realm and inspired social activism. Khatami and his reformist cadre promoted a democratic vision for Iran, offering the populace the promise of renewed social, economic, and political opportunities. Yet in spite of victory at the ballot box, it soon became clear that this potent momentum would be stifled. Limitations to presidential and parliamentary power imposed by conservative opponents slowly truncated prospects for change.[6]

An analysis of the developments of this period is critical to understanding the dynamics and evolution of factionalism and activism at work within the Islamic Republic. Women would be at the center of these trends. Despite the optimism surrounding Khatami's election, his eight years in office would be marked by intense struggles between the conservative leaders who wanted to consolidate clerical power, and moderate democratic proponents who sought to strengthen power in civil society institutions. This period would create openings and opportunities for increased activism. Sidney Tarrow suggests, "When institutional access opens, rifts appear within elites, allies become available, and . . . challengers find opportunities to advance their claims . . . opportunities produce episodes of contentious politics."[7] The ideological challenge of the reform movement inevitably led to a conservative backlash with the election of a conservative parliament in 2004 and the hard-line President Mahmoud Ahmadinejad in 2005 further opening the field to activism. This growing factional divide coupled with popular discontent in the aftermath of the reform period would prove fertile ground for the emergence of the reactionary Green Movement in 2009.

Socioeconomic and demographic swings contributed to the shift in electoral politics. The gains in literacy and education including female economic participation impacted society, as did the trends of mass urbanization and population growth. The doubling of the population had enormous socioeconomic and political consequences for the state. Not only was the burden of a young population taxing with regards to social services, employment, and economic demands, but this young generation reared in the aftermath of the revolution had political expectations unexpected by the regime. Youthful expression of greater freedom, economic disenchantment of the middle class, and growing social demands came to the fore in Khatami's election.

During Khatami's two-term presidency, women and reformists attempted to use the electoral and institutional system to effect social and political change, but cooperation and conciliatory measures were often fruitless in a government that was mired in contradiction. Appreciating these dynamics is again crucial to exposing the incongruities and transformations effecting women's activism and social change. Nevertheless, the growth of civil society, the blossoming of the press, the spread of the Internet, the momentum of student activism, and closer coordination among women all fueled greater cohesion in civil society and women's activism, opening a new, promising chapter in the fight for women's rights.

The conservatives viewed the 1997 elections as a routine exercise necessary to validate the Islamic government and its ability to guarantee a smooth and legitimate change of leadership. Through the ballot box, the government preserved its Republican facade while also drawing from popular legitimacy. During this period, the conservative establishment sought to contain growing popular discontent exacerbated at the end of the Rafsanjani period by allowing moderates a voice and an opportunity to contest the presidential elections. To this end, the Guardian Council approved the candidacy of Muhammad Khatami. The conservative establishment envisioned that the selection of Khatami, who was known for his reformist background foreshadowed during his appointment as Rafsanjani's minister of culture, and his message of tolerance and change would placate popular discontent without threatening the ruling order. They underestimated the possibility that elections could mobilize large numbers of Iranians into the political process and challenge the conservative monopoly of power.[8]

Khatami's character and message appealed to a broad cross section of Iranians. His personal style, manners, and way of communication sharply contrasted with the grim expression of many among the clerical elite, and quickly earned him a following. His supporters were men, women, young, old, rich, middle class, and poor, diverse in ethnicity and religiosity yet all sharing a demand for political reform and social change.[9] Khatami had had limited involvement in the revolution and the administration of the state throughout the 1980s. He was elected as a member of the first parliament. He had served as director of the National Library and Minister of Culture and Islamic Guidance from 1982 to 1992. He was well versed in Western political literature and philosophy, and known for his frequent references to Kant and Rousseau. He was credited for policies at the Ministry of Culture that led to the cultural opening of the 1990s, where he also built bridges with the secular intelligentsia. His writings on Islam reflected and promoted a humanistic and tolerant vision of the faith in contrast to the conservative interpretations advocated by the clerical leadership. Khatami's campaign and speeches were infused with references to "democracy," "civil society," "social liberalization," "equal opportunities," "political tolerance," "women's rights," "rule of law," and "dialogue of civilizations."[10] He particularly emphasized civil society, advocating cultural freedoms, and legal protections to empower its growth. His promise of relaxing the state's ideological vigilance also gained him support among women, youth, civil society forces, and secular voters. At the same time, he was considered attractive to the pragmatic faction, including Rafsanjani, for his seemingly moderate political views.[11] Khatami "came to represent the totality of repressed frustration with the system," stated one female university student, who recounted that she and her circle of friends trusted his promises for more social and political freedom particularly for women deciding to support his campaign.[12]

Khatami definitively courted a female constituency. Most helpful to his campaign was an interview he gave to *Zanan* magazine in advance of the election in which he provided a candid assessment of his goals as president while also revealing intimacies about his personal life including information about his wife and daughters.[13] Khatami's attitude on gender issues distinguished him from his hard-line competitor. He openly recognized that women's issues were controlled by a "male chauvinist attitude" yet he sought to eliminate "male supremacy" offering women a presence in political, social, and religious forums.[14] His gender views were best summarized in a July 2005 statement in Tehran, when he said, "We should have a comprehensive view of the role of women and before anything else, should not regard women as second-class citizens . . . We should all believe that both men and women have the capability to be active in all fields, and I emphasize, in all fields."[15]

Conversely, the conservative candidate Nateq Nouri did not respond to a request for an interview to be published in *Zanan* and only belatedly realized the power and importance of the female vote. He clambered to counter a rumor that if elected he would impose more stringent veiling requirements, and made public his role in passing a bill that established a parliamentary women's committee in the fifth Majlis.[16] To cultivate his appeal with women, he marshaled through parliament several bills that improved women's status including a law that permitted women to work three-fourths time and receive full compensation.[17]

While some women, particularly traditional ones, supported Nateq Nuri, most activist women were drawn to Khatami, who received widespread support throughout Iranian society, including among a diverse spectrum of women of various political, social, and age groups. These were women from upper, middle- and working-class backgrounds, from secular and Islamist households, and in urban and rural areas of Iran. Unique to his campaign was the presence and participation of younger women, who enthusiastically canvassed for Khatami. Young women, in particular, sought more social freedom and less harassment by the morals police, increased legal protections, and revisions to the family and civil codes, as well as female appointments to Khatami's cabinet and political inner circle.[18]

Polls and public opinion expected that Khatami would pose a significant challenge to Nateq Nuri, but few predicted his victory. Indeed, his win was a humiliating rejection of the entrenched policies and practices of the conservative elite. Many interpreted the election, dubbed the "second revolution," as a referendum on change, and the date of the election, May 23rd or *Dovome Khordad* became synonymous with that of the reform movement signaling a new era known as the Third Republic.[19]

The most immediate effect of the election was evidenced in the optimism and hope among Iran's activist society. A new frontier was opened, where the results of the elections mandated an accelerated pace of change. Such momentum facilitated the birth of what became known as the "Tehran Spring." During this time, Iran's relations with the international community improved significantly. Equally noteworthy was the expansion of press and social freedoms that generated a burst of social, political and economic activity.[20]

Reaction from the conservative establishment was initially muted, as a slow and intense debate waged through the halls of the conservative dominated revolutionary institutions. Initially, the conservative elite was shocked by Khatami's triumph and uncertain of the implications of such a victory. Moreover, many felt threatened by the popular demand and prospects for reform that would ultimately weaken or divide their power.[21] The conservatives drew a decisive line, separating and pitting themselves against this new reformist wave. Khatami became an advocate of change, while the Supreme Leader became the primary defender of revolutionary values, bringing to light the ultimate political conflict in which opposing forces would struggle over the ideological future of the Islamic Republic. Again this struggle would involve and revolve around women.

In this period, like the preceding decades, the road to female reform continued to be tied to political reform. Through the years of war and subsequent economic stagnation, the popular tide turned against the Islamic government. The tangible reasons for this included authoritarianism, corruption, and state interference in the private lives of citizens. Moreover, there was widespread disappointment over the failure of the state to meet the economic and political promises pledged during the revolutionary fervor. Amidst declining purchasing power and growing popular economic strain, Iran's population proved desperate for change. These factors gradually eroded genuine mass support for the Islamic Republic and amounted to a crisis of legitimacy for the hard-liners in control of the state apparatus.[22]

Khatami's move to allow greater freedom of expression to the press changed the face of the media in Iran. Although he did not control all the levers of power, Khatami exercised control over the Ministry of Culture, which oversaw censorship and regulation of the print media. Reformist Culture Minister Ataollah Mohajerani led the charge against the stricture governing various cultural activities. By relaxing government control of newspapers, the arts, and cinema, the Khatami years brought a flowering of intellectual and political discourse in Iran that rapidly reshaped the style and content of Iranian politics.[23] Newspapers were permitted to cover previously avoided subjects such as political repression, corruption, and bureaucratic administration. The greater openness not only increased the number of newspapers in circulation but also facilitated a vibrant atmosphere of literary and political debate. In turn, such discussion generated much popular enthusiasm for reform, leading to further electoral victories for the reformists in the 1999 municipal elections and parliamentary elections of 2000.[24]

Khatami's strong mandate at the polls did not translate into robust executive powers, though. The conservative leadership accepted the verdict of the elections but quickly moved to limit Khatami's room to maneuver. The conservative elite had miscalculated the potential for the reform movement to garner popular support. As such, they interpreted the results as a challenge to their power, and reacted defensively to mitigate the effectiveness of the reform movement. Indeed, the power of the president was already constitutionally restricted when compared to the overarching influence of the Supreme Leader, yet a conservative strike came in the form of institutional, legal, and forceful confrontation. The response to Khatami was meticulous and multifaceted. It also came at a time when the electorate was increasingly politically conscious, literate, and urban. The growth of economic and cultural activism coupled with the growing assertiveness of women and youth only exacerbated the conservative reaction and backlash.

The conservative response was a calculated and coordinated design to protect the traditional strongholds of power. Most immediately, Supreme Leader Khamenei swiftly reshaped the leadership of the IRGC bolstering his power with allies who shared a commitment to the integrity and ideology of the Islamic Republic. Khamenei also increased the IRGC defense funding, including budgets for salaries and benefits, in order to strengthen his ties with the leadership. Not surprisingly, the new commander, in allegiance to the Supreme Leader and the IRGC's constitutional mandate "as guardians of the revolution and its achievements,"[25] Yahya Rahim Safavi, quickly became a strong critic of Khatami calling his supporters "diseased people."[26] The strengthened ties with the military would only increase after this period. The IRGC and its commanders were elevated to prominent decision making positions and assumed a larger role in the political process gaining 30 percent of the parliamentary seats in the 2004 elections.[27]

Khamenei also attempted to consolidate control of the Assembly of Experts, the Guardian Council, the judiciary and key seminaries in Qom using his power and influence to appoint loyalists who would defend his ideological vision. In doing so, he sought to constrict Khatami's influence. The Guardian Council and the judiciary limited the ability of the government to carry out reforms as well as curbed the scope of press freedoms and civil society activism by refuting legislation and pursuing legal action against those who challenged the system.

Another tactic designed to constrain the reform movement came from the security forces that set out to threaten dissidents. This tactic of intimidation had been utilized by the state since its inception and would become a recurrent tool of popular coercion. Most shocking were the brutal murders of political reformer Darioush Forouhar and his wife, Parvaneh Eskandari Forouhar, in 1998.[28] In 1999, reformist strategist and Khatami advisor Said Hajjarian was also the target of an assassination attempt leaving him disabled. The same violent ploys were used against the student demonstrations that began in 1999 and continued through 2003.[29] These tactics went hand-in-hand with judicial efforts to cripple the government's reforms. This included the arrest and trial of various elected officials, beginning with Tehran mayor Gholamhussein Karbaschi, who was charged with corruption in 1998.[30] Next came the blatant attack on the reformist press, in which a number of popular newspapers were shut down. The conservative leadership increased pressure on Minister of Culture Mohajerani, eventually forcing him from office through impeachment proceedings. By May 1999, 19 reformist newspapers were shut down and a number of reformist leaders were arrested.[31]

In reaction, student demonstrations broke out in opposition to the growing conservative backlash. In July 1999, protests swept through the country, leaving the establishment fearful of such a powerful wave of public denunciation. Known as Iran's Tiananmen Square, students were repressed with ferocity including attacks on universities dormitories. Moreover, Khatami himself was warned by the IRGC that should he not contain the violence and demonstrations, the IRGC, backed by a constitutional mandate to defend the integrity of the Iranian revolution, would aggressively suppress the populace, stating in a letter that "our patience has run out. We cannot tolerate this situation any longer."[32] In the end, Khatami refused to break with core of the Islamic Republic, and proved unwilling to defend the students, going so far as to admonish them for their disobedience. Despite Khatami's clear dissatisfaction with the political constraints on his power, evidenced through his repeated threats to resign, he remained faithful to the Supreme Leader. More importantly, he remained loyal to the Islamic Republic and the Supreme Leader stating, "The main axis and the central pillar of our system is the Great Leader and the vali-e faqih, around whom other institutions and organs take shape."[33] Such messages ran counter to his lofty speeches promoting civil society and the rule of law. Clearly, the promises and talk of democracy and reform could not be translated into reality. "Khatami did not provide leadership for the reformists—he was more like a spokesman, and no one else had the authority or the mandate to lead."[34] As such, reformist forces were increasingly marginalized and lost hope in the project of reform from within. These sentiments and experiences were not limited to the political establishment, but also affected and impacted women and the youth who felt betrayed by Khatami. Such disappointment created two distinct reactions among the populace in general and activists in particular. Many young hopefuls and activists abdicated from political participation while others shifted gears pursuing a confrontational approach.

Women's status during Khatami's initial years in office was rife with contradictions reflecting the tensions of factionalism in domestic politics. Khatami's election had demonstrated that politicians could no longer ignore or marginalize women, yet the political elite continued to obstruct reforms that were designed to improve women's legal status.[35] Disappointingly, Khatami did not appoint women to any ministerial positions, signaling another tenure of contradictory policies to come. During his campaign when asked if he would appoint women as ministers, he suggested, "In this regard, I make no distinction between men and women."[36] In a poll conducted by *Zanan*, 78 percent stated that they had no objection to the appointment of women as ministers.[37] He did, however, appoint Massoumeh Ebtekar[38] as the Vice President on environment and women's issues, and Zahra Shojai as his advisor and the head of his coordination body on women, the Center for Women's Participation (*Markaz Mosharekat Zanan,*). The Center for Women's Participation was created by Khatami to promote women's rights as part of the President's office. The director was included as a cabinet member.[39] Boosting this position further was a cabinet vote to increase the budget of the department by 800 percent.[40] The journalist, Jamileh

Kadivar, wife of Minister of Culture and Islamic Guidance Ataollah Mohajerani, was appointed as his special advisor on press affairs. Zahra Rahnavard, wife of former Prime Minister Mir Hussein Musavi, became chancellor of the women's Al Zahra University. Khatami's wife, Zohreh Sadeghi, was appointed to oversee a special committee designed to address the needs of rural women.[41] Khatami also maintained each ministerial office and provincial governor's office for women's affairs established by Rafsanjani.[42] At the same time, the number of female parliamentarians increased to 14 in the mid-term parliamentary elections after Fatemeh Karroubi's election in 1997. All three branches of the judiciary, the legislature, and the executive had special institutions to advise them on women's issues. Further, Zahra Shojai implemented a plan for the decentralization of provincial governance where a 12-member committee of women in each province, would add 336 women to government posts.[43] The approach of establishing separate women's units came from Khatami's belief that "women should also try to put their full weight behind their demands, presenting and specifying their requests, finally molding them as law."[44] In December 1998, a group of Islamist women all active in the government bureaucracy formed the Islamic Women's Association. The founders described themselves as "activist, thoughtful Muslim women" dedicated to helping women realize their full potential in society. Parliamentarian, Fatemeh Karroubi, was named their secretary general.[45]

During this period, parliament worked in coordination with the presidency passing important female oriented legislation. The first provided a readjustment of the *mehrieh* or monetary sum promised to a woman in her marriage contract and payable upon divorce (or at anytime she requests during the marriage), adjusted for inflation.[46] A second law allowed for female civil servants to retire after 20 years of service.[47] At the same time, though, conservatives sought to assert themselves on women's issues through the passing of laws regarded by the reformers as retrograde. The first, an amendment to the press law, which was designed to curtail the reformist press, made it a criminal offense to publish photos or exposing material of women.[48] The second law supported a segregated health-care system where medical practitioners were only allowed to treat patients of their own sex. The Guardian Council rejected the medical bill on the grounds that the state lacked the funding to create a dual health-care system.[49]

These bills revived earlier attempts of state sponsored gender segregation and pointed to the lack of unanimity within the political establishment regarding women. During these years, there were also no changes seen to the family law, inheritance law, or law of retribution. Khatami alluded to the discrimination suffered by women due to "certain prejudices upheld under the pretext of religion."[50] However, activists were quick to acknowledge that as long as conservatives dominated the parliament and other important institutions, it would be impossible to effectively challenge laws based on an Islamic precedence.[51]

Nevertheless, Khatami continued to push for greater female integration. In 1998, he announced the establishment of the first women's police academy. The graduates would serve throughout regular police units. Ironically, these female graduates have become part and parcel of the government's contradictory approach to women. As women have become more active through protests and demonstrations, it is these policewomen who are dispatched to contain such unrest. Astutely, the regime has pitted women against women.[52]

Inspired by the growing momentum of this time, seven women attempted to run in the Assembly of Experts election in 1998. All of the candidates were rejected based upon their lack of religious qualifications.[53] At the same time, women participated in the municipal local council elections, held for the first time in February 1999. An estimated 5,000 women were approved by the Guardian Council to run for 220,000 positions throughout the country, and 300 of them won.[54]

In the legal sphere, female participation also increased. During President Rafsanjani's tenure, women served as consultants to clerical judges presiding over special clerical courts that address family issues.[55] In 1997, the head of the judiciary, Muhammad Yazdi, appointed Mahindokht Daoodi as undersecretary to the office responsible for the implementation of rulings issued by family courts. While the ban against women serving as judges was not lifted, women's judicial rights were extended to serve as investigative magistrates or consulting judges. At the same time, women were given licenses to open and head notary offices, a profession conventionally held by men.[56]

A consequence of Khatami's program of expanding civil society and freedom of expression was the blossoming of Iran's press. New publications—among them women's newspapers and magazines—briefly flourished. Faezeh Hashemi's newspaper *Zan* provided social and political news. *Huquq-e-Zanan,* (Women's Rights), was the first magazine devoted exclusively to female legal matters. While these publications thrived in the more open environment created by Khatami, they generated opposition from hard-liners. *Salam, Tous,* and *Jameeh* were closed down and Hashemi and *Zanan* publisher Shahla Sherkat summoned to answer charges of slander.[57]

Khatami's presidency also provided Iranians with a sense of freedom in the public sphere. Men and women experienced greater freedom of movement, to mingle on university campuses and throughout towns and parks. The streets became vibrant and colorful as women exchanged their traditional black veils for bright colored scarves. They also began wearing more makeup and exposing more skin. In reaction, the state returned the morals squads to the streets forcing women to adhere to conservative dress.[58]

Despite the creeping conservative backlash evidenced through the crackdowns and violence, the parliamentary elections of 2000 added greater momentum to the reform movement, as Khatami and the parliament pursued coordinated reform efforts. Indeed, this election was perceived to be a further threat to the conservative establishment as the parliament put forward legislation to liberalize the press, moderate women's rights, and protect civil society. In reaction, using institutional means, the Guardian Council blocked most reformist efforts. By the end of Khatami's first term as president, it was clear that the reform movement had limited legal and institutional power to affect political change. The conservatives had successfully used state institutions to resist these efforts. The frustration with the pace of change and Khatami's reluctance to lead the charge was reflected in the fact that although Khatami received 78 percent of the votes in the 2001 presidential elections, voter turnout declined.[59] Public political apathy had become a common reaction toward the reformist failures. For women, too, the lack of change in their legal status during Khatami's presidency led to the disenchantment of many secular and Islamist-educated activist women. Such sentiments facilitated trends such as lack of participation and even boycotting of the subsequent legislative and presidential elections after 2004. Female and public political apathy further enabled the elections of hard-line candidates. Conversely, other activists abandoned their cooperative efforts acknowledging that state sponsored piecemeal reform was too gradual and unfruitful.[60]

Khatami's second term as president was marked by an unimpeded period of conservative consolidation of power not seen since the aftermath of the revolution. This drive for power reached its apogee in 2004 when conservatives regained control of parliament using the institutional power of the Guardian Council to disqualify most reformist candidates. The council disqualified 3,600 reformist candidates—including 84 incumbents. Their goal of restricting reformist advances in an effort to reassert their power was effective. During the tenure of the new parliament, these parliamentarians reversed reformist legislation, advancing their own conservative mandate.

The combination of conservative tactics effectively weakened the momentum of reform. With Khatami unwilling and unable to directly challenge the conservative apparatus of the state, reform activists and their female counterparts slowly recognized that new pressure tactics were needed. Activist women in particular acknowledged that their years of collaboration and conciliation had yielded little gain in the fight for equal rights. Secular and some Islamist women in particular ceded from this sphere of female unity, deciding to confront the government more directly. Non-activist women became disenchanted by the political process and failed promises of the reformists, surrendering to trends of political apathy. A large percentage of Islamist women though, remained loyal to the hope of working within the system. Indeed, these women were also disappointed by the pace and prospect of change. However, unlike their secular counterparts, Islamist women retained a stake in the system because of their familial or professional ties and because of their continued loyalty to the Islamic system of government. So, while the former group sought to challenge the regime through direct confrontation on issues of equality, the latter continued to lobby and pressure the political elite and challenge patriarchal interpretations of Islam.[61]

Some scholars suggest that this rupture among women's groups took place around and after the Berlin Conference of 2000, sponsored by the Heinrich Böll Foundation, to assess Iran's parliamentary election and the reform movement's future. The conference drew controversy not only due to the list of participants, which included secular lawyer Mehrangiz Kar, reformist cleric Hassan Eshkevari, feminist publisher Shahla Lahiji, *Zanan* publisher Shahla Sherkat, and investigative journalist Akbar Ganji, but also because of the anti-regime comments and protests from Iranian exiles.[62] The conference was disrupted by Iranian exiles, one man stripped naked while a female in short sleeves danced around the room in a direct challenge to Islamic dress. After a videotape of the conference was broadcast repeatedly by Iranian state television, the Iranian judiciary declared the gathering anti-Islamic and arrests began, mostly on charges of "acting against national security." Penalties ranged from four to ten years in prison. After punishments were issued, secular female activists such as Kar criticized the reaction of her Islamic activist female contemporaries, who did not rise to their defense. It became clear that Sherkat did not display overt support for her colleague in criticizing the government in order to protect her publication rights in the tense atmosphere of the conservative backlash. Shahla Lahiji later commented, "This was an interesting experience that revealed the limits of our cooperation."[63] At the same time, though, this also highlighted the limitations of Islamist female strategies. By not supporting their secular counterparts and continuing their non-confrontational relationship with the state, these women were enabling the government crackdown on secular reformers to go unchallenged, thereby undermining their own reform goals.[64]

While there were clear rifts among women's groups during this period, one should not discount their continued cooperation. Indeed, both sides have been critical of the ideological differences separating them. At the same time, though, there is an acknowledgement that the pervasive issue of gender equality affects all Iranian women and is not limited to one group or one ideological vision. Moreover, as Islamist women were impacted by the marginalization policies of the state, evidenced most prominently at the electoral level as the number of women elected to parliament repeatedly declined since 2000, they have woken to the reality that greater cooperation was needed to combat patriarchal state policies. Faezeh Hashemi reflected on these problems, stating that: "I lost my seat because of party politics. My position as a woman who was involved in women's issues was completely ignored because my position as a member of the Majlis was seen as a political issue. Women's issues and political issues are interrelated and will continue to limit women until there is a reconciliation that women are not a political problem."[65]

For many, the disappointments of reform quickly translated into greater activism. The culminating effect of the reform movement, the political marginalization of the reformist leadership and the impact of growing female activism in the political, social, and religious arenas all contributed to greater gender consciousness throughout society. The effect was circular as activism amplified awareness and awareness augmented activism. Indeed, this consciousness did not develop in a vacuum but can be attributed to a myriad of social and political variables at work within Iranian society. "Movements . . . engage in a variety of other actions ranging from providing 'selective incentives' to members, building consensus among current or prospective supporters, lobbying and negotiating with authorities to challenging cultural codes through new religious or personal practices . . . movement leaders have become skilled at combining contention with participation in institutions."[66] This model is apropos in considering Iranian activism. The impact of female education has already been discussed, as has the impact of female support for the revolution and its consolidation. The government's contradictory policies with regards to women have undoubtedly helped women recognize the double standards rife throughout the Islamic system. However, one should not discount the impact of the growth of civil society witnessed in the media, including the Internet, the effect of parliamentary politics, the blossoming of NGOs, student activism in tandem with the reform movement, and the awarding of the Nobel Peace Prize in 2003 to human rights activist Shirin Ebadi—all of which contributed to greater female consciousness. Together these issues added new fuel to the female activist fire connecting action and reaction.

Parliament and Party Politics

The formation of political parties since the death of Khomeini has produced mixed results for female politicians. In the immediate aftermath of the revolution, over 100 political organizations emerged. This flourishing of political activity was perceived as a threat to the new republic. The Iranian constitution stipulates that the "formation of parties, societies, political or professional associations as well as religious societies, whether Islamic or pertaining to one of the recognized religious minorities, is permitted provided that they do not violate the principles of independence, freedom and national unity, the criteria of Islam or the basis of the Islamic Republic."[67] Yet Khomeini permitted a crackdown on parties, and in 1981 a new law was passed defining political parties and the scope of their activities. The new law made the creation of parties dependent on the acquisition of a permit from the Ministry of Interior. In 1987, Khamenei and Rafsanjani dissolved the clerically dominated Islamic Republic Party, whose mandate was directed toward institutionalizing the *velayat-e faqih*.[68] Since the 1997 presidential election, party organizations or factional groups began to play a more prominent role in electoral politics. "Quasi parties" such as the powerful conservative Militant Clergy Association (*Jame'eh-ye Rowhaniyat-e Mobarez*) initially created in 1936 in opposition to Reza Shah and the leftist Militant Clerics Society (*Majma-e Rowhaniyun-e Mobarez*) and the Executives of Construction Party (*Hezb e Kargozaran*), a group of moderate technocrats founded by officials of the Rafsanjani government were also active in parliamentary politics. Resembling parties, several were affiliated with or owned newspapers and hence had effective tools of public mobilization. The Islamic Iran Participation Front (*Jebheye Moshakerate Iran Islami*) was formed in 1998 as the principle reformist party.[69] President Ahmadinejad is a founding member of the Islamic Revolution Devotees Society (*Jamiyat-e Isargara-e Enghelab-e Islami*).

Among the principal limitations of party politics is their domination or affiliation with a political personality. As such, many factions have struggled to develop cogent, issue oriented political platforms. Moreover, politicians can be linked to more than one political group. Haleh Afshar has suggested that the absence of political parties has been a mixed blessing for women enabling them to campaign individually without platform constraints. However, the parochial competition has also forced women into factional groups to increase their support. Additionally the fluidity of factionalism in absence of defined political parties has also been a "mixed blessing" for politically active women who have been unconstrained by formal party politics but equally dependent on male benefactors.[70] At the same time factional considerations play an important role in committee appointments. Faezeh Hashemi commented, "I have repeatedly said that members of the Commission for Women were chosen according to factional considerations. The [dominant faction] wants those parliamentarians who are tame and passive, whereas those who represent different groups of women should have been chosen."[71]

In 2010, there were an estimated 240 registered political groups, 18 of which are women's organizations, these include Maryam Behrouzi's Zeinab Society, Azam Taleghani's WSIR, and the Forum of Reformist Women. Despite their Islamist leanings and loyalty to the Islamic Republic, these organizations have kept women's issues at the forefront of the national debate by advocating novel interpretations of Islamic law pertaining to women while also supporting female candidacy for parliament, president, and other elected office. Only two reformist parties, the Islamic Iran Participation Front (*Jebheye Moshakerate Iran Islami*) and Islamic Workers Party (*Anjoman-e Islami-e Kargaran*), have a women's wing or gender platform. The Participation Front has uniquely implemented a 30 percent quota for women in their decision-making bodies. Female members have created a coalition to encourage female political participation particularly in small towns and rural areas where the conservative parties have stronger support. They have also lobbied other parties to implement a quota system.[72] In general, most factional groups have been reluctant to develop a gender platform despite the importance of the female vote as revealed in the limited female victories in the presidential and parliamentary elections from 1997 to 2004.

The Sixth Majlis elected in 2000 was an important bastion of reformist influence and momentum. The members of parliament took office at the peak of the reformist movement's power with 13 female representatives.[73] They implemented some cosmetic but important gender related reforms within the Majlis, including removing the curtain that separated their dining area at parliament, and joined the men at a separate table in the corner. They also refused assigned seats for women in the assembly. Some of the new women deputies appeared in more informal headscarves and coats. Conservative members objected and demanded their dismissal, but the women argued that they had campaigned in this dress and people had voted for them in spite of their choice of dress. The energy of these women was important, as they linked the reform movement with women's activism.[74] Unlike their predecessors in the previous parliament, the new female deputies entered office boldly, declaring their intention to amend the laws in favor of women.[75] Along with male reformist allies, they formed a women's faction to push through their agenda.[76] Elaheh Koolaee, a female parliamentarian elected from Tehran, was among the most energetic and prominent members of the parliament. She wrote, "The Women's coalition of the Sixth Parliament took its job seriously. We worked hard to frame arguments in Islamic terminology ... to make a lasting impact on women's rights in Iran."[77] Their three-pronged strategy focused on the executive, judiciary, and legislative branch where parliamentarians made institutional appeals to reverse retrograde gender law. Within the executive, they pressured President Khatami to appoint female ministers to his second administration. They also lobbied for equal compensation for men and women. Discussions with judges and clerics were centered on reversing patriarchal interpretations of gender legislation and women parliamentarians focused on repealing both the law of retribution and death by stoning. These efforts proved unsuccessful though.[78] Part and parcel of the challenge for reformist female parliamentarians was convincing their male colleagues to support gender reform. Most of these men who were influenced by the combination of patriarchal Islamic norms and Iranian culture were unwilling to compromise on their values. Others considered women's issues to be secondary to larger economic policy concerns. Some reformist men though, did support their female colleagues and their legal initiatives. Only with their assistance were women able to redress gender reform.[79]

Legislatively, they focused on reversing laws related to inheritance, divorce, child custody, and insurance. Their principle effort was directed in support of the important UN Convention on the Elimination of Discrimination Against Women (CEDAW) of 1979, which Iran has never signed. Secular female activists were the initial proponents of CEDAW provisions as a means to legalizing improved women's rights. With time, the Convention had become an important initiative for all activists, as it was believed that if approved, it would strengthen women's rights through the elimination of discriminatory laws.[80] With increasing public pressure, the state officially considered the convention. The government debate pitted the parliament and president against the conservative organs of the state. In 1997, the High Council of Cultural Revolution reviewed and rejected the adoption of CEDAW by a majority vote. The Supreme Leader and other high-ranking clerics also assessed the Convention. They concluded, "Unless certain provisions were removed, the Convention's contents were in contradiction with Islamic laws."[81] In December 2001, Zahra Shojai stated that the Cabinet had approved Iran's joining CEDAW, providing that it did not contradict Islamic law. "As long as enforcement of the Convention's contents does not transgress the red line of religious principles, there is no reason for concern. Not only do we not stray from the demands of religion and allow women to enjoy the benefits and power contained in international documents, but at the same time, the government's credibility is saved in terms of its international responsibilities."[82] In a letter addressed to the parliament, Khatami declared that, "With the recommendation of the Foreign Ministry in a session held on [December 19, 2001], the government approved joining the Convention."[83] Proponents of the bill hoped that the ratification would further clarify the government's position with regards to women's rights.[84] With presidential approval, the women's faction succeeded in pushing CEDAW through the Cultural Affairs Committee of the Parliament. Opposition to CEDAW was considered inevitable as conservative clerics such as Ayatollahs Mazaheri and Makarem-e Shirazi had objected to Iran's joining of the convention due to its non-compliance with Shariah law. Other opponents to the bill suggested that CEDAW would pave the way for the separation of religion and politics confirming that religion is insufficient and inefficient in solving gender issues while also undermining the policies of Khomeini and the authority of the *velayat-e faqih*.[85]

After intervention by the Expediency Council, 16 of the 33 gender bills proposed by this parliament became law.[86] However, most of the liberal gender elements were removed. Among the legislation, there was included a bill calling for the removal of the education discrimination against women traveling abroad, another for amendments to the civil code to increase the minimum marriage age for girls from 9 to 13, and one to increase the age up to which mothers have custody rights of sons from 2 to 7. Those not supported included a proposal that Iran join CEDAW, a proposal to create a Majlis Commission to address issues relating to family, youth, and women, and a plan to give the right of residence and nationality to non-Iranian spouses of Iranian women.[87]

In December 2002, 11 of the women parliamentarians submitted a bill to the Majlis that would impose a moratorium on executions by stoning of women and men accused of engaging in extramarital or premarital sex.[88] Stoning and other forms of "Islamic punishment" are written into the 1995 penal code, and although their practice has not been routine, they have stood as a powerful emblem of the backwardness and violence of the Islamic Republic's legal system, both inside and outside Iran.[89] The bill was not approved, but shortly after the government held trade talks with the European Union later in the month, Hojjatoleslam Mohsen Gharavian, a leading figure in the conservative dominated judiciary, stated that "stoning has been provisionally suspended due to its negative effects." [90] This verbal commitment was not matched with legal changes, leaving application of the law unchanged.

Initially, the apparent moratorium was widely heralded as an important victory for human rights and women's rights. However, the judicial action forced women to take heed of the apparent limitations of their activism. Female activists recognized the confines of the parliamentary process where years of work to expand women's rights in other areas had been rendered moot by Guardian Council fiat. Female lobbying to end stoning was stonewalled until the state was spurred into action by international and domestic pressure. This process left women's rights activists with limited satisfaction in regard to the reformist era and in their own ability to force gender reform.[91]

In February 2004, the reformist ascendancy was dealt an electoral blow as conservative candidates regained control of parliament. Through the Guardian Council, thousands of candidates including 84 incumbents were disqualified. What ensued after a 26-day sit-in was the mass resignation of 124 parliamentarians who accused the government of an institutional takeover of parliament.[92] Among those who resigned was female parliamentarian, Fatemeh Haghighatjoo. Known as the *lion woman* for her courageous move as the youngest and first parliamentarian to resign, Haghighatjoo grew up in a traditional, devout, middle-class family that supported the revolution. Haghighatjoo was raised by her mother after her father died in an accident when she was 6. She observed the hijab even after she moved abroad in 2004. She became a student leader and was shaped by the political transformation experienced by students in the aftermath of the 1999 protests as she earned her university degree in psychology, and went on to study for a doctorate in counseling. In her resignation statement, she stated, "after 25 years, I now witness a fundamental departure of the rulers from the ideals of the revolution and Imam [Khomeini] ... with a 26-day sit-in we warned the heads of the system that a rogue group are slaughtering the nation's security and people's right to sovereignty ... They want people to be unable to choose their representatives directly, republicanism to cease, and the Islam of the Taliban to take primacy over pure Mohammadan Islam."[93] Haghighatjoo's speech earned her a 20-month prison sentence for misinterpreting the words of Ayatollah Khomeini and insulting the Supreme Leader and Guardian Council. Initially, Haghighatjoo showed little interest in women's issues seeking to represent both men and women equally. She opposed the formation of the Women's Faction, yet upon its establishment she became an active member. Additionally she was critical of Khatami for not appointing a female minister.[94] The irony is that she has become a foremost champion for gender equality.

The Seventh Majlis was dominated by a new class of conservatives bent on reviving the principles of the Iranian Revolution. Unlike their predecessors, the Seventh Majlis was not receptive to women's rights or the flourishing of civil society supported by reformists. A legislative backlash became inevitable. The first strike attacked both women and reformists in one move. An article in the right-wing newspaper *Jomhuri-yeh Eslami* (*Islamic Republic*) assailed women's rights groups and NGOs as agents of the West foreshadowing the new strategy of the conservative factions. What followed were a series of arrests designed to send targeted messages to the activist and reformist communities. Female activists such as Mahboubeh Abbasgholizadeh were among those charged. The message that civil society participants would no longer have a free voice and access to the political and public sphere was clear. The shift led women's rights activists to acknowledge that their limited gains would soon be reversed.[95]

The women of the Seventh Majlis promoted a conventional, traditional image for Iranian women.[96] Indeed, the ideological composition in parliament halted all progressive gender legislation. In this vein, they ignored and abandoned the legislation pursued by their reformist predecessors. The Zeinab Society, which had supported female candidates in the Fourth and Fifth parliaments, had sponsored the candidacy of 10 of the 12 women parliamentarians.[97] One elected representative, Fatemeh Aliya, spoke of polygamy as a blessing for women particularly in combating poverty and alleviating the plight of widows. Many defined themselves by criticizing the women of the previous Majlis for introducing bills defying the teachings of Islam, such as joining CEDAW or sending female students to study abroad.[98] When the Fourth Economic, Social, and Cultural Plan approved by the Sixth Majlis was recalled by the Seventh, the revisions included elimination of the pledge to maintain gender justice—a motion that received no objection from the female deputies.[99]

Communication and Media

Efforts against the passage of these bills, while obviously disappointing, had some positive effects. Most apparently, there was a more open debate in the media and the public regarding gender. Senior clerics were forced to discuss, comment on, and take positions on women's issues, thus involving society at large. Here the diffusive nature of the Shi'a establishment facilitated the activist cause as a range of views emerged from hard-line and moderate clerics. Moreover, the fact that women's issues became controversial and were debated publicly in the legislature, judiciary, and in the seminaries was a significant development, revealing the effectiveness of women's activism in influencing the public discourse.

Despite growing restrictions in the political sphere, women continued to rely on the media to publicize their efforts, draw support, and educate the populace. The number of women writers, novelists, journalists, publishers, and movie directors flourished. Women had begun to use the camera to highlight the mechanisms of patriarchal control and to demonstrate women's struggles against gender disparities. Their collective creative emphasis on women's legal and social problems and portrayal of women as active and courageous people with strong personalities brought more social awareness to gender issues. The important success of movies revealed that the urban population was indeed interested in more modern interpretations of gender questions. Rakhshan Bani-Etemad, Tahmineh Milani, Pouran Derakhshandeh, Manijeh Hekmat, Marziyeh Meshkini, Samira Makhmalbaf, and Nikki Karimi are the most recognized of these movie directors that addressed controversial issues of women's rights. But it is in the realm of literature where women have found their true voice. Some of these writers, such as Simin Daneshvar, Goli Taraqi, and Shahrnoush Parsipour, had started publishing prior to the revolution. Yet others, such as Qazaleh Alizadeh, Monirou Ravanipour, Fariba Vafi, Zoya Pirzad, Lili Farhadpour, Sepideh Shamlou, and Mahsa Moheb-Ali are among the many female authors who started writing from the 1990s onward. The aim of these novelists is to occupy the public space through written expression and to give greater visibility to women, their problems, and their struggles. In their literary works, women also deal with the issues of sexuality and the body that are usually considered to be taboo subjects and are prohibited in the movies.

During this period, the media became a direct vehicle of dissent for activists and reformists. Shifting tactics in response to a government crackdown and closure of the print media, activists used the Internet as a new vehicle of communication. With some 20 million people accessing the Internet, Iran has one of the biggest Internet communities in the Middle East. While the government or hard-line conservatives controlled much of the official media, for Iran's well-educated and inquisitive younger generation the Internet became the favored and most accessible way of communicating. Indeed, as suggested by Iranian and Islamic studies professor Babak Rahimi, "the Internet and in particular the blogsphere, have offered an alternative public discourse to the state-controlled media and Internet outlets."[100]

Early on, the Internet was an unregulated outlet in Iran. Under both the Rafsanjani and early Khatami administrations, the government encouraged and sponsored expansion of the Internet even using the Internet as a tool of Islamic propagation. Conservative authorities concentrated their censorship on the print media and TV, not officially sanctioning Internet websites or filtering content until 2003.

While politically sensitive websites were banned as early as 2001, official response to the Internet was generally muted at first, mainly because the government was using the Internet for its own purposes. From clerics in the holy city of Qom to President Mahmoud Ahmadinejad, Iran's myriad of authorities and religious leaders set up personal websites to promote their ideas and communicate with the public. Moreover, the government has tried to cultivate its image as one that encourages new modern, technology. Censoring of online content became commonplace only because of the growing threat of the reform movement.

Pressure came to a head in 2000 as conservatives sought to constrain the reformist press in another effort to contain their advances. Using the 1986 press law, media outlets that were deemed to have violated Islamic principles and the national civil codes were banned. Such restrictions were then extended and applied to the World Wide Web.[101] As many reformist, dissident, and female activists began to rely on the Internet as an outlet for their discontent, it became clear that a new battleground was being exploited at the government's expense. Harsh criticism of Khamenei and other authorities was circulated online, rousing the interest and attention of the Western media. Students opposed to the regime used the Internet as a mobilizing link. Particularly during the summer of 1999, the Internet played a critical communication role, providing students with an outlet to set up meetings, organize demonstrations, and generate and exchange ideas. An excerpt from editor and pro-democracy journalist Bijan Saffari's weblog highlighted in Narsin Alavi's *We Are Iran* poignantly demonstrated the importance of the Internet as a means of free expression and communication. "There are those such as Abtahi [Iranian Parliamentary ex-Vice President Muhammad Ali Abtahi] who have called our virtual community too political and have put that we should use weblogs for their intended use . . . that is to say, for clichéd daily diaries. . . . So what if we use our blogs in ways not intended for or defined during the distant conception of this media. . . . At a time when our society is deprived of its rightful free means of communication, and our newspapers are being closed down one by one—with writers and journalist in the corners of our jails . . . the only realm that can safeguard and shoulder the responsibility of free speech is the weblog."[102]

And despite all the blocks, filtering, and other restrictions, blogging became increasingly popular. According to reports, Iran is home to the world's second largest blogging community with some 65,000 bloggers. Many avoid discussion of political issues, focusing instead on social, art, family, and other neutral topics. But the popularity of the Internet, especially among the youth, and its impact on society has aroused concern. Some Iranian leaders have warned that the West is trying to provoke a "Velvet Revolution" in Iran using the Internet. Alongside Iranian music, news, and political websites, the regime has made efforts to block access to popular foreign sites such as YouTube and Facebook.[103]

For women in particular, the Internet has also facilitated greater activism, communication and cooperation. Female bloggers, both secular and conservative, use the Internet as a tool of expression, publicizing details of their lives and voicing their opinions about the political system and religious interpretation of their legal and social rights. The Internet has also enabled greater international access and publicity for campaigns against the government, as well as allowed for news of arrests and detentions of activists. Most important has been the greater communication with the international community that has brought media and political attention to these growing movements.

The Student Network

Students have played an integral role in both supporting the revolution and in challenging the status quo since 1979. The student movement was active in the 1970s embracing Marxist, Islamist, and revolutionary discourse in support of the overthrow of the shah. In the aftermath of the revolution university campuses were hotbeds of radical activity providing fertile ground for Islamic student groups who cleansed campuses of dissident faculty and students. Indeed, the Student Followers of the Imam Line were responsible for the November 1979 take over of the U.S. embassy. The state affiliated Office of Consolidation and Unity of Islamic Associations (*Daftare Tahkim va Vahdat-e Anjomanha-ye Islami*) supported the government Islamization initiative. Tahkime Vahdat was the operating arm of official politics, enforcing the administration's policies throughout Iran's universities. In the group's mission statement, Tahkime Vahdat was committed to the *velayat-e faqih*. The students of Tahkime Vahdat explicitly thought of themselves as protectors of and protected by the Supreme Leader. As the revolutionary fervor began to subside and the war with Iraq ended in 1988, students embraced the realities of Islamic education, leading to a transformation of student activism.

In the 1990s, students distanced themselves from the ideological orientations of the past, "becom[ing] ordinary . . . they lived their lives, studied, worked and worried about their future."[104] In this period, student activism was propelled by a variety of sources including urbanization, demographic shifts, and increased levels of education combined with growing disappointment with the culturally and economically restrictive environment. Students embraced the reflective discourse of intellectuals and reformers such as Abdol Karim Soroush and were inspired by the growing discourse of reformism. Students overwhelmingly supported the election of Khatami in 1997 becoming a critical constituency for the president. They embraced Khatami's promises of civil society and democracy in the hope of enjoying new freedom and opportunity. Many students campaigned for Khatami and his reformist party in the presidential and parliamentary elections hopeful that reformism would lead to political and social transformations.[105] The trends of cultural liberalization, the growth of the press, and reformism converged to give more momentum to the student movement.

Students, though, were the first of Khatami's constituency to cede support. The July 1999 Tehran University protests, which ignited a chain of protests throughout the country where students were repressed, arrested, beaten, and killed, proved to be a turning point for students who recognized early on that reformists had limited means to change the political system due to the constitutional constraints on the offices of the presidency and parliament. No longer willing to provide legitimacy to the system, student groups and organizations under the umbrella of Tahkime Vahdat began to criticize the state and the constitution, taking an independent stance. The protests were the first massive outpouring since the revolution.[106] The government backlash that ensued would be one of many confrontations between the state and the students. In 2002, students again took to the streets protesting the death sentence of university lecturer Hashem Aghajari for blasphemy. In 2003, they protested against government plans to privatize universities.

Tahkime Vahdat was divided over boycotting the 2005 elections. Needless to say, the election of President Ahmadinejad fueled tensions between the state and student groups. Students were not excluded from the repressive conservative strike at civil society and reformist groups. As universities had again become harbingers of anti-government support, student activism was directed against the president and his policies. In repeated student demonstrations in December 2006 and 2007, students denounced the president and the Islamic system of government and many were arrested and detained. In reaction, Ahmadinejad instituted a purge of the university system removing faculty and students who were disloyal to the regime while promoting state allegiance and patronage through the revival of the student basij militias designed to monitor students and professors.

Tahkime Vahdat also evolved during this period. The association provided a bridge linking civic groups, including those representing women, labor, minorities, and teachers. Through its alumni organization *Advar*, the group united former students and leaders of the past giving more strength to membership and student activism. Tahkime Vahdat's evolution, organizational structure, and culture has been reflective of Iran's patriarchal society. Only in 2007 was a woman, Bahareh Hedayat, elected to the Central Council leadership. The student organization tried to justify its lack of female representatives within its leadership by pointing to a lack of interest among female students, conservative attitudes of women, or a lack of competence necessary for such positions. Ali Afshari political secretary and former board member explained: "From its inception, Tahkime Vahdat was a male-dominated group. The few women there had low-profile positions and did not participate actively in the Central Council's activities. This context defined Tahkime Vahdat's view towards its female members. Also, until the second half of the 1990s, gender-segregation dominated Tahkime Vahdat. Local offices had a women's branch and their activities were managed separately. Later, Tahkime Vahdat changed this arrangement."[107]

Former parliamentarian Fatemeh Haghighatjoo, in her student days was a member of the Central Council of Tahkime Vahdat, was propelled into activism and reformist politics through her student activities. She identified two main reasons for the lack of female participation in the organization: "Women, in general assemblies and various offices, had always been in the minority and this minority was not active. I was elected as a board member thanks to my activities in the Islamic Student

Organization of Tarbiat Moallem University. At the time, the Supreme Leader's liaison in the university had abandoned the university's Islamic student organization. I actively opposed this decision and succeeded in reviving the organization. Having demonstrated my potential, I was elected to two terms as a Tahkime Vahdat board member. The environment in the university was not conducive to female students becoming active and visible in student organization activities. Also, in a male-dominated place, men have fewer competitors."[108]

In 2006, a women's commission was established with Hedayat elected to its head. The women's commission was to limit its activities to Tehran, however, Hedayat discovered that student organizations around the country had also followed suit implementing their own female commissions. Hedayat reflected on some of the challenges to women and cooperation with the female activists in an interview in *Zanestan* stating,

> The women's movement must be supported by the student movement—specifically Tahkime Vahdat—to bring about a mutual dialog of understanding. If people from the women's movement think that we still have a long way to go, they should take action themselves. I think it is each group's duty to do its own part in establishing a discourse of women's issues. Even I, a politically active student, cannot find you [the women's movement] easily. If you think that we should join forces at some point, you should convince me to accept your manifesto and disseminate it. I, as a politically-active student who monitors civil society, have no reason to not accept the additional responsibility of becoming involved with social movements like that of women. I think the discernable gap between the student movement and the women's movements needs to be closed. Social movements should understand that political parties can not be eliminated. Politically active people should also understand how useful social movements are and work directly with them. Were any political parties present at this rally last June to support those women? The political parties just issued statements stating that the police should not have assaulted women; no one discussed the merits of the demands of the women's movement. As it happens, parties closer to the student movement—specifically Tahkime Vahdat—are parties which could interact more with the women's movement. There should be a direct dialogue between these parties and the women's movement. As a member of the Women's Commission, I can help establish this link, but the women's movement should identify the issues to be discussed.[109]

While this link is nascent, female activists and students have continued to cooperate in creating awareness on issues of civil society human and women's rights.

Among the important functions of the student movement is its role as a link to other social movements including the workers' and women's movement. Women's activism has benefited in particular from its connections to students who have taken their first experiences of student activism and transferred them to women's issues.

Grassroots organizations, NGOs, and gender awareness campaigns have also made use of this network of political and socially active youth.[110] "The initial experience of student activism gave a voice to many Iranian students during the reform period," stated one female secular activist who was a member of the student organization of Amir Kabir University.[111] She described her politicization as women's activists and students worked on the political campaigns of 2005—each lobbying for their own political and social objectives. She said that despite cooperation, "divisions between the two groups exist and are primarily methodological as women are forced to confront the patriarchy and Shariah law while students are focused on political issues and democratic change."[112]

The Ebadi Effect

The awarding of the 2003 Nobel Peace Prize to Shirin Ebadi, a female Iranian lawyer, university professor, and human rights advocate, added further momentum to the growing women's movement. The award signaled a striking success for Ebadi's persistent efforts in the past quarter century to champion the rights of women and children. This recognition was significant not only for Ebadi's work, but also in bringing greater attention to her causes of human and women's rights—the latter of which is integral to the former. Ebadi is credited with being a driving force behind the reform of family laws in Iran by seeking changes in divorce and inheritance legislation. But she has also come into conflict with the law in Iran and jailed on numerous occasions.[113]

Ebadi graduated from law school at the University of Tehran in 1969, and spent the next decade rising through the ranks as one of Iran's youngest female judges. The Islamic Revolution quickly halted Ebadi's ambitions, demoting her and all other female judges to secretarial positions. In this vein, Ebadi rechanneled her energies on activism. In 1993, she was reinstated as an attorney spending the past decade and a half promoting human rights in Iran—through efforts and lobbying both inside and outside of the courtroom.

Ebadi has dedicated her career to protecting Iranian dissidents and other victims of human rights abuses. She is perhaps best known in Iran for her work on behalf of the family of political reformers Dariush and Parvaneh Forouhar, who were stabbed to death in their home in 1998. Ebadi was able to help connect the murders to the Iranian Ministry of Intelligence; the head of the agency, Saeed Emami, committed suicide before he could be formally charged.

In all her roles, she has sought to interpret and harmonize Islam with Western thought, particularly focusing on the ideals of human rights, democracy, freedom of speech, and religious freedom. This stance has often put her in opposition to the conservative elements in the government and has led to her repeated imprisonment. But as she said, "Any person who pursues human rights in Iran must live with fear from birth to death, but I have learned to overcome my fear."[114]

Despite intimidation and harassment, Ebadi has continued her fight for human rights. As she said at the conclusion of her Nobel acceptance speech, "There is no other way except by understanding and putting into practice every human right for all mankind, irrespective of race, gender, faith, nationality, or social status." She also argues that "with a correct interpretation of Islam we can have equal rights for women," adding that women in Iran "haven't had the opportunity . . . to demonstrate their capabilities." Expounding on women's activism she has said, "This is the reason the feminist movement in Iran has become very strong. These women want equal rights. Small steps have been taken for equality, but these steps are not satisfying for Iranian women. They want absolute equality of rights."[115]

After the Nobel award ceremony, a crowd of 10,000 greeted Ebadi in Tehran. Her victory and the publicity surrounding her work though has been a thorn in the side of the conservative establishment. In fact, much of the conservative press ignored or criticized the award. Even reformist president Khatami did not greet Ebadi upon her return to Tehran. However, Ebadi has continued to champion human and women's rights, lending her voice and energy to bring global attention to these important issues in Iran.

"Women have been motivated by Ebadi and her prize," commented a women's rights activist. "She has shown women that challenging the system can yield success not only for her personally but also for her causes."[116] Many of the female activists I interviewed both Islamist and secular drew attention to Ebadi as a major source of influence. Her incremental efforts inspired many activists that through perseverance they could affect gender reform.[117] Ebadi was also instrumental to the female parliamentarians of the sixth Majlis providing innovative interpretations to Islamic law on gender issues.[118] In a *Zanan* interview in 2003, Ebadi spoke of the challenges to women stating, "One of the major problems for Iranian women is the inappropriate law that damages their identity. The other is the lack of government support. In my opinion, it is useless to give women the right to divorce if we don't give them widowhood insurance. Repeatedly, I have come across women who had the right to divorce but could not use this right because they did not have the necessary financial means. . . . and the law says that girls—just like boys—must study. But we see that the number of girls who are allowed to study is less. As a matter of fact, women's problems stem from cultural, executive, and legal issues."[119] Yet, Ebadi maintains that "I am not the leader of the women's movement and do not know any such person. The beauty of the women's movement is that it is spontaneous, self-reliant and doesn't have any such leader. As a result it will not fail."[120] Drawing inspiration from Ebadi's commitment to Iran and human and women's rights in the face of intimidation and government pressure, particularly since the election of Ahmadinejad, many activists have become more dedicated. In fact, since Ebadi was awarded the Nobel Prize, women's activism experienced a major transition away from cooperation with the government, and toward greater confrontation.[121]

Shifting Ground and Turning Corners

The disillusionment with the reform movement fostered a shift in female and political activism. Most notably, the change in tactics of female activism has facilitated a greater challenge to the regime. The decisive turn was evidenced on the March 8, 2003, public gathering of women in commemoration of International Women's Day. Women came together then for the first time since the 1980 protests to demand equal rights—a move that was interpreted as a direct shift in activist strategy. As a first step, in March 2000, activist women commemorated International Women's Day at the Women's Cultural Center, a non-governmental organization.[122] The event was a watershed, as women's groups shifted to public claim making. This change was also designed to mobilize non-activist women through increased public awareness. Ritualization through demonstrations and commemorations of women's events became part of the two-pronged strategy to increase gender consciousness. For secular women activists, this day served as a dividing line, recognizing that the past efforts of institutional and conciliatory lobbying were no longer viable.[123] Activists also acknowledged that after years of cooperation and collaboration rallying for reform from within, it had become clear that the regime intended to obstruct any change, particularly that which threatened the conservative bastion of power. Moreover, another more important realization was made recognizing that should change in fact be implemented it would come from the regime itself and not as a direct response to popular lobbying efforts.[124] What would ensue in the aftermath of this strategic reorientation was a new and direct method of activism consisting of claim making, gender awareness, and lobbying through targeted campaigns.

At the end of the reform period, it became clear to many activists that it was the Islamic Republic's constitution that was the primary obstacle to gender reform. The constitution did not explicitly provide for equality of rights between men and women, unlike that evidenced in CEDAW. Rather, Article 20 of the constitution stated that men and women "enjoy equal protection of the law . . . in conformity with Islamic criteria" while at the same time Article 21 stipulated that "the government must ensure the rights of women in all respects, in conformity with Islamic criteria."[125] Most of the personal status laws that discriminate against women in marriage, divorce, inheritance, and child custody, however, derive their legitimacy from the clause effectively subordinating women's rights to the state's interpretation of Islamic law. Drawing from the years of collaboration in the first two decades of Islamic government had revealed the futility of activist efforts. While offering new interpretations of Islamic jurisprudence that encourage gender equality has promoted innovative public discussion, limited legal change was evidenced as the Guardian Council and judiciary consistently propagated their own concept of gender legislation. Disheartened by the failures of the reformist parliament to achieve legal reform, many secular and Islamist activist women supported a boycott of the 2005 presidential elections—and instead advanced a new strategy—a gendered critique of the constitution.[126]

In advance of the June 2005 presidential elections women took to the streets. Seeking to broadcast their dissatisfaction with the gender segregation policies of the state, hundreds of activist women protested. Inevitably, the demonstration was met with a forceful response from the state particularly since one week earlier women had also challenged the three-decade ban on women watching soccer games at the stadium. Women forced themselves into the stadium to watch the Iran-Bahrain game foreshadowing yet another looming conflict for the state. The significance according to Parastoo Dokouhaki, a blogger, activist, and organizer is that "Today most of the group experienced their most serious example of gender discrimination. But we achieved something bigger than just going to the stadium—gender consciousness."[127]

The decisive shift in marking the new activist strategy was a sit-in that took place on June 12, 2005. By exploiting the state's relaxation of restrictions during the election season, the informal network of women's NGOs and independent associations decided to assert their grievances and demands through civil disobedience. In a protest declaration, members of NGOs, male and female student activists, journalists, and bloggers added their signatures and brought attention to the declaration demanding that the nation's laws secure women's "fundamental and equal rights" and comply with international conventions such as CEDAW. Until the government complied with these demands, the activists stated that they would continue a campaign of peaceful protest.[128] Shirin Ebadi, who was abroad at the time, announced her support for the sit in criticizing the "unequal treatment of half of the Iranian population." The petition bearing Ebadi's name also featured the signatures of four other Nobel Peace Prize recipients, including Archbishop Desmond Tutu.

The June 2005 protest was a definitive turning point for female activism where new activist strategies and patterns were established.[129] Firstly, despite the lack of government approval for the sit-in, participation was high. Notwithstanding the encirclement by police officers, the incidence of violence was limited as the police opted for a strategy of containment of the demonstration. The participation and perceived success of the rally gave momentum to female activism such that from 2005 to 2009 activism would reach its highest peak in three decades. Secondly, a tactic of non-violent confrontation with the state was established. Noushin Ahmadi Khorasani, one of the principal secular activists and organizers wrote a protest song set to an old Joan Baez tune especially for the sit-in. Copies of the lyrics and protest slogans were distributed throughout the crowd of women, who enthusiastically chanted and sang throughout the one-hour event. The support of Simin Behbahani, Iran's most famous living woman poet and longtime supporter of women's rights participation and a message from Ebadi strengthened the resolve of the activists.[130] Finally and most importantly, the activist message was not limited to a certain class or age group of women but rather extended to *all* Iranian women. They declared that Iranian women of all classes, ages, and religious background shared: "The constitution's belittlement of women as citizens and active social participants has blocked their ability to secure their rights," their statement read. "The potential for reactionary movements and political extremism has forced the women's movement to face the reality that under the current state of affairs, seeking civil justice from the constitution and protesting the breach of women's rights of citizenship can be an effective step toward achieving democracy, peace and self-determination of the citizenry." Organizers stressed that legal reform was the absolute precondition for securing the end goal. In the words of a slogan repeatedly chanted at the sit-in: "Equal rights is our minimum demand."[131]

To the dismay of many female activists though, politically active and elected Islamist women including the female members of the reformist parties who had served in the Sixth Majlis were absent from the demonstrations. Their participation would have required them to break from their male counterparts who, for the most part, have privately and publicly opposed the women's movement's confrontational stance toward the constitution.[132] Maintaining political cooperation with the political institutions and Islamic system was considered more important for these women who sought to maintain open lines of political communication and pressure with on the government. Retaining the support of their male counterparts, particularly those in the reformist camp has been challenging for Islamist women. Many reformist men often suggest that the struggle for democracy has priority over the struggle for women's rights.[133] In retaliation to this collaborative thinking, the declaration also stated that: "Democracy cannot be achieved without freedom and equal rights."[134] Azam Taleghani was also not in attendance at the event. In solidarity with her female activists, she had held a much smaller sit-in protesting women's exclusion from the presidential races held earlier in the month. But she like most Islamist women was against the strategy of direct confrontation.[135] Despite the disunity among women's groups on how to achieve their goals, this gathering pointed to a newfound accord among activist women where they acknowledged the failures of the past, turning a new page towards the future. From here, activists increased their collaboration strategizing on new methods to redress gender issues.

In advance of the 2005 presidential elections, many women's activists along with disaffected students, intellectuals and prominent reformist politicians planned to boycott the elections. For many the idea of a boycott was the only means to register their dissatisfaction with the state and its policies of reformist suppression. Since the revolution, the state made use of high public turnouts and participation in Friday prayers, public events, and elections to highlight the public's endorsement for clerical rule. While attendance at prayer ceremonies grew ever more sparse through the years, turnout in presidential elections remained high. Through non-participation activists hoped to whittle down the state's legitimacy.

A secondary consequence of the Khatami era took the form of an "individualist revolt" experienced predominantly among the urban and middle- to upper-class youth. This defection from political participation was the culmination of years of political and social frustration where the young had limited outlets of expression. For many, reformist politics and promises offered prospects of political change, economic opportunity, and social liberalization. The failures of the movement to translate their pledges into reality resulted in a social backlash among the youth. Pardis Mahdavi documented this recoiling through the rise of sexual promiscuity, drug use, and challenge of Islamic and social mores. Her analysis concludes that this social revolution is a "new act of political rebellion where the state regulates morality and social behavior, fashion and sexuality in extreme ways . . . therefore when a large portion of the population (the young people) is enacting a counter-revolution by creating its own moral values, the very fabric of the regime and what it stands for are threatened."[136] Publicly visible changes such as the pervasiveness of plastic surgery among women and men, provocative hairstyles and hair color, excessive attention to dress, superficial status symbols, and physical perfection have been part of this social transformation. In private homes, I have witnessed, similar to Mahdavi, wild sexual behavior and pervasive drug use, not seen so openly in the West. I have often contemplated the difference between native middle and upper middle class Iranian society where families and children are more liberal and permissive to the Iranians who grew up in the diaspora and are now seemingly more stagnant. The latter has sustained much of the pre-revolutionary tradition and culture in terms of social customs while the former has evolved due to restrictive life in the Islamic Republic. The notoriety of this social and cultural shift among the youth has also created a backlash as many young men have expressed disdain for the sexual promiscuity evidenced among young, urban women.[137] Many young men I spoke with lamented that they could not no longer find "a good Iranian girl to settle down with." In general, marriage is no longer enforced upon the youth but has become an individual choice. The youth and particularly women are marrying later than previous generations. The average age of female marriage was 19.5 years in 1976 and was 22.5 years in 2006.[138] Moreover, the divorce rate had climbed ten percent.[139] Prostitution, drug addiction, and suicide have also become more pervasive in light of the national economic impediments. A 2005 study conducted by the United Nations concluded that Iran had the highest drug addiction rate in the world at 2.8 percent of the population.[140] Temporary marriage (sigheh) reinforced by the state in 2007 has become a legal means to prostitution.[141] In 2000, the average suicide rate was 25 to 30 percent per 100,000.[142] This culture clash has also forced changes in the political sphere evidenced in the 2005 presidential elections where presidential candidates Hashemi Rafsanjani and Muhammad Bagher Qalibaf tried to curry favor with this constituency using techno music, CDs, and young female supporters to display their progressive positions.

The reformist era provided a space for civil society and particularly women to study, organize, develop a gender analysis, and create a vocabulary of resistance. Building on the institutional, political, socioeconomic, and religious gains of the past decade, women were further motivated and encouraged by the open social spaces and opportunities presented by the reform movement. The trickle down effect of socioeconomic changes and political stagnation had impacted activist and non-activist women alike. The byproduct of this period was a merger of increased gender consciousness and political disillusionment. For many activists, this consciousness provided new forums of mobilization. The disappointment with reform also facilitated the development of targeted gender activism. For the disenchanted youth though many sought refuge through individual expression. Despite reformist failures it was amidst the factional discord of Khatami's two presidential terms that the political and social landscape opened allowing for greater discourse and criticism. As stated by Ziba Mir Hosseini, "a burgeoning, if fragile civil society had emerged."[143] Ahmadinejad's election also added to the contentious mix. The resulting outgrowth led to a shift in strategy away from collaboration toward confrontation. Indeed, this move galvanized activist women. While political and religious differences and regime pressures prevented the establishment of a disciplined and organized women's front, the drive for equal rights and the greater visibility of women in the public sphere increasingly brought elements of the women's movement together. The effect of the 2005 sit-in was a declaration that the system's fundamental legal structure precluded the possibility of realizing women's full rights, and by extension meaningful democracy—ultimately challenging the regime. At the same time, the close of the Khatami era foreshadowed increased repression for activists and women, as the domestic political dynamics would continue to color women's advances. It was also clear that a new era of activism and conflict with the regime would also be on the horizon.

Notes

1. Michael Hillmann. *A Lonely Woman: Forugh Farrokhzad and Her Poetry*, 1987.

2. Ali Gheisari and Vali Nasr, *Democracy in Iran: History and the Quest for Liberty,* 2006.

3. Haleh Esfandiari, "The Politics of the 'Women's Question' in the Islamic Republic, 1979–1999," in *Iran at the Crossroads*, edited by John L. Esposito and R.K. Ramazani, 2001.

4. *Iran News,* June 2, 1997.

5. Ibid. For more on Khatami, his election and tenure as president see David Menashri's, *Post Revolutionary Politics in Iran: Religion, Society and Power*, 2001.

6. Ibid., 82–3.

7. Tarrow, 2002, 71.

8. David Menashri, *Post Revolutionary Politics in Iran: Religion, Society and Power*, 2001, 80.

9. Ibid., 87.

10. Tehran TV, May 10, 1997.

11. Said Amir Arjomand, *After Khomeini: Iran Under his Successors,*" 2009, 94.

12. Personal interview with female university student, Tehran February 23, 2007.

13. *Zanan,* April 1997, 4–8.

14. *Islamic Republic News Agency,* February 22, 1997.

15. Fars News Agency, July 4, 2005.

16. Esfandiari, "The Politics of the 'Women's Question' in the Islamic Republic, 1979–1999," 2001, 86.

17. *Zanan,* April 1997, 4–8.

18. Esfandiari, "The Politics of the 'Women's Question' in the Islamic Republic, 1979–1999," 2001, 87.

19. Arjomand, *After Khomeini: Iran Under his Successors,* 2009, 92.

20. Menashri, *Post Revolutionary Politics*, 2001, 88.

21. Arjomand, *After Khomeini,* 2009, 94–6.

22. Ibid.,120–2.

23. Menashri, *Post Revolutionary Politics*, 2001, 134.

24. Ali Gheissari and Vali Nasr, *Democracy in Iran: History and the Quest for Liberty*, 2006, 135. See also, Nazanin Shahrokni, "Voroode Zanan be Shoraye Islami Shahr va Roosta," [Women are Represented in the Islamic City and Village Councils,] *Zanan*, 54, 10–14.

25. Asghar Schirazi, *The Constitution of Iran: Politics and the State in the Islamic Republic*, 1998, 151.

26. Quoted in Menashri, *Post Revolutionary Politics*, 2001, 96.

27. Mohammad Ghouchani, "Nasle Dovvome Sepah Dar Rah" [The Coming of the Second Generation of the Guards], *Shargh*, April 12, 2005.

28. Menashri, *Post Revolutionary Politics*, 2001, 138.

29. Ibid., 142–7.

30. *Keyhan International,* June 17, 1998.

31. Menashiri, *Post Revolutionary Politics*, 2001, 141.

32. *Jomhuri-ye Islami,* July 19, 1999.

33. Tehran TV, May 23, 1998.

34. Quoted in Nasr and Gheissari, 2006, 140.

35. Elaheh Koolaee, "Women in Public Sphere, a Case Study of Islamic Republic of Iran," *Journal of Faculty of Law & Political Science*, Tehran University, No. 61, Fall 2001, 228–32.

36. *Iran*, March 17, 1997.

37. *Zanan*, August 1997.

38. Ebtekar, an immunologist, is most widely known as Mary, who served as the official translator for the Iranian students during the 1979 hostage crisis.

39. Parastoo Dokouhaki, "Hasht Sale Kar Baraye Zanan: Dar Miyane Afkare Sonnati va Shoarhaye Modern" [The Results of Eight Years Work for Women: In the Midst of Traditional Thought and Modern Slogans], *Zanan* 121, 15–21. This article includes great detail on the budget and outlook of the Center for Women's Participation.

40. Ibid.

41. Ibid.

42. Esfandiari, "The Politics of the 'Women's Question' in the Islamic Republic, 1979–1999," 2001, 88.

43. Parastoo Dokouhaki, "Hasht Sale Kar Baraye Zanan: Dar Miyane Afkare Sonnati va Shoarhay-e Modern" [The Results of Eight Years Work for Women: In the Midst of Traditional Thought and Modern Slogans], *Zanan* 121, 15–21.

44. Quoted in Parvin Paidar, "Gender of Democracy: The Encounter Between Feminism and Reformism in Contemporary Iran," United Nations Research Institute for Social Development, Democracy, Governance and Human Rights, Program Paper Number 6, October 2001, 11.

45. Esfandiari, "The Politics of the 'Women's Question' in the Islamic Republic, 1979–1999," 2001, 88.

46. Nazanin Shahrokni, "Majles Baraye Zanan Che Kar Kard?" [What Has the Parliament Done for Women," *Zanan* 41, 2–4.

47. Ibid.

48. "Jostojoo dar Parvandehye Zanane Namayandeh Majlis 5" [Investigating the Background of the Women of the 5th Majlis], *Zanan* 60, 3–7.

49. Esfandiari, 2001, 91.

50. Quoted in Esfandiari, 2001, 92. Only two of the fourteen female parliamentarians voted against these two measures.

51. Nazanin Shahrokni, "Majles Baraye Zanan Che Kar Kard?" [What Has the Parliament Done for Women," *Zanan* 41, 2–4.

52. Noushin Tarighi, "Khabardar be Jaye Khod: Zanane Police be Peesh," [Women Police Officers Advance,] *Zanan* 95, 2–7.

53. Esfandiari, "The Politics of the 'Women's Question' in the Islamic Republic, 1979–1999," 2001, 89.

54. Ziba Mir-Hosseini, "Women and Elections in the Islamic Republic of Iran," *Iranmania*, February 1, 2000.

55. Mina Yadigar Azadi, "Ghezavat-e Zan" [Women's Judgement], *Zanan* 4, 20–26.

56. Ibid.

57. Gholam Khiabany and Annabelle Srebeney, "The Women's Press in Contemporary Iran: Engendering the Public Sphere," in *Women and Media in the Middle East*, Naomi Sakr (ed.), 2004.

58. Azadeh Moaveni, *Lipstick Jihad: A Memoir of Growing up Iranian in America and American in Iran*, 2005, 161.

59. Esfandiari, 2001, 94.

60. Personal interview with female journalist, Tehran, May 12, 2008.

61. Personal interviews with secular and Islamist activists, journalists, and former politicians, Tehran, May 12, 14, and 21, 2007.

62. Lily Faradpour, *Zanan-e Berlin* [Women of Berlin], 2000.

63. Gholam Khiabany and Annabelle Srebeney, "The Women's Press in Contemporary Iran," in *Women and Media in the Middle East*, Naomi Sakr (ed.), 2004.

64. "Na Goftehaee az Conference Berlin" [The Berlin Conference: What Remained Unsaid,] *Zanan* 63, 3–5.

65. Quoted in Elaheh Rostami-Povey, "Feminist Contestations of Institutional Domains in Iran," *Feminist Review*, Vol. 69, No. 1, 2001, 51.

66. Tarrow, 2002, 5.

67. Asghar Schirazi. *The Constitution of Iran: Politics and the State in the Islamic Republic*, 1998, 125.

68. Mehdi Moslem, *Factional Politics in Post Khomeini Iran*, 2002, 60–1.

69. Stephen Fairbanks, "Theocracy Versus Democracy: Iran Consider Political Parties," *Middle East Journal*, 52, 1, 1998, 17–21.

70. Haleh Afshar, "Competing Interests: Democracy, Islamification and Women Politicians in Iran," *Women, Politics and Change*, K. Ross (ed.), 2002, 112.

71. Afarin Shahriari, "Cheezhaee Ke Dar Majlis Didam Ta'asofbar Ast," [What I Have Seen in the Parliament is Deplorable,] *Zanan* 56, [awaiting year] 4–5.

72. Homa Hoodfar and Shadi Sadr, "Can Women Act as Agents of a Democratization of Theocracy in Iran?" United Nations Research Institute for Social Development, October 2009, 17.

73. Parastoo Dokouhaki, "Dar Kaheshe Taedad Zanan-e Namayandeh-ye Majlis Ghorohaye Siyasi Moghaserand," [Reduction in the Number of Female Parliamentarians Is Due to Political Groups,] *Zanan*, 64, 2–5.

74. Elaheh Koolaee, ""Yeh Negah Jenah Zanan Majlis Sheeshom," [A Glance at Women's Faction Performance in 6th Parliament,] *Shargh*, Nos. 215 and 223, 2002, 3.

75. "In Yazdah Zan Keystand?" [Who are these 11 women?], *Zanan*, 64, 6–9.

76. Ziba Mir-Hosseini, "Fatemeh Haghighatjoo and the Sixth Majles: A Woman in Her Own Right," *Middle East Research and Information Project*, 2003, 233.

77. Elaheh Koolaee, "The Prospects for Democracy: Women Reformists in the Iranian Parliament, in *On Shifting Ground: Muslim Women in a Global Era* edited by Fereshteh Nouaie-Simone, New York: The Feminist Press at CUNY, 2005, 212.

78. Shahla Sherkat, "Eslahtalaban va Sokhangooee az Jense Digar: Gofto Goo ba Dr. Elaheh Koolaee" [Reformists and a Discussion on the Other Sex: A Conversation with Dr. Elaheh Koolaee], *Zanan*, 120.

79. Farideh Farhi, "Jonbeshe Zanan va Mardane Eslahtalab" ("The Women's Movement and the Reformist Men"), *Zanan*, May 2003, www.zanan.co.ir/culture/000047.html. Accessed November 27, 2008.

80. Parvin Ardalan, "Joining on the Condition to Discriminate," *Bad Jens,* May 22, 2002.

81. *Azad,* February 6, 2002.

82. *Aftab-e Yazd,* January 27, 2002.

83. *Zanan,* 84, 18.

84. Zahra Ebrahimi, "Hoghughe Zanan va Rahe Doshvar Peyvastan be Convension," [Women's Rights and the Difficult Path of Joining the Convention,] *Zanan* 102, 22–27.

85. Ibid.

86. Ziba Mir-Hosseini, "Fatemeh Haghighatjoo and the Sixth Majles: A Woman in Her Own Right," *Middle East Report,* 233.

87. Elaheh Koolaee, "The Prospects for Democracy: Women Reformists in the Iranian Parliament," in *On Shifting Ground: Muslim Women in a Global Era* edited by Fereshteh Nouaie-Simone, 2005, 212–3.

88. Shadi Sadr. "Mane'e Sang Sar ra Ghanooni Konid" [Abolishing Stoning Should Become Law] *Zanan* 134, 26–34.

89. Many Muslim jurists in Iran are of the opinion that while stoning is considered a form of Islamic punishment, the conditions under which it is used as a method of punishment are rare. Because of the large burden of proof needed to reach a guilty sentence of adultery, its penalty is hardly ever applicable. Furthermore, while legally on the books, because of the enormity of both domestic and international controversy and outcry over stoning in the early years of the Islamic republic, the government placed official moratoriums on the punishment and, as a result, it was rarely practiced. Nevertheless, much of the public was outraged that such a cruel ritual became instituted in Iranian laws. In 2002, Iran's judiciary indicated that stoning would no longer be practiced in Iran. Yet, it has continued under President Ahmadinejad. In 2006, in reaction to two stonings in Mashad, the "Stop Stoning Forever" campaign was launched. This campaign has not limited its work to Iran but merged with international groups to bring greater attention to their cause. In 2008, Iran's judiciary once again committed to stop stoning as a form of punishment and the parliament introduced a change to the penal code where stoning would be more difficult to implement. In May 2009, the judicial commission in the parliament had further amended the bill to eliminate stoning. For more see the campaign website http://www.meydaan.com/english/default.aspx Accessed September 12, 2008. The movie *The Stoning of Soraya M* has brought international attention to this issue.

90. Mahsa Sherkarloo, "Iranian Women Take on the Constitution," *Middle East Reports Information Project,* July 21, 2005.

91. Personal interviews with female activist and journalist, Washington DC, November 12, 2007, and Tehran, February 14, 2007.

92. Zahra Ebrahimi, "Zanan, Tahason, Estefa," [Women, Sit-in, Resignation,] *Zanan* 106, 2–10.

93. Zahra Ebrahimi, "Fatemeh Haghighatjoo: Aval" [Fatemeh Haghighatjoo, The First!] *Zanan* 107, 8–10.

94. Ibid.

95. Personal interview with secular activist, Tehran, April 28, 2008.

96. "One Month with Women in the Parliament," *Zanan* 133, 20–3.

97. Homa Hoodfar and Shadi Sadr, "Can Women Act as Agents of a Democratization of Theocracy in Iran?" United Nations Research Institute for Social Development, October 2009, 21.

98. Elham Gheytanchi, "Women against Women: Women in Iran's Seventh parliament," *TheIranian.com,* November 5, 2004.

99. "Omit the Gender, Justice and its Reflections," *Reyhaneh,* No. 8, 2005, 177–88.

100. Babak Rahimi, "Politics of the Internet in Iran," in *Media, Culture and Society in Iran: Living with Globalization and the Iranian State,* Mehdi Semati (ed.), 2008, 37.

101. Ibid.

102. Nasrin Alavi, *We are Iran: The Persian Blogs,* 2005, 5.

103. Ibid., 10–12.

104. Asef Bayat, "A Women's Non Movement: What It Means to be a Women's Activist in an Islamic State," *Comparative Studies of South Asia, Africa and the Middle East,* Vol. 27, No.1, 2007, 69.

105. Mohammad Tahavori, "The Evolution of Iran's Student Movement: An Interview with Abdollah Momeni," *www.gozaar.org,* July 1, 2007, accessed March 6, 2010.

106. Mehrdad Mashayeki, "The Revival of the Student Movement in Post-Revolutionary Iran," *International Journal of Politics, Culture and Society,* Vol. 15, No. 2, 2001, 297.

107. Quoted in Fariba Davoodi Mohajer, "Challenging Tradition: Women Inside Iran's Student Organizations," www.gozaar.org, February 1, 2007.

108. Ibid.

109. Farnaz Seyfi, ""Rally on June 12, 2006 Was an Opportunity for the Women's Commission,"*www.zanestan.net,* December 18, 2006.

110. Personal interviews with secular and Islamist women, Tehran, April 12, 14, and 27, 2008.

111. Personal interview with female secular activist and university student, April 25, 2008.

112. Ibid.

113. Fereshteh Nouaie-Simone, "Shirin Ebadi: A Perspective on Women's Rights in the Context of Human Rights," in *On Shifting Ground: Muslim Women in a Global Era,* Fereshteh Nouaie-Simone (ed.), 2005.

114. Shirin Ebadi, *Iran Awakening: A Memoir of Revolution and Hope,* 2006.

115. Ibid.

116. Brian Schott, "Iran Awakening: An Interview with Shirin Ebadi," *New America Media,* May 20, 2006.

117. Personal interview with female activist and journalist, Washington, D.C., February 17, 2008 and secular activist Tehran, April 27, 2008.

118. Personal interview with female activist and journalist, Washington, D.C., February 17, 2008.

119. Shahla Sherkat, "Talkhy Siyasat, Shirin Solh: Dar Goftogoo ba Shrini Ebadi," [Bitterness of Politics, Sweetness of Peace: An Interview with Shirin Ebadi], *Zanan* 105, 6–19.

120. Ibid.

121. Personal interview with female activist and journalist, Washington, D.C., February 17, 2008.

122. Fariba Davoudi Mohajer, "From New York to Tehran: International Women's Day," www.gozaar.org, March 6, 2009.

123. Personal interview with secular female activist, Tehran, April 27, 2008.

124. Personal interview with female blogger and journalist, London, April 23, 2006.

125. Asghar Schirazi. *The Constitution of Iran: Politics and the State in the Islamic Republic* 1998, 139–42.

126. Personal interview with former female parliamentarian, New Haven, Connecticut, February 16, 2006.

127. Personal interview with female blogger and journalist, London, April 23, 2006.

128. Mahsa Sherkarloo, "Iranian Women Take on the Constitution," *Middle East Research Information Project,* July 21, 2005, 4.

129. Personal interview with female activist, Tehran, February 2007.

130. Sherkarloo, "Iranian Women Take on the Constitution," 2005, 5.

131. Ibid., 5.

132. Personal interview with Islamist activist and former female politician, Tehran, April 27, 2008.

133. Ibid.

134. Shekarloo, "Iranian Women Take on the Constitution," 2005, 6.

135. Ibid.

136. Mahdavi, 2008 , 300.

137. Personal interviews with young Iranian men Tehran, February 12, 17, 2007.

138. Iran statistics center, National yearbook 2006.

139. Ibid.

140. United Nations World Drug Report, 2005.

141. Afary, 2008, 364.

142. Ibid., 366.

143. Ziba Mir-Hosseini, "Is Time on Iranian Women Protesters Side?" *Middle East Research and Information Project*, June 16, 2006.

7

Ahmadinejad: Claim Making and Stagnating Reform

With soft words
I draw a childhood dream
On a nascent memory.
I write in peace
So that the silky dream of the notebook
Will not tear apart.
But the blooming words declare
The storm with bravery.

Sylvanna Salmanpour[1]

In a much-hailed public move, Mahmoud Ahmadinejad announced in April 2006 that Iranian women should be permitted to attend football matches. Banned from Iranian stadiums since the revolution, women were shocked that one of their many activist demands was arbitrarily being granted by the Islamic state. Ahmadinejad couched his new pronouncement as an effort to "improve soccer-watching manners and promote a healthy atmosphere" in the stadium.[2] Public and government reaction to this change of policy was widespread, as analysts both international and domestic speculated that the president's strategy had little to do with gender issues and rather was part and parcel of his attempts to deflect attention from Iran's controversial nuclear program, ailing economy, and looming international isolation.

While Ahmadinejad had earned a reputation as a provocateur, his political moves were more often than not carefully calculated political advances. Indeed, women activists have been rallying against the female soccer ban for decades. In 2004, women launched a targeted campaign known as the White Scarf Campaign (also known as the Women for Public Access to Stadium Campaign) to redress gender segregation and sport issues.[3] The subject drew much international attention, as female demonstrations against the ban were widely reported and a film on the subject, Jafar Panahi's *Offside,* about a group of women who dress as men so they can enter football stadiums, won the Silver Bear award at the Berlin Film Festival. Despite such attention, it is unlikely that public pressure influenced Ahmadinejad. Instead, his decision was a reflection of the president's populist political style. Seeking to garner more female political support, Ahmadinejad has attempted to distinguish himself from his rigid political contemporaries in defense of a popular social issue. Such acquiescence toward women pointed to a repeated government trend of offering piecemeal concessions to win female support.

Iranian women were caught off guard by the president's symbolic gesture. Indeed, amidst the conservative political revival that culminated with Ahmadinejad's presidential election in June 2005, most activists expected and predicted a dramatic rollback of women's rights and advances. Ahmadinejad's campaign foreshadowed renewed social restrictions for women, including more stringent veiling requirements and gender segregation, although gender was scarcely mentioned as part of Ahmadinejad's political platform. Unlike his electoral rivals, Ahmadinejad did not even try to curry favor with women. He justified this stating, "We are all part of a nation and should not have a gender gaze."[4]

Initially these restrictions were slow to be implemented, leaving women both surprised and optimistic about the prospects for change. Eventually, though, the feared limitations surfaced, and women found themselves confronting the same challenges and contradictory policies experienced with past administrations. Despite Ahmadinejad's headline-grabbing pronouncement permitting women to reenter football stadiums, this decision was quickly quashed through Iran's consensus-driven decision making system. Disapproval from the clerical authorities in Qom and from the Supreme Leader himself forced the president to renege on his promise. A number of ayatollahs issued fatwas stating that "looking at the uncovered bodies of unrelated members of the opposite sex is sexually stimulating and the mixing of men and women leads to social corruption."[5] For women, the decision confirmed that gender politics would be dominated by the arbitrary nature of politics as usual. The outcome reflected the need to push ahead with new strategies and tactics. Ahmadinejad's gender policies coupled with the fallout of Iran's dubious 2009 presidential election would set the stage for renewed momentum toward female activism.

It was President Muhammad Khatami's 1997 landslide election that drew worldwide attention to the factional divide and debates taking place within the Islamic Republic of Iran. Khatami and his allies brought to the fore a domestic push for reform with new emphasis on democratic principles of civil society, pluralism, and human rights. While popular among the predominantly youthful population, the politics of change led to a domestic backlash against the reform movement. Conservatives seeking to preserve the structure of the Islamic Republic and with it their place within the system implemented a strategy to systematically marginalize and limit reformist politicians access to the institutional levers of power. Indeed, reformists were overwhelmingly and repeatedly defeated in the parliamentary elections of February 2004, in the presidential election of June 2005 and in the disputed presidential elections of June 2009.

While the reform movement had galvanized Iranian society, so too had it shocked the conservative political establishment. Realizing the fragility of their monopoly of power and institutions, conservative politicians—particularly those surrounding and supporting Supreme Leader Khamenei—began to strike back against reformist political gains. Finding allies in the Islamic Republic Guards Corps (*Sepahe Pasdaran*) and other ideological supporters of the revolution, Khamenei consolidated his power by surrounding himself with a cadre of loyalists willing to adhere to the revolutionary creed that would protect and preserve the umbilical cord of the Islamic Republic. From the rank and file of this devoted group came the son of a blacksmith, Mahmoud Ahmadinejad, the ever-devoted revolutionary stalwart.[6]

Ahmadinejad's 2005 election dramatically altered Iran's domestic and international dynamic. After eliminating six candidates in a first round of voting, Ahmadinejad defied predictions of a close run-off contest against born-again moderate ex-President Hashemi Rafsanjani, trouncing him with 62 percent of votes. Ahmadinejad canvassed on a conservative Islamic platform promising to embark on a campaign against corruption and the Western decadence that had yet again come to pervade Iranian society. Seeking to revive Ayatollah Khomeini's revolutionary doctrine, Ahmadinejad drew strength from the regime's ideological foundations promising that a return to the traditional ideology of the revolution would provide Iranians with redemption and hope for a new future.

Unlike Ahmadinejad's opponents, the president was a child of the Iranian Revolution. Having fought ardently in the Iran-Iraq war as a member of the Revolutionary Guards, the president rose to the ranks of the elite *Qods* (Jerusalem) forces, and participated in targeted assassinations. The impact of the war in particular had fostered a new mind-set among this younger generation who were devout, ideological, and contemptuous of the veterans of the revolution. In April 2003, Ahmadinejad was elected mayor of Tehran. As a hard-line conservative and Revolutionary Guard veteran, he mounted a surprisingly strong challenge with a populist message aimed at the economically disadvantaged. Ahmadinejad capitalized on his Spartan and Islamist image to draw support from a disillusioned population.

While there is much speculation around the degree of political influence and even corruption that enabled Ahmadinejad's election, there can be no doubt that upon election, Ahmadinejad had significant popular support. Unlike Khatami's election that was propelled by urban, youthful, and secular supporters, Ahmadinejad generally received support from a diverse and discrete constituency of provincial, rural, and devout enthusiasts. He also had the backing of a group of younger, second-generation revolutionary elites known as the *Abadgaran*, (Developers,) who were dominant in the Iranian parliament. His presidential campaign focused on poverty, social justice, and the redistribution of wealth inside Iran. Indeed, Ahmadinejad canvassed as a humble religious man. When compared to the frivolities and corruption associated with his opponent Hashemi Rafsanjani, many Iranians were attracted to Ahmadinejad's appeal. After his election as mayor in 2003, Ahmadinejad continued to live in a lower-middle class neighborhood in South Tehran where he shopped among the masses and drove his own aged car. His religious allure coupled with his promises of providing for the *mosta'zafin,* or dispossessed members of society, resonated loudly with many Iranians who felt that the revolution had neglected to provide the promised economic munificence. To charm this large portion of the populace, Ahmadinejad revived populist politics promising to "return oil money to the people's tables." With an additional pledge to tackle corruption, Ahmadinejad offered the hope of economic relief and reinforcements—a much-needed diet after eight years of inflated, failed promises of democracy and civil society which fell miles short of facilitating political, social, or economic change. The people's choice of Ahmadinejad reflected both the growing trend of political apathy and the imperative of economic necessity.

Despite this conservative political resurgence witnessed by Ahmadinejad's stunning 2005 electoral victory, factional disunity continued to be rife. The conservative establishment did not wholly embrace the new president. Moreover, during the first term of his leadership, corruption levels heightened and the economy spiraled downward. The president, while supporting the conservative ascendancy and ideological rigidity, also proved to be unpredictable on the public stage, particularly in the foreign policy realm. Seeking to roll back Khatami's conciliatory diplomatic approach, principally with regards to Iran's nuclear program, Ahmadinejad pursued a confrontational and defiant stand, withdrawing from the nuclear negotiation process—a move that resulted in three United Nations Security Council resolutions against Iran, including widespread sanctions and economic and financial isolation. Furthermore, he shocked the international community with his aggressive anti-Semitic rhetoric towards Israel. While these moves were championed in Arab capitals, where the "street" applauded Ahmadinejad's confrontational challenge to the West, in Tehran the president earned the ire of many detractors—both conservative and reformist—who feared he had made a mockery of Iran abroad. In addition to losing the support of many in the clerical leadership, he also lost much of his base.[7] As a reaction, conservative groups split into two factions—the United Principalist Front that continued to defend and support the president and the Broad Principalist Coalition represented by Ali Larijani, the former nuclear negotiator and current speaker of the parliament. The latter, dominated by old guard conservatives, contested Ahmadinejad's confrontational foreign policy and expansionary economic measures accusing the president of tarnishing the government's standing.

Notwithstanding the seething attacks against the president's foreign policy pronouncements, Ahmadinejad also met significant criticism for his domestic policies, particularly related to his economic plans. Initially, soaring oil revenues helped Ahmadinejad distribute patronage and financial subsidies with government measures such as cheap loans for small businesses, as well as the establishment of a "Love Fund" to assist young men and women defray the cost of marriage. He traveled around the country approving construction projects and distributing largesse. This lavish spending was responsible for increasing the double-digit inflation rate, causing concerns among politicians and economists that his economic policies coupled with his hard-line stance on the nuclear dispute and approach to foreign policy would inflict long-term damage to the country. Some economists argued that while the country's economy was being pressured externally by sanctions, the government was spending money as though there were an abundance of resources. With inflation rapidly approaching critical levels, economists and politicians began to sound the alarms. The country's leading economists, who numerous times had condemned the president's inflationary programs, publicly criticized Ahmadinejad. A 2008 letter addressed to the president accused Ahmadinejad of being responsible for "meager economic growth, widespread jobless rate, chronic and double-digit inflation, crisis in capital markets, government's expansionary budget, disturbed interaction with the world, [along with] inequity and poverty [that] have combined with the global economic downturn to leave undeniably big impacts on exports and imports."[8] With the world's fourth-largest oil reserves and second-largest natural gas reserves, the government is highly dependent on energy resources. The decline in oil prices inevitably added more pain to Iran's rising inflation and unemployment rates.[9]

In the midst of these shortfalls, the government was burdened by a whirlwind of activism and dissent evidenced through strikes, protests, and demonstrations. Economic inequity became an agent of discord. In response, the Iranian labor movement became increasingly active. Textile workers in Isfahan, teachers in Tehran, bakery workers in Kurdistan, and Haft Tapeh sugarcane workers in Khuzestan walked off their jobs in 2008 and 2009. The most significant and visible challenge came from the Vahed bus company in Tehran. Under the leadership of Mansour Ossanlou, these drivers struggled to form the Islamic Republic's first independent trade union. The government tried to contain the impact of this movement, imprisoning Ossanlou and much of Vahed's leadership, but the trend of labor strife continued to spread. After a prolonged strike over unpaid wages and working conditions, Haft Tapeh workers in Khuzestan followed suit forming an independent union. In November 2008, bazaar merchants around the country, which have traditionally supported the regime and were instrumental during the revolution, went on strike in protest of a proposed government value-added tax. Like workers, merchants have also suffered from the growing economic crisis, leading to increased discontent. Regime officials have acknowledged the danger of an independent labor power base evident in the heavy-handed response to union activity.[10]

At the same time, ethnic violence and disruption also became more pronounced. Iran is home to a myriad of ethnic and religious minorities who, since the revolution, have suffered at the mercy of the central government. Such ethnic unrest is located primarily in the Arab-dominated Khuzestan province in the southwest and in the Kurdish region in the northwest. Iran's diverse ethnic minorities include Arabs, Azeris, Baluch, Kurds, and Turkmans. These groups harbor irredentist dreams and have never embraced the regime's particular brand of Islamic revolution. Iran's Persian-dominated culture and language perpetuate a sense of discrimination—professionally, socially, and economically. And the minority groups have been largely neglected by the government's mostly urban-based development initiatives. In Iran's strained domestic environment, social and economic tensions among minorities have been rising. Since the summer of 2005, Kurdish unrest—propelled by the 2003 Iraq War and feelings of solidarity with Iraqi Kurdistan—increased, partly in the hope that more attention would be given to local development and political representation. Kurdish activists comprise the largest group of dissidents operating in Iran. In the southwestern city of Ahvaz in Khuzestan province, rioting and bombings have led to clashes with security forces, along with arrests. Khuzestan, located on the Iran-Iraq border, is home to most of Iran's ethnic Arab population.[11] The Sunni minority in Sistan-Baluchistan province near the Pakistani border—an impoverished area, and also a smuggling crossroads—agitated against the government as well, forming the Baluch group *Jundallah*, also known as God's Soldiers, or the People's Resistance Movement of Iran. Jundallah has been responsible for numerous attacks on Iranian security forces.[12]

This ongoing domestic strife must also be placed in the context of Iran's geostrategic alignment and tense relationship with the United States. At the forefront of the issues affecting Iranian politics is Tehran's tumultuous relationship with Washington. United States–Iranian relations, hostile for 32 years, have been on a fast-paced collision course since the United States launched its "war on terror" in response to the terrorist attacks of September 11, 2001. Washington has considered Tehran a challenge to its Middle East interests. Tehran stands accused of maintaining financial and military links to Lebanon's Hezbollah, Palestinian Hamas, and Shi'a groups in Iraq, while also promoting Iranian interests in Afghanistan. Its clandestine nuclear energy program has earned the ire of the international community. Its opposition to the state of Israel is yet another issue straining relations.[13]

At the advent of the war on terror, Iran and the United States engaged in several cooperative military and political endeavors. Iran was among the few countries that lauded the American campaign against the fundamentalist Taliban in 2001. Indeed, the Taliban's radical Salafist interpretation of Islam is shunned in Iran. Iran, which shares a border with Afghanistan, has struggled to contain the flow of refugees and drugs coming through this porous frontier. In 1998, tensions reached new heights as the Iranian regime mobilized its troops on the border in retaliation for the murder of nine Iranian diplomats that occurred during the Taliban's takeover of Mazar-i-Sharif. Despite Iranian efforts of collaboration in the war against the Taliban, the Bush administration as part of its democracy agenda in the Middle East lumped Iran in as part of the infamous "axis of evil"—a move that led to the abrupt termination of this short-lived U.S.-Iranian cooperation. With the outset of the war in Iraq, relations soured further as Tehran felt threatened by an increasing encirclement of American troops. During the eight-year tenure of the George W. Bush administration, Washington implemented a strategy of applying economic, political, and military pressure in the hope of moderating the Iranian threat. In response, Tehran seized on America's criticism and menacing rhetoric as justification for its aggressive strategy of domestic and international confrontation.[14]

At the same time, American troops in Iraq and Afghanistan were deployed around Iranian territory to the north, south, east, and west—too close for Iranian comfort. American troops in Iraq were also building bases in close proximity to the Iranian border. U.S. aircraft carriers in the Persian Gulf coupled with verbal threats from Washington lent credence to rumors that a "surgical" military strike could one day become a reality. The Bush administration's repeated statements that "all options are on the table" were taken by the regime at face value, and have contributed to Iran's hostile posturing. Tehran has increased its hostile rhetoric as well as attempted to prepare for any attack scenario.[15]

Equally troubling for Tehran has been Washington's democracy promotion program. The State Department requested $75 million, although $63 million was allocated, for 2007 and expanded its request for 2008 to $109 million for efforts to stimulate domestic change in Iran through civil society initiatives. These efforts included promotion of free expression and women's rights and funding for broadcasting services. Similar to American efforts during the Cold War, this American strategy was directed toward promoting civil society in Iran. These initiatives were ill received in Tehran and perceived as unmistakable attempts at regime change, further exacerbating the security concerns that linger in the clerical mind-set.[16] The Bush administration in its public statements repeatedly distinguished between the Iranian regime and the Iranian population. But it was not evident that U.S. policies benefited the Iranian people. On the contrary, a direct correlation was observed between American investment in democracy projects and the increased repression in Iran. Tehran successfully turned the tables on Washington, capitalizing on the possibility of U.S. infiltration to justify its purging of dissidents.

In the name of national security, Tehran initiated a clampdown that has undermined the operations of political, opposition, and nongovernmental organizations. New censorship laws prohibited journalists from writing on public security, oil price increases, new international sanctions, inflation, civil society movements, or negotiations with the United States over Iraq. A multitude of reformist newspapers and websites were closed. Further, the 2007 detention of four Iranian-Americans with ties to the United States think tanks and foreign news outlets drew international attention and condemnation. Although the detained scholars were released after a number of months, moves such as this—along with the arrests of students, professors, scholars, women activists, trade unionists, and journalists—sent clear signals that the door to political openness and freedom of expression evidenced during the reformist apogee were closed.

Government elites were not excluded from the onslaught of repression. In May 2006, Hossein Mousavian, the regime's former nuclear negotiator under Khatami, was arrested on espionage charges. He had played a central role in talks that saw Iran strike a deal with Europe, under which it agreed to suspend its uranium enrichment activities. At the time of his arrest, Mousavian was accused of exchanging information with foreigners. The regime, by going after one of its own, revealed its paranoia. Mousavian was among the long list of elites, journalists, academics, students, and activists arrested as part of the campaign to silence dissent. Officials accused those arrested of fomenting a "soft revolution" against the Islamic government. Tehran claimed that the Bush Administration's funds for democracy promotion were used to create a network that would force the regime into political change and ultimately facilitate a "velvet" or "color" revolution as was seen in Georgia and Ukraine.[17]

A morality drive complemented the political repression. In the past, the government targeted political activists but avoided antagonizing the general population. In June 2007, however, the regime extended its security operations to a new frontier by initiating a widespread crackdown on "immoral" behavior. Over the summer, the crackdown led to the temporary detainment of an estimated 150,000 people for various "social vices." Women were advised to adjust clothing that revealed too much of their hair or female contours. Young men were cautioned for wearing short-sleeved shirts or for their provocative immodest hairstyles. The public morality clampdown came amid a broader law-and-order offensive, where the government aimed at increasing domestic security. Large numbers of "hooligans" were arrested in police raids. In the past years, executions dramatically increased—some public—for crimes including murder, rape, armed robbery, and drug trafficking. Ultimately, external security threats provided the justification for rampant popular suppression.[18] In 2009, Iran executed 338 people, the second highest in the world after China.

Women were not excluded from this crackdown. It was expected by many female activists that the cumulative effect of their efforts coupled with the endogenous and exogenous threats facing the regime would result in a backlash.[19] While the general female population has been subjected to more stringent vigilance in response to the government "morality" campaign, more specifically, the government has targeted activist women and particularly secular ones who initiated and actively participated in a direct confrontation with the government—through collaborative, organized women's activism. Through arrests and detentions many secular women and female oriented NGOs, journals, and organizations were removed from public access. As a consequence, female activism relocated into the virtual world of the Internet.

The November 2008 American election of Barack Hussein Obama marginally eased tensions with Iran as Obama offered "to extend a hand if you unclench your fist"[20] in open engagement with the Iranian regime. Obama went further than any American president offering direct engagement without preconditions even disavowing regime change efforts. He furthered with Persian New Year greetings in March 2009 calling for "engagement that is honest and based on mutual respect."[21] Obama's election and proposition posed a distinct challenge for the Iranian regime that had relied on anti-American antagonism to bolster its rhetoric and international and domestic policy positions. Iranians, like their Arab neighbors, were enamored and encouraged by Obama's new policy direction. Iranians creatively suggested that "Oo-ba-mast or he is with us"—the literal translation of Obama's name. President Ahmadinejad congratulated Obama on his election and the Iranian policy institutions declared their intent to partake in negotiations.[22] This dramatic shift in American policy led to the first high-level bilateral talks in Geneva in October 2009 over Iran's nuclear program. The outcome of this meeting however was muted as Iran stalled on nuclear concessions, a move that has led to increased Western pressure and sanctions on the regime. Yet, the Iranian response toward the Obama Administration and their continued obstructionism over their nuclear program is ultimately a reflection of the mounting tensions of domestic politics—that have only become more polarized during the tenure of President Ahmadinejad.

Strategy Shifts—The One Million Signatures Campaign

While women's activism shifted in focus and method during this decisive time of Ahmadinejad's first administration, gaps dividing women continued to exist, if not widen. In fact, as evidenced during the early days of the revolution, the state made every effort to divide women against themselves. Again, the division between Islamist and secular women was brought to the fore, facilitating "their further autonomization and radicalization."[23] In 2006, Noushin Ahmadi-Khorasani, Parvin Ardalan and Mansoureh Shoja'i of the Women's Cultural Center, part of the younger generation of secular feminists strategically distanced themselves from elite and state institutions. They called upon women like themselves to embrace a new strategy of challenging the state through demonstrations, non-violent tactics, and direct confrontation on gender issues. Their intent was to extend beyond their activist contemporaries to reach non-activist women, whose large scale access and mobilization would force the elite to acknowledge the public endorsement for reform of gender based legislation. In effect, by drawing larger numbers to support their efforts, they could pressure the regime collaboratively to revise the constitution and remove the unequal gender provision that legalized gender discrimination.[24]

Islamist activists including Shahla Sherkat, editor of *Zanan*, as well as politically active reformist women initially disapproved of these new tactics.[25] They argued that the price of such acts of defiance would outweigh the results. More importantly, they insisted that such confrontation would not increase popular support for women's activism, but instead would result in the alienation of non-activist women, who would be targeted by the regime for their participation. This cautious approach flamed tensions between the two groups as secular activists accused Islamist women of allying with the political system and supporting the piecemeal change in gender laws through gradual lobbying.[26] In repeated media interviews and in my private ones, activist women have acknowledged the ongoing ideological and strategic divisions among women as among the principle obstacles to their activism.

These divisions would not impede the total effect of female activism though. In particular, the former group would come to accept the diversity of views, ideologies, and politics among women and would make use of the multiplicity of opinions to expand the focus of their mandate. To increase the base of female support, these women activists reoriented their objectives from issue-based gender reform to encompass grievances affecting *all* women, regardless of religious, political, ideological, ethnic social, and class backgrounds. Moves such as this were meant to further enshrine the egalitarian nature of women's activism.[27] Constituent and issue-based gender reform had proved to be a limited strategy—one that was dependent on the political will of politicians rather than a legally sanctioned process. Real gender reform was predicated on changing the fundamental gender bias institutionalized in the Constitution. Only with constitutionally certified equality would women succeed in amending, reinterpreting, and combating the patriarchal constructs in Islamic law. It was also recognized that gender activism and reform of gender laws were intimately linked to the issues pursued by other social and civil society movements. No group could afford isolation. Thus, a universal message applying to all women was essential to 1) facilitate greater cooperation among women's and activist groups, 2) pursue direct issue-based campaigns, and 3) lobby for constitutional revisions and the acceptance of CEDAW—moves that would impact all society as a whole.[28]

After numerous demonstrations protesting unequal gender laws and efforts to urge the state to accept CEDAW, secular women activists recognized that repeated state disruptions of their peaceful public demonstrations called for a change of tactic. Initial cooperation bore fruit in the 2004 and 2005 protests, where women actively agitated against discriminatory laws. At the June 12, 2006 anniversary of past female demonstrations, women again gathered in solidarity.[29] An educational booklet entitled "The Effect of Laws on Women's Lives" was distributed detailing the legal discrimination against Iranian women. As stated by one female activist, "For the first time, it seemed that the world was watching women's rights activists and civil society in Iran, and we felt at the time that we should come together to work collaboratively to address women's issues on a broader scale. We came together in the form of a Forum, or *Hamanidishi Zanan*, where women's rights activists met to discuss issues of importance to women and approaches toward joint strategies for addressing women's concerns."[30] From there, women's activists collaborated from June to August 2006 concluding that a grassroots operation would be an effective means to achieve their objective. On August 27, 2006, secular activists launched the One Million Signatures Campaign Demanding Changes to Discriminatory Laws. Modeled after a similar effort in Morocco, the aim of the Campaign is to collect one million signatures on a petition protesting the lack of gender equality in Iran.[31] The Campaign began with 54 organizers and was launched with 118 signatures supporting legislative reform.[32]

The principle objective was to collect one million signatures on a petition that will ultimately be submitted to the Majlis calling for the revision of discriminatory laws against women such as those relating to divorce, child custody, inheritance rights, equal testimony in court, among others. The intention of this endeavor was designed to address the social, cultural, political, religious, and economic inequities with regards to women.[33] While the petition was the ultimate goal, the initiative was also directed toward changing discriminatory gender laws, empowering women in society, developing profound gender consciousness, and confronting the sources of the social and legal discrimination against women—both in public and private domains.[34]

Since its inception, the Campaign has been oriented to challenging laws and restrictions against women. Because of the unique methods and all-embracing objectives, activists received strong support from youth, students, workers, human rights and civil society activists as well as Islamist and politically active women, both inside and outside of the country. Through female participation and collaboration, activists advocated gender reform particularly relating to issues of child custody, marriage and divorce terms, inheritance allocation, resistance to male aggression, protection against stoning, polygamy, equal compensation for injury or death, equal testimony rights in court, and equal opportunity issues. Rather than relegating such decisions to the patriarchal Islamic interpretations of Shariah law, activists have argued in favor of collaborative forums of discussion where women partake in effecting change.[35] Ideological and political affiliations have not divided women in this forum as the foundation of the Campaign is directed toward the "minimum demand of gender equality."

I conducted a number of interviews with Campaign members who were willing and eager to discuss Campaign activities and reiterated the methods and motivation of the organization. One young activist's participation came to the Campaign by way of her journey to Tehran from Mashad. She had been raised in a middle-class religious family, but her decision to go to Tehran and pursue women's studies, like many young secular Campaign activists, slowly facilitated her evolution from Islamist to secularist activism. After university, she had pursued a career in journalism. Her combined exposure to women's issues both in the university environment and in the capital coupled with her work as a journalist motivated her to actively engage on gender issues. She projected that the Campaign was built on strong bonds. These bonds linked together activist women in their efforts and in coordinated strategies to circumvent the government while also connecting with non-activist women through the dialectic of direct interaction.[36]

Campaign pursuits included practical and consciousness-raising activities. The Campaign has been divided into committees where coordinated efforts on civil issues, strategies for local and provincial outreach, lobbying strategies with parliament, and other institutions, media, and education are addressed.[37] Functional measures included education on non-violent resistance, offering legal assistance to women in distressed situations, capacity and confidence building among women and defending imprisoned activists. Cultural activities consisted of research on laws affecting women and public debates on gender issues, media outreach, networking, and advocacy. Through a two-pronged strategy of promoting greater education of women and generating publicity on gender issues, the Campaign endeavors to transform discriminatory gender relations in public and private arenas ultimately improving the conditions for female participation and leadership in decision-making.

The Campaign was effective in attracting attention and publicity due to its innovative methods of engagement and implementation of reactive strategies of empowerment and education—all designed to facilitate common fertile ground among women. The Campaign has sought out new opportunities to stimulate and contact women. In a national grass roots endeavor, female activists travel door-to-door and engage in a face-to-face contact to garner as many signatures—both male and female—as possible. The productive method of "dialectical interaction," in which the activist and the woman engage and learn from each other in dialogue on women's rights and personal experience—also provides a significant contribution to the movement and the growth of female activism. In this vein, while many women have been reluctant to sign the petition for fear of government or spousal reprisal, they benefit through the exchange of opinions and knowledge acquired in the interaction. Such an interaction is considered sufficient progress to fuel further education and action for women. Moreover, each woman receives a pamphlet detailing the objectives and initiatives of the Campaign as well as a detailed explanation of the laws affecting women's lives. Additional topics for dialogue and information exchange have included collaboration with other movements, sports activities, CEDAW, and the imprisonment of activists. Campaign activists have approached women in female religious gatherings, and have regular encounters in female spaces such as taxi cabs, the metro, student dormitories, on the streets, in beauty salons, exercise facilities, and private homes. In each case, Campaign activists strategized and mobilized resources according to their goals and objectives.[38] Activists have met with people, discussed issues, provided literature that explains laws affecting women, and encouraged them to support the Campaign. The idea should gain momentum through a sequence of activities that build successively on each other, thus moving closer to the desired change. According to the Campaign, nearly 1,000 people have been trained in its methods of legal awareness and face-to-face outreach, while countless others have downloaded the petition from the campaign-for-equality.org site or have received it from others engaged in signature collections. The Campaign stated that it has been active in more than 15 of Iran's 30 provinces.[39]

Modern technology has been a critical and effective tool to increase the Campaign's global network and connectivity with new members and participants. The Internet has facilitated communication and outreach as well as provided a safe haven for discussion and organization away from government interference.[40] At the same time, reliance on the Internet has intensified interest both domestically and internationally in the Campaign's progress and objectives. Because of such media attention, including from controversial American outlets such as Voice of America and Radio Free Europe, it has come under government scrutiny. Its website has been subject to continual filtering and blockage by the state. More dramatically, member activities are monitored by security and intelligence organizations such that many Campaign activists have been arrested, detained, imprisoned, and barred from traveling outside the country.[41]

Strictly confined to constructive social and legal changes, the Campaign has tried to avoid ideological affiliations and labeling. Permitting the infiltration of ideological and factional concerns to shape its strategy and tactics, the Campaign would be subject to similar challenges that have crippled previous efforts of women's activism. Activists have acknowledged that they would welcome reform of the legal system "by anyone or any power or faction in any context or with any motivation . . . because the activists of the Campaign are not after gaining any personal or partisan benefits and do not intend to place themselves on one side of the table in the existing tensions between governments."[42] Campaign activists have recognized the broad diversity of views both among themselves and women activists of other orientations. With this understanding, they stand at the forefront of gender reform directed to improve the status of all women, regardless of their individual religious and political orientation. They have worked alongside Islamist women, who advocate the reinterpretation of Shariah laws regarding women supporting alternate modes of female activism. As stated on the website,

> While the Campaign seeks to bring Iranian law addressing women's status in line with international human rights standards, these demands are in no way in contradiction to Islam . . . Shiite Islam, on which the interpretations of Shariah rely with respect to Iranian law, claims to be dynamic and responsive to the specific needs of people and time. Iranian society has changed much since 1,400 years ago, but the interpretations of Shariah on which the Iranian law is based remain rather conservative. We ask that the laws come in line with international human rights standards and recognize the important role that religious scholars can play in facilitating our demand. In fact, long before the start of the Campaign, religious scholars, including Ayatollahs Sanei'i and Bojnourdi, for example, using dynamic jurisprudence and *ijtihad* had addressed some of our demands by offering new and progressive interpretations of Shariah with respect to women's rights.[43]

Grand Ayatollahs Sanei'i and Bojnourdi are among the frequent defenders of women's equality. Sanei'i has declared that a woman should be allowed to hold any job—president, supreme religious leader, even judge. He has permitted sex-change operations under certain conditions and first-trimester abortion for the mother's health or if there are fetal abnormalities. What has raised perhaps the most debate is his ruling that compensation for loss of life—so-called blood money or *diyeh*—should be the same for men and women, even though current religious law considers the life of a woman or a non-Muslim to be worth half that of a Muslim man. "Blood money is the price for a human life and the essence of life is driven from the soul," he has said. "The soul that God gave women is no less than the soul God gave men. How can we agree that women are equal to men, as the Qur'an has decreed, then say that the women's diyeh is half the sum of the compensation received for killing a man? How can we say that if a man kills a woman he can only be executed on condition that her family pays his family financial compensation that is the equivalent of half the sum of the diyeh but if a woman kills a man she is immediately sentenced to execution? How can we say that men can be judges but that women cannot be?

The fundamental criterion is knowledge of the law and of the procedures. Women, like men, can acquire that knowledge."[44] Ayatollah Sanei'i has suggested that legal changes similar to the ones he proposes are slowly being incorporated but he suggests that domestic politics continue to obstruct such changes, "The views I have about Islam have started to become law but it takes time. There are two reasons why they are not becoming law more swiftly: First, Imam Khomeini is not there and you know he had a high level of understanding of these issues which inspired our understanding. Secondly, political games are obstructing them, which the Imam would have prevented."[45]

Bojnourdi has made similar statements on female equality such as, "Women have all the God-given rights. A woman can certainly be president." Bojnourdi has also argued in favor of CEDAW, "Islam supports the emancipation of women so we have no difficulty signing up to the convention except for certain parts which the religious leaders are opposed to."[46] These opinions along with a number of others on women's rights alone have pitted Bojnourdi against many of his contemporaries, while enhancing his stature among women and activists who refer to his rulings regularly.[47]

Despite such clerical support, there has also been a limitation to female cooperation. During this period, most Islamist and reformist women supported the aims and objectives of the Campaign, even conceding the existence of legal and constitutional limitations to gender reform. Yet, many of these women objected to the confrontational and direct nature of the movement.[48] However, as restrictions on female activism and gender reform increased under President Ahmadinejad, Islamist women were again marginalized from the elite discourse. Initially, unwilling to compromise their personal political influence and positions providing moral rather than physical support, with time, this encouragement has become more overt. [49] Many Islamist women chose not to sign the petition but some reformist politicians and former parliamentarians including Shirin Ebadi publicly declared their support for the Campaign and its ambitions.

Taking a page from history, Campaign activists pursued egalitarian over elitist strategies—overcoming a debilitating trend evidenced in past women's activism in Iran. The current model employed by women activists dispels the old image of the women's movement as an exclusive effort distant from the average citizen. In fact, unlike efforts evidenced during the Pahlavi era, this grassroots organization is designed to include, involve, and even recruit all Iranian women in common cause. As suggested by Shirin Ebadi, "By getting one million signatures, the world will know we object to these conditions. . . . And I can't help but think that instead of one courageous woman for the government to contend with, it will have reaped a million."[50] Equally important is the structure of the organization. While the Campaign was initiated by a younger, more secular, group of women's activists, the organization is considered leaderless. In this vein, activists work collectively and collaboratively in committees.[51] As part of this strategy, without identifiable leadership, the Campaign cannot be effectively dismantled by the state. Indeed, volunteers and activists are regularly targeted but similar to other horizontally structured groups and associations, this structure protects the organization and fosters a culture of commonality and teamwork. Many activists suggest that this is among the greater strengths of the organization.[52] At the same time though, the horizontal structure has proven challenging for decision making. Moreover, the concept of ambiguous leadership has resulted in slow response to the government repression.

Finally, while maintaining its focus, the Campaign has collaborated with other civil rights community-based efforts. Many Campaign activists are also involved in NGO activities and are members of student and women's groups outside the Campaign. Women involved in the Campaign have often partnered with workers, students, and human rights activists as all these movements represent collective efforts toward improved human and civil rights.[53] Campaigners are connected with other non-governmental organizations to help address various social problems. Many have worked with people in disaster areas, AIDS patients, earthquake victims, abused children, and victims of sexual violence. Collaboration across the spectrum of groups has not only helped promote greater solidarity for civil society and human rights, but also facilitated close learning and cooperation on various efforts.[54] Yet activists have also distinguished their objectives from those of other social movements. The Campaign addresses controversial issues around Islamic law targeting the core of the Islamic Republic.[55]

Campaign members have repeatedly affirmed that ideology and politics are not part of the Campaign, nor do they publicly seek to challenge the regime or Islamic law. Ahmadi Khorasani has stated Islam "whether one likes it or not is part of people's lives."[56] Mahboubeh Abbasgholizadeh has furthered, "We want to change the behavior of the state in its relations with women, and we believe the people of the country and Iranian women can do this. More importantly, these changes must come by relying on our own domestic resources."[57] However, at the same time, the Campaign is inevitably engaged in politics. A number of my interviewees suggested that by virtue of the goals of the Campaign—to revise the Constitution—Campaign activities were indeed political.[58] As has been demonstrated through the review of female activism in Iranian history, women's activism is inextricably linked to politics. There is no exception here. The goals of changing Islamic laws, amending provisions of the constitution and improving women's rights pose a direct challenge to the institutional framework of the Islamic Republic and provoke instinctual opposition from both the dominant patriarchal culture and the theocratic state. To counteract accusations against its work, the Campaign has sought to counter the notion that it is working as a political party. It has done so by adopting flexible tactics including a strategy of democratic education. The website states "The Campaign is not an opposition group or opposed to the government. It seeks to work within the existing system to create change and to express the demands of a major segment of the Iranian population to the government. The Campaign's petition is directly addressing the Iranian public and the Iranian legislature."[59]

Notwithstanding such protestations and regular statements from Campaign members who insist that they are not against nor attempting to thwart the Iranian government, its members have experienced threats and attacks, particularly accusing members of receiving foreign and American funds to support their initiative. President Bush's democracy agenda had brought increased scrutiny to the Campaign. Female activist Parvin Ardalan has poignantly stated, "It is interesting to note that the continuity of the Campaign is not reliant on its financial resources [rather] the movement is supported by its human resources."[60] The Campaign website also clearly states:

> It was decided, and the Campaign stands firm on this issue to this day, that no funding support from international organizations, foundations or governments whether overt or covert would be accepted. . . . From the start however, we faced accusations from security forces, whether official or spread in the form of rumors, or published untruths in news outlets associated with security apparatuses, in regards to receiving support or direction from the West. The saving grace for the Campaign here has been that all its members understand and fully believe that the Campaign is a homegrown effort, which relies on the ideas, and energies of Iranians, especially young women and men, for its sustenance, and on the personal contributions of individual members and supporters to meet its financial obligations.[61]

Most acutely, the Campaign has been targeted by the administration of President Ahmadinejad. Its activities have been curtailed; its center's office has been searched and closed; its demonstrations canceled or disrupted by police; and its members have been intimidated, harassed, arrested, fined, jailed, and sentenced to imprisonment; members have been accused of espionage, writing for banned websites, spreading propaganda against the state, and endangering national security.[62] Government forces have broken up subsequent meetings to promote the Campaign and arrested and jailed many of its leaders, as well as some other women's rights activists. Steps taken against the group have raised its profile, including publicity of the numerous court cases and "national security" charges. The Campaign's website has been blocked dozens of times. A spike of interest came when Parvin Ardalan was named winner of the 2007 Olof Palme prize, but was prevented from collecting it when she was ordered off the plane moments before takeoff. The prize is for "making the demand for equal rights for men and women a central part of the struggle for democracy in Iran." Ardalan was among four activists sentenced to six months in jail September 2008 for "spreading propaganda."[63] The Campaign also won the 2009 Simone de Beauvoir prize for women's freedom, but the group decided, given the current atmosphere in Iran, that they could not accept the €30,000 ($40,000 at exchange rate of $1.36) in prize money. Indeed such scrutiny has proved challenging for the Campaign. Government tactics designed to neutralize its outreach have made it more difficult for activists to circulate their petition and increase public awareness. In the wake of arrests, detentions, and voluntary exile of Campaign leadership particularly since the June 2009 election, the Campaign has yet to advance new strategies to circumvent government control.

A further blow to the Campaign came as the Iranian leadership rejected its objective to realign Iranian gender laws with international norms. In July 2007, Ayatollah Khamenei suggested that the Campaign's activities designed to "harmonize Islamic laws with international conventions is wrong." At the same time, though, Khamenei indicated "some Islamic rules regarding women could change if jurisprudence research led to a new understanding."[64] A function of this contradiction is that the government takes pride in legal and progressive changes affected since 1990—changes that were opposed by the same government in the 1980s. Most of these changes, though limited and conditional in scope, have come as a result of efforts by women despite government restrictions and policy orientations. Arenas such as sports, education, arts, literature, and sciences—all inaccessible to women in the early years of the revolutionary government—are now burgeoning with women.

Like their activist predecessors, campaigners are under no illusion that the changes they seek will come about quickly. Moreover, among my interviewees, not one conceded that the patriarchal laws would disappear altogether or even soon or that judges and lawmakers would be arbitrarily willing to reverse gender discrimination.[65] The task for women then is a two-fold challenge against the discriminatory laws imposed on women and against the entrenched sociocultural norms. Some Campaign activists have acknowledged that government-inspired gender reform is arbitrary and will come at the will of the regime, not as a result of female and political pressure.[66]

Yet, the task of the Campaign is to generate consciousness, expectation, demand, and mobilization for change. The hope expressed by one young activist is that as gender issues become more public and the demand for change becomes widespread, the movement will take center stage and produce a new energy and momentum much stronger than those found among the early activists.[67] While the goals of the Campaign are further reaching, its capacity to generate change through education and interaction is more promising. The desired impact "will be gradual, cumulative, tangible and practical."[68] The ultimate goal is to make a difference, be it changing one person's mind at a time, winning one person over in a day, or forcing open just one closed door.

In addition to the One Million Signatures Campaign other female-oriented issue-based initiatives also lobby in tandem with the Campaign for changes to gender laws and policies. They include the Stop Stoning Forever Campaign, the Women for Equal Citizenship Campaign, that lobbies for an Iranian woman who is married to a foreigner being able to pass citizenship to her children, the Women's Access to Public Stadiums Campaign (also known as the White Scarf Campaign), the National Women's Charter Campaign, the Young Lawyers Campaign for Gender Equality in Family Law, Mothers for Peace, and Mournful Mothers Campaign.[69] The National Women's Charter Campaign in particular has been a two-year collaboration among female activists who drew on the aspirations and demands of women for political and social change. Through meetings and discussion, activist women have issued a women's charter detailing their comprehensive goals for social, political, and economic reform.[70]

These examples of claim making evidenced in the various campaigns are important components of a social movement as suggested by Tilly. The synthesis of three elements is needed to account for the presence of a social movement: 1) the *campaign* where a sustained, organized public effort makes claims on target authorities, 2) the *repertoire* where the creation of associations and coalitions and the use of public meetings, vigils, rallies, media statements, and demonstrations are used to convey the message of the claimants, and 3) *worthiness, unity, numbers, and commitment* on the part of the participants.[71] Indeed, these characteristics combined with the growth of a women's discourse and gender consciousness suggest that Iranian women's activism evolved during this period into a 'conventional' social movement.

State Backlash

In the wake of this growing grassroots movement, Ahmadinejad reacted to such female activism with more stringent efforts to restrict women's social, political, and economic presence. Resurrecting the initial pro-natalist views of Ayatollah Khomeini, Ahmadinejad encouraged women to return to their natural role as nurturers. Unlike President Khatami, who invited some women into his inner circle and cabinet as advisors, Ahmadinejad stifled female participation in his first administration. Among the visible cosmetic changes was the renaming of the Center for Women's Participation to the Center for Women and Family Affairs. He also replaced the Center's head, Zahra Shojai, with Nasrin Soltankhah and then her successor, Zohreh Tabibzadeh Nouri, who declared that Iran would not ratify CEDAW as long as she remained in her post. The budget for governmental institutions affecting women was also significantly reduced.[72] Some activists also say Iran's minister of culture and Islamic guidance, Muhammad Hossein Saffar Harandi, encouraged women to leave work early so they can attend to their familial duties.[73]

Within the parliament, there has been little example of progressive change for women as championed by its reformist predecessors. Since the election of the seventh parliament in February 2004, the majority of its members have been fundamentalist, far-right politicians.[74] A similar ideological group has succeeded in monopolizing the eighth parliament elected in 2008 as well. The conservatives have regularly accused women's organizations and NGOs of being either subgroups of political parties or of exhibiting Western influences.[75] Yet, in a noticeable shift, during the eighth parliamentary elections, Islamist female activists formed political coalitions to press for a gender agenda among the candidates as well as press for a 30 percent quota for female candidates.[76] Since 1979, traditional and Islamist women have repeatedly defied government policy and expectation demanding political, social, and economic empowerment. Training sessions were organized for female candidates and a gender platform advocated the empowerment of women in economic, social, and familial spheres, the removal of discriminatory laws against women, and the appointment of women to national decision-making levels. Despite such pressure, only eight women were elected. The outcome had produced limited results for women's activists. Through the process, women had officially introduced the quota concept while also conditioning their support for political parties—a decisive strategy shift for Islamist women.[77]

At the same time, a number of progressive measures on gender issues have been passed by the eighth parliament again highlighting the paradoxes inherent in state politics. Under consideration in November 2010 at the Expediency Council is a bill designed to amplify the requirements for a presidential candidate. Such clarification is necessary to clear the path for women's candidature. In the past, female presidential candidature has been forbidden due to a legal interpretation of the term *rejal* [man or person], a qualification for candidacy denoted in the constitution as applying to only men.[78] While women have argued that the term refers to a person's political and religious competence without regard to gender this debate has hampered women's past presidential bids. Azam Taleghani, chairwoman of the Women's Islamic Society and repeated presidential candidate, welcomed the bill's possible approval by the State Expediency Council suggesting that factional politics was the cause of past legislative attempts designed to clarify women's political opportunities. She stated, "Interpreting the term rejal in a manner that allows women's candidature had been proposed by the Sixth Parliament as well. Why did the Council reject the bill then, only to consider its approval now? The Council's membership hasn't changed. Has there been a change in opinion or was it not approved then because the reformists were in power?"[79] Additionally, in the 2009 presidential elections 42 women declared their candidacy. While the Guardian Council disqualified all, they did so on the grounds of their qualifications rather than their gender, opening the door for future female candidacy.

Another important change has been evidenced in women's inheritance and citizenship rights. In August 2006, the parliament passed an amendment to the citizenship law allowing women married to foreign nationals to pass on their citizenship to their children. The new legislation permits this transfer of citizenship as long as the child is 18, the father is Muslim and the parents have a legalized marriage.[80] While the legal change has been applauded, activists have criticized the measure as half-hearted as children would continue to be "stateless" until the age of 18 rendering them ineligible for public benefits and social services.[81] In January 2009, the Iranian parliament passed legislation making it possible for women to inherit up to a quarter of the land and standing property from their husbands.[82] The previous law only allowed women to inherit a portion of portable property prohibiting their inheritance of real estate. Ahmadinejad issued a decree that instructs all government bodies to enforce this recently passed law, despite the Guardian Council's silence over the issue.[83] The Guardian Council must approve all parliamentary legislation. If the Council decides to avoid taking an official stance on any legislation in a set period of time, the legislation becomes automatically official, as in the case of the new legislation on women's inheritance rights. The Guardian Council's decision to remain silent on the issue follows heavy criticism from several top religious figures, who view the legislation as in clear contradiction with the Islamic law.[84]

Simultaneously, the president sponsored a number of initiatives affecting women. The first, known as the Social Morality Plan (*Tarhe Amniyat Ejtema'i)*, was officially launched in March 2007. The program is designed to combat immorality and criminality. The first and most visible component of this program included a campaign addressing lax adherence to Islamic hejab standards.[85] Through increased police vigilance, police have identified and detained women who fail to comply with the Islamic dress code. The police are strategically dispatched to congested locations where they can target women. The targets of these crackdowns are commonly detained until family members can bring them clothing deemed to be in compliance with the law. They are generally given warnings and forced to sign a commitment that obliges them to dress appropriately. Repeat offenders are referred to the judicial system, where sentences can include fines and even lashings.[86]

A second measure advocated by the Ahmadinejad Administration has been a stringent effort to change the provisions of the Family Protection Act (*Layehe Hemayate Khanevadeh)*—renamed by women activists as the 'Anti-Family bill'. This legislation was originally submitted to the parliament in August 2007 and designed with the intention of allowing women to serve as judges. As initially drawn up, it would also impose prison sentences for men who marry girls before they have reached the legal age of nine. But the government push to add articles, including Article 23 permitting multiple marriages without the first wife's consent, has raised controversy.[87] Under Islamic law, a man is entitled to marry up to four wives, and many countries in the Middle East allow polygamy. However, Iran is one of the few Islamic countries that require the consent of the first wife before a husband can take another. Polygamy is not commonly practiced in Iranian society, but the government of President Ahmadinejad has pursued these amendments to enshrine traditional elements of Islamic law and advance the state's maternal image of women into the country's legal system. Another stipulation, Article 25, would set a standard rate for *mehrieh,* or bridal dowry, as well as impose a tax on this dowry should it exceed the standard rate. The bill also reduced the female eligibility for marriage age from 16 to 13.

A positive result of this negative legislation has led to greater solidarity among secular and Islamist women. In September 2008, over 50 secular and Islamist activists decided to prevent the bill's ratification, including Shirin Ebadi. A broad array of women's associations including The One Millions Signatures Campaign, the Zeinab Society, and the Women's Organization of the Islamic Revolution collaborated in mobilizing women against the bill. They demanded to meet the members of parliament presenting proposals to change the controversial provisions. Ultimately, they succeeded in convincing the parliament to postpone ratification pending further investigation. Their action provoked debates among the more moderate parliamentarians, who did not support the government of President Ahmadinejad and agreed to modify the bill, and pro-government hardliners who support the bill. Judiciary chief Ayatollah Mahmoud Hashemi Shahroudi and Ayatollah Sanei'i disparaged the government's amendments, saying the changes were harmful to women. A recent survey conducted by a Shahla Ezazi from Allameh Tabatabai University, revealed that 96 percent of Iranian women do not approve of polygamy.[88]

The fierce debate on the bill highlights rising social tensions in Iran, where the Ahmadinejad government has targeted women's rights activists. In reaction to such uproar, the parliament indefinitely delayed voting on the bill. The conservative-controlled assembly was due to vote on the government proposal on August 31, 2008, but it was sent back to its legal committee for more work where the polygamy and mehrieh clauses were said to be withdrawn. Despite the delay, it is important to note that this bill has yet to be withdrawn, and could be sent back for a vote at any time. Indeed, in January 2010, the spokesperson of the Law and Legal Affairs Committee of the parliament announced that the Committee had reinstated the polygamy clause with some modifications including that a "man can marry a second wife under ten conditions."[89] The new version still requires the first wife to give permission, though controversially this would not be required under certain conditions, such as if she is mentally ill, or suffers from infertility, has a chronic medical condition, or is addicted to drugs, in which case the husband can marry another woman. Also if the first wife does not cooperate sexually, the husband can take another wife. Another provision to the bill that would encourage temporary marriage—which has become more common in Iran, particularly under the encouragement of the clerical establishment, was removed in 2010.[90] The legal changes have been promoted by conservative members of the parliament in their efforts to strengthen Islamic law. A conservative deputy, Ali Motahari, said in parliament last year, "Polygamy is Islam's honor."[91]

The paradox here is that Ahmadinejad campaigned on the promise to strengthen the family and family values. However, a bill that legalizes polygamy and "gives a free pass to polygamists," as suggested by Shrin Ebadi, in effect weakens the structure of the family.[92] For Ahmadinejad though, it is clear that strengthening the family implies strengthening the position of men. Ebadi asserted "This bill damages the institution of the family . . . it further weakens the position of women within society. In the case of inheritance, the second or third wife as well as women from temporary marriages and their children are financially disadvantaged."[93] At the same time, though, the bill points to the patriarchal norms and ideology advanced by the Ahmadinejad government and values still shared by many within Iranian society.

Women's rights activists were appalled by the prospective reversal in the polygamy law, among others. However, traditional women, even those in the parliament, have also argued in favor of this measure, defending polygamy as stipulated in the Qur'an on the condition that husbands treat their wives equally and justly. Also, these women suggest that polygamous families are helpful to women in particular as wives can assist each other in their matrimonial duties and can benefit from their respective companionship. A 2008 film released in Iran, *Second Wife* (*Zan-e Dovom*) also encouraged support for the polygamist message.

An added restrictive measure has been implementation of gender quotas within the university system. Ahmadinejad's government has advanced the notion of "gender equilibrium" and "appropriate gender roles" as an essential component of social stability eschewing religious arguments and as such preventing female legal challenges within an Islamic framework.[94] In April 2008, the government announced its intention to limit acceptance of female students in specific fields of university study.[95] The program, which seeks to redress the disproportionately high number of female university students, drew attention to the government's obvious gender bias. While no official legislation has been submitted or passed, in February 2008, the *Sazeman Sanjesh,* (government admissions organization), confessed that it had already been enforcing a de facto quota system restricting female admission since 2006.[96] The organization's leaders acknowledged that they had been promoting a male priority acceptance policy. Since September 2009, female students have been required to study at universities in their towns or cities, thereby restricting their free access to higher education. No such requirement exists for male students.[97] Mousa Ghorbani, the head of judiciary commission of parliament stated that female localization provides a solution to social problems generated "When girls move to other cities to study, it causes some problem for their families as well as society. If they stay with their families they help to improve the peace of society and themselves."[98]

Another blow was evidenced in the January 2008 ban of the feminist monthly magazine *Zanan.* The grounds for this closure was that it "endangered the spiritual, mental and intellectual health of its readers" promoting "insecurity in society, disturbed public rights, weakened military and revolutionary institutes." It was also accused of publishing articles that "led people to believe that the Islamic Republic is unsafe for women."[99] The closure is notable in that the monthly *Zanan* is widely regarded as a moderate magazine that cautiously avoids politics and focuses exclusively on women's issues. With its shutdown, *Zanan* joined a long list of publications banned in the past decade, such as the daily *Zan* and *Payam-e Hajar* closed down in 1999 and 2001 respectively. However, as opposed to its predecessors, *Zanan* had managed over the years to overcome difficulties and survived the extensive press purge of 2000 to 2001. *Zanan's* last published volume online, numbered 152, marking 16 years of publication—an impressive achievement given the short life of most independent publications in Iran, especially those for women during the last century.[100] *Zanan's* closure, coming a few months prior to the Majlis elections held in March 2008, suggested a continuous campaign of repression directed at the reform movement and at the independent press. This drive dates back to the elections for the seventh parliament in 2004, which was dominated by members of the ultra-conservative faction. The government's move to shut down *Zanan* reverberated throughout Iran and around the world, prompting international petitions that called on Iran's leadership to renew the journal's license. *Zanan's* legal advisor even claimed that the order to shut down the publication was illegal, since it did not meet the procedures stipulated by law. "Events that have taken shape since the license revocation suggest that the decision was motivated more by the personal and ideological animosity of a few individual members and not the whole Press Supervisory Board, which presumably ordered the license revocation."[101]

In acknowledgement of the growing relevance of women, particularly in the aftermath of the 2009 elections, Ahmadinejad nominated three women to his cabinet in June 2009. It was presidential candidate Mehdi Karroubi that introduced this issue into his political platform thereby recognizing the importance of his female constituency. Ahmadinejad who had surprised women with his call to allow females into soccer stadiums in 2006 did so again with these nominations. Indeed, in the 2009 election campaign, Ahmadinejad had yet again neglected gender issues. Some accused the president of using this deflective strategy to distract from the election dispute and public protests.[102] Others suggested that Ahmadinejad sought "to pull the rug out from under women's activism" by using women to contain women.[103] Marzieh Vahid Dastjerdi was designated for the position of minister of health, Fatemeh Ajorlou as minister of social security and welfare, and Sussan Keshavarz as minister of education. Keshavarz had served as a deputy to the previous education minister in a department devoted to mentally challenged students and was considered a newcomer to the political scene. Dastjerdi, a gynecologist and former parliamentarian belonging to the Principalist Women Faction who opposed CEDAW, was elected in 1992 to 1996 and 1996 to 2000. Ajorlou, also equally conservative, was a parliamentarian in the eighth parliament. Ajorlou and Dastjerdi have explicitly defended the idea of gender segregation in hospitals, universities, public transportations, parks, and other public places and have supported Ahmadinejad's family oriented measures including reducing a married woman's workday and the legislation in support of polygamy. Ajorlou was a leading advocate of gender quotas to stem the rise of female students in Iranian universities and an ardent supporter of the chador as a defense of female chastity. The selection of these women agitated considerable opposition among conservatives and women's rights advocates alike.[104] From high-ranking Ayatollahs in Qom to conservative parliamentarians, Ahmadinejad's female nominees provoked significant debate. Women's rights activists also expressed their reservations as the three female nominees would likely perpetuate Ahmadinejad's restrictive gender policies. In the end, only Dastjerdi's candidacy was approved linking the president to the appointment of the first female cabinet member in 32 years.[105] Such a feat however has been bitter for female activists who have stated, "having women ministers does not mean or guarantee a better position for women in our society."[106]

A final state strategy has been directed at promoting gender-segregated environments and in enforcing his "Plan of Mercy." In May 2008, Tehran mayor Muhammad Baqir Qalibaf opened a new sex-segregated park known as Mothers' Paradise, where women are encouraged to engage in sports and exercise. This park is not the only sex-segregated park in Iran. Similar parks exclusively for women have already been established in other Iranian cities, including Mashad and Qom. Developments such as this are overseen by the Center for Women and Family Affairs. Their mandate includes the "Plan of Mercy," a program supported by a 10 billion rial budget, designed to implement the center's grassroots program promoting marriage, domesticity, and Islamic values. In essence, this scheme has been the government's cultural strategy to counterbalance the one pursued by the One Million Signatures Campaign. Using similar local outreach strategies, the government has drawn on its female Basij network to spread the official policy of modesty and family values throughout the country.[107] At the same time, through such incorporative measures, these women are involved in the social and economic sustenance of the country, moves designed to empower women within the Islamic system. One Basiji woman recently argued that, "one of the most effective ways to combat the misinterpretation of women's role in Islam would be to accommodate the active participation of women in the Islamic and revolutionary organizations."[108]

Nasrin Sotoudeh, a Tehran-based lawyer and women's-rights activist, stated that such moves represent clear discrimination against women. "They set up separate taxis for women, separate parks for women, separate hospitals for women . . . Female patients can only be attended to by female medical workers. In the short-term future, we may see entire cities being divided into women's sections and men's sections. Or how about creating women-only and men-only cities? The [sex-segregated park] contradicts the international convention on human rights."[109] In November 2007, Iran's second female university, Hazrat-e Ma'soumeh University, was opened in Qom. Other initiatives such as female-only police stations have been set up in Mashad, with plans to extend the design to Tehran. Female police officers are used in the government effort to crack down on those flouting Islamic dress codes and social mores.[110]

Indeed, these government maneuvers speak to the inherent paradox surrounding women's issues. It is clear that there is no collaborative understanding or unified vision of women's role in society either among women activists or non-activists, or within the political system. Such polarization undoubtedly affects and limits the impact of women's activism. From a state perspective, more often than not, women's issues and women's activism is invoked and promoted on a state level when politically expedient. Otherwise, as ideological and factional struggles continue to dominate the political landscape, women's issues are subordinated to general political ones. In the Ahmadinejad government, these trends are ever applicable, as the president has advanced his Islamic agenda while also attempting to reverse previous rulings on women when convenient. At the same time, the growing crackdown on civil society and women's activism in particular is a reflection of the growing perception of public dissent and the widening cleavages between state and society.

The government reaction to female activism evidenced in the repeated crackdowns, arrests, and civil society contraction also points to the inherent weaknesses of the Iranian regime. On March 8, 2007, International Women's Day, Iranian women were prevented from standing in solidarity with their female counterparts worldwide in recognition of women's rights. At the same time, women activists continue to be government targets as more and more women have received prison sentences for their participation in the One Million Signatures Campaign. Shirin Ebadi has also been subjected to intimidation. Both her home and office were vandalized as a crowd of hardliners chanted slogans against her. Authorities shut down her Center for the Defense of Human Rights, which had recently compiled a report cited by United Nations Secretary General Ban Ki-moon that led to a nonbinding December 18, 2009, U.N. resolution calling on Iran to improve its human rights record.[111]

In the midst of international crises over the country's nuclear program and expansionist regional role, Iran has been beleaguered with domestic dissent and economic pressure. This pressure is more potent when one weighs the impact of demographic and social shifts that have occurred over the last 32 years—which prominently affected and impacted women. Active in social, political, economic, and religious spheres, women have evolved into a political pressure point to be reckoned with. Years of experience, growth, networking, collaboration, and claim making had laid the foundations of a women's movement. Charles Kurzman argued "Observers have noted that a feminist generation of educated women appears to be emerging in Iran, despite the anti-feminist discourse of the Iranian government. Revolutionary mobilization may have generated a heightened sense of efficacy among women. The policies of the Islamic Republic may have also generated a backlash among women. Education may have generated gender-egalitarian values in spite of the patriarchal content of instruction. Economic difficulties may have pushed women into assuming greater responsibilities."[112] It is this new generation having learned from the errors of female activism of the past, having benefitted from the paradoxes of Islamic politics, having seized on the opportunities offered through education, employment, and technology and having merged together in common cause that will continue to build on this momentum of confrontation—exposing the contradictions and posing the biggest contest for the Islamic Republic of Iran. This challenge would rear its head earlier than expected. The June 2009 election campaign season, presidential elections, and post-electoral protests would reflect the totality of social and political frustration on behalf of society as well as the strains of factionalism and ideological disunity among the elite. The impact of these tensions would have profound consequences for the future of the Islamic Republic and for women's activism.

Notes

1. Sheema Kalbasi, *Seven Valleys of Love: A Bilingual Anthology of Women Poets from Middle Ages Persia to Present Day Iran*, 2008, 70.

2. Nasser Karimi, "Iran's Women Barred from Soccer Games," *Reuters*, May 8, 2006.

3. For more see Rochelle Terman, "Sport and Segregation in Iran: The Women's Access to Public Stadiums Campaign," Women Living Under Muslim Laws, forthcoming.

4. Noushin Tarighi, "Mardan Reghabat Baraye Raye Zanan" [Men Competing for Women's Votes], *Zanan* 121, 4–7.

5. *BBC Persian*, April 26, 2006.

6. For more on Mahmood Ahmadinejad see Kasra Naji, *Ahmadinejad: A Secret History of Iran's Radical Leader*, 2008; Ali Ansari, *Iran under Ahmadinejad*, 2008; Yossi Melman and Meir Javedanfar, *The Nuclear Sphinx of Tehran: Mahmood Ahmadinejad and the State of Iran*, 2007, Anoushiravan Ehteshami and Mahjoob Zweiri, *Iran and the Rise of the Neoconservatives: The Politics of Tehran's Silent Revolution*, 2007, Anoushiravan Ehteshami and Mahjoob Zweiri, *Iran's Foreign Policy from Khatami to Ahmadinejad*, 2008; Abbas Milani, "Pious Populist: Understanding the Rise of Iran's President," *Boston Review*, November/December 2007, Jahanghir Amuzegar, "The Ahmadinejad Era: Preparing for the Apocalypse," *Journal of International Affairs*, 2007, Vol. 60, No. 2.

7. Akbar Ganji, "The Latter Day Sultan," *Foreign Affairs*, 2008, Vol. 87, No. 6, 45–66.

8. Borzou Daragahi, "Iran Economists Denounce Ahmadinejad's Policies," *Los Angeles Times*, November 10, 2008. Also see, Jahanghir Amuzegar, "Islamic Social Justice, Iranian Style," *Middle East Policy*, 2007, Vol. 14, No. 3, 60–78. Patrick Clawson, "The Islamic Republic's Economic Failure," *Middle East Quarterly*, 2008, Vol. 15, No. 4, 15–26.

9. Ali Ansari, "Iran Under Ahmadinejad: Populism and its Malcontents," *International Affairs*, 2008, Vol. 84, No. 4, 696.

10. Peter Tatchell, "Iran's Union Heroes: Tehran's Anti-union Repression Is Symptomatic of the Fascistic Nature of the Clerical Regime," *The Guardian*, March 6, 2008.

11. Abbas William Samii, "Ethnic Tensions Could Crack Iran's Firm Resolve Against the World," *The Christian Science Monitor*, May 30, 2006.

12. Sanam Vakil, "Tehran Gambles to Survive," *Current History*, December 2007, 415.

13. For more details on the evolution and issues at the heart of United States-Iranian relations see James Bill, *The Eagle and the Lion: The Tragedy of American-Iranian Relations*, 1989. Barbara Slavin, *Bitter Friends, Bosom Enemies: Iran, the U.S., and the Twisted Path to Confrontation*, 2007; Ray Takeyh, *Hidden Iran: Paradox and Power in the Islamic Republic*, 2006; and Ali Ansari, *Confronting Iran: The Failure of American Foreign Policy and the Next Great Crisis in the Middle East*, 2006.

14. Abbas Milani, "Russia and Iran: An Anti-Western Alliance?" *Current History*, 2007, Vol. 106, No. 702, 328–32. Fariba Adelkhah and Zuzanna Olszeska, "The Iranian Afghans," *Iranian Studies*, 2007, Vol. 40, No. 2, 137–65.

15. Barbara Slavin, *Bitter Friends, Bosom Enemies: Iran, the U.S. and the Twisted Path to Confrontation*, 2007, 197–8.

16. Sanam Vakil, Tehran Gambles to Survive," *Current History*, December 2007.

17. Ibid., 418.

18. Farangis Najibullah, "Iran: Wrapping Up for Winter, and the Morality Police," *Radio Free Europe Radio Liberty*, December 13, 2007. Katherine Butler, "Lipstick Revolution: Iran's Women Are Taking on the Mullahs," *The Independent*, February 26, 2009.

19. Personal interviews with female activists, Washington DC, November 12, 2007, Tehran, Februrary 4, 2007.

20. Barack Obama's Inauguration Address, Washington, D.C., January 20, 2009.

21. http://www.whitehouse.gov/the_press_office/Videotaped-Remarks-by-The-President-in-Celebration-of-Nowruz/ Accessed March 18, 2009.

22. Ahmadinejad's letter can be accessed at http://www.farsnews.com/newstext. php?nn=8708160754 Accessed March 18, 2010.

23. Azadeh Kian, "Social Change, the Women's Rights Movement and the Role of Islam," *Viewpoints* Special Edition, The Iranian Revolution at Thirty, Middle East Institute, Washington, DC, 2009.

24. These issues were discussed at length in *Zanan*, 137 and 138.

25. Personal interviews with Islamist activists and politicians, Tehran, May 14, 2008 and May 17, 2008.

26. See *Zanan*, 137 and 138.

27. Mahboubeh Abbasgholizadeh, "Dar Iran Jonbeshe Zanan bi Sar Ast" [The Iranian Women's Movement Is Leaderless], *Zanan*, September 2003, www.zanan.co.ir/culture/000153. html. Accessed October 23, 2008.

28. Ziba Mir-Hosseini, "Is Time on Iranian Women Protesters' Side?" *Middle East Research and Information Project*, June 16, 2006.

29. "Face to Face Approach, the Symbol of Struggle in the One Million Signature Campaign: An Interview with Noushin Ahamdi Khorasani," http://zanschool.net/english/spip.php?article327, August 26, 2009. Accessed March 21, 2010.

30. Personal interview with journalist and activist, Washington, DC, November 12, 2007.

31. Maura J. Casey, "Challenging the Mullahs, One Signature at a Time," *The New York Times,* February 7, 2007.

32. "Face to Face Approach, the Symbol of Struggle in the One Million Signature Campaign."

33. Noushin Ahmadi Khorasani, "Jonbesh Yek Million Emza: Ravayati az Daroun" [The One Million Signatures Campaign: A Narrative from Inside], Summer 2007, http://www.femschool.info/campaign/spip.php?article86. Accessed March 25, 2010.

34. http://campaign-for-equality.org/eFAQ.php. Accessed March 15, 2010.

35. Personal interview with Campaign activist, Tehran May 12, 2008.

36. Personal interview with Campaign activist, Tehran, April 27, 2008.

37. Ibid.

38. Personal interviews with Campaign activists, Tehran May 12 and 13, 2008.

39. http://campaign-for-equality.org/eFAQ.php. Accessed March 15, 2010.

40. Personal interview with Campaign activist, Tehran April 27, 2008.

41. Elham Gheytanchi, "Lashing Out on Iranian Women's Rights Activists," huffington-post.com, November 2007.

42. "Face to Face Approach, the Symbol of Struggle in the One Million Signature Campaign."

43. http://campaign-for-equality.org/eFAQ.php. Accessed March 15, 2010.

44. Ayatollah Saanei began his religious studies at the age of 9 and attended the classes of Ayatollah Ruhollah Khomeini, at 25, when he also joined the struggle against the old government under the shah. The two men developed such a bond that Ayatollah Saanei still talks of it with pride, and even displays a sign on one wall quoting the Ayatollah Khomeini as saying, "I raised Ayatollah Saanei like a son." Ayatollah Saanei was very much a part of the religious establishment in the early days of the revolution. He was on the 12-member Guardian Council that drafted the Constitution. Later he was appointed chief prosecutor, and he was part of the religious establishment that replaced the secular legal code with Islamic law. Since withdrawing from the government in 1984, Ayatollah Saanei has devoted his career to clarifying his position that men and women enjoy equal rights in the Koran. He has also moderated some of his views, with his most liberal rulings coming in the last several years, since the rise of the reformist president, Muhammad Khatami. See Nazila Fathi, "Ayatollah, Reviewing Islamic Law, Tugs at Ties Constricting Iran's Women," *New York Times,* July 29, 2001. Also see Manal Lutfi, "The Women's Mufti: Interview With Grand Ayatollah Yousef Sanei'i," *Asharg Alawsat,* June 4, 2007; Roya Karimi-Majd, "Islam Deene Adl Ast: Goftogoo Ekhtesasy ba Ayatollah Sanei'i" [Islam Is the Religion of Justice: Exclusive Interview with Ayatollah Sanei'i], *Zanan* 96, 2–7; For more on Sanei'i ruling see the Ayatollah's website at http://www.Saanei.org/index.php?lang=en. Accessed March 15, 2010.

45. Najmeh Bozorgmehr, "Grand Ayatollah Yusef Sanei'i: A Liberal Voice Among Clerics," *Financial Times,* February 6, 2009.

46. To bolster his reasoning, he said that the game of chess is banned in Islam until now but that the late Imam Khomeini pronounced an exception by lifting the ban with due consideration to time and place. "Ayatollah Bojnourdi Says Iran May Sign the Women's Convention With Reservations," IRNA, August 18, 2003.

47. Hooman Majd, *The Ayatollah Begs to Differ: The Paradox of Modern Iran*, 2008, 213.

48. Personal interviews with Campaign activists, Tehran, April 27 and 28, 2008.

49. Personal interview with Campaign activist, Tehran April 27, 2008.

50. Maura J. Casey, " Challenging the Mullahs, One Signature at a Times," 2007.

51. Personal interview with Campaign activist, Tehran April 27, 2008.

52. Personal interviews with Campaign activist, Tehran, May 12 and 13, 2008.

53. Personal interview with Campaign activist, Tehran, April 27, 2008.

54. Personal interviews with Campaign activists, Tehran, May 12 and 13, 2008.

55. Personal interview with Campaign activist, Tehran, April 27, 2008.

56. Afary, 2009, p. 368.

57. Omid Memarian, "Interview with Abbasgholizadeh: They Are Against Civil Society, www.Roozonline.com, July 7, 2007. Accessed July 10, 2007.

58. Personal interviews with secular and Islamist activists, Tehran April 12 and 13, 2008.

59. http://campaign-for-equality.org/eFAQ.php. Accessed March 15, 2010.

60. Parvin Ardalan, "The Women's Movement in a Game of Snakes and Ladders, http://fairfamilylaw.info/spip.php?article412 , November 25, 2008. Accessed April 7, 2010.

61. http://campaign-for-equality.org/eFAQ.php. Accessed March 15, 2010.

62. For further details on the arrests and detentions of Campaign activists see "Detentions and Summons Against Campaigners for Gender Equality," February 24, 2008. http://www.change4equality.com/english/spip.php?article225.

63. "Jayezeh Olaf Palme Baraye Parvin Ardalan" [Olaf Palme Prize Awarded to Parvin Ardalan], *BBC Persian*, February 14, 2008.

64. "Iranian Leader Tells Women's Rights Activists Not to Try to Change Laws: Ayatollah Decries West as a Model," *Reuters*, July 5, 2007.

65. Personal interviews with secular and Islamist activists, Tehran April 12 and 13, 2008.

66. Personal interviews with blogger and journalist, London, April 27, 2006 and secular Campaign activist and journalist, Tehran, May 5, 2008.

67. Personal interview, activist, Tehran, April 12, 2008.

68. Ali Akbar Mahdi, "A Campaign for Equality and Democratic Culture," August 6, 2007, www.we-change.org/english/spip.php?article130. Accessed September 12, 2009.

69. Rochelle Terman, "The Contemporary Iranian Women's Rights Movement."

70. Personal interview, women's activist, March 16, 2010. Lida Hosseininejad, "Nemi Khaheem Charkh Motalebat Zanan Az Aval Ekhtera Shavad: Ghoftogoo ba Mahboubeh Abbasgholizadeh" [We Do not Want the Wheels of Women's Demands Invented From the Start: An Interview with Mahboubeh Abbasgholizadeh], *Radio Zamaneh*, February 7, 2007.

71. Charles Tilly, *Social Movements, 1768–2004,* 2004, 3–4.

72. Zahra Ebrahimi, "Zanan dar Boodjeye 1386 Jaee Nadashtand" [Women Had No Place in the Budget of 2007], *Zanan* 143, 6–9.

73. Ziba Mir-Hosseini, "Is Time on Iranian Women Protester's Side?" *Middle East Report,* June 16, 2006.

74. Zahra Ebrahimi, "Eeteraze Shadeed be Ozveat Nadashtan dar Heeyat Raeese" [Women's Objection to Not being in the Parliament's Board of Directors], *Zanan* 124, 22–26.

75. Elahe Koolaee, "Iranian Women After Reform," *Ayeen Monthly* No. 9, 2007, 46–50. Nazila Fathi, "Iranian Women Should Have More Children," *New York Times*, October 24, 2006.

76. Zahra Ebrahimi, "Sahmiyeh 30 Dar Sad Baraye Zanan dar Entekhabat," [Women's Fraction Demand 30% Quota for Women in the Election," *Zanan* 104, 18–24.

77. Homa Hoodfar and Shadi Sadr, "Can Women Act as Agents of a Democratization of Theocracy in Iran?" *United Nations Research Institute for Social Development*, October 2009, 24.

78. "Tajamo'e Zanan dar E'teraz be Shoraye Negahban" [Women Gathering to Protest the Guardian Council], *BBC Persian*, June 1, 2005.

79. Shabnam Ghafourian, "One Step Away From Legalizing Women's Candidacy for President," *Bamdad News*, March 17, 2009.

80. "Tarhe Majles Baraye Akhze Tabe'yat Irani Az Madar Rad Shod" [Majles' Plan to Obtain Citizenship Through the Mother is Not Approved,] *BBC Persian*, May 16, 2006.

81. The Women for Equal Citizenship Campaign launched in August 2006 has lobbied to further amend this law. For more on this Campaign see Rochelle Terman, "The Women for Equal Citizenship Campaign," Women Living Under Muslim Laws, forthcoming.

82. "Mosavabe Sahme Erse Zanane Iran Ejraye Shod" [Iranian Women's Inheritance Share Was Ratified], *BBC Persian*, March 11, 2009.

83. "Tarhe Namayandegane Majles Baraye Afzayeshe Sahme Zanane Iran" [The Majles' Plan for Increasing Women's Share], *BBC Persian*, December 1, 2008. Accessed December 28, 2009.

84. "Iran Enforces New Women's Inheritance Law," *Press TV*, March 12, 2009.

85. Arash Behmanesh, "Eejad Amniyate Ejtemaee Ba Roosari va Chador" [Creation of Social Morality with a Scarf and a Veil], *BBC Persian*, September 14, 2007.

86. "Tarhe Aminayate Ejtemaee Esrat Manfee Dashte Ast" [Social Morality Plan has Negative Effects], *BBC Persian*, August 12, 2008.

87. "Nameh Fa'alan Hoghoghe Zanan be Namayendeye Zane Majlise Iran" [Letter by Women's Rights Activists to Iranian Female Parliamentarians], *BBC Persian*, December 5, 2007.

88. Sahar Sepehry, "Dava Bar Sar Zan Dovom dar Owj-e Bohran-e Siasi" [Battle over Acquiring a Second Wife at the Peak of Political Turmoil], *Mianeh*, February 1, 2010. www.mianeh.net/fa/articles/?aid=252. Accessed March 12, 2010.

89. Statement by Amnesty International March 5, 2010. http://www.amnesty.org/en/library/asset/MDE13/028/2010/en/8513eb97-f106-4ca0-809f-4c3a9cb15336/mde130282010en.pdf. Accessed March 23, 2010.

90. Fatemeh Sadeghi, "Ezdevaje Movaghat va Eghtesade Lezat," [Temporary Marriage and the Economy of Pleasure,] January 9, 2010, http://www.alborznet.ir/Fa/ViewDetail.aspx?T=2&ID=275. Accessed April 14, 2010.

91. Sahar Sepehry, "Dava Bar Sar Zan Dovom dar Owje Bohrane Siyasi" [Battle over Acquiring a Second Wife at the Peak of Political Turmoil], *Mianeh*, February 1, 2010.

92. Dorna Hatamlooy, "Protest Against Planned Family Law in Iran: Free Pass for Polygamous Men," *Qantara.de*, 2008.

93. Ibid.

94. Hoodfar and Sadr. "Can Women Act as Agents of a Democratization of Theocracy in Iran?" 2009, 13.

95. Elaheh Koolaee, "Sahmieh Bandi Jensiaty bar Zede Zanan," [Gender Quota Against Iranian Women,] Ayeen, No. 10, 2007, 54–57.

96. "Elam-e Sahmieyehbandy Jensiaty Dar Daneshgahaye Iran" [The Official Announcement of Gender Quotas in Iranian Universities], *BBC Persian*, February 25, 2008.

97. Taraneh Baniyaghoub, "Tahseele Dokhtaran dar Daneshgahaye Markaz ba Ejazeh Khanevadeh Hayeshan" [Girls Education in Main Cities' Universities Only With Parents Permission], March 5, 2009, www.irwomen.info/spip.php?article6488. Accessed March 12, 2010.

98. Ibid.

99. *Iranian Student News Agency* (ISNA), Tehran, 28 January 2008.

100. Liora Hendelman-Baavur, "Iran Bans 'Women'—The Shutting Down of Women," *Iran Pulse* 21, April 15, 2008; Farangis Najibullah, "Iran: Women's Magazine Felled By Latest Government Closure," *RFERL*, February 13, 2008; Wendy Kristiansen, "Stop the Presses," *Le Monde Diplomatique*, April 2008.

101. Farideh Farhi, "The Attempted Silencing of Zanan," *Informed Comment Global Affairs Blog*, February 1, 2008.

102. Nahid Tavassoli. "Entekhab Vazire Zan, Chera Hala?" [Election of a Woman Minister, Why Now?] August 21, 2009, www.feministschool.com/spip.php?article3065. Accessed March 22, 2010.

103. Personal Interview with Islamist activist and former politician, Tehran, April 30, 2008.

104. "Mokhalefate Oosolgarayan ba Vezarate Zan: Kamy ta Ghesmaty Shari'e" [Principalists' Opposition to Female Ministers: Some of it Religious] *BBC Persian*, August 26, 2009, www.bbc.co.uk/persian/iran/2009/08/090826_ka_women_minister-iran.shtml accessed March 22, 2010.

105. Ibid.

106. Fatemeh Govaree, "Never Mind Women Ministers, Where Are the Women's Votes?" September 15, 2009, www.iranfemschool.com/english/spip.php?page=pint&id_article=eee. Accessed October 23, 2009.

107. Fatemeh Sadeghi, "Foot Soldiers of the Islamic Republic's 'Culture of Modesty,'" *Middle East Report 250*, Spring 2009.

108. Quoted in Sadeghi, "Chera Hijab?" [Why We Say No to the Compulsory Hijab], trans. Frieda Afary, *Meydaneh Zan* [Women's Field], 2008, 54.

109. Farangis Najibullah, "Iran: Tehran Opens Controversial Women-Only Park," *Radio Free Europe Radio Liberty*, May 17, 2008.

110. "Tehran to get Special Police Stations for Women," *Agence Free Press*, December 7, 2007.

111. Shirzad Borzorgmehr, "Nobel laureate's Tehran home attacked," *CNN News*, February 26, 2009.

112. Charles Kurzman, "A Feminist Generation in Iran?" *Iranian Studies*, Vol. 41, No. 3, 2008.

8

The Circles of Confrontation, Conciliation, and Contradiction

In February 2009, with much fanfare, Iran celebrated the thirtieth anniversary of the Iranian Revolution trumpeting its success and endurance as a revolutionary state surviving amidst much adversity. The symbolism associated with this celebration was poignant. Indeed, observers had repeatedly questioned the durability of the revolutionary, theocratic regime that shunned both East and West in the hope of maintaining its commitment to "independence, freedom and the Islamic Republic." Despite such resilience, the Islamic Republic bears the mark of a country in transition—suffering stagnation as a result of its many internal contradictions. Notwithstanding the taxing years of consolidation, war, and isolation, the Islamic Republic has faced mounting challenges both from within and from without. Iran remains a regional menace flouting United Nations and U.S. sanctions over its nuclear program while also strengthening its regional hand through the support of proxy powers such as Hezbollah and Hamas. Domestically, a demographic explosion has exacerbated the burdens of securing and maintaining a cohesive revolutionary leadership and the subsequent socioeconomic pressures associated with it. At the same time, Iran's population, which has been bound by the political and social constraints of living in an Islamic Iran, is no longer fiercely revolutionary or committed to the restrictive life in the Leviathan state. Instead, the restive youth and dynamic society long for greater freedom of expression and greater opportunity of representation. Indeed during these 30 years, this population has become overwhelmingly educated and incorporated not only in the domestic and regional realm but also in reaping the benefits of modernity and technology in a globalized world. These paradoxes would unexpectedly rear their head in May 2009 only three months after this momentous anniversary when the totality of 30 years of popular frustration would collide with the coercive power of the state in post-election protests. The convergence of these trends—widespread social and political disenchantment, factional divisions, pervasive economic dislocations, and increasing international

198

pressure on the Islamic regime—would merge together in the aftermath of the tenth presidential elections forming an almost insurmountable list of challenges for the regime. Women, who had been vigorous participants in past political movements, were again vanguard activists.

The 2009 Presidential Election: Everything Green and the Women In Between

The 2009 Presidential election and post-election upheaval caused tectonic shifts in Iran's domestic and international political landscape. Months before the election, most Iranians expected Ahmadinejad's reelection to be a forgone conclusion. Public political apathy further corroborated these predictions. During the first weeks of the campaign season, the four candidates approved by the Guardian Council on May 20, 2009, incumbent Mahmoud Ahmadinejad, former Prime Minister Mir Hussein Musavi, former Speaker of the Parliament Mehdi Karroubi, and former Revolutionary Guard commander Mohsen Rezai, garnered little enthusiasm.[1] Yet, by the first week of June 2009, the candidates participated in six live debates offering the public a unique opportunity to observe interactions among the candidates. President Ahmadinejad's debate with Mir Hussein Musavi was particularly impassioned as the President criticized Musavi's wife, Zahra Rahnavard. Ahmadinejad also attacked former President Rafsanjani accusing him publicly of corruption.

In the subsequent weeks, Musavi appeared to experience a surge in public support. His campaign had gained momentum as he offered a more progressive program for political change. Supporters embraced his platform and rallied in favor of the former prime minister by donning his "green" campaign color. Many prominent reformist politicians and activists also publicly endorsed Mehdi Karroubi. Both reformist candidates had promised to curb social restrictions, improve the rights of women and ethnic minorities, resuscitate the ailing economy, and moderate foreign policy.

It is within this atmosphere that women's activists collaborated to compel each candidate to address gender issues and delineate a gender policy. Drawing from the lessons of their years of activism, women recognized that boycotting, as had been experienced in the 2005 election, had failed to bring attention to women's concerns. Moreover, the lack of female participation in past elections had also enabled conservative victories in the 2005 presidential election and 2008 parliamentary elections. In this vein, building upon their collaborative efforts in advance of the 2008 parliamentary elections and the new wave of collective activism evidenced through the various campaigns, 700 women's activists and 42 women's groups, both Islamist and secular, came together forming a coalition known as Convergence of Women (*Hamgarayee Zanan*). The goal of the group was not to endorse one political candidate but rather force the candidates to establish "fundamental demands" for the amelioration of gender laws. The coalition encapsulated their two demands as: 1) the ratification of CEDAW and 2) the revision of Articles 19, 20, 21, and 115 in the constitution that enshrined gender discrimination.[2] Alongside establishing defined gender priorities was the cooperation of all activist women regardless of ideological, political, and religious orientation. Moreover, the equal embrace of these demands displayed the newfound unity among women's activists.[3] Filmmaker Rakhsan Bani Etemad documented the mobilization and collaboration of women including interviews with activists in her film *We are Half of Iran's Population* that was shown to all the presidential candidates except Ahmadinejad. Musavi, Karroubi, and Rezai responded by developing a gender platform that was committed to addressing women's issues and appointing female cabinet ministers.

Throughout the campaign Musavi's wife Zahra Rahnavard regularly accompanied him oftentimes holding his hand. Moves such as this were unprecedented in Iran's gender segregated society. Rahnavard's stature as a prominent and outspoken women's activist, academic, and artist also enhanced Musavi's appeal among women. Considered by many to be the more charismatic of the two, Rahnavard committed that if her husband were elected she would make Iran a signatory to CEDAW. For many women, Rahnavard became a public symbol of women's activism. Karroubi, too, offered a gender friendly alternative. Compared to his last presidential bid in 2005, Karroubi acknowledged the importance of the female vote. He was supported by a number of prominent women's activists as well. Karroubi's spokeswoman Jamileh Kadivar even openly questioned the mandatory hijab. These decisive shifts set the stage for greater female and popular participation.[4]

On Election Day, June 12, 2009, reports of high voter participation and long lines at polling stations circulated. By the evening, the government had declared Ahmadinejad the victor having won 62 percent of the vote with Musavi having garnered 34 percent.[5] The three opposing candidates immediately contested the official results calling for a recount amid accusations of fraud. In reaction, spontaneous clashes erupted the following day in Tehran and other major cities as the allegations of deceit resonated among Musavi supporters. Over the subsequent weeks and months, demonstrations would continue to engulf Tehran and other principal cities as popular disappointment over the opaque election translated into larger political grievances against the repressive and coercive arm of the state. Protesters draped in Musavi's campaign color of green, became more fearless in challenging the regime's status quo. The opposition under the de facto leadership of Musavi, Karroubi, and Khatami revived tactics used during the 1979 revolution by calling for demonstrations on days of mourning, and symbolic days of importance such as the anniversary of the American hostage crisis and the mourning celebrations of Ashura to bring people into the streets. By highjacking the state's revolutionary symbols, in using the color green, traditionally associated with Islam, and in employing non-violent tactics, the movement proved to be an enormous challenge to those currently in power.

Undoubtedly, the spontaneous outpouring of dissent was a shock to the conservative establishment that proved initially slow to respond. The Guardian Council ordered a partial recount of the votes only to recertify Ahmadinejad's triumph.[6] Supreme Leader Khamenei's public affirmation of support for Ahmadinejad and declaration that the election was a victory for democracy cemented divisions among the elite. Khamenei whose position as Supreme Leader required him to remain above the fray had intervened in the election displaying his hidden hand. Khamenei indicated that protests would no longer be tolerated foreshadowing the state backlash to come. Drawing a lesson from Alexis de Tocqueville who wrote, "the most perilous moment for a bad government is one when it seeks to mend its ways,"[7] Khamenei maintained a hard-line position to protect the longevity of the Islamic Republic. Yet despite his pronouncement that the elections were over, protests continued in Tehran and in other cities, as protesters chanted, "Where is my vote?" Public anger toward the conservative bastions of the state peaked as chants against the Supreme Leader could also be heard. Nightly chants of *Allah o Akbar* (God is great) could also be heard on the rooftops reminiscent of similar calls heard during the 1979 revolution.

The government crackdown was implemented through a multifaceted strategy of violent tactics, intimidation, surveillance, arrests of demonstrators and reformist elite, detentions of activists, a purge of the bureaucracy and universities, the expulsion of the foreign media, and blockage of Internet and mobile phone access. With no respite from the protests after ten days of upheaval and confusion, the Basij and Revolutionary Guard were deployed throughout Tehran and other cities as the government crackdown on demonstrations intensified. These security forces began using violence, tear gas, and live ammunition to disperse crowds. On June 20, demonstrators clashed with Basij militia, who used violence to dispel the protesters. Neda Agha Soltan, a 27-year-old philosophy student, was shot becoming the first martyr of many in what became known as the Green Movement. Neda's death, captured on mobile phones and videos was distributed on the Internet through the online networking sites Facebook and YouTube drawing worldwide attention and outrage to both her death and the uprising.[8] As the foreign media was expelled from Iran, it was "citizen journalists" who took the mantle of journalism and reporting to new heights using Facebook and Twitter to communicate with the outside world and to coordinate amongst themselves. Arrests of over 150 prominent reformists, former political officials, and journalists further exacerbated tensions revealing the widening cleavages among the political elite. Members of former President Rafsanjani's family were reportedly arrested, as were members of Musavi and Karroubi's family. Over 100 reformists were put on trial and jailed for a number of month's accused of endangering national security. Thousands of demonstrators and activists were arrested and an estimated 107 people were killed.[9] Nine months later, by the thirty-first anniversary of the Islamic Republic on February 11, 2010, the state, through its tactics, had neutralized the opposition. Although few protests had taken place since February 2010, which allowed the state breathing room, it remains unlikely that the Green Movement will disappear. The sentiments and disappointment that culminated in the election protests continued to aggravate despite government suppression. Without any wholesale acknowledgement and reconciliation of popular social, economic, and political grievances, such opposition will continue to fester.

Women's activists were not excluded from the onslaught. Women, both young and old, secular and religious, were prominent among the demonstrators. Women's activists were also targeted and arrested, including former parliamentarian Faezeh Hashemi, lawyer and activist Shadi Sadr, lawyer Nasrin Sotoudeh, student activist Bahareh Hedayat among many others. That women were willing to take risks and be jailed alongside their male counterparts signified their power of presence and commitment to social and political change.[10] For women, the Green Movement was a reflection not only of popular disenchantment but also a merging of the hopes seen through reformism, secularism, and the blossoming of civil society. Activists linked the improvement in women's rights to the trends of political liberalization. Indeed, the increasing number of arrested and indicted women—estimated to be over 600—highlights the perceived threat of women's activism. A growing government suppression that had commenced in reaction to the One Million Signatures Campaign extended to other female initiatives, greatly impacting the network of women's activism. In reaction, "women's groups have taken refuge under the shadow of the Green Movement," stated one women's activist.[11] Consequently, the women's network built around the campaign broke into smaller groups and many activists went underground or fled into exile to survive the government onslaught. As such, women's activists have not had an opportunity to strategize or regroup. According to Mahboubeh Abbasgholizadeh, "the goal of destroying civil society . . . the real culprit behind the Green movement has been highly successful. Women's groups face a crisis of operation." [12]

Such paralysis has not impeded activist women from criticizing the Green Movement and its leadership though demonstrating a decisive break from the past. Some activists continue to be disappointed by the lack of a decisive gender platform. A recent statement signed by a group of women activists accused defeated presidential contenders Mir Hossein Musavi and Mehdi Karroubi of ignoring women's rights and paying limited tribute to gender issues in their political manifestos. "We believe that women's issues are a major part of the current crisis and no solution will be achieved unless this issue is included," they wrote. Other disagreed suggesting that women were already expressing their demands and were not in need of politicians' support.[13] Zahra Rahnavard who has continued to challenge the regime alongside her husband has in response called upon women to learn from the lessons of history. She stated that while "there is considerable overlap between the two movements. On more specific issues, there is a need for the women's rights movement to branch out and push its own agenda above and beyond the support that it gleans from the Green Movement. . . . general political reform movements and revolutions have shown that women's fight for equality needs to be distinguished from the general political movement for democracy.[14] This dynamic interaction has been an integral part of women's activism. Indeed, women continue to be united on the ends, yet the means continue to be debated.

This debate has also affected the future of the campaigns. Since the apogee of the government backlash, the campaign has been most effective in the virtual world. Unable to organize and network, activists have retreated into cyberspace. With limited ability to attract new activists or engage in public interfacing, the reach of the campaign has been contained. At the same time, activists continue to deliberate over their long-term strategies. Activist, Parvin Ardalan reported on this stalemate, suggesting that women's groups were reconsidering their strategy of negotiation with the an illegitimate government that had lost popular support. Those in the One Million Signatures campaign who had planned to submit their demands to parliament no longer sought to do so. She stated, "The situation has changed—people want gender equality but they don't think the approach is to go to this government to get it. So currently even the groups that did have contact with the government, no longer do." [15] Indeed, women's activists are at an impasse. Stunted by government repression on the one hand, they too remain impeded by the lack of future direction a daunting prospect when many believe that their gender ambitions can only be achieved with a change of government.

Such ongoing restrictions and examples of intimidation toward women represent the unending dichotomy lingering between state and society. Clearly, while the Islamic Republic has struggled amidst adversity so too have Iranian women. Over the 30 year evolution, women have moved through the phases of collaboration, conciliation, and confrontation using diverse tactics to advance their agenda for women's equality. Their narrative is critical to understanding these changes. More importantly, their story is decisively linked to the legitimacy of the Islamic Republic and at the same time exposes the contradictions of the regime and its leadership. Indeed, just as there have been setbacks for women, there have also been gains. But clear to this story is the ongoing divide over the regime's paradoxical approach toward gender issues. Iran's women have quietly steered a course through the restrictions of politics, religion, and tradition over the last three decades to bolster their status and advance into positions of power. Although the conservative clerics hoped to solidify a traditional role for women, conversely they institutionalized the dynamics that liberated them. "It's one of the ironies of the revolution that women's sense of self became stronger. The revolution has given birth to a stronger women's movement." [16]

These contradictions are a function of the many unrestrained paradoxes that reign free in the Islamic Republic. Through this study it is clear that the Iranian leadership remains not only at odds with itself but also with its population. The recent post-election protests and the presence of the Green Movement are clear reflections of such cleavages. However, in spite of these competing factional trends and unresolved ideological vision, these uncontrolled contradictions have ironically also held the regime together in the face of continued obstacles. The result is often evidenced in stagnation or in contradictory and incoherent policies advanced by various elites, factions, and institutions. Because of the flexible decentralized political and religious structure, the state has been able to balance and navigate through unmitigated waters. The fragmented political and religious system whereby elected branches of government beholden to the public are frequently at odds with nonelected bodies belies the notion of a clear demarcation between the regime and the public. Also among the religious institutions, where individual clerics retain their rights of interpretation, paradoxes emerge over contending religious readings, again widening the divide between state and society. However, without impending reconciliation of these contending policies, including those that relate to women, the future of the Islamic Republic will be mired in continued political stagnation. In the short run, continued stagnation can be good for the regime providing the illusion and hope of power as well as greater political inclusion to the various factional groups. In the long run, though, disavowing the demands of the state, particularly economic and social ones, will ultimately perpetuate the vicious cycle of domestic instability.

Thirty-one years in, the Islamic Republic soldiers on as a "state, which is neither revolutionary nor fully pragmatic."[17] It has survived in the face of these obstacles mainly through a delicate balancing of its intractable ideological façade with its malleable pragmatic core. Such a balancing act has been the essential keystone holding the Islamic state and its appendages together and enabling the leadership to navigate through the rough seas. At the outset of the revolution, Ayatollah Khomeini's presence and stature provided the necessary cohesion for the nascent revolutionary state. His charisma and authority elicited compromise and collaboration among the diverse ideological groups that supported his leadership. However, upon his death, the regime's paradoxes and factional groups could no longer be contained. The void was replaced by intense factional competition among the myriad of ideological groups. The much-heralded revolutionary consensus seemed to fray amidst burgeoning economic, social, and demographic challenges.

Revolutionary loyalists held fast to the values and commitments of the revolution—social justice, independence, and Islam—promises designed to sustain an ideological commitment to Khomeini's dictum. Pragmatists offered a middle-ground solution of economic moderation aimed at reviving Iran's economy and accommodating the demands of Iranian society. Reformers who were disillusioned by the failed revolutionary promises advanced new strategies of political moderation, social openness and economic liberalization designed to breathe new life into the stagnating republic. For them, popular support would give new legitimacy and sustainability to the Islamic Republic. These divisions brought to the fore new intellectual and ideological discourse among Iran's vibrant civil society. These debates opened new ground for competing political, social, and intellectual trends including the emergence of a secular one. Within the Islamic landscape, it is the growing trend of secularism evidenced most prominently since the election of Muhammad Khatami in 1997 that has gained the most ground threatening the ideological foundation of the Islamic Republic.

In this atmosphere, civil society has experienced a flourishing of expression. Iranian society has changed dramatically and bears little resemblance to the expectations of the leadership of the Islamic Republic. Internal and external social and political transformation have fueled greater awareness, greater activism. The "demographic gift" of the post-revolutionary period resulted in a doubling of the population to 71 million, and more specifically a burgeoning of the youth population. As reflected by Iran's 85 percent literacy rate among the highest of Muslim countries, young Iranians are much better educated than previous generations. However, fewer than one in three can remember the revolution, and the young suffer disproportionately from the regime's failures. Unemployment, inflation, urbanization, and demographic shifts have added pressure to both state and society. The revolution has come full circle as students, women, workers, writers, artists, musicians, journalists, environmentalists, and intellectuals among others have worked in spite of the revolutionary restrictions. They have reaped the paradoxical benefits of education and development using creative means to assert their ideas and attitudes.

This study has examined the trajectory of women's activism since the Iranian Revolution. A number of conclusions can be made about the changes evidenced among women and women's activism and the state. It has been argued that in a similar transformation evidenced in Iranian civil society and domestic politics, women's activism has moved through various phases—from the collaborative, to the conciliatory to the confrontational. Exploiting the contradictions within the political and social polity has enabled women to make gains despite the control of the patriarchy. Evidenced through this chronological review of women's activism is that the state has offered women piecemeal advances over its three-decade tenure. Ideological orientation of the leadership from conservative pragmatist Khomeini and Rafsanjani to reformist Khatami and conservative Ahmadinejad cannot account for the gains and losses for women.[18] Rather the state has offered gradual legal and political gains when expedient or in response to public pressure. Moreover, each leader promoted gender reform within the context of their policy programs, but various leaders have yet to develop a comprehensive gender platform. Instead, their policies remain reactive.

It has been suggested by other scholars before and repeated here that states have absorbed and controlled gender policies to promote their national interests.[19] In Iran, this has been no exception. Indeed, the state's gender policy has been among the ideological pillars of the Islamic Republic. Under the Pahlavi monarchy, gender was used to promote the Shah's modernization and Westernization campaigns, such that the inclusion of the Iranian woman was critical to the projection of a modern Iran. Within the Islamic Republic, gender has been used to convey the ideological goals of independence associated with the revolution. Islam and the state's Islamicization of society were the mechanisms of such a message. The use of gender to define Iran's domestic and even international policies was essential to the legitimacy of the regime and the strength and permanence of the revolution. Women have become the symbolic guardians of the revolution as the state constructed an identity that linked the female role of a wife and mother to the defense of the revolutionary values. Using the Prophet's daughter Fatemeh as a paragon of tradition and motherhood, this image has been juxtaposed against the sexual, exploitative one of Western women. At the same time, as women have emerged alongside men in political demonstrations, in universities and in the work place, the image of a modern, Islamic woman has also served the government's purposes.

Yet, the regime has been forced to compromise. From the early days under Khomeini's authority through the presidencies of Rafsanjani, Khatami, and even

Ahmadinejad we have witnessed repeated examples of moderation towards the restrictive policies of gender. For each of the leaders, the issue of gender became a salient feature of domestic development, modernization, and an example of the pragmatic politics evidenced in the Islamic Republic. Such examples of pragmatism have slowly reversed or advanced alternative gender visions. Moreover, the policies of Khomeini, Rafsanjani, Khatami, and Ahmadinejad have exposed the contradictory tendencies with regards to women while at the same time have uncovered the evolutionary trends in Iranian domestic politics. Here, the state, political factions, and ideological groups have used women's issues as a platform to advance their alternative visions for the future of the Islamic Republic. Indeed, the legislative, social, economic, political, and cultural issues surrounding gender equality have been caught up in Iran's domestic political tug of war.

Women too learnt the lessons and drawbacks of history. Through the stages of revolutionary leadership women established the foundations and building blocks for their activism. During Khomeini's consolidation tenure, the Imam was forced to concede to women as he confronted the realities of war and statecraft. Early on, to retain female support, women were enfranchised. Women were also encouraged to become educated and were equally important to the economic sustenance of many families. Offering amendments to the traditional Islamic interpretations of Shariah law, Khomeini placated women in return for their political support by allowing widows to retain custody of their children rather than bequeath them to the paternal family. Women have ironically used Khomeini's early dispensations toward women in an effort to reverse patriarchal legal interpretations and secure political, economic and social concessions.

President Rafsanjani was forced to address the political, social, and economic post-war realities. In an effort to stimulate the economy while simultaneously mollifying the restive, youthful population; Rafsanjani presented further conciliatory olive branches to women. For Rafsanjani, the eternal pragmatist, women were essential to the economic development of Iranian society. Politically, female support was essential for the government's legitimacy. Economically, women were called upon to assist in the national economic regeneration campaign. Socially, too, women were beneficiaries of the less restrictive environment where they could thrive academically and professionally through the growing support of the state apparatus. Gradual accommodation on issues of marriage and divorce were also witnessed. The growing secular and reformist discourse also gave secular women greater space to return to the political and social scene where they joined the ranks of civil society as journalists, artists, and agitators. However, Rafsanjani was constrained by a growing ideological divide. This political partition would only harden, creating obstacles for political, economic, and social development.

Overwhelming female support bolstered Khatami's term. His reform movement offered possibilities to women who were mobilized by his promise of civil society and political liberalism. Indeed, the demographic boom coupled with the growth of female education had given strength to women's demands. Together with the election of the 2000 reform parliament, women gained more political authority during this period through elections and political appointments. Through their presence and with increased pressure they attempted to reverse legislative limitations on gender equality. While much disappointment is associated with the Khatami presidency, it is also acknowledged that the reform momentum and political support given to women's issues enabled women to assume greater social and activist roles during this period. Winning publication permits, reformist, gender journals, and magazines blossomed. Through these mediums, women addressed their political, social and economic demands as well as discussed cultural gender inequities. Such dialogue and dissemination was also enhanced by the growth of the Internet. NGO networks supported by the government spread the seed of female activism, which in turn facilitated a growing female association and collaboration. Legislative gains evidenced in the reversal of study bans on female students and the return of women to the courts as consultative judges among others were coupled with defeats over CEDAW. Growing inspiration from the publicity and recognition of Shirin Ebadi's activities propelled women forward. Linkages with the student movement and other nascent social groups laid the groundwork for future collaboration. As conservatives lashed out against the reform movement, the fallout extended toward much of Iran's vibrant civil society and toward the growing momentum of women's activism. For women, past policies of collaboration and conciliation with the regime had proved frustrating. Many activist women, particularly secularist ones, emerged from this period ready to assume a confrontational approach to change.

The election of Ahmadinejad signaled a new trend in domestic politics. Reflecting the hardened ideological divide cemented between conservatives and reformists, Ahmadinejad tried to return to the traditional values embraced by the revolution. The women parliamentarians of the Seventh Majlis vowed not to discuss women's rights except as they related to Islamic jurisprudence and to increase monitoring of strict veiling requirements. Indeed, the Eighth parliament was forced to amend a bill allowing for polygamous marriages. Women mounted a strong opposition to the bill lobbying the parliament against such moves. At the same time though, the president tried to reverse a three-decade ban preventing women from entering sports stadiums. His effort was met with fierce resistance among the religious community resulting in a decree against the move from Ayatollah Khamenei as well. He has however attempted to revive the traditional gender imagery associated with the revolution to counter the changing face of women's activism. New legislation passed through the parliament on blood money and inheritance has provided women equal privileges. Clearly, amidst the growing strains of domestic politics, even for Ahmadinejad, isolating women and ignoring gender issues has not been a viable option. In the aftermath of the 2009 elections, Ahmadinejad was the first Iranian president to appoint a female cabinet member. Amidst the domestic factional infighting that continues to dominate the political fray, women's issues are likely to be included in this contested agenda, but offered piecemeal or *gham be gham*.[20] As one activist maintained, this approach does not compromise the integral vision of the state and its Islamic ideology.[21] Still the issue of women exposes the fragile fault lines and contradictions that threaten the viability of the Iranian regime.

Women have been active in all major Iranian political and social transformations since the nineteenth century. Their political and social convergence alongside men during the past three decades bears witness to the growing momentum behind their efforts. Agitating alongside their male counterparts in the Constitutional Revolution, women sought to gain equal standing and representation. While dismissed in these early efforts, pioneering women such as Bibi Khanoom Astarbadi and Taj al Sultaneh translated female grievances into political ones where they criticized the patriarchal norms regarding women. To further their goals for gender equality, some women articulated their demands through journalistic endeavors while others advanced the campaign for female education by sponsoring and opening their own schools for girls. Women continued to be active as agents of social and political change throughout the twentieth century. Taking part in demonstrations and lobbying for political and legal rights, women continued to draw from the examples and lessons of their ancestor activists. At the same time though, similar to their predecessors, women were forced to subsume their gender goals in favor of larger political ones. Such moves were expedient in order to retain male and government support, but in making such compromises women's issues were regularly neglected among the larger political or social platforms for change. These patterns while established decades ago have been perpetuated by activists in the early days of the revolution as again women, especially Islamist and traditional ones, collaborated with the new Islamic government hoping that their participation would result in greater political and social inclusion. At the same time, women used similar strategies of organizational, journalistic, and educational expansion in order to articulate and challenge the contemporary political, legal, religious, and social norms. In 2010, there was greater awareness among activists to avoid the pitfalls of the past. A major achievement is that activists are no longer willing to subordinate their aim of gender equality in favor of political priorities. The goals of political change, democracy, and liberalization are interconnected with gender equality, but activists insist that these larger ambitions are dependent on gender reform.

For female activists, the greatest feat to emerge from the Iranian revolution was the unification of women in common cause. While such cooperation is by no means monolithic or universal in Iran, the birth of a gender conscious society has greatly assisted the foundation of women's activism. Indeed, two shifts have occurred. The first has taken hold at the popular level where gender consciousness has influenced society at large. The second has impacted elites who through the years have merged forces to challenge the state's gender policy. At the outset of the revolution, despite a show of force in demonstrations and political participation, women were ideologically and politically divided amongst themselves. Different political associations, parties, and groups pushing their divergent ideologies for the new government led to contests among factional groups and even women on the future of the Islamic Republic. Further partitions among women were exacerbated by the imposition of Shariah law and revocation of legal gains obtained under the Pahlavi monarchy. Secular women were essentially marginalized from the political scene while Islamist women split into two groups—those who advocated reform and progressive interpretations of Islamic law and traditional women who fully supported the Islamic agenda with restrictions on women. In the first decade of the revolutionary government, little cooperation was evidenced among these groups. Moreover, Islamist women subscribed to collaborative strategies with the government in the hope of participating and affecting the debate on women's issues.

This common cause, the shared challenges, the sense of struggle experienced among all women from divergent political, religious, social, and economic backgrounds facilitated greater bonds and collaboration among women. It is not only secular women who must struggle to prove their grounds for divorce, but all women. It is not only traditional women who must fight to retain custody of their children, but all women. It is not only urban women who face challenges in the work force, but all women. It is not only rural women who struggle against abuse, violence, and a patriarchal culture, but all women. Clearly, the unintended consequence of the revolution, the imposition of an Islamic legal system and government, and the contradictory gender policies of the state, has been the alliance of women bound by their collective experiences and their collective presence. Indeed, as suggested by Bayat, "women were part of passive networks that served as the most important medium for the construction of collective identities. [These] networks signified instantaneous and unspoken communication between atomized individuals established through the gaze in public space by tacit recognition of commonalities expressed in style, behavior or concerns." [22] Bonds of affinity and empathy in effect has facilitated female solidarity.

In recognizing these shared bonds, activist women both secular and Islamist have moved away from the patterns of the past. Since 2009, there is greater cooperation evidenced among activists despite ideological or political orientation. There have been limitations to this cooperation as Islamist women have oftentimes chosen to pursue collaborative governmental tactics while secular activists have diverged towards confrontational strategies. This divergence is particularly evidenced in the tactics pursued by the One Million Signatures Campaign. However, while the means might differ the ends endure. In advance of the 2009 presidential election, collaboration among women's groups was evidenced in the collective effort to promote gender platforms. Ideological orientation was no longer a barrier to cooperation. Moreover, such divisions did not prevent women from endorsing the same goals. This shift is significant, as women's activism has evolved away from the Islamist and secularist typologies. Rather, women's activism has embarked upon post-Islamist and post-secularist period. For female activists, from all walks of life, the struggle for gender equality has transcended the boundaries of the past and the barriers of belief—another monumental feat.

Over this 32-year period, female activism has flourished in response and in reaction to the contradictory policies of the Iranian government. Despite this evolution that has given birth to a gender conscious society, there remain numerous obstacles ahead for women and women's activism. Primarily, as women's issues remain linked to the legitimacy of the Islamic revolution, prospects for radical changes including constitutional amendments recognizing gender equality remain dim. This possibility is further constrained by the stagnating factional disputes stalling progress on domestic politics. Indeed, a major ideological reconciliation on the future of the Islamic Republic is needed to resolve the political, economic, and social stagnation—much of which impacts women. But, domestic reconciliation in Iran is equally tied to Iran's international relations principally in light of the state's ongoing enmity with the United States, Iranian obstruction over its nuclear program and sanctions. Domestic paralysis and factional infighting will likely perpetuate as long as Iran continues to feel threatened by American regional interests as the state uses these issues to justify their control of society. Limited or piecemeal compromise will likely be the continued government response to civil society pressure particularly while international tensions remain unresolved. With regards to women's activism, the state will be unlikely to accept CEDAW despite ongoing pressure, but continue to gradually adjust gender legislation.

Today, the challenge for female activists extends beyond their confrontational demands with the state. Iranian activism still remains largely confined to the educated urban middle class limited to large cities. In bustling Tehran, one can easily be consumed by the pressure and promise of activist momentum. I certainly was. One should also not neglect the role and visibility of traditional women who remain loyal to the state and the tenets of the Islamic Republic. When traveling to the provinces or small towns, the network and impact of women's activism fades. There, it is easy to disregard the strength of tradition and religion that are dominant fixtures for women outside urban centers. Indeed, the secularization of society should be contextualized amidst the expectations of the clerical establishment who hoped to spawn a devout revolutionary generation. While the latter has not taken pervasive hold, the importance of religion as a personal, spiritual, and traditional marker in Iranian society is still quite apparent. For example, taking the popular issue of veiling into consideration, some interviewees insisted that should veiling become a matter of personal choice in Iran, still half of the female population would adhere to the veil.[23] Yet, the adherence to Western ideals and images of veiling should not color one's understanding of female activism. Many women, while traditional, are also supportive of gender equality and activism. Studies of Basiji women also reveal a newfound gender consciousness that seeks to reconcile support for the regime with fair interpretations of Islamic law.[24] To further advance, activists must strengthen ties with lower class, rural, and ethnic minority women and women in mid-size and small towns where the majority of the population live. This majority population is barely represented, although rural younger generation Iranians share the egalitarian demands of women's rights activists. While this group of women, particularly traditional mothers, housewives, and war widows are less inclined to agitate; their social and economic grievances are articulated in a passive yet effective manner.

In the aftermath of the war, their political support and participation facilitated government compromise over child custody issues for example. Despite the lack of robust relations between these non-activist women and the activists, the women's movement overwhelmingly reflects the demands of an increasing number of women. "Thanks to their better education, their increasing social and economic participation as well as their common cause, women have become aware that the current laws and institutions tend to strengthen the patriarchal order, and that the struggle for women's citizenship rights and democracy are intertwined."[25]

At the same time, many activists and interviewees acknowledged that changes in women's rights, the growth of women's activism, and the future of the Iranian women's movement is not only tied to female strategies and goals but also dependent on the support of men. The impact of Iran's patriarchal culture cannot be discounted or ignored. Such an observation can be considered redundant and obvious in the face of the male dominant Islamic Iran. However, Iran's social transformation has impacted men alongside women. Indeed, evidenced in the generational divide, young men share a sense of gender consciousness. Students involved in civil society activism lend support to their counterparts involved in the women's arena. Fathers, brothers, uncles, and husbands have also experienced a gender awakening and/or greater awareness having witnessed the legal, social, and cultural hardships experienced by their daughters, sisters, wives, and mothers. This awakening is again tied to the many paradoxical results of the revolution, as the clerical establishment has reconsidered dated legal precedents adjusting them to modern times. At the same time, while gender consciousness is more socially pervasive, one cannot overstate the impact of Iran's patriarchal culture. Obstruction to gender equality is enshrined in the patriarchal interpretations of Islamic law—a pillar of the revolution, the state's legitimacy and national culture.

This analysis of female activism in Iran has highlighted specific trends and developments in state-gender relations. At the same time, this study sheds light on domestic political and civil society transformations through the examination of women's activism. In recent years, conducting primary research in Iran has become increasingly challenging due to the domestic tensions surrounding civil society. Yet, the prospects for future research amidst the dynamic political and social changes in Iran remain vast. Further examinations should focus on rural versus urban shifts in gender consciousness, female voting behavior, more detailed analysis of institutional gains and losses for women, and a concise study on female seminaries among other issues. Equally important would be a study focusing on the impact of education in influencing female activism and gender consciousness as well as on focusing on the changes and impact of the revolution on traditional, religious women. Today, women in Iran continue to negotiate within the Islamic discourse in order to bring about change. Further analyses on these debates can serve as a model for discussing democracy within the context of Islam and not as separate from it. Comparative models of Iranian civil society development with that of its regional neighbors would also contribute to an understanding of the regional and Muslim advances toward gender equality.

Iran's neighbors are quickly catching up in addressing women's issues. In Kuwait, women voted and ran for the first time in local and national elections in 2006. While Saudi Arabia lags behind its neighbors and while women there live in a gender segregated and unequal society, the Kingdom is inching forward allowing women to study law, check in to hotels alone, and obtain their own identification cards. Saudi King Abdullah bin Abdul-Aziz ibn Saud went further, appointing his first female cabinet official to the post of education minister in March 2009.[26] Other countries have paved the way for female acceptance into the political world through the introduction of political quotas.

Quotas for women in government suggest that women must constitute a certain number or percentage of a candidate list or parliamentary assembly. It is the adoption of quotas that has enabled women to make gains across Africa and some Middle Eastern countries. Two recent successes were seen in Iraq and Afghanistan. In Iraq, a quarter of the seats in the parliament are reserved for women. In Afghanistan, 25 percent of seats in the lower house of parliament are reserved for women. Morocco provides another successful example of how quotas have helped promote female political participation. In 1993, less than one percent of the parliament was female, putting it at number 118 internationally in amount of women in government. However, nine years later in 2002, that figure increased to ten percent. In the Arab world, it is surpassed only by Tunisia, where 14 percent of the legislators are women.[27] Among the many options for reform in Iran, the imposition of quotas is indeed on the agenda of female activists particularly as female parliamentary representation has declined in the midst of the factional infighting.[28] This quota system should be extended to political groups, businesses, and civic associations suggest many activists.[29] The legally enforced inclusion of women would help adjust patriarchal norms.

In 2010, Iranian women's activism had built the foundations of a conventional social movement amidst some limitations. In accordance with Tilly's characterization, women's activism has traveled through the phases of collaboration, conciliation, and confrontation creating the building blocks of a social movement. Distinctly in the aftermath of the reform movement, women pursued an organized strategy of claim making or campaigns. Activism initially benefited from the mobilization of women at the outset of the revolution, during the Iran-Iraq war and through the educational system. Economic and social inclusion under Rafsanjani enabled women to make further gains. Such foundations were further cemented during the Khatami presidency and from gender consciousness evident in civil society as women were pivotal in the reformist ascendancy. The "changing political opportunities" of the reform period further enabled women to fuse together an interactive campaign. Adding to these trends, women have overcome ideological differences and defined their discourse and demands revealed through the 2009 gender platform. They employed direct means of political action through the creation of organization and coalitions, public meetings, rallies, demonstrations, and petitions. Important to this element is the overlap between women's activism and that of electoral activity, and the student and labor movement. Building bridges with other movements has been essential for the foundations of women's activism. In adherence with Tilly's characterization, they have demonstrated the *worthiness* and commitment to their cause, *unity* as activists as Islamists and secularists have merged forces and work in collaboration with other activist groups, their *numbers* through petitions and demonstrations and their *commitment* evidenced in the resistance to repression and willingness to agitate despite the costs.

Yet, particular attributes of Iranian women's activism revealed in the horizontal or collective concept of leadership could pose a challenge for the prospects of the movement. This concept of leadership on the one hand is reflective of the negative impact of Iranian history and the government of the Islamic Republic where the *rahbar* (leader) has had ultimate and arbitrary control. In the wake of ongoing government suppression of civil society and of women's activists though, the lack of distinct leadership has advantages as the state cannot identify and neutralize the leadership. But at the same time, gender activists are in need of direction to maintain the coherence and organization of their efforts. The effectiveness of the government clampdown has already impeded activist efforts at large-scale mobilization. Most importantly, the elite nature of women's activism continues to be a limitation to the movement's effectiveness. Outreach and recruitment of non-activist, ordinary women is needed for the women's movement to proactively and effectively pressure the state on gender equality. A long-term strategy is also needed for women's activism to survive government repression. Targeted economic, political, social, and legal aims must be delineated coupled with a plan for gaining mass support. Only with continued pressure on the state, will women succeed in forcing gender reform.

The wheels of civil society continue to spin amidst political and social constraints and contradictions. In spite of government restrictions, clampdowns, and repressions, activists of all kind continue to confront, cooperate, and collaborate in anticipation of greater rights. For women in particular, their revolution has come almost full circle. Over a century's worth of protest, participation, and agitation has brought them out of the shadows. It is here, in plain sight that they will continue to push forward, unabatedly bound by their common cause and cohesive presence. The growing divide between state and society, conservative and reformist, Islamist and secularist, young and old, is only adding greater pressure and urgency to the mix and morass of domestic politics. Within this gulf so too will women persevere in their quest for equal rights. For the Islamic Republic, the presence and potency of these changes will continue to pose challenges among the regime's incongruities. Reflecting on these paradoxical events and transformations, the celebrated Iranian poet Simin Behbahani, known as the "Lioness of Iran," wrote "An Homage to Being," in 1983, celebrating women's presence and influence. Her cogent words synthesize the ultimate contradictions between state and society and between women and the Islamic Republic of Iran.

> Sing, Gypsy, sing.
> In homage to being you must sing.
> Let ears register your presence.

Eyes and throats burn from the smoke
that trails the monsters as they soar in the sky.
Scream if you can of the terrors of this night.
Every monster has the secret of his life
hidden in a bottle in the stomach of a red fish
swimming in waters you cannot reach.
In her lap every maid holds a monster's head
like a piece of firewood set in silver.
In their frenzy to plunder, the monsters
have plundered the beautiful maidens
of the silk and rubies of their lips and cheeks.
Gypsy, stamp your feet.
For your freedom stamp your feet.
To get an answer,
send a message with their beat.
To your existence there must be a purpose under heaven.
To draw a spark from these stones,
stamp your feet.
Ages dark and ancient
have pressed their weight against your body.
Break out of their embrace,
lest you stay a mere trace in a fossil.
Gypsy, to stay alive, you must slay silence.
I mean, to pay homage to being, you must sing.[30]

Notes

1. "Zendegi Namehye Candidha" [The Biography of the Candidates,] *BBC Persian*, May 21, 2009.

2. Shahab Nikzad, "Jonbeshe Zanan dar Sal 88" [The Women's Movement in the Year 1388], *BBC Persian*, March 24, 2010.

3. Personal interview with journalist and activist, Washington, D.C., April 16, 2010.

4. Nikzad, "Jonbeshe Zanan dar Sal 88", 2010.

5. "Netayej Entekhabate Riyasate Jomhuri Iran bar Asas Elam Vezarate Keshvar" [The Results of the Presidential Election Publicized by the Interior Ministry], *BBC Persian*, June 12, 2009.

6. "Shoraye Negahban Sehate Entkhabate Riasate Jomhuriye Iran ra Taeed Kard" [The Guardian Council Confirmed the Accuracy of the Iranian Election], *BBC Persian*, June 29, 2009.

7. Alexis de Tocqueville, *The Old Regime and the French Revolution*, translated by Stuart Gilbert, 1955, 176–177.

8. Nikzad, "Jonbeshe Zanan dar Sal 88," March 24, 2010.

9. Muhammad Sahimi, "Martyrs of the Green Movement," *Tehran Bureau*, April 7, 2010. www.pbs.org/wgbh/pages/frontline/tehranbureau/2010/04/martyrs-of-the-green-movement.html. Accessed April 19, 2010.

10. Personal interview with journalist and activist, Washington, D.C., April 16, 2010.

11. Ibid.

12. "Suppression has changed Iranian women's priorities," http://en.irangreenvoice.com/article/2010/mar/12/1469. Accessed April 12, 2010.

13. Jane Gabriel, "Iran: Time to Change the Question," *Opendemocracy,* March 8, 2010.

14. Translated by http://khordaad88.com/?p=1302.

15. Jane Gabriel, "Iran: Time to Change the Question," *Opendemocracy,* March 8, 2010.

16. Pardis Mahdavi, *Passionate Uprisings: Iran's Sexual Revolution*, 2008.

17. Takeyh, 2006, 219.

18. See Appendix A.

19. See Sedghi, 2007, Afshar 1998, Paidar 1995 and 2001, among others.

20. Personal interview with journalist and activist, Washington DC, April 16, 2010.

21. Ibid.

22. Bayat, 2010, 110.

23. Interviews with activists, journalists, professors, and former politicians, Tehran 2007 and 2008.

24. Fatemeh Sadeghi, "Foot Soldiers of the Islamic Republic's 'Culture of Modesty,'" *Middle East Report 250*, Spring 2009, 55.

25. Nikki R. Keddie. "Women and 30 Years of the Islamic Republic." *Viewpoints* Special Edition, The Iranian Revolution at Thirty, Middle East Institute, Washington, DC, 2009.

26. "Kuwaiti Women Vote for first time," BBC News, April 4, 2006. Julian Borger, "Saudi Appoints First Female Minister," *The Guardian*, February 16, 2009.

27. K. Annan, "Afghan Women May Still Suffer", Associated Press. Online. 2002; A. Nordlund, "Demands for Electoral Gender Quotas in Afghanistan and Iraq," The Research Program on Gender Quotas, Working Paper Series 2004: 2, 2004; John Leicester, "Women to Take Seats in Morocco Government," Associated Press. September 27, 2002.

28. Mohammad Hossein Hafezian, "Political Participation of Women in Iran," *Discourse: An Iranian Quarterly*, Vol. 4, No.1, 2002.

29. Interviews with secular activist and Islamist professor and former politician, Tehran, May 12 and 13, 2008.

30. Simin Behbahani, *A Cup Of Sin: Selected Poems*, translated by Farzaneh Milani and Kaveh Safa, 1999.

Selected Bibliography

Abbasgholizadeh, Mahboubeh. "*Dar Iran Jonbesh-e Zanan bi Sar Ast*" [The Iranian Women's Movement Is Leaderless]. *Zanan*, September 2003, www.zanan.co.ir/culture/000153.html. Accessed October 23, 2008.

Abdo, Geneive. "Re-Thinking the Islamic Republic: A 'Conversation' with Ayatollah Hossein 'Ali Montazeri'," *The Middle East Journal*, Vol. 55, No. 1, 2001, 9–24.

Abedin, Mahan. "The Origins of Iran's Reformist Elite," *Middle East Intelligence Bulletin*, Vol. 5, No. 4, April 2003.

Abisaab, Rula Jurdi. *Converting Persia: Religion and Power in the Safavid Empire*. London: I.B. Tauris, 2004.

Abrahamian, Ervand. *Iran between Two Revolutions*. Princeton, NJ: Princeton University Press, 1982.

—. *Khomeinism: Essays on the Islamic Republic*. Berkeley, CA: University of California Press, 1993.

Adelkhah, Fariba, and Zuzanna Olszeska. "The Iranian Afghans," *Iranian Studies*, Vol. 40, No. 2, 2007, 137–65.

Afary, Janet. *The Iranian Constitutional Revolution: 1906–1911*. New York: Columbia University Press, 1996.

—. "*Jonbeshe Zanane Iran: Gheire Motamarkez va Gostardeh*" [Iranian Women's Movement: Decentralizeded and Vast]. *Zanan*, April 2003, www.zanan.co.ir/culture/000059.html. Accessed April 8, 2008.

—. *Sexual Politics in Modern Iran*. Cambridge: Cambridge University Press, 2009.

Afkhami, Mahnaz. "Women in Post-Revolutionary Iran: A Feminist Perspective," in *In the Eye of the Storm: Women in Post Revolutionary Iran*. Mahnaz Afkhami and Erika Friedl, eds. Syracuse, NY: Syracuse University Press, 1994.

Afshar, Haleh. "Behind the Veil: The Public and Private Faces of Khomeini's Policies on Women," in *Structures of the Patriarchy: State, Community and Household in Modernizing Asia*. B. Agarwal, ed. London: Zed Books, 1988.

—. "Competing Interests: Democracy, Islamification and Women Politicians in Iran," in *Women, Politics and Change*. K. Ross, ed. Oxford: Oxford University Press, 2002.

—. *Islam and Feminisms: An Iranian Case Study.* New York: St. Martin's Press, 1998.

—. "Women and the Politics of Fundamentalism in Iran," in *Women and Politics in the Third World.* Haleh Afshar, ed. London: Routledge, 1996.

—. "Women and Reproduction in Iran," in *Women, Nation, State.* N. Yuval-Davis and F. Anthias, eds. London: Macmillan, 1989.

Afzali, Nasrin. "*8 Mars Emsal: Payane Tardeedha darbareye Jonbeshe Zanan*" [March 8 this year: End of doubts about the women's movement]. *Zanan,* 119, 19–23.

Afzali, Nasrin, and Zeinab Peyghambarzadeh. "*8 Mars dar Daneshghahaye Sarasare Keshvar Che Gozasht?*" [March 8: What Took Place at the Universities Around the Country?]. *Zanan,* 143, 24–7.

Agence Free Press. "Iranian Leader Warns Women Against Copying Western Feminist Trends," October 22, 1997.

—. "Tehran to Get Special Police Stations for Women," December 7, 2007.

Ahmadi, Fereshteh. "Islamic Feminism in Iran: Feminism in a New Islamic Context," *Journal of Feminist Studies in Religion,* Vol. 22, No. 2, 2006, 33–53.

Ahmadi Khorasani, Noushin. "*Jonbesh Yek Million Emza: Ravayati az Daroun*" [The One Million Signatures Campaign: A Narrative from Inside]. Summer 2007, www.femschool.info/campaign/spip.php?article86. Accessed March 25, 2010.

—. *Zanan Zir-e Sayeh-e Pedar Khandeh-ha* [Women Under the Protection of Step-fathers]. Tehran: Tose'eh, 1380, 2001.

Ahmed, Leila. *Women and Gender in Islam.* New Haven: Yale University Press, 1992.

Akhavi, Shahrough. "Elite Factionalism in the Islamic Republic of Iran," *Middle East Journal,* Vol. 41, No. 2, 1987.

—. "The Ideology and Praxis of the Iranian Revolution," *Comparative Studies in Society and History,* Vol. 25, No. 2, 1983.

—. *Religion and Politics in Contemporary Iran: Clergy–State Relations in the Pahlavi Period.* Albany, NY: SUNY Press, 1980.

al-Ahmad, Jalal. *Gharbzadeghi: Westruckness.* Costa Mesa, CA: Mazda Publishers, 1982.

al Sadat Zahidi, Shams. "*Moghiyate Zanan dar Jame'e Daneshgahi*" [Status of Women at University]. *Zanan,* 24, 3–6.

Alavi, Nasrin. *We are Iran: The Persian Blogs.* New York: Soft Skull Press, 2005.

Alavitabar, Ali Reza. "*Masaele Zanan dar Iran*" [The Problems of Women in Iran]. *Zanan,* 65, 44–5.

Albert, David H. *Tell the American People: Perspectives on the Iranian Revolution.* Philadelphia, PA: Movement for a New Society, 1980.

Alfoneh, Ali. "The Revolutionary Guards' Role in Iranian Politics," *Middle East Quarterly,* Vol. 15, No. 4, 2008.

Algar, Hamid. *The Constitution of the Islamic Republic of Iran.* Berkeley, CA: Mizan Press, 1980.

—. *Islam and Revolution: The Writings and Declarations of Imam Khomeini.* Berkeley, CA: Mizan Press, 1981.

Alizadeh, Parvin, and Barry Harper. "The Feminization of the Labor Force in Iran," in *Iran Encountering Globalization: Problems and Prospects*. Ali Mohammadi, ed. London: Routledge, 2003.

Amanat, Abbas. *Pivot of the Universe: Nasir al-Din Shah Qajar and the Iranian Monarchy, 1831–1896*. Berkeley, CA: University of California Press, 1997.

—. *Resurrection and Renewal: The Making of the Babi Movement in Iran, 1844–1850*. Ithaca, NY: Cornell University Press, 1989.

Amanat, Abbas, ed. *Taj al Saltaneh, Crowning Anguish: Memoirs of a Persian Princess from the Harem to Modernity: 1884–1914*. Washington, D.C.: Mage Publishers, 1993.

Amini, Asieh. "Battle of the Blogs," *Payvand News*, September 11, 2008.

Amuezegar, Jahanghir. "The Ahmadinejad Era: Preparing for the Apocalypse," *Journal of International Affairs*, Vol. 60, No. 2, 2007, 35–53.

—. "Islamic Social Justice, Iranian Style," *Middle East Policy*, 2007, 60–78.

Ansari, Ali. *Confronting Iran: The Failure of American Foreign Policy and the Next Great Crisis in the Middle East*. New York: Basic Books, 2006.

—. *Iran, Islam and Democracy: The Politics of Managing Change*. London: The Royal Institute of International Affairs, 2001.

—. *Iran Under Ahmadinejad, the Politics of Confrontation*. Abingdon: Routledge, 2008.

—. "Iran Under Ahmadinejad: Populism and its Malcontents," *International Affairs*, Vol. 84, No. 4, 2008, 683–700.

—. "Iranian Nationalism Rediscovered," *Viewpoints* Special Edition, The Iranian Revolution at Thirty, Middle East Institute, Washington, D.C., 2009.

Arastoo, Bardia. "*Amniyate'e Mardane, Amniyate'e Zanane*" [Male Security, Female Security]. *Zanan*, 131, 13–16.

Arayan, Hossein. "Iran's Basij Force—The Mainstay of Domestic Security," *Radio Free Europe Radio Liberty*, December 7, 2008.

Ardalan, Parvin. "Joining on the Condition to Discriminate," *Bad Jens*, May 22, 2002.

—. "*Shoma Dar Bareye een Bande Taze Che Migooid*" [What Do You Have to Say About This New Bill?]. *Zanan*, 42, 7–11.

—. "The Women's Movement in a Game of Snakes and Ladders," November 25, 2008, http://fairfamilylaw.info/spip.php?article412. Accessed April 7, 2010.

—."*Zanan Nashriyate Zanan ra Mo'arefi Mikonad: In Bar Farzaneh*" [Zanan Introduces Women's Journals: This Time Farzaneh]. *Zanan* 69, 2000, 16–17.

—. "*Zanan Nashriyate Zanan ra Mo'arefi Mikonad: In Bar Payam-e Hajar*" [Zanan Introduces Women's Journals: This Time Payam-e Hajar]. *Zanan*, 1999, 53.

Ardalan, Parvin, Mohajer, Firouzeh, and Ahmadi Khorasani, Noushin. *Fasl-e zanan: Majmu'e ara va Didgahayeh Femiiniisti [The Season of Women: A Compilation of Feminist Viewpoints and Opinions]*. Tehran: Roshangaran and Women's Studies Publication, 2004.

Arjomand, Said Amir. *After Khomeini: Iran Under his Successors*. Oxford: Oxford University Press, 2009.

—. "The Reform Movement and the Debate on Modernity and Tradition in Contemporary Iran," *International Journal of Middle East Studies*, Vol. 34, 2002, 719–31.

—. "The Rule of God in Iran," *Social Compass*, Vol. 36, No. 4, 1989, 539–48.

—. *The Shadow of God and the Hidden Imam*. Chicago: Chicago University Press, 1984.

—. *The Turban for the Crown: The Islamic Revolution in Iran*. Oxford: Oxford University Press, 1988.

Ashraf, Ahmad. "Theocracy and Charisma: New Men of Power in Iran," *International Journal of Politics, Culture, and Society*, Vol. 4, 1990, 139.

Azari, Farah, ed. *Women of Iran: The Conflict with Fundamentalist Islam*. London: Ithaca Press, 1983.

Badran, Margot. *Feminism in Islam: Secular and Religious Convergences*. Oxford: Oneworld Press, 2008.

—. "Islamic Feminism: What's in a Name?" *Al Ahram Weekly*, January 17, 2002.

Bahramitash, Roksana. "Revolution, Islamization, and Women's Employment in Iran," *Browns Journal of World Affairs*, Vol. IX, No. 2, 2003.

—. "Women's Employment in Iran: Modernization and Islamization," in *Iran: Between Tradition and Modernity*, Ramin Jahanbegloo, ed. Lanham: Lexington Books, 2004.

Bakhash, Shaul. "Islam and Social Justice in Iran," in *Shi'ism, Resistance and Revolution*. Martin Kramer, ed. Boulder, CO: Westview Press, 1987.

—. *Reign of the Ayatollahs: Iran and the Islamic Revolution*, rev. ed. New York: Basic Books, 1986.

—. "Sermons, Revolutionary Pamphleteering and Mobilization: Iran, 1978," in *From Nationalism to Revolutionary Islam*. Said Amir Arjomand, ed. London: Macmillan Press, 1984.

Baktiari, Bahman. "Iranian Society: A Surprising Picture," *Viewpoints* Special Edition, The Iranian Revolution at Thirty, Middle East Institute, Washington, D.C., 2009.

—. *Parliamentary Politics in Revolutionary Iran: The Institutionalization of Factional Politics*. Gainesville: University Press of Florida, 1996.

Bamdad, Badrol-Molouk. *From Darkness into Light: Women's Emancipation in Iran*. Trans. and ed. F. R. C. Bagley. Smithtown, NY: Exposition Press, 1977.

Baniyaghoub, Taraneh. "*Tahseele Dokhtaran dar Daneshgahaye Markaz ba Ejazeh Khanevadeh Hayeshan*" [Girls Education in Main Cities' Universities Only with Parents Permission]. March 5, 2009, www.irwomen.info/spip.php?article6488. Accessed March 12, 2010.

Bayat, Asef. *Life as Politics: How Ordinary People Change the Middle East*. Stanford, CA: Stanford University Press, 2010.

—. "Revolution without Movements, Movement without Revolution: Comparing Islamic Activism in Iran and Egypt," *The Comparative Studies in Society and History Book Series*, Vol. 40, No. 1, 1998.

—. *Street Politics: Poor People's Movement in Iran*, New York: Columbia University Press, 1997.

—. "Un-civil Society: The Politics of the Informal People," *Third World Quarterly*, Vol. 18, No. 1, 1997.

—. "A Women's Non Movement: What It Means to Be a Women's Activist in an Islamic State," *Comparative Studies of South Asia, Africa and the Middle East*, Vol. 27, No.1, 2007.

Bayat, Mangol. "Mahmud Taleghani and the Iranian Revolution," in *Shi'ism, Resistance, and Revolution*. Martin Kramer, ed. Boulder, CO: Westview, 1987.

—. "Women and Revolution in Iran, 1905–1911," in *Women and the Muslim World*. Lois Beck and Nikki Keddie, eds. Cambridge: Harvard University Press, 1978.

BBC. "*Elame Sahmieyehbandy Jensiaty Dar Daneshgahaye Iran*" [The Official Announcement of Gender Quotas in Iranian Universities]. *BBC Persian*, February 25, 2008.

—. "Kuwaiti Women Vote for first time," *BBC*, April 4, 2006.

—. "*Namehe Fa'alan Hoghoughe Zanan be Namayendeye Zane Majlis Iran*" [Letter by Women's Rights Activists to Iranian Female Parliamentarians]. *BBC Persian*, December 5, 2007.

—. "*Netayeje Entekhabate Riyasate Jomhouri Iran bar Asas Elame Vezarate Keshvar*" [The Results of the Presidential Election Publicized by the Interior Ministry]. *BBC Persian*, June 12, 2009.

—. "*Shoraye Negahban Sehate Entkhabate Riasate Jomhuriye Iran ra Taeed Kard*" [The Guardian Council Confirmed the Accuracy of the Iranian election]. *BBC Persian*, June 29, 2009.

—. "Women Police on Parade in Iran," *BBC*, October 10, 2000.

Behbahani, Simin. *A Cup of Sin: Selected Poems*. Trans. Farzaneh Milani and Kaveh Safa. Syracuse, NY: Syracuse University Press, 1999.

Beheshti, Ahmad. *Zanan-i Namdar dar Qur'an Hadith va Tarikh* [Important Women in the Qur'an, Hadith and History]. Vol. 1. Tehran: Sazmane Tablighate Islami, 1989.

Behmanesh, Arash. "*Eejad Amniyate Ejtemaee Ba Roosari va Chador*" [Creation of Social Morality with a Scarf and a Veil]. *BBC Persian*, September 14, 2007.

Behnam, M. Reza. *Cultural Foundations of Iranian Politics*. Salt Lake City: University of Utah Press, 1986.

Betteridge, Anne. "To Veil or Not to Veil: A Matter of Protest or Policy," in *Women and Revolution in Iran*. Guity Nashat, ed. Boulder, CO: Westview Press, 1983.

Bill, James. *The Eagle and the Lion: The Tragedy of American-Iranian Relations*. New Haven, CT: Yale University Press, 1989.

Bill, James, and Louis, W. Roger, eds. *Mussadegh, Iranian Nationalism and Oil*. London: I.B. Tauris, 1988.

Bojnourdi, Ayatollah Seyed Mohammad Mousavi. "Gender Justice in Islam," *Reynameh, Center for Women's Participation and Cultural Research Quarterly*, No. 8, 2005.

Borger, Julian. "Saudi Appoints First Female Minister," *The Guardian*, February 16, 2009.

Boroujerdi, Mehrzad. *Iranian Intellectuals and the West: The Tormented Triumph of Nativism*. Syracuse, NY: Syracuse University Press, 1996.

Bozorgmehr, Najmeh. "Grand Ayatollah Yusef Saanei: A Liberal Voice among Clerics," *Financial Times*, February 6, 2009.

Borzorgmehr, Shirzad. "Nobel Laureate's Tehran Home Attacked," *CNN News*, February 26, 2009.

Brumberg, Daniel. "Khomeini's Legacy: Islamic Rule and Islamic Social Justice," in *Spokesmen for the Despised: Fundamentalist Leaders of the Middle East*. Scott Abbleby, ed. Chicago: University of Chicago Press, 1997, 19.

—. *Reinventing Khomeini: The Struggle for Reform in Iran*. Chicago: University of Chicago Press, 2001.

Buchta, Wilfried. *Who Rules Iran? The Structure of Power in the Islamic Republic*. Washington D.C.: Washington Institute for Near East Policy, 2002.

Butler, Katherine. "Lipstick Revolution: Iran's Women Are Taking on the Mullahs," *The Independent*, February 26, 2009.

Casey, Maura J. "Challenging the Mullahs, One Signature at a Time," *New York Times*, February 7, 2007.

Center for Women's Participation. *Women's Participation and Seventh Government*. Tehran: Author, 2001.

Chubin, Shahram, and Charles Tripp. *Iran and Iraq at War*. Boulder, CO: Westview Press, 1988.

Clawson, Patrick. *Iran Under Khatami: A Political, Economic, and Military Assessment*. Washington, D.C.: Washington Institute for Near East Policy, 1998.

—. "The Islamic Republic's Economic Failure," *Middle East Quarterly*, Vol. 15, No. 4, 2008, 15–26.

Cottam, Richard. *Nationalism in Iran*. Pittsburgh, PA: University of Pittsburgh Press, 1979.

Cronin, Stephanie. *The Making of Modern Iran: State and Society Under Riza Shah 1921–1941*. New York: Routledge, 2007.

Dabashi, Hamid. *Theology of Discontent: The Ideological Foundations of the Islamic Revolution in Iran*. New York: New York University Press.

Dabbagh, Marzieh. "*Zanan va Naghshe Anan dar Majlis*" [Women and Their Role in the Majlis: A Round Table]. *Nida*, Winter 1996, 17–18.

Daragahi, Borzou. "Iran Economists Denounce Ahmadinejad's Policies," *Los Angeles Times*, November 10, 2008.

Davoudi Mohajer, Fariba. "Challenging Tradition: Women Inside Iran's Student Organizations," *www.gozaar.org*, February 1, 2007.

—. "From New York to Tehran: International Women's Day," *Gozaar*, March 6, 2009.

de Tocqueville, Alexis. *The Old Regime and the French Revolution*. Trans. Stuart Gilbert. Garden City, NY: Doubleday Anchor, 1955.

Deutsche Welle. "*Madreseh Dosheezegan*" ["The School for Girls"] Interview with Dr Mah-Laghā Mallah Maternal Granddaughter of Bibi Khatoon Astarabadi. *Deutsche Welle Persian*, August 11, 2006.

Dokouhaki, Parastoo. "*Dar Kaheshe Taedad Zanane Namayandehye Majlis Gorouhaye Siyasi Moghaserand*" [Reduction in the Number of Female Parliamentarians Is Due to Political Groups]. *Zanan*, 64, 2–5.

—. "*Hasht Sale Kar Baraye Zanan: Dar Miyane Afkare Sonnati va Shoarhaye Modern*" [The Results of Eight Years Work for Women: In the Midst of Traditional Thought and Modern Slogans]. *Zanan*, 121, 15–21.

—. "*Voroode Dolat be Kabeene Zanan Mamnoo Ast!*" [The Government Entrance in the Women's Cabinet is Forbidden!]. *Zanan*, 124, 15–19.

Dokouhaki, Parastoo, and Tarighi, Noushin. "*In Khanoom Chadar Sar Mikonad ya Na?*" [Does This Woman Wear the Chador or Not? A Report on Disqualifying Women Candidates for Parliamentary Election]. *Zanan*, 59, 2–6.

—. "*Sale 1383: Onkeh bar Zanan Gozasht*" [What Happened to Women?]. *Zanan*, 2004, 118, 22–31.

Ebadi, Shirin. *Iran Awakening: A Memoir of Revolution and Hope*. New York: Random House, 2006.

Ebrahimi, Zahra. "*Dar Naharkhori-ye Majles Dor-e Zanan Pardeh Keshidand*" [They Have Drawn a Curtain Around the Women's Lunch Room in the Majles]. *Zanan*, 11, 26–31.

—. "*Davazdah Zane Majlise Haftom: Ghodrat Bedoone Eghtedar*" [Twelve Women From the Majlis: Strength Without Power]. *Zanan*, 111, 33–39.

—. "*Eeteraze Shadeed be Ozveat Nadashtan dar Heeyat Raeese*" [Women's Objection to Not Being in the Parliament's Board of Directors]. *Zanan*, 124, 22–26.

—. "*Entekhabe Osoolgarayan Azme Meli Baraye Mobareze ba Fesad va Bad Hejabi Ast*" [The Election of a Principalists Candidate Shows National Resolution in Fighting Moral Corruption and Veiling]. *Zanan*, 117, 28–31.

—. "*Ezame Dokhtarane Daneshjoo be Kharej Keshvar Tasveeb shod*" [Ratification of Legislation Permitting Female Students to Study Abroad,] *Zanan*, 74, 8–9.

—. "*Ezdevaje Mojadad Bee Ejazeyeh Zane Aval*" [Second Marriage Without Permission of the First Wife]. *Zanan*, 147.

—. "*Fatemeh Haghighatjoo: Aval*" [Fatemeh Haghighatjoo, The First!]. *Zanan*, 107, 8–10.

—. "*Hoghoughe Zanan va Rahe Doshvar Peyvastan be Convension*" [Women's Rights and the Difficult Path of Joining the Convention]. *Zanan*, 102, 22–27.

—. "*Jostojoo dar Parvandehye Zanan Namayandeh Majlis Panjom*" [Searching the Files of the Female Representatives of the Fifth Parliament]. *Zanan*, 60, 3–7.

—. "*Ma Vazeefeye Ghanoonyee Khod Midaneem*" [Confrontation Is Our Legal Duty]. *Zanan*, 42, 3–5.

—. "*Payan Chahar Sal ba Ta'beez Jensy*" [End of Gender Discrimination after Four Years of Struggle]. *Zanan*, 109, 3–6.

—. *"Porsesh az Zanan-e Nemayandeh-ye Majles-e Sheshom"* [Questions for Female Parliamentarians From the Sixth Majles]. *Zanan*, 75, 27–29.

—. *"Sahmiyeh 30 dar Sad Baraye Zanan dar Entekhabat"* [Women's Fraction Demand 30% Quota for Women in the Election]. *Zanan*, 104, 18–24.

—. *"Talash Zanane Majlis Baraye Jelogiree az Tasveebe Convension"* [Women's Efforts Against the Ratification of the Convention," *Zanan*, 113, 35–40.

—. *"Yek Zane Digar Varede Majlis Shod: Yek Mah ba Zanane Majlis"* [Another Woman Joins the Parliament: One Month With the Women of the Parliament]. *Zanan*, 139, 26–30.

—. *"Yek sal ba Jedal Zanan dar Majles"* [A Challenging Year for Women of the Parliament]. *Zanan* 73, 18–23.

—. *"Zanan dar Boodjeye 1386 Jaee Nadashtand"* [Women Had No Place in the Budget of 2007,] *Zanan*, 143, 6–9.

—. *"Zanan, Tahason, Estefa"* [Women, Sit-in, Resignation]. *Zanan*, 106, 2–10.

Ebtekar, Massoumeh. "Women's NGOs and Poverty Alleviation: The Iranian Experience." *Farzaneh*, Vol. 4, No. 9, 1998.

—. "The Women's Quest for Reform," *Farzaneh*, Vol. 5, No.10, 2000.

Eftekhari, Roza. *"Chahar Mabhase Asasi dar Feminism"* [Four Essential Discussions in Feminism]. *Zanan*, 1996, 32, 30–4.

Ehteshami, Anoushiravan. *After Khomeini: The Iranian Second Republic.* London: Routledge, 1995.

Ehteshami, Anoushiravan, and Mahjoob Zweiri. *Iran and the Rise of the Neoconservatives: The Politics of Tehran's Silent Revolution.* London: I.B. Tauris, 2007.

—. *Iran's Foreign Policy from Khatami to Ahmadinejad.* Ithaca: Cornell University Press, 2008.

Enayat, Hamid. "Iran: Khumayni's Concept of the 'Guardianship of the Jurisconsult,'" in *Islam in the Political Process.* James Piscatori, ed. Cambridge: Cambridge University Press, 1983.

Erdbrink, Thomas. "Iranian Parliament Delays Vote on Bill that Upset Judiciary, Women's Activists," *Washington Post*, September 3, 2008, A09.

Esfandiari, Golnaz. "Iranian Police Forcibly Disperse Women's Rights Protest in Tehran," *Payvand News*, June 14, 2006.

Esfandiari, Haleh. "The Majles and Women's Issues in the Islamic Republic of Iran, 1960–90," in *In the Eye of the Storm: Women in Post-Revolutionary Iran.* M. Afkhami and E. Friedl, eds. London: I.B. Tauris, 1994.

—. "The Politics of the 'Women's Question' in the Islamic Republic, 1979–1999," in *Iran at the Crossroads.* John L. Esposito and R. K. Ramazani, eds. New York: Palgrave, 2001.

—. *Reconstructed Lives: Women and Iran's Islamic Revolution.* Washington, D.C.: Woodrow Wilson Center Press, 1997.

Eshkevari, Hasan Yousefi, Ziba Mir Hosseini, and Richard Tapper. *Islam and Democracy in Iran. Iran: Eshkevari and the Quest for Reform.* New York: I.B. Tauris, 2006.

Fairbanks, Stephen. "Theocracy Versus Democracy: Iran Consider Political Parties," *Middle East Journal*, Vol. 1, 1998.

Fallaci, Orianna. *Interview with History*. New York: Houghton Mifflin, 1977.

Faradpour, Lily. "Women, Gender Roles and Journalism in Iran," A paper presented at the Development Studies Association, Women and Development Study Group 6 May, 2006, UK: York University.

—. *Zanan-e Berlin* [Women of Berlin]. Tehran: Me'reaj Publishers, 2000.

Faramazi, Scheherezade. "Iran's Rising Conservatives Roll Back Women's Rights," *Los Angeles Times*, April 29, 2007.

Farhi, Farideh. "The Attempted Silencing of Zanan," *Informed Comment Global Affairs Blog*, February 1, 2008.

—. "The Contending Discourses on Women in Iran," *Third World Network, Third World Resurgence*, No. 94, June 1998.

—. "*Jonbeshe Zanan va Mardane Eslahtalab*" [The Women's Movement and the Reformist Men]. *Zanan*, May 2003, www.zanan.co.ir/culture/000047.html. Accessed November 27, 2008.

—. "Sexuality and the Politics of Revolution in Iran," in *Women and Revolution in Africa, Asia and the New World*, M. A. Tetrault, ed. Columbia: University of South Carolina Press, 1994.

Farman Farmaian, Sattareh, and Dona Munger. *Daughter of Persia: A Woman's Journey from her Father's Harem through the Islamic Republic*. New York: Crown Publishers, 1993.

Farrokhzad, Forough. *Sin: Selected Poems of Forough Farrokhzad*. Little Rock: University of Arkansas Press, 2007.

Fathi, Nazila. "Ayatollah, Reviewing Islamic Law, Tugs at Ties Constricting Iran's Women," *New York Times*, July 29, 2001.

—. "Hundreds of Women Protest Sex Discrimination in Iran," *New York Times*, June 13, 2005.

—. "Iranian Women Should Have More Children," *New York Times*, October 24, 2006.

Fattahi, Kambiz. "Women's Bill United Iran and US," *BBC News*, July 31, 2007.

Fifield, Anna. "Girls Allowed," *Financial Times*, April 18, 2008.

Gabriel, Jane. "Iran: Time to Change the Question," *Opendemocracy*, March 8, 2010.

Ganji, Akbar. *Ghosts' Darkhouse: Pathology of Transition to the Developmental Democratic State*. Tehran: Tarh-e, 1999.

—. "Half a Man," *Boston Review*, November/December 2007.

—. "The Latter Day Sultan," *Foreign Affairs*, Vol. 87, No. 6, 2008, 45–66.

Gasiorowski, Mark, and Malcolm Bryne. *Mohammad Mosaddeq and the 1953 Coup in Iran*. Syracuse, NY: Syracuse University Press, 2004.

Ghafourian, Shabnam. "One Step Away From Legalizing Women's Candidacy for President," *Bamdad News*, March 17, 2009.

Ghani, Cyrus. *Iran and the Rise of Reza Shah: From Qajar Collapse to Pahlavi Power*. London: I.B. Tauris, 2001.

Gheisari, Ali, and Vali Nasr. *Democracy in Iran: History and the Quest for Liberty*. Oxford: Oxford University Press, 2006.

Gheytanchi, Elham. "Chronology of Events Regarding Women in Iran since the Revolution of 1979," *Social Research*, 67, Summer 2000.

—. "Civil Society in Iran: Politics of Motherhood and the Public Sphere," *International Sociology, Vol.* 16, No. 4, 2001.

—. "Lashing out on Iranian Women's Rights Activists," www.huffingtonpost.com, November 2007.

—. "Women against Women: Women in Iran's Seventh Parliament," *TheIranian.com*, November 5, 2004.

Gholamreza Kashi, Mohammad Javad, "*Zan dar Kalame Siyasi: Tahleely az Olgooye Zan dar Negahe Dr. Ali Shariati*" [Women in Political Words: Analysis of the Model of Women in the View of Dr. Ali Shariati]. *Zanan*, 70, 54–59.

Ghorashi, Halleh. *Iranian Islamic and Secular Feminists—Allies or Enemies?* Amsterdam: *Middle East Research Associates*, 1996.

Ghouchani, Mohammad. "*Nasl-e Dovvom-e Sepah Dar Rah*" [The Coming of the Second Generation of the Guards]. *Shargh*, April 12, 2005.

Gieling, Saskia. *Religion and War in Revolutionary Iran*. London: I.B. Tauris, 1999.

Gorjin, Iraj. "Does Iran Fear Educated Women?" *Radio Free Europe Radio Liberty*, February 10, 2008.

Govaree, Fatemeh. "Never Mind Women Ministers, Where Are the Women's Votes?" September 15, 2009, www.iranfemschool.com/english/spip.php?page=pint&id_article=eee. Accessed October 23, 2009.

Haeri, Shahla. *Law of Desire: Temporary Marriage in Shi'a Islam*. Syracuse, NY: Syracuse University Press, 1989.

Hafezian, Mohammad Hossein. "Political Participation of Women in Iran," *Discourse: An Iranian Quarterly*, Vol. 4, No.1, 2002.

Haleem, M. A. S. Abdel, trans. *The Quran*. Oxford: Oxford University Press, 2008.

Hegland. Mary Elaine. " 'Traditional' Iranian Women: How They Cope," *The Middle East Journal*, Vol. 36, No. 4, 1982, 483–501.

Hendelman-Baavur, Liora. "Iran Bans 'Women'—The Shutting Down of Women," *Iran Pulse 21*, April 15, 2008.

Hillmann. Michael. *A Lonely Woman: Forugh Farrokhzad and Her Poetry*. Washington D.C.: Three Continents Press and Mage Publishers, 1987.

Hoodfar, Homa. "Activism Under the Radar: Volunteer Women Health Workers in Iran," *Middle East Report, 250*, Spring 2009.

—. "Bargaining with Fundamentalists: Women and the Politics of Population Control in Iran," *Reproductive Health Matters*, Vol. 8, November 1996.

—. "The Veil in Their Minds and on Our Heads: The Persistence of Colonial Images of Muslim Women," in *The Politics of Culture in the Shadow of Capital*. David Lloyd and Lisa Lowe, eds. Durham, NC: Duke University Press, 1997.

—. "The Women's Movement in Iran: Women at the Crossroad of Secularization and Islamization," Women Living Under Muslim Laws. The Women's Movement Series No. 1, Winter 1999.

Hoodfar, Homa, and Shadi Sadr. "Can Women Act as Agents of a Democratization of Theocracy in Iran?" *United Nations Research Institute for Social Development*, October 2009.

Hoodfar, Homa, and Fatemeh Sedeghi. "Against All Odds: The Women's Movement in the Islamic Republic of Iran," *Development*, 52, 2009, 215–23.

Hosseininejad, Lida. "*Nemi Khaheem Charkh Motalebate Zanan az Aval Ekhtera Shavad: Ghoftogoo ba Mahboubeh Abbasgholizadeh*" [We Do Not Want the Wheels of Women's Demands Invented From Scratch: An Interview With Mahboubeh Abbasgholizadeh]. *Radio Zamaneh*, February 7, 2007.

Imani, Parvin. "*Mardha Daeman Mikhahand az Man Sebghat Begirand: Goftogoo ba Shahin Rejai, Avaleen Zane Irani Ranandeh Transit*" [Men Always Want to Take Advantage: A Conversation with Shahin Rejai, the First Female Transit Driver] *Zanan*, 122, 8–11.

Islamic Republic of Iran Ministry of Interior. "*Ettela'iyeh Shomarehye 8 Setade Entekhabate Keshvar Adar Khosouse Amare Ghat'iye Sabtenam Shodeh Gane Entekhabate Majlise Hashtom*" [Bulletin Number VIII of the Headquarters for Elections on the Final Statistics of Registered Candidates for the Eighth Parliamentary Elections]. Jafarzadeh, Suad. "Iranian Women Take Front and Center," *The Washington Times*, July 23, 2009.

Jahanbaksh, Forough. *Islam Democracy and Religious Modernism in Iran*. Leiden: Brill, 2001.

Jamy, Mehdi. "*Az Shahr Khoda ta Shahr-e Donya: Zanan-e Hozeh Dar Marzhaye Mardaneh*" [From the City of God to the City of the World: Female Seminarians in a Male Domain]. *BBC Persian*, August 7, 2005.

Kadivar, Mohsen. *Vela'ie Based State*. Tehran: Nashreh Ney, 1999.

Kalbasi, Sheema. *Seven Valleys of Love: A Bilingual Anthology of Women Poets from Middle Ages Persia to Present Day Iran*. Martinez, GA: PRA Publishing, 2008.

Kamrava, Mehran. *Iran's Intellectual Revolution*. Cambridge: Cambridge University Press, 2008.

Kandiyoti, Deniz, ed. "Contemporary Feminist Scholarship," in *Gendering the Middle East: Emerging Perspectives*. Deniz Kandiyoti, ed. Syracuse, NY: Syracuse University Press, 1996.

—. *Women, Islam and the State*. Basingstoke: Macmillan, 1991.

Kar, Mehrangiz. *Crossing the Red Line: The Struggle for Human Rights in Iran*. Costa Mesa, CA: Blind Owl Press, 2007.

—. "*Hoghoughe Siyassie Zanane Iran*" [Women's Political Rights in Iran]. Tehran: Entesharat-e Roshangaran va Motale'at-e, *Zanan*, 1997.

—. "*Jaygahe Zan dar Ghavanine Keyfari Dar Iran*" [The Position of Women in Criminal Law in Iran]. *Zanan*, Vol. 11, 1No. 6, 1993.

—. "*Mosharekate Siyassie Zanan: Vagheiyyat ya Khial*" [Political Participation of Women: Reality or Ideal?]. *Zanan*, 1998, No. 47, 12–13.

—. *Tose'h va Chalesh haye Zanan-e Iran* [Women's Participation in Politics: Obstacles and Possibilities]. Tehran: Roshangaran and Women's Studies Publication, 2000.

—. "Women and Civil Society in Iran," in *On Shifting Ground Muslim Women in the Global Era*. Fereshteh Nouraie-Simone, ed. New York: The Feminist Press at the City University of New York, 2005.

—. "Women's Strategies in Iran from the 1979 Revolution to 1999," in *Globalization, Gender and Religion: The Politics of Women's Rights in Catholic and Muslim Contexts*. Jane H. Bayes and Nayereh Tohidi, eds. New York: Palgrave, 2001.

Kar, Mehrangiz, and Homa Hoodfar. "Personal Status Law as Defined by the Islamic Republic of Iran: An Appraisal," *Women Living under Muslim Laws* Special Dossier, 1996, 7–35.

Karimi-Majd, Roya. *"Islam Deene Adl Ast: Goftogoo Ekhtesasy ba Ayatollah Saanei"* [Islam Is the Religion of Justice: Exclusive Interview with Ayatollah Saanei']. *Zanan*, 96, 2–7.

Karimi, Nasser. "Iran's Women Barred from Soccer Games," *Reuters*, May 8, 2006.

Karsh, Efraim. "From Ideological Zeal to Geopolitical Realism: The Islamic Republic and the Gulf," in *The Iran-Iraq War: Impact and Implications*. Efraim Karsh, ed. New York: St. Martin's Press, 1989.

Katzman, Kenneth. *The Warriors of Islam: Iran's Revolutionary Guard*. Boulder, CO: Westview Press, 1993.

Kazemi, Farhad. "Civil Society and Iranian Politics," in *Civil Society in the Middle East, Leiden*. Augustus Norton, ed. The Netherlands: Brill, 1996.

Keddie, Nikki R. "Foot Soldiers of the Islamic Republic's 'Culture of Modesty.'" *Middle East Report 250*, Spring 2009.

—. *Modern Iran: Roots and Results of Revolution*. New Haven, CT, and London: Yale University Press, 2003.

—. "Women and Religious Politics in the Contemporary World," *ISIM Newsletter, Vol. 3*, 1999, 6.

—. "Women in Iran since 1979," *Social Research*, Vol. 67, No. 2, 2000.

Keddie, Nikki R., and Lois Beck, eds. *Women in the Muslim World*. Cambridge: Harvard University Press, 1978.

Keshavarz, Nahid. "Interview with Jelve Javaheri: From a Reading Group to the Campaign for One Million Signatures," *Changeforequality.org*, January 1, 2008.

—. *"Kare Khanegiye Zanan: Moshkeli keh Tamami Nadarad"* [Women's Household Labor: A Problem Without End]. *Fasle Zanan: Majmoo'ye Ara va Didgah-e Feministy* [Women's Chapter]. 2003.

Khalaji, Mehdi. "Apocalyptic Politics: On the Rationality of Iranian Policy," The Washington Institute for Near East Policy, Policy Focus No. 79, 2007.

—. "The Last Marja: Sistani and the End of Traditional Religious Authority in Shi'ism," The Washington Institute for Near East Policy, Policy Focus No. 59, 2006.

Khiabany, Gholam. "The Iranian Press, State and Civil Society," in *Media, Culture and Society in Iran: Living with Globalization and the Iranian State*. Mehdi Semati, ed. New York: Routledge, 2008.

—. "Politics of the Internet in Iran," in *Media, Culture and Society in Iran: Living with Globalization and the Iranian State*. Mehdi Semati, ed. New York: Routledge, 2008.

Khiabany, Gholam, and Annabelle Sreberny. "The Women's Press in Contemporary Iran: Engendering the Public Sphere," in *Women and the Media in the Middle East: Power Through Self Expression*. Naomi Sakr, ed. London: I.B. Tauris, 2004.

Khomeini, Ruhollah. *A Clarification of Questions: An Unabridged Translation of Resaleh Towzih al-Masael*. J. Borujerdi, trans. Boulder, CO: Westview Press, 1984.

—. *Highlights of Imam Khomeini's Speeches (Nov 5, 80–Apr 28, 81)*. Albany, NY: Muslim Student Association, 1981.

—. *Imam Khomeini's Last Will and Testament*." Washington, D.C.: Interests Section of the Islamic Republic of Iran, 1989.

Khosrokhavar, Farhad. "New Intellectuals in Iran," *Social Compass*, Vol. 51, No. 2, 2004.

—. "New Social Movements in Iran," *ISIM Newsletter*, No. 7, 2001, 17.

—. "Postrevolutionary Iran and the New Social Movements," in *Twenty Years of Islamic Revolution: Political and Social Transition in Iran Since 1979*. E. Hooglund, ed. Syracuse, NY: Syracuse University Press, 2002.

Kian, Azadeh. "From Islamicization to Individualization," in *Women, Religion and Culture in Iran*. Sarah F. D. Ansari, Vanessa Martin, eds. London: Routledge, 2002.

—. "Islamist and Secular Women Unite," *Le Monde Diplomatique*, November 1996.

—. *Les Femmes Iraniennes entre Islam, Etat et Famille*. Paris: Maisonneuve & Larose, 2002.

—. *Secularization of Iran: a Doomed Failure? The New Middle Class and the Making of Modern Iran*. Paris: L'Institut d'Etudes Iraniennes Peeters, 1998.

—. "Social Change, the Women's Rights Movement and the Role of Islam," *Viewpoints* Special Edition, The Iranian Revolution at Thirty, Middle East Institute, Washington, D.C., 2009.

—. "Women and Politics in Post-Islamist Iran: A Gender Conscious Drive to Change," *British Journal of Middle Eastern Studies*, Vol. 24, No. 1, 1997, 75–96.

—. "Women and the Making of Civil Society in Post-Islamist Iran," in *Twenty Years of Islamic Revolution: Political and Social Transformation in Iran since 1979*. Eric Hoogland, ed. Syracuse, NY: Syracuse University Press, 2002.

—. "Women's Religious Seminaries in Iran," *ISIM Newsletter* Vol. 6, 2000, 23.

Koolaee, Elaheh. "The Prospects for Democracy: Women Reformists in the Iranian Parliament," in *On Shifting Ground: Muslim Women in a Global Era*. Fereshteh Nouaie-Simone, ed. New York: The Feminist Press at CUNY, 2005.

—. "*Sahmieh Bandi Jensiaty bar Zede Zanan*" [Gender Quota Against Iranian Women]. *Ayeen Monthly*, No. 10, 2007, 54–7.

—. "Women in Public Sphere, a Case Study of Islamic Republic of Iran," *Journal of Faculty of Law & Political Science*, No. 61, Fall 2001.

—. *"Yeh Negah Jenah Zanan Majlis Sheeshom"* [A Glance at Women's Faction Performance in 6th Parliament]. *Shargh,* Nos. 215 and 223, 2002.

—*"Zane Irani Bad az Eslahat"* [Iranian Women After Reform]. *Ayeen Monthly,* No. 9, 2007, 46–50.

Kristiansen, Wendy. "Stop the Presses," *Le Monde Diplomatique,* April 2008.

Kurzman, Charles. "A Feminist Generation in Iran?" *Iranian Studies,* Vol. 41, No. 3, 2008.

—. *The Unthinkable Revolution in Iran.* Cambridge: Harvard University Press, 2004,

Leicester, John. "Women to Take Seats in Morocco Government," *Associated Press,* September 27, 2002.

Lutfi, Manal. "The Women's Mufti: Interview with Grand Ayatollah Yousef Saanei," *Asharg Alawsat,* June, 2007.

Mahdavi, Pardis. *Passionate Uprisings: Iran's Sexual Revolution.* Palo Alto, CA: Stanford University Press, 2008.

Mahdi, Ali Akbar. "A Campaign for Equality and Democratic Culture," August 6, 2007, www.we-change.org/english/spip.php?article130. Accessed September 12, 2009.

—. "Caught between Local and Global: Iranian Women's Struggle for a Civil Society," paper presented at the CIRA annual meeting, Bethesda, MD, April 2000, www.owu.edu/~aamahdi/globalization-final.doc.

—. "The Iranian Women's Movement: A Century-Long Struggle." *The Muslim World,* Vol. 94, October 2004.

—. *Women, Religion, and the State: Legal Developments in Twentieth Century Iran.* Office of Women in International Development. East Lansing: Michigan State University, 1983.

Mahmood, Saba. *Politics of Piety: The Islamic Revival and the Feminist Subject.* Princeton, NJ: Princeton University Press, 2004.

Majd, Hooman. *The Ayatollah Begs to Differ: The Paradox of Modern Iran.* New York: Doubleday, 2008.

Maleki, Sina. *"Zan Irani dar 8 Mars: Hamgahm ba Jonbeshe Zananie Jahan"* [Iranian Women on March 8: In Step with the International Women's Movement]. *Zanan,* 131, 17–30.

Martin, Vanessa. *Creating an Islamic State: Khomeini and the Making of a New Iran.* London: I.B. Tauris, 2000.

Mashayeki, Mehrdad. "The Revival of the Student Movement in Post-Revolutionary Iran," *International Journal of Politics, Culture and Society,* Vol. 15, No. 2, 2001.

Matin-Asghari, Afshin. "Abdol Karim Soroush and the Secularization of Islamic Thought in Iran," *Iranian Studies,* Vol. 30, No. I-2, 1997, 95–115.

Mayer, Ann Elizabeth. *Islam and Human Rights: Tradition and Politics.* Boulder, CO: Westview Press, 1991.

Mehran, Golnar. "Lifelong Learning: New Opportunities for Women in a Muslim Country (Iran)," *Comparative Education,* Vol. 32, No. 2, 1999.

—. "The Paradox of Tradition and Modernity in Female Education in the Islamic Republic of Iran," *Comparative Education Review*, Vol. 47, No. 3, 2003.

—. "Socialization of School Children in the Islamic Republic," *Iranian Studies*, Vol. 22, No.1, 1989.

Mehrpour, Hasan, "A Brief Review of Women's Economic Rights in the Iranian Legal System," *Farzaneh*, Vol. 2, No. 7, 1995/1996.

Melman, Yossi, and Meir Javedanfar. *The Nuclear Sphinx of Tehran: Mahmood Ahmadinejad and the State of Iran*. New York: Basic Books, 2007.

Memarian, Omid. "Interview with Abbasgholizadeh: They Are Against Civil Society," *Roozonline*, July 8, 2007.

Menashri, David. *Iran: A Decade of War and Revolution*. Tel Aviv: Holmes & Meir Publisher, 1990.

—. *Post Revolutionary Politics in Iran: Religion, Society and Power*. London: Frank Cass, 2001.

Mernissi, Fatima. *Beyond the Veil: Male-Female Dynamics in a Modern Muslim Society*. Bloomington and Indianapolis: Indiana University Press, 1987.

—. *The Veil and the Male Elite: A Feminist Interpretation of Women's Rights in Islam*. New York: Basic Books, 1991.

Middle East Forum. "Roundtable on Middle Eastern Women: The Experience of Iranian Women," *Middle East Studies Quarterly*, Vol. 8, No.2, 2001.

Middle East Research and Information Project. *Iran in Revolution: The Opposition Reports*. Middle East Reports Nos. 75 and 76, March/April 1979.

Milani, Abbas. "Pious Populist: Understanding the Rise of Iran's President," *Boston Review*, November/December 2007.

—. "Russia and Iran: An Anti-Western Alliance?" *Current History*, Vol. 106, No. 702, 1007, 328–32.

Milani. Farzaneh. "Islamic Bicycle Can't Slow Iranian Women," *USA Today*, June 29, 2007.

—. "Revitalization: Some Reflections on the Work of Saffar-Zadeh," in *Women and Revolution in Iran*. Guity Nashat, ed. Boulder, CO: Westview Press, 1983.

—. *Veils and Words: The Emerging Voices of Iranian Women Writers*. Syracuse, NYLondon: Syracuse University Press, 1992.

Milani, Mohsen M. *The Making of Iran's Islamic Revolution: From Monarchy to Islamic Republic*. Boulder, CO: Westview Press, 1994.

Mira Elmi, Zahra. "Educational Attainment in Iran," *Viewpoints* Special Edition, The Iranian Revolution at Thirty, Middle East Institute, Washington, D.C., 2009.

Mir-Hosseini, Ziba. "Debating Women: Gender and the Public Sphere in Post-Revolutionary Iran," in *Civil Society in the Muslim World*. Amyn Sajoo, ed. London: I.B. Tauris, 2002.

—. "Divorce, Veiling, and Feminism in Post-Khomeini Iran," in *Women and Politics in the Third World*. H. Afshar, ed. London: Routledge, 1996.

—. "Fatemeh Haghighatjoo and the Sixth Majlis: A Woman in Her Own Right," *Middle East Research and Information Project*, No. 233, April 23, 2003.

—. "Is Time on Iranian Women Protesters Side?" *Middle East Research and Information Project*, June 16, 2006.

—. "Islam, Women and Civil Rights: The Religious Debate in the Iran of the 1990s," in *Women, Religion and Culture in Iran*. Sarah F. D. Ansari, Vanessa Martin, eds. Royal Asiatic Society of Great Britain and Ireland. London: Routledge, 2002.

—. *Islam and Gender: The Religious Debate in Contemporary Iran*. Princeton, NJ: Princeton University Press, 1999.

—. "The Rise and Fall of Faezeh Hashemi: Women in Iranian Elections," *Middle East Research and Information Project*, Middle East Report, No. 218, Spring 2001.

—. "Women and Elections in the Islamic Republic of Iran," *Iranmania*, February 1, 2000.

Moaddel, Mansoor. *Class and Ideology in the Iranian Revolution*. New York: Columbia University Press, 1993.

Moaveni, Azadeh. *Lipstick Jihad: A Memoir of Growing Up Iranian in America and American in Iran*. New York: Public Affairs, 2005.

Moghadam, Fatemeh. "Commoditization of Sexuality and Female Labor Force Participation in Islam: Implications for Iran, 1960–1990," in *In the Eye of the Storm: Women in Post-Revolutionary Iran*. Mahnaz Afkhami and Erika Friedl, eds. Syracuse, NY: Syracuse University Press, 1994.

Moghadam, Valentine. "Islamic Feminism and Its Discontents: Toward a Resolution of the Debate," *Signs*, Vol. 27, 2002.

—. "Islamic Populism, Class and Gender in Postrevolutionary Iran," in *A Century of Revolution: Social Movements in Iran*. John Foran, ed. Minneapolis, MN: University of Minnesota Press, 1994.

—. *Modernizing Women: Gender and Social Change in the Middle East*. Boulder, CO: Lynne Rienner, 2003.

—. *Revolution En-Gendered: Women and Politics in Iran and Afghanistan*. North York, Ontario: York University Department of Political Science, 1990.

—. "Women in the Islamic Republic of Iran: Legal Status, Social Positions, and Collective Action," *Woodrow Wilson International Center for Scholars Conference*. November 16–17, 2004.

—. "Women, Work, and Ideology in the Islamic Republic," *International Journal of Middle East Studies*, Vol. 20, No. 2, 1988, 221–43.

—. "Women's NGOs in the Middle East and North Africa: Constraints, opportunities, and priorities," in *Organizing Women: Formal and Informal Women's Groups in the Middle East*. Dawn Chatty and A. Rabo, eds. Oxford: Berg, 1997.

Moghissi, Haideh. *Populism and Feminism in Iran*. New York: St. Martin's Press, 1996.

—. "Women in the Resistance Movement in Iran," in *Women in the Middle East: Perceptions, Realities and Struggles for Liberation*. Haleh Afshar, ed. New York: St. Martin's Press, 1993.

Mohajer, Fariba Davoudi. "From New York to Tehran: International Women's Day," *www.gozaar.org*, March 6, 2009.

Mohammadi, Majid. *"Jensiyat: Khat-e Ghermez-e Roshanfekran-e Dini"* [Gender: The Red Line of Religious Intellectuals]. *Zanan*, 58, 39–40.

Moin, Baqer. *Khomeini: The Life of the Ayatollah*. New York: St. Martin's Press, 1999.

Moruzzi, Norma Claire and Fatemeh Sadeghi. "Out of the Frying Pan, Into the Fire: Young Iranian Women Today," *Middle East Report, 241*, Winter 2006.

Moslem, Mehdi. *Factional Politics in Post Khomeini Iran*. Syracuse, NY: Syracuse University Press, 2002.

Motahari, Morteza. *Masaele Hejab* [The Problem with the Hejab]. Tehran: Sadra Publishing, 1979.

—. *Nezam Hoghugh Zan dar Eslam* [The System of Women's Rights in Islam]. Qom: Entesharat Sadra, 1978.

Mottahedeh, Roy. *The Mantle of the Prophet: Religion and Politics in Iran*. Oxford: One World Publications, 2000.

Naji, Kasra. *Ahmadinejad. The Secret History of Iran's Radical Leader*. Berkeley, CA: University of California Press, 2008.

Najibullah, Farangis. "Iran: Tehran Opens Controversial Women-Only Park," *Radio Free Europe Radio Liberty,* May 17, 2008.

Najibullah, Farangis. "Iran: Women's Magazine Felled by Latest Government Closure," *Radio Free Europe Radio Liberty*, February 13, 2008.

—. "Iran: Wrapping Up for Winter, and the Morality Police," *Radio Free Europe Radio Liberty,* December 13, 2007.

Najmabadi, Afsaneh, ed., *Bibi Khanum Astarabadi's Ma'ayib al-Rijal: Vices of Men*. Chicago, IL: Midland Printers, 1992.

—. "Feminism in an Islamic Republic: Years of Hardship, Years of Growth," in *Islam, Gender, and Social Change*. Yvonne Yazbeck Haddad and John L. Esposito, eds. Oxford: Oxford University Press, 1998.

—. "Hazards of Modernity and Morality," in *The Modern Middle East*. Albert Hourani, Phlip S. Khoury, and Mary C. Wilson, eds. Berkeley, CA: University of California Press, 1993.

—. *Women with Mustaches and Men Without Beards*. Berkeley, CA: University of California Press, 2005.

Namazi, Bagher. *Non-Governmental Organizations in the Islamic Republic of Iran: A Situation Analysis*, Tehran: UNDP, 2000.

Nashat, Guitty, and Judith Tucker. *Women in the Middle East and North Africa: Restoring Women to History*. Bloomington: Indiana University Press, 1988.

Nasr, Vali. *The Shia Revival: How Conflicts Within Islam Will Shape the Future*. New York: W.W. Norton, 2006.

Nikzad, Shahab. *"Jonbeshe Zanan dar Sal 88"* [The Women's Movement in the Year 1388]. *BBC Persian*, March 24, 2010.

Nordlund, A. "Demands for Electoral Gender Quotas in Afghanistan and Iraq," The Research Program on Gender Quotas, Working Paper Series. Stockholm: Stockholm University Department of Political Science, 2004.

Nouaie-Simone, Fereshteh. "Shirin Ebadi: A Perspective on Women's Rights in the Context of Human Rights," in *On Shifting Ground: Muslim Women in a Global Era*. Fereshteh Nouaie-Simone, ed. New York: The Feminist Press at CUNY, 2005.

Olmstead, A. T. *History of the Persian Empire*. Chicago: University of Chicago Press, 1959.

Pahlavi, Muhammad Reza. *Mission for My Country*. London: Hutchinson, 1960.

Paidar, Parvin. "Feminism and Islam in Iran," in *Gendering the Middle East*. Deniz Kanidyoti, ed. Syracuse, NY: Syracuse University Press, 1996.

—. "Gender of Democracy: The Encounter between Feminism and Reformism in Contemporary Iran," United Nations Research Institute for Social Development, Democracy, Governance and Human Rights, Program Paper Number 6, October 2001.

—. "Iran: Ayatollah Support Women's Right to Inheritance and Abortion," *Payvand News*, February 18, 2008.

— "The Position of Women from the Viewpoint of Imam Khomeini." Juliana Shaw and Behrooz Arezoo, trans. Tehran: *The Institute for Compilation and Publication of Imam Khomeini's Works*, 2001.

—. *Women and the Political Process in Twentieth-Century Iran*. Cambridge: Cambridge University Press, 1995.

Potter, Lawrence, and Gary Sick eds. *Iran, Iraq and the Legacy of War*. New York: Palgrave Macmillan, 2004.

Poya, Maryam. *Women, Work and Islamism: Ideology and Resistance in Iran*. London: Zed Books, 1999.

Price, Massoumeh. "A Brief History of Women's Movement in Iran 1850–2000." Iran Chamber Society, 2002.

Rahimi, Babak. "Politics of the Internet in Iran," in *Media, Culture and Society in Iran: Living with Globalization and the Iranian State*. Mehdi Semati, ed. New York: Routledge, 2008.

Rahnema, Ali. *An Islamic Utopian: A Political Biography of Dr. Ali Shariati*. London: I.B. Tauris, 2000.

Rajaee, Farhang. *The Iran-Iraq War: The Politics of Aggression*. Gainesville: University of Florida Press, 1993.

Ramazani, Nesta. "Women in Iran: The Revolutionary Ebb and Flow," *Middle East Journal*, Vol. 47, No. 3, 1993.

Reeves, Minou. *Female Warriors of Allah: Women and the Islamic Revolution*. New York: E. P. Dutton, 1989.

Ridgeon, Lloyd, ed. *Religion and Politics in Modern Iran: A Reader*. London: I.B. Tauris, 2005.

Rostami Povey, Elaheh. "*Azam Alaee Taleghani*," in *Biographical Encyclopedia of the Modern Middle East and North Africa*, Vol. 1. Michael R. Fischbach, ed. Detroit: Gale Group, 2008.

—. "*Dastavarde Jonbeshe Zanane: Barabareye Jensiati be Nafe Har Do Jens*" [Achievements of the Women's Movement: Gender Equality Is in the Interest of Both Genders]. *Zanan*, 147, 1–9.

—. "Feminist Contestations of Institutional Domains in Iran," *Feminist Review*, Vol. 69, No. 1, 2001, 44–72.

—. "Trade Unions and Women's NGOs: Diverse Civil Society Organizations in Iran," *Development in Practice*, Vol. 14, 2004, 1–2.

Rubin, Michael. *Into the Shadows: Radical Vigilante's in Khatami's Iran*. Washington, D.C.: Washington Institute for Near East Policy, 2001.

Rupp, Leila, and Taylor, Verta. "Forging Feminist Identity in an International Movement: A Collective Identity Approach to Twentieth Century Feminism," *Signs*, Vol. 24, 1999.

Saba, Sadeq. "Iran Awaits Verdict on Women Judges," *BBC News*, August 1, 2000.

Saberi, Roxanna. "Women's Rights on Iranian Agenda," *BBC News*, March 9, 2006.

Sadeghi, Fatemeh. "*Chera Hijab?*" [Why We Say No to the Compulsory Hijab]. Frieda Afary, trans. *Meydaneh Zan* [Women's Field]. April 14, 2008.

—. "*Ezdevaje Movaghat va Eghtesade Lezat*" [Temporary Marriage and the Economy of Pleasure]. January 9, 2010, www.alborznet.ir/Fa/ViewDetail.aspx?T=2&ID=275. Accessed April 14, 2010.

—. "Foot Soldiers of the Islamic Republic's 'Culture of Modesty,'" *Middle East Report 250*, Spring 2009.

Sadjadpour, Karim. *Reading Khamenei: The World View of Iran's Most Powerful Leader*. Washington, D.C.: The Carnegie Endowment for International Peace, 2008.

Sadr, Shadi. "*Aya Hokoomate Masool Bi Hejaby Ast?*" [Is the Government Responsible for Bad Hijab?]. *Zanan*, 103, 14.

—. "*Mane'e Sang Sar ra Ghanooni Konid*" [Abolishing Stoning Should Become Law]. *Zanan*, 134, 26–34.

—. "Women's Gains at Risk in Iran's New Parliament," Womeniniran.org, June, 9, 2004, www.onlinewomeninpolitics.org/archives/04_0608_iran_wip.htm. Accessed January 27, 2010.

Sahimi, Muhammad. "Martyrs of the Green Movement," *Tehran Bureau*, April 7, 2010, www.pbs.org/wgbh/pages/frontline/tehranbureau/2010/04/martyrs-of-the-green-movement.html. Accessed April 19, 2010.

Saikal, Amin. *Islam and the West: Conflict or Cooperation?* London: Palgrave, 2003.

Samii, Abbas William. "Ethnic Tensions Could Crack Iran's Firm Resolve against the World," *The Christian Science Monitor*, May 30, 2006.

Sansarian, Eliz. "The Politics of Gender and Development in the Islamic Republic of Iran," *Journal of Developing Societies*, Vol. 8, January–April 1992, 56–68.

—. *Religious Minorities in Iran*. Cambridge: Cambridge University Press, 2000.

—. *The Women's Rights Movement in Iran: Mutiny, Appeasement, and Repression from 1900 to Khomeini*. New York: Praeger, 1982.

Schacht, Joseph. "Law and Justice," in *The Cambridge History of Islam*. Vol. 2. P. M. Holt, Ann Lambton, and Bernard Lewis, eds. Cambridge: Cambridge University Press, 1977.

Schirazi, Asghar. *The Constitution of Iran: Politics and the State in the Islamic Republic*. London: I.B. Tauris, 1998.

Schott, Brian. "Iran Awakening: An Interview with Shirin Ebadi," *New America Media*, May 20, 2006.

Schuster, W. Morgan. *The Strangling of Persia: A Story of European Diplomacy and Oriental Intrigue*. Washington D.C.: Mage Publishers, 2007.

Sciolino, Elaine. "Daughter of the Revolution Fights the Veil," *New York Times*, April 2, 2003

Scott, James. *Weapons of the Weak: Everyday Forms of Peasant Resistance*. New Haven, CT: Yale University Press, 1985.

Sedghi, Hamideh. *Women and Politics in Iran: Veiling, Unveiling and Reveiling*. Cambridge: Cambridge University Press, 2007.

Semati, Mehdi. "Communication, Media and Popular Culture in Post-revolutionary Iran," *Viewpoints* Special Edition, The Iranian Revolution at Thirty, Middle East Institute, Washington, D.C., 2009.

Sepehry, Sahar. "*Dava Bar Sar Zan Dovom dar Owje Bohrane Siasi*" [Battle Over Acquiring a Second Wife at the Peak of Political Turmoil]. *Mianeh*, February 1, 2010, www.mianeh.net/fa/articles/?aid=252. Accessed March 12, 2010.

Seyfi, Farnaz. "Rally on June 12, 2006 was an Opportunity for the Women's Commission," *www.zanestan.net*, December 18, 2006.

Shabestari, Muhammad Mojtahed. *Iman va Azadi* [Faith and Freedom]. Tehran: Tarh-e Naw, 1997.

—. *Naghdi bar Ghira'at-e Rasmi-e Din* [A Critique of the Official Reading of Religion]. Tehran: Tarh-e Naw, 2000.

—. "*Zanan, Ketab va Sonnat*" [Women, Books and Tradition]. *Zanan*, 57, 19–22.

Shaditalab, Jaleh. "Iranian Women: Rising Expectations," *Critique: Critical Middle Eastern Studies*, Vol. 14, No.1, 2005, 35–55.

—. *Mosharekat-e Siasi Zanan, Mavane' va Emkanat* [Development and Challenges of Iranian Women]. Tehran: Ghatreh Press, 1381, 2002.

—. "*Zandar Tose'eh*" [Women through Development]. *Zanan*, 172, 3–5.

Shahidian, Hammed. *Women in Iran: Gender Politics in the Islamic Republic*, Vol. 1. Westport, CT: Greenwood Press, 2002.

Shahriari, Afarin. "*Cheezhaee Ke Dar Majles Didam Ta'asofbar Ast*" [What I Have Seen in the Parliament is Deplorable]. *Zanan*, 56, 4–5.

—. "*Jeloye Harekate Zanan dar Majles Gerefteh Shod*" [Women's Activities in Parliament is Blocked]. *Zanan*, 58, 14–15.

Shahrokni, Nazanin. "*Az Nardebane Ghodrat va Shohrat-e Mardhaye Khanevadeh Bala Nayamadam: Goftogoo ba Jamila Kadivar*" [I Did Not Ascend the Ladder of Familial Power: A Conversation With Jamila Kadivar]. *Zanan*, 63, 7–12.

—. "*Majlis Baraye Zanan Che Kar Kard?*" [What Has the Parliament Done for Women]. *Zanan*, 41, 2–4.

—. "*Voroode Zanan be Shoraye Islami Shahr va Roosta*" [Women are Represented on Islamic City and Village Councils]. *Zanan*, 54, 10–14.

—. "*Zanan-e Khabarnegar: Zendegi az No'eh Digar*" [Women Journalists: A Different Life]. *Zanan*, 54, 2–7.

Shakerhosseini, Shakiba. "*Layeheye Hemayate Khanevadeh Tavaghof-e Tavanmandi-yeh Zanan*" [The Family Protection Act Prevents the Strength of Women]. *Zanan*, 148, 12–18.

Shariati, Ali. *Fatima is Fatima*. Trans. Laleh Bakhtiar. Tehran Foundation: The Shariati Foundation, 1980.

Sheikholeslami, Pari. *Zanane Rooznameh va Negar va Andishmande Iran* [Female Iranian Journalists and Intellectuals]. Tehran: Mazgrafic, 1351, 1972.

Sherkarloo, Mahsa. "Government Newspaper? What Government Newspaper? An Interview with Journalist Lily Farhadpour," *Bad Jens, Iranian Feminist Newsletter*, November 21, 2000, www.badjens.com/fourthedition/farhadpour.htm. Accessed July 23, 2009.

—. "Interview with Mehrangiz Kar: Settling the Score," *Bad Jens*. Fourth Edition, November 21, 2000, www.badjens.com/fourthedition/kar.htm. Accessed August 27, 2008.

—. "Iranian Women Take on the Constitution," *Middle East Research Information Project*, July 21, 2005.

Sherkat, Shahla. "*Chashmahe Agahi Agar Bejushad . . .*" [If Opened Eyes Only Boiled . . .]. *Zanan*, February 1992.

—. "*Eslahtalaban va Sokhangooee az Jense Digar: Gofto Goo ba Dr. Elaheh Koolaee*" [Reformists and a Discussion on the Other Sex: A Conversation With Dr. Elaheh Koolaee]. *Zanan*, 120, 3–16.

—. "*Faezeh Hashemi Che Migooyad?*" [What Does Faezeh Hashemi Say?]. *Zanan*, 28, 8–17.

—. "*Talkhy Siyasat, Shirini Solh: Dar Goftogoo ba Shirin Ebadi*" [Bitterness of Politics, Sweetness of Peace: An Interview with Shirin Ebadi]. *Zanan*, 105, 6–19.

—. "*Zanan dar Dadgah*" [Women in the Courts]. *Zanan*, 43, 2–4.

Shirazi, Faegheh. *The Veil Unveiled: The Hijab in Modern Culture*. Gainesville: University Press of Florida, 2001.

Shojai, Zahra. "Muslim Women: Politics, Leadership and Civil Society," Presented at the Second Annual Arab International Women's Forum Conference, London, October 24, 2003.

Siavoshi, Sussan. "Islamist Women Activists: Allies or Enemies," in *Iran: Between Tradition and Modernity*. Ramin Jahanbegloo, ed. Lanham: Lexington Books, 2004.

Slavin, Barbara. *Bitter Friends, Bosom Enemies: Iran, the U.S., and the Twisted Path to Confrontation*. New York: Macmillan, 2007.

Soroush, Abdolkarim, and M. Sadri, *Reason, Freedom and Democracy: The Essential Writings of Abdolkarim Soroush*. Oxford: Oxford University Press, 2000.

Sotoudeh, Nasrin, "*Hoghoughe Zanan dar Ghanoon, dar Gharardad*" [Women's Rights: In Law, in Contract]. *Zanan*, 116, 22–3.

Spellman, Kathryn. *Civil Society and the Women's Movement.* Tehran: Volunteer, Iran CSO's Training and Research Center, 2005.

Statistical Center of Iran. *Iran Statistical Yearbook 1379.* Tehran: Author, 2001.

—. *Iran Statistical Yearbook 1385.* Tehran: Author, 2006.

Sykes, Hugh. "Iran Rejects Easing Polygamy Law," *BBC News,* September 2, 2008.

Taati, Poopak. "Iranian Women's NGOs: A Case for Feminine Leadership," presented at XV World Congress of Sociology, Brisbane Australia, July 2002.

Tabari, Azar, and Nahid Yeganeh, eds. *In the Shadow of Islam: The Women's Movement in Iran.* London: Zed Press, 1982.

Tahavori, Mohammad. "The Evolution of Iran's Student Movement: An Interview with Abdollah Momeni," July 1, 2007, *www.gozaar.org.* Accessed March 6, 2010.

Tahmasebi, Sussan. "Interview with Elnaz Ansari: Iranian Women Activist," Change for Equality.org, September 17, 2008.

Takeyh, Ray. *Hidden Iran: Power and Paradox in the Islamic Republic.* New York: Times Books, 2006.

Taleghani, Azam. *"Mikhaham Taklife Rejal ra Roshan Konam"* [I Want to Clarify the Role of Statesmanship]. *Zanan,* 34, 1997, 6–7.

Tarighi, Noushin. *"Khabardar be Jaye Khod: Zanane Police be Peesh"* [Women Police Officers Advance]. *Zanan,* 95, 2–7.

—. *"Mardan Reghabat Baraye Rai'e Zanan"* [Men Competing for Women's Votes]. *Zanan,* 121, 4–7.

—. *"Shirin Ebadi: Zan Boodan dar Iran Aasoon Neest"* [Shirin Ebadi: Being a Woman in Iran Is Not Easy]. *Zanan,* 103, 12–13.

—. *"Yek Eshtebahe Ghanoonee"* [A Legal Mistake]. *Zanan,* 112, 2–6.

—. *"Zanane Namayandeh Che Migooyand? In bar Elaheh Koolaee, Fatemeh Rakei, Akram Mosavery Manesh"* [What Do Female Parliamentarians Have to Say This Time? Elaheh Koolaee, Fatemeh Rakei, Akram Mosavery Manesh]. *Zanan,* 105, 32–4.

—. *"Zanan va Shoraha"* [Women and the Councils]. *Zanan,* 139, 2–5.

Tarrow, Sidney. *Power in Movement: Social Movements and Contentious Politics.* Cambridge: Cambridge University Press, 2002.

Tatchell, Peter. "Iran's Union Heroes: Tehran's Anti-union Repression Is Symptomatic of the Fascistic Nature of the Clerical Regime," *The Guardian,* March 6, 2008.

Tavakoli-Targhi, Mohamad. "Women of the West Imagined: The Farangi, Other and the Emergence of the Woman Question in Iran," in *Identity Politics and Women.* Valentine M. Moghadam, ed. Boulder, CO: Westview Press, 1994, 105.

Tavassoli. Nahid. *"Entekhab Vazire Zan, chera Hala?"* [Election of a Woman Minister, Why Now?]. August 21, 2009, www.feministschool.com/spip.php?article3065. Accessed March 22, 2010.

Terman, Rochelle. *The Contemporary Iranian Women's Rights Movement.* London: Women Living Under Muslim Laws, forthcoming.

—. *Sport and Segregation in Iran: The Women's Access to Public Stadiums Campaign.* London: Women Living Under Muslim Laws, forthcoming.

Tilly, Charles. *Social Movements, 1768–2004*. London: Paradigm Publishers, 2004.

Tohidi, Nayereh. "Beacon's of Hope: Iran's Women's Rights Movement and the One Million Signatures Campaign," *Iranian.com*, December 23, 2006.

—. " 'Fundamentalist' Backlash and Muslim Women in the Beijing Conference," *Canadian Women Studies*, Vol. 16, No. 3, 1996.

—. "Gender and Islamic Fundamentalism: Feminist Politics in Iran," in *In Third World Women and the Politics of Feminism*. Chandra Mohanty, ed. Bloomington: Indiana University Press, 1991.

—. "International Connections of the Iranian Women's Movement," in *Iran and the Surrounding World 1501–2001: Interactions in Culture and Cultural Politics*. Nikki Keddie and Rudi Matthee, eds. Seattle: University of Washington Press, 2002.

—. "The Issue at Hand," in *Women in Muslim Societies: Diversity within Unity*. Herbert Bodman and Nayereh Tohidi, eds. Boulder, CO: Lynne Rienner, 1998.

—. "*Peyvande Jahaniye Jonbeshe Zanane Iran*" [The Iranian Feminist Movement's Global Connections]. *Journal of Goft-o-Gu*, No. 38, December 2003, 25–49.

—. "*Ta`amol Mahali-Jahani Feminism dar Jonbeshe Zanane Iran*" [The Local-Global Intersection of Feminism in the Women's Movement in Iran]. *Arash: A Persian Monthly of Culture and Social Affairs*, No. 100, 2007,163–8.

—. "Women's Rights in the Middle East and North Africa: Iran Draft Chapter," *Gozaar.org*, September 2, 2009, www.gozaar.org/template1.php?id= 1343&language=english. Accessed March 25, 2010.

Torab, Azam. "The Politicization of Women's Religious Circles in Post-revolutionary Iran," in *Women, Religion and Culture in Iran*. Sarah F. D. Ansari and Vanessa Martin, eds. London: Routledge, 2002.

United Nations Development Program, *Non-Governmental Organizations in the Islamic Republic of Iran: A Situation Analysis*. Tehran: UNDP, 2000.

Vahdat, Farzin. "Post-revolutionary Discourses of Mohammad Mojtahed Shabestari and Mohsen Kadivar: Reconciling the Discourses of Mediated Subjectivity, Part 1: Mojtahed Shabestari," *Critique Journal for Critical Studies of the Middle East*, Vol. 16, Spring 2000.

—. "Post-revolutionary Discourses of Mohammad Mojtahed Shabestari and Mohsen Kadivar: Reconciling the Discourses of Mediated Subjectivity, Part 2: Mohsen Kadivar," *Critique Journal for Critical Studies of the Middle East, Vol.* 17, Fall 2000.

Vakil, Sanam. "Tehran Gambles to Survive," *Current History*, December 2007.

Vakili, Valla. *Debating Religion and Politics in Iran: The Political Thought of Abdolka-rim Soroush. Occasional Paper Series*, No. 2. New York: Council on Foreign Relations, 1996.

Varzi, Roxanne. *Warring Souls: Youth, Media, and Martyrdom in Post-Revolutionary Iran*. Durham, NC: Duke University Press, 2006.

Vaziri, Pershang. "Caught in the Middle: Women and Press Freedom in Iran," *Middle East Research Information Project*, February 16, 2001.

Weber, Charlotte. "Between Nationalism and Feminism: The Eastern Women's Congresses of 1930 and 1932," *Journal of Middle East Women's Studies*, Vol. 4, No.1, 2008, 83–106.

Weber, Max. *The Sociology of Religion*. Boston: Beacon Press Books, 1993.

Wright, Robin. *The Last Great Revolution: Turmoil and Transformation in Iran*. New York: Alfred Knopf, 2000.

Yadigar Azadi, Mina. "*Ghezavate Zan*" [Women's Judgement]. *Zanan*, 4, 20–26.

—. "*Ijtehad va Marja'iyate Zanan*" [Level of Religious Learning and Jurisprudence among the Women's Clergy]. *Zanan*, 29, 7–9.

Zabih, Sepehr. *The Mossadegh Era: Roots of the Iranian Revolution*. New York: Lake View Press, 1986.

Zahedi, Ashraf. "Contested Meaning of the Veil and Political Ideologies of Iranian Regimes," *Journal of Middle East Women's Studies*, Vol. 3, No. 3, 2007, 75–98.

Zahedi, Zohreh. "*Agar Zanan ba Mardan Barabarand pas Chera!!!?*" [If Women are Equal with Men, Then Why!!!?]. *Zanan*, 11, 18–29, 1993.

Appendix: Highlights of the Gains and Losses in Women's Activism, 1960–2010

Highlights of the Gains and Losses in Women's Activism, 1960-2010

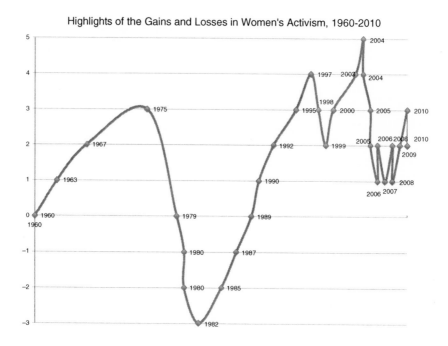

Highlights of the Gains and Losses in Women's Activism

1960	Muhammad Reza Pahlavi's White Revolution
1963	Female enfranchisement
1967	Family Protection Act (FPA)
1975	Enhanced FPA
1979	Revolution
1980	Gender segregation
1980	Hijab mandated
1982	Law of retribution
1985	Custody law enhanced
1987	Women's Social Cultural Council established
1989	Divorce law amended
1990	Family planning instituted
1992	Zanan established
1995	Women permitted to serve as consulting judges
1997	Khatami election with overwhelming female participation
1998	Press law enacted
1999	Student crackdown begins
2000	International Women's Day celebrated for first time since 1979
2003	Nobel Prize awarded to Shirin Ebadi
2004	Women permitted to study abroad without male guardianship
2004	CEDAW rejected
2005	International Women's Day celebrated
2005	Center for Women's participation changed to Center for Women and Family Affairs
2006	Female activists arrested
2006	One Million Signatures Campaign begins
2007	Family Protection Act revisions include legalization of polygamy
2008	Right to receive equal blood money in car accidents granted to women
2008	Closure of Zanan magazine
2009	Women granted right to inherit land
2010	First female minister appointed
2010	Mass arrests of female activists

Index

CPSIA information can be obtained at www.ICGtesting.com
Printed in the USA
266084BV00003B/54/P